ORIGINS OF COGNITIVE SKILLS

The Eighteenth Annual Carnegie Symposium on Cognition

ORIGINS OF COGNITIVE SKILLS

The Eighteenth Annual Carnegie Symposium on Cognition

edited by
CATHERINE SOPHIAN
Carnegie-Mellon University

LEA LAWRENCE ERLBAUM ASSOCIATES, PUBLISHERS
1984 Hillsdale, New Jersey   London

535 26356

Lawrence Erlbaum Associates, Inc., Publishers
365 Broadway
Hillsdale, New Jersey 07642

This work relates to Grant No. BNS82-17804 from the National Science Foundation.
However, the content does not necessarily reflect the position or policy of the National Science
Foundation or the Government and no official endorsement should be inferred.

The United States Government has a royalty-free, nonexclusive and irrevocable license
throughout the world for Government purposes to publish, translate, reproduce, deliver, perform, dispose of, and to authorize others so to do, all or any portion of this work.

Library of Congress Cataloging in Publication Data

Symposium on Cognition (18th : 1983 : Carnegie-Mellon
  University)
  Origins of cognitive skills.

  Bibliography: p.
  Includes indexes.
  1. Cognition in children—Congresses. 2. Infant
psychology—Congresses. I. Sophian, Catherine.
II. Carnegie-Mellon University. III. Title.
BF723.C5S95 1983   155.4'22   84-10215
ISBN 0-89859-390-5

Printed in the United States of America
10 9 8 7 6 5 4 3 2 1

For mothers,
and for every woman who deserves
better than she gets

Contents

Preface

How does the infant develop into a child? Despite accumulating research on both infant cognition and cognitive development in childhood, the course of development linking the two is not well understood. The chapters in this volume represent an initial effort to integrate research with infants and young children into a more coherent picture of early cognitive development.

The volume is based on the proceedings of the Eighteenth Annual Carnegie Symposium on Cognition, which was held in Pittsburgh in May, 1983. The book, like the symposium, is divided into three parts, each addressing a different area of early cognitive development. A final commentary then raises some general issues that span all the papers.

The three topics around which the book is structured are spatial development, number development, and the development of categorisation. These topics were chosen because they represent areas that are currently receiving active study both with infants and with young children. Each section of the book spans these age groups, presenting both infancy research and research on later cognitive development, often in the same chapters. A commentary at the end of each section brings together the different lines of research discussed in the preceding chapters.

The section on spatial development includes chapters by Lockman and Pick, Sophian, Deloache, and Huttenlocher and Newcombe. They consider abilities ranging from the young infant's perception of how far away an object is to the elementary school child's (still limited) ability to infer how an array of objects would look from a different perspective. In between, we see a whole progression of skills for getting from one place to another and for finding objects that have been moved from one place to another. In his commentary, Harris focusses on the recurrent problems of how children cope with movements and how they make use of landmarks.

The section on number development includes chapters by Strauss and Curtis, Cooper, Miller, and Siegler and Shrager. They discuss abilities ranging from infant's discrimination between two small numerical quantities to elementary school children's selection of appropriate addition and subtraction strategies for problems of varying difficulty. Among the interesting issues raised are questions about the relationship between children's understanding of continuous and discontinuous quantities and about the relationship between acquisition of functional skills and development of a conceptual understanding of the principles underlying those skills. In his commentary, Klahr considers the kinds of solutions that are emerging from this work to the classic problem of developmental mechanisms.

The section on the development of categorisation includes chapters by Bornstein, Mervis, and Markman. They review developments from infants' early perception of color categories to children's acquisition of an understanding of hierarchical relationships among taxonomic categories. Relationships between conceptual and linguistic development are central here, and the contribution of other people, particularly the mother, to the child's development is highlighted. MacWhinney's commentary discusses the developmental ordering of different types of categories and their origins in biological, cognitive, social, and linguistic functioning.

Looking across all of these chapters, one gets a richly-textured view of the very young child and the first steps in his or her development. Even the youngest children considered here are not the helpless and virtually mindless creatures that accounts of infancy once described, yet they are also not yet the accomplished cognizers that they will become. Much of the content of the chapters in this volume consists of a chronicle of the many small (and not so small) achievements that will mark their cognitive progress over the next several years. This chronicle does not in itself tell us *how* the infant becomes a child, but it does give us a clearer picture of the kinds of developments which any answer to that question will have to explain. In addition, the authors do offer some initial suggestions about how the developmental changes they describe may come about. More complete answers will only emerge as they continue their work and as other investigators join them in their efforts to link infancy with subsequent cognitive development. This volume, and the symposium that led to it, will have served their purpose if they have even posed the problem well enough to encourage more work on it in the future.

Many people have contributed to the organization of the symposium on which this book is based and to the preparation of this volume. I would especially like to thank Betty Boal for her expert handling of the arrangements for the symposium and for her unflagging good cheer. I also thank Jill Larkin, Margaret Clark, Sharon Carver, Diane Briars, Celia Brownell, Ken Kotovsky, Carl Johnson, Joe Stemberger, and Alice Siegler for helping with many tasks during the symposium. Financial support for the symposium was provided by the National Science Foundation (through their program on Memory and Cognitive Processes) and by the Department of Psychology of Carnegie-Mellon University. Finally, I am grateful for the co-operation and hard work of the contributors whose chapters make up this volume. Thank you all.

Catherine Sophian

ORIGINS OF SPATIAL SKILLS

1 Problems of Scale in Spatial Development

Jeffrey J. Lockman
Tulane University

Herbert L. Pick, Jr.
*Institute of Child Development,
University of Minnesota*

What role does *size* play in spatial behavior? Our answer to this question may help us to understand not only the development of spatial cognition but also the origins of some basic quantitative skills and the ability to use representations. Issues relating to size or scale are implicated in a variety of spatial problems including how young children choose the shortest route to a goal, learn environmental layouts, and read maps. As a first step in considering the role of size in spatial behavior, we would like to review evidence on children's *direct* responsivity to size information. In this discussion size refers to linear measures of both objects and distances. Beyond direct responsivity to linear extent, size may also affect behavior *indirectly* when the scale of a space simply elicits different kinds of behavior or engages different modes of information processing. In the second step of our answer we adduce evidence that this is true for children and we suggest possible underlying reasons. Given that differences in scale do affect how information is processed, problems may also occur when information must be coordinated across scales. The concluding step of our analysis cites some examples of these difficulties and relates them to more general problems of cross-domain coordination and the perception of representations.

DIRECT SENSITIVITY TO SIZE

How do infants demonstrate sensitivity to information regarding size or distance in their spatially coordinated behavior? This sensitivity, of course, depends on the ability to pick up information about the real size of objects or distances

3

between objects. Traditional studies of infant space perception indicate that perception of size and distance develops during the first 6 months of life. In research on depth perception, for example, young infants have been shown to be sensitive to a variety of cues specifying the distance of objects. By 3 months of age, infants show a defensive reaction such as blinking or head withdrawal to an expanding optical field that specifies an approaching object (Yonas, Pettersen, Lockman, & Eisenberg, 1980), and they are also sensitive to disparity information in random dot stereograms (Fox, Aslin, Dumais, & Shea, 1980); by $6\frac{1}{2}$ months of age they are sensitive to linear perspective and will reach toward the large side of a trapezoidal window viewed monocularly (Yonas, Cleaves, & Pettersen, 1978). All these kinds of experiments indicate perception of distance relative to the subject, a kind of egocentric sensitivity that we have referred to as sensitivity to self–object relations (Pick & Lockman, 1981). Even the stereoscopic sensitivity amounts to a judgment of whether the target figure is the same distance or closer than the background surface.

The classic size-constancy experiment of Bower (1964) comes closer to a demonstration of an infant's nonegocentric perception of size. In that study infants of 10 to 12 weeks of age were conditioned to turn their heads to a stimulus cube 30 cm. on a side positioned at a distance of 1 meter. After stable conditioning was achieved the infants were tested for generalization with a 90-cm. cube at a distance of 3 meters (thus projecting the same size retinal image as the conditioned stimulus), a 90-cm. cube at a distance of 1 meter, and a 30-cm. cube at a distance of 3 meters (thus preserving the original size of the conditioned stimulus). Moderate degrees of generalization occurred when either the original size or the original distance of cube was tried. However, very little generalization was exhibited when both the size and distance of the cube were changed even though this preserved the size of the retinal image of the conditioned stimulus.

Given this early sensitivity to size and distance, how do infants use such information in executing spatially coordinated acts? In research on the development of spatially coordinated behavior, this question has been approached in two somewhat different ways. One approach has been to investigate whether infants are in fact capable of visuomotor coordination as such—that is, whether they indeed relate their motor movements to visually perceived information about size or distance. Considerable interest has been devoted to this issue because of its implications for determining what role experience plays in the development of spatially coordinated behavior (see Lockman & Ashmead, 1983). Research on the development of eye–hand coordination, for example, has been concerned with the earliest age at which infants appropriately adjust the frequency, extent, or form of their arm movements as a function of object distance (Field, 1976; Gordon & Yonas, 1976) or object size (Bruner & Koslowski, 1972). Similarly, research with the visual cliff has centered on when infants begin to use distance information to avoid locomoting to the cliff's deep side (Gibson & Walk, 1960; Rader, Bausano, & Richards, 1980).

In contrast, the second approach to studying the early use of magnitude information in spatially coordinated behavior focuses not on whether infants are capable of visumotor coordination, but rather on whether this coordination is manifest in a spatially efficient manner. For example, given the ability to relate distance information to motor responses, when will infants do so in a way that minimizes physical effort? Can infants use visually perceptible information about magnitude to go from one point to another by the shortest route? Surprisingly, little is known about the development of this ability, yet it is important for understanding not only the origins of efficient spatial behavior, but also the origins of some very basic quantitative skills for combining and comparing different amounts.

The early use of magnitude information in skilled action can be examined by looking at infants' and toddlers' shortest-route behavior. Our own and others' recent research suggests that locomotor infants are able to use magnitude information to perform spatial tasks in an efficient manner but that certain constraints, associated with stimulus and response factors, affect the use of this information. On the stimulus side, infants may demonstrate the ability to locomote from one place to another by the shortest route when magnitude information is unambiguously available. However, when magnitude information must be represented rather than directly sensed (e.g., in large-scale environments that cannot be apprehended from a single vantage point) and/or when it conflicts with other sources of information (e.g., with event information about an object's disappearance trajectory), spatial efficiency may break down. On the response side, the tendency of infants to make perseverative errors may also mask rudimentary forms of efficient spatial behavior. Let us consider evidence for these proposals.

When do infants use information about relative magnitude to go from one place to another by the shortest route? Surprisingly, there have been few systematic studies on the development of this ability. In recent work, we have begun investigating how this skill emerges during the toddler period. In one study, 12- and 18-month-olds were tested on their ability to go around an 8-foot long barrier to get to their parent by the shortest route. Initially, the child and parent were positioned 2 feet from either the right or left end of the barrier. The parent then stepped over the barrier, faced the child, and called to him or her to come around. The barrier was low enough for the child to still see the parent, but too high for the child to climb over and simply follow the parent's route. After the trial had ended, the parent held the child and returned to the next starting point by stepping over the barrier. Each child was presented six trials—three beginning on the left, three on the right—with starting position alternating between trials and counterbalanced across children within each age level.

The results indicated that even 12-month-olds could use relative magnitude information that is perceptually available to go from one place to another by the shortest route. However, this ability may be masked by a tendency to repeat previously successful responses. In particular, analysis of the first trial data revealed little difference in the performance of 12- and 18-month-olds. Children from both age groups almost always went to the parent by the shortest route. However, when looking at performance across trials, age differences emerged. Whereas 18-month-olds generally continued to go to the parent by the shortest route, 12-month-olds did not. Instead, they tended to repeat a previously successful response, and often went to the parent via the same side across trials. This result is consistent with the general finding that on a variety of manual and locomotor search tasks, infants often respond in a perseverative fashion (Harris, 1975; Piaget, 1954; Rieser, Doxsey, McCarrell, & Brooks, 1982; Sophian, this volume). Moreover, in the present context the results suggest that although the ability to use relative magnitude information can be found in rudimentary form at 12 months, it is subject to certain response constraints. We do not know when infants first use relative magnitude information to locomote from one place to another by the shortest route or what role experience plays in the development of this ability, but these questions could be investigated with infants who have just begun to crawl or with prelocomotor infants in walkers.

Although the present results indicate that by 12 months infants can use relative magnitude information in a spatially efficient manner, this ability undergoes important changes. One such change involves being able to demonstrate efficient spatial behavior when relative magnitude information is not immediately perceptible—that is, when it must be represented to some extent. This situation often arises as a child moves about a more complex environment that cannot be apprehended from a single vantage point. To act in a spatially efficient way in such settings, both magnitude and direction of movement must be coordinated. The child must not only represent information about the relative distances between locations, but must also code his or her current position with respect to a stable frame of reference or one that has been reliably updated as he or she moves about the space.

Rieser and Heiman (1982) have developed a procedure to investigate how these components of shortest-route behavior are coordinated early in development. In one experiment 18-month-olds and a select group of 14-month-olds were placed in the center of a cylindrical room and were trained to go to one of eight identical choice windows on the surrounding wall (see Fig. 1.1). They were then turned (either 135° or 315°) to a new position and from there had to find the original target window. Based on the patterning of the child's search behavior, spatial efficiency could be examined in terms of both magnitude and direction of movement. The results indicated that both groups of toddlers generally turned in the direction of the shorter route (reversing the direction of self-movement in the case of a 135° turn and continuing in the same direction after a 315° turn) but tended to undershoot the target location. Although toddlers may have difficulty in precisely representing magnitude information in these situations, they nevertheless demonstrate a relative sensitivity to it. In a similar experiment, Rieser and Heiman found that 18-month-olds would appropriately adjust the magnitude

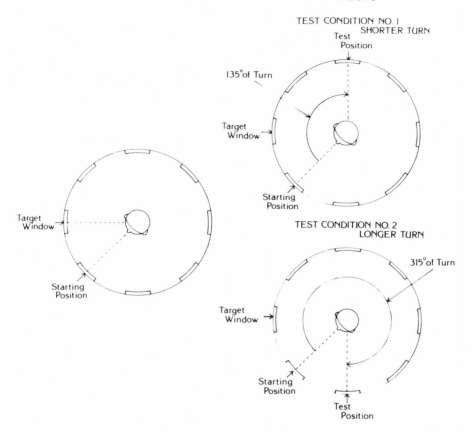

FIG. 1.1.   Schematic representation of shortest-route task used in Rieser and Heiman (1982) study. Training is depicted in the left half of the figure; the two test conditions are shown on the right. See text for additional explanation. (From Rieser & Heiman, 1982. Reprinted by permission.)

of their turns in relation to the magnitude of their movements away from the target. These results suggest that by 18 months, toddlers have begun to develop the ability to determine the shortest route to a location by coordinating updated self-reference information (no relevant distinctive landmarks were present in these settings) with represented magnitude information.

When young children must infer relative magnitude information from limited experience in a more complex environment and coordinate this information with their current position in that environment, spatial efficiency may break down. Hazen (1982), for example, trained 2-and 3-year-olds to learn an indirect route to a goal through a three-room layout arranged in a zig-zag pattern. They were then tested on their ability to go directly to the goal from various points along the route or from new starting positions in the space. Three-year-olds had few problems in performing these tasks but 2-year-olds experienced more difficulty, related both to the magnitude and direction of their movements. They often went indirectly to the goal, sometimes relying on body cues by turning in the same directions that they had learned to reach the goal, again showing a type of perseveration.

These studies suggest that the extent to which infants behave in a spatially efficient manner depends in part on the direct availability of relative magnitude information. Spatial efficiency may also depend on the degree to which relative magnitude information conflicts with other sources of route information. One potentially important source of conflict is associated with spatiotemporal factors—namely, information about events. Reliance on the path by which an object was hidden or where one of a series of objects was most recently hidden may interfere with efficient spatial search patterns. In fact, Piaget (1954) suggested that when infants first make locomotor detours to find a hidden object (i.e., when part of the detour path must be represented), they do so by retracing the object's disappearance trajectory.

There have been few investigations of how event *and* relative magnitude information influence the performance of efficient spatial behavior. Traditional studies of early search behavior have been concerned with where infants believe objects to be located rather than the way by which they get to those locations. However, we have recently initiated research on whether event information affects the way by which infants search for hidden objects (Lockman, 1983). Most relevant to the present discussion is whether infants base their searches for hidden objects on the objects' disappearance paths. Initial results indicate that they do to some extent, but that they are also able to overcome this event information. In one part of the study, 8-month-olds were tested weekly on two detour-reaching tasks, differing in how an object disappeared. In one problem, infants watched an object go *around* a tall, upright, opaque barrier, centered at midline, and could retrieve the object by making a detour reach in a similar manner. In the other problem, infants watched an object go *over* and behind the same barrier and could only retrieve the object by making a detour reach around the barrier—that is, by a path different from the object's disappearance trajectory. Infants generally began solving both problems at the same time, indicating that their first manual detours are not necessarily limited by an object's disappearance trajectory. Nevertheless, they often relied on this information in planning their reaching paths. When the object disappeared around a side of the barrier, infants were more likely to reach around that side to obtain the object. This even occurred when awkward reaches resulted; for example, infants sometimes reached around the right side of the barrier with the left hand. Thus, infants can search for hidden objects by overcoming the object's disappearance trajectories; yet, they tend to rely on this information and, in doing so, sometimes reach in an awkward and inefficient manner.

Event information may also conflict with relative magnitude information when a series of objects needs to be found. That is, information associated with the order in which several objects are hidden may not coincide with the most spatially efficient strategy for retrieving those objects (Menzel, 1978). When these sources of information do conflict, young children may have difficulty in demonstrating efficient spatial behavior. Cornell and Heth (1983) found that 16-month-olds often relied on recency information in retrieving two hidden objects in a large room. Rather than generally using a least-distance strategy, they tended to search first where the most recent hiding had occurred. In contrast, 3-year-olds used a minimal-distance strategy regardless of the hiding order.

In more complex tasks, when more objects are hidden in larger environments, preschoolers may have difficulty in demonstrating efficient search patterns even though they do not solely rely on information about hiding order (Cornell & Heth, 1983; Wellman & Somerville, 1982; Wellman, Somerville, Revelle, Haake, & Sophian, in press). As more information about relative magnitude between locations must be represented and/or coordinated, it might become harder for young children to generate spatially efficient patterns of search behavior. To overcome this problem, an adaptive strategy would be to cluster locations rather than to consider individual distances between locations when generating search patterns. Wellman et al. (in press) adduced evidence that young children may adopt such a strategy on more complex multiple-object search tasks. Preschoolers had to retrieve several objects after observing an adult hide them in a playground by walking a circuitous route. Although the preschoolers did not search for the objects by the shortest possible route, neither did they follow the adult's route. They minimized their search patterns to some extent by grouping locations into clusters, and by searching one cluster more or less exhaustively before searching the others. Preschoolers thus appear able to overcome event information associated with hiding order to generate search patterns that take into account some information about relative magnitude.

Summary

Early in life, infants are sensitive to size information and appear able to use information about relative magnitude to guide their spatial behavior. They will demonstrate appropriate kinds of visuomotor coordination for distance information—for example, by reaching more frequently for near rather than far objects. They will also use this information to behave in a spatially efficient manner—for example, by locomoting around a simple barrier by the shorter route. We noted, however, that little is known about how children's use of relative magnitude information in skilled action changes with age. Based on existing research, we suggested that during the infancy and toddler periods certain stimulus and response constraints are overcome. Young children may initially have difficulty in using relative magnitude information in an efficient manner if it is not directly available and/or it conflicts with other sources of route or distance information.

And even if the information is perceptually available, a tendency to respond in a perseverative fashion may mask a sensitivity to relative magnitude information. Additional work is needed to uncover the processes by which young children arrive at decisions of relative magnitude. In more complicated problems involving the combination and comparison of several distances, knowledge of these processes may provide us with insights into the early development of some basic quantitative skills (also see Strauss & Curtis, this volume).

Up to this point, we have been focusing attention on how children respond directly to size or relative magnitude information. Size or distance, however, may also have indirect effects on other aspects of spatial behavior. We next examine what these effects might be and their implications for the development of spatial cognition.

PROBLEM OF SCALE AND INDIRECT EFFECTS OF SIZE ON SPATIAL BEHAVIOR

When differences in size of spatial layout result in different modes of behaving, conceiving of space, or processing spatial information, we speak of differences in scale. In fact, one approach to describing the indirect effects of size or scale on spatial behavior has been to categorize the properties of spaces differing in size or scale and to demonstrate that these properties have some empirical consequences for spatial cognition. Acredolo (1981), for example, compared large- and small-scale spaces, distinguishing between them on the basis of whether the space surrounds the observer *and* requires multiple viewpoints for its apprehension. Using this distinction, Acredolo pointed out that the impact of landmarks is similar for both large- and small-scale spaces. On the other hand, egocentric responding persists till a much later age in a landmark-free large-scale space than in a model of that space. Weatherford (1982) extended Acredolo's criteria and distinguished between model and navigable spaces and between large- and small-scale spaces. According to Weatherford, navigable spaces differ from model spaces in that the latter can only be observed and manipulated from the outside; small-scale spaces differ from large-scale spaces in that the former can be viewed from one vantage point whereas the latter require multiple viewpoints for complete exposure.[1] The utility of this distinction is illustrated in the work of Weath-

---

[1]Weatherford combines these characteristics into a three-member classification: model/small-scale, navigable/small-scale, and navigable/large-scale. Weatherford does not use the qualifier navigable for his large-scale space although it is clear from his discussion that he means this. Logically and practically, it would also be possible to have model/large-scale spaces completing a 2 × 2 classification. These would, of course, be spaces that were so small that they could only be viewed from the outside but that were constructed such that they have to be viewed from multiple points of view. At present, there is little research that uses spaces of this last type.

erford and Cohen (1981), who compared interpoint distance judgments of children given experience with navigable small- or large-scale spaces. The experience with the space consisted either of walking through it or viewing it from four stationary points along the perimeter. Third-grade children did better in the large-scale space with the walking experience than with the stationary viewing; type of experience did not make a difference in the small-scale space. In contrast, none of these variables affected performance of fifth-grade children.

Although size and scale of space as defined here do indeed seem to have the kinds of empirical consequences that Acredolo and Weatherford point out, it seems that the actual effective or process variables are not the size nor the scale (nor multiple viewing) per se but rather the consequences these factors have for the spatial cognizer. Weatherford (1982) indeed anticipates this point by suggesting that spaces of different scale impose differential processing demands on observers trying to master them. Following this idea we feel that it might be better to try to describe these demands than to simply categorize the nature of the space in a very general way. Indeed, a person's spatial behavior is affected by the way information about a spatial layout is acquired and by the response demands of the task being performed. Although in most situations both of these factors are operative, we would want to consider how size or scale affects these factors individually.

How might size and scale affect the way information is acquired? Perhaps the first place to look is at the initial registration of spatial information. Does the size of the space make any difference in what information is registered? At an almost sensory level we can ask if the visual field of the subject places any constraints on the size of space over which spatial information can be handled. Here, too, there is not a lot of evidence about this from a developmental perspective. However, a very suggestive experiment was described by Enns and Girgus (1983), who showed subjects of different ages (7, 9, and 22 years) Escher-like impossible figures of rectangular frames in which the left and right halves of the frame were incompatible. Subjects were asked to detect these impossible figures in the context of foils of depictions of possible frames. By making the horizontal connecting parts of the frame different lengths, they were able to vary the effective visual field. For stimuli subtending small visual angles, children of all ages and adults were equally fast at identifying the possible and impossible figures. However, at the larger visual angles children were much slower than adults to detect the nature of the figures. These results seem to suggest that there are developmental changes in the size of the visual field across which configurational information is quickly processed.

This finding is consistent with the developmental trend we noted some time ago for increasing sensitivity with age to more and more remote frames of reference (Yonas & Pick, 1975). That generalization was based on experiments in which subjects were shown a spatial layout and were then tested for recall of particular locations when various aspects of the frames of reference originally present were placed in conflict. For example, Acredolo (1976) brought children between 3 and 7 years of age into a relatively bare room with a window at one end and a table on one side. The children were taken to a corner of the table and blindfolded. They were then led via a circuitous path back to the door end or to the window end of the room. During their blindfold walk the table might or might not have been moved to the other side of the room. The blindfold was removed and the children were asked to return to the place in the room where they had originally been blindfolded. Three frames of reference could possibly be operative in this situation: egocentric (going left or right), object-landmark (table), shell or container (walls of room). Acredolo's procedure permitted pitting all pairs of two reference systems against the third and teasing out which frame of reference is preferred at different ages. In returning to the place where blindfolded they might have oriented on the basis of egocentric responses—turning right or left when they first came in the room—on the basis of objects in the room—the table—or on the basis of the shell of the room—the walls. The younger children tended to respond in terms of an egocentric reference system; the older children in terms of the shell, and children of intermediate age, more in terms of the objects.

There is no reason at present to doubt this generalization about the sensitivity to more and more remote frames of reference. However, it is also the case that differences in size or scale of a layout may be accompanied by differences in the distinctiveness of the locations of interest within the space. Such differences may be associated with differences in how information is registered and encoded. An example of this can be taken from a recent report by Hazen and Volk-Hudson (1983) on the ability of children of different ages to use spatial layouts of different sizes to aid the recall of a set of objects in the fashion of the method of loci. One space was a 3 $\times$ 3 matrix of small boxes on the top of a table in front of the subject. Three- and 4-year-old children observed the objects being hidden in the boxes and were then asked to recall as many as possible, either in a free-recall manner or with the context of the matrix layout present. In an analogous experiment the nine locations were places around a preschool classroom. In each location was a familiar object that the children observed and named. The objects were then removed and the children were asked to recall them either inside the original room or in a different room. Recall was facilitated for the 4-year-olds by the original spatial context with both spatial layouts. However, for the 3-year-olds it was only facilitated with the larger layout. What is it about the larger layout that could account for the more general facilitating effect? There were a number of differences between the two spaces but an obvious one is the greater distinctiveness of the locations in the larger space. Part of that distinctiveness involved the different actions that the subjects had to perform in dealing with the objects in the different locations. For the matrix space all locations were on a table top in front of the subjects. Looking at the different locations when the objects were being labeled did not even involve very different eye movements.

With the larger space the subjects turned around to each location as they named the object. Thus the responses with respect to an egocentric frame of reference were very similar in the small-scale space and very different in the large-scale space. With respect to an external frame of reference, looking at the locations in the small-scale space was also very similar. All the locations were confined to the table top, which was at approximately the same place in the context of the larger room. On the other hand, in the condition involving objects in the pre-school room, the locations were in rather different places with respect to the shell of the room considered as a frame of reference

Scale differences can also implicate differences in modality of processing and thus can affect what spatial information is acquired. For example, spatial information acquired through reaching may differ from the spatial information acquired through locomotion even though the tasks themselves might be formally similar. This can be illustrated by an experiment reported by Garfin (1983). In this work, 8-year-old children and adults learned two spatial layouts. One was a table-top layout involving reaching among locations while blindfolded. The other was a locomotory layout on the floor of an unusually complex building. In both cases the layout consisted of a home base and three target locations. And in both cases the subjects learned to go from the home base to each of the three locations until they could do this quickly and accurately. They were then asked to judge the direction of each location from every other location. There were no age differences in the small proprioceptive space, but the adults were more accurate in inferring the directions (of the out-of-sight targets) in the locomotory space. More revealing for the purposes of the present discussion, however, was that the correlations between spatial performance in the reaching and locomotory spatial tasks were low and insignificant for both the children and adults (.13 and .14, respectively). Apparently, the spatial processing in these formally similar tasks with different modalities is quite different.

Even when the modalities of processing spatial information are similar across scales, increase of scale of a space may also be accompanied by increase of complexity of the space. Thus, changes in spatial performance may well be due to this correlated variable. A dramatic example of the effect of this correlated change occurs when the size of the space is increased by adding another level to a single-level environment. In a recently completed study we investigated this problem by asking children (4- to 6-year-olds) and their parents to aim a sighting tube directly at target locations that were out of sight behind walls on the same floor or at locations also out of sight upstairs or downstairs from where they were standing (Lockman & Pick, in preparation). The layout of this two-level space is shown in Fig. 1.2. In both cases spatial inferences were required because the direct angle and the functional path to the target locations were quite different. Children were just about as accurate as adults when the target locations were on the same floor but their accuracy deteriorated markedly when they were aiming at targets on different floors. The adults' performance was just about as good for between-floor as for within-floor judgments (see Fig. 1.3) The experimental space in this case was the subjects' own duplex apartments. The difficulty the subjects had with the between-floor judgments might be due to the general increase of complexity of the space when several new locations must be considered. However, there would be no reason for the between-floor judgments to be systematically more difficult if the issue was simply overall complexity. Two

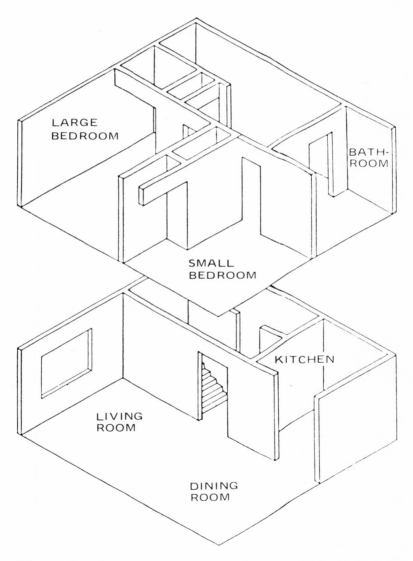

FIG. 1.2. Layout of the duplex apartments used in the study by Lockman and Pick (in preparation).

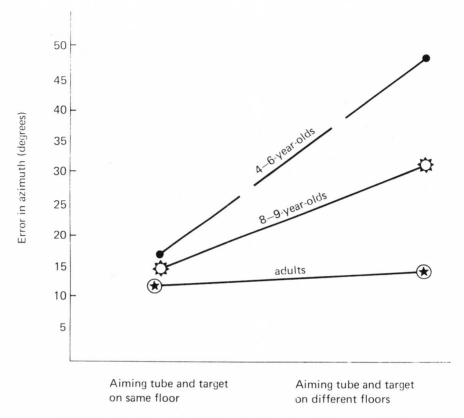

FIG. 1.3.   Azimuth errors by children and adults when pointing at out-of-sight locations from the same floor as the target location or from a different floor. (From Lockman & Pick, in preparation.)

other possibilities should be considered. One is that any increase of size of space by trying to relate a separately organized layout would lead to this kind of result. The other is that increasing the size or scale of space by adding a new dimension—that is, the vertical dimension—causes the increased difficulty found here.

Suggestive evidence in support of the first possibility was obtained by Garfin and Pick (1981) trying to use reaching spaces as analogues. In this work, adult subjects were familiarized with two spatial layouts. In each case a subject learned to reach, for example, from home base *L* to locations *A, B,* and *C,* and then from home base *N* to each of locations *1, 2,* and *3.* During the familiarization period, subjects never reached between the letter locations or between the number locations. After this familiarization, subjects were given specific information about how the two spaces overlapped and were then asked to make spatial inferences within a space—for example, between *A* and *C*—and between spaces—for example, between *B* and *3*. The within-space inferences were made more accurately than the between-space inferences. This result is consistent with the idea that it is not the fact that the two spaces to be integrated involve a new third dimension but rather that any additional space that must be integrated imposes difficulty. Additional support for this hypothesis would be provided if similar results were obtained in a locomotor version of this experiment.

Besides affecting spatial behavior through the way information about a layout is initially acquired, size or scale can affect spatial behavior by the response demands of a task. These response demands could affect behavior in various ways. If the response has been recently learned, simple performance may require so much processing capacity that retrieving spatial information or sophisticated use of it might be impaired. This is perhaps the case in a study of infants' detour behavior by Lockman (in press). Twelve infants were tested every 3 weeks from approximately 8 to 12 months of age on corresponding reaching and locomotor detour tasks. In the detour tasks, infants had to either reach or locomote around an upright opaque or transparent barrier to retrieve an object that they had just seen disappear over and behind the barrier. The barrier was too tall for the infants to retrieve the object by simply retracing the object's trajectory. In general, the results indicated that infants began solving the reaching task before the corresponding locomotor one, by about a month's time.

Of most interest here, however, is the reason for the differential reaching and locomotor detour performance. One possible explanation directly implicates size rather than the different motor responses. That is, the reason for the lag in performance may be due to the different lengths of the barriers rather than to the different responses required in the two tasks. In an ideal test of this explanation, barrier length should be equated across reaching and locomotor problems. However, with barrier lengths equal, it is unlikely that infants would make a reaching detour in one situation and a locomotor detour in the other. To overcome this problem, the effect of barrier length on detour behavior could be investigated within one type of response. Thus, another group of twelve infants were tested every 2 to 3 weeks on two locomotor detour tasks, one with a narrow barrier not much wider than the breadth of the infant's shoulders and the other with a longer barrier, the same length as used in the previous experiment. The results clearly indicated that barrier length had no effect on when detours were first made. All twelve infants first solved both detour problems during the same session. This finding suggests that the lag in first making reaching and locomotor detours is probably not a function of barrier length. Rather, it lends support to the idea that the difference is associated with the motor responses themselves. Possibly because reaching is a more practiced and earlier-developed skill than crawling, infants are freer to attend to the spatial demands of problems and can readily use this skill to establish desired spatial relationships. In any event, the results suggest that it is not size or scale per se but rather the response demands associated with the different scales that are responsible for these early patterns of spatial behavior.

Summary

In this section, we have considered how size or scale may have indirect effects on spatial behavior. Our focus has not been to provide a taxonomy of spaces in terms of size or scale, but rather to consider the processing demands entailed by scale differences. In doing so, we have examined how scale differences may affect the acquisition of spatial information and impose different response demands on young children. Scale differences may be associated with differences in the distinctiveness of locations within each space, in the complexity of the space, and in the mode of processing and responding to information contained in each space. It appears that developmental differences in spatial behavior may be better understood by considering these correlated variables rather than simply considering the size or scale variable by itself.

COORDINATING INFORMATION BETWEEN SCALES

Up to this point, we have considered how young children may show direct sensitivity to size or magnitude information in their spatial behavior and how size or scale variables may affect other aspects of spatial behavior. In some sense, all the individual behaviors that have been examined have involved the use of information that is present within a given scale. Yet some sophisticated kinds of spatially coordinated behavior require coordination of information from different scales. For instance, instrumentation tasks involving the magnification or minification of perceptual information often require a person to coordinate information perceived in one scale with actions performed in another. This problem occurs when performing actions under a microscope—visual information apprehended under one scale is being related to proprioceptive information perceived along a different scale. A different type of scale coordination or translation problem occurs when people construct or use external representations in spatial tasks—for example, when building models of large-scale environments or when using maps to navigate through them. Here, too, information acquired under one scale must be related to actions that are being performed in a different scale. Although the ability to coordinate spatial behavior with respect to information in different scales is clearly an important aspect of skilled action, we know little about its development. If, as was suggested in the previous section, scale differences affect the acquisition of spatial information and impose different response demands, then we might also expect coordination problems to arise as a result of these differential processing demands.

The following discussion concerns what happens when spatial behavior must be coordinated with respect to information from different scales. An attempt is made to examine the types of information and correspondences that are present within and between scales and how the child may detect and relate them. In some ways, this approach resembles those used for studying cross-modal perception, which emphasize the equivalence of information across modalities rather than the discrete nature of the modalities or the information from them (Gibson, 1966; Goodnow, 1971; see also Bornstein, this volume). Here, the focus is on how children relate information across scales by looking at the correspondences they establish within and between scales. This framework is employed to describe how coordination problems may arise when children construct or use representations of large-scale environments. In doing so, we hope also to gain some insights into the general processes by which young children perceive and understand representations.

Much of the literature on the development of spatial cognition has been concerned with determining what is the most appropriate method for externalizing children's spatial representations (Liben, 1982; Newcombe, in press; Siegel, 1981). Some methods have been questioned because they require children to demonstrate their spatial knowledge in a scale that is different from the one in which the knowledge was originally acquired. Yet these same methods may be of interest precisely because they offer insights into how children translate spatial information from one scale to another. In fact, some studies employing these methods suggest that scale-coordination problems do cause difficulty for children. Liben, Moore, and Golbeck (1982) found that when preschoolers had to reconstruct the layout of their classroom by replacing either full-size furniture in the actual classroom or miniaturized furniture in a model of it, they performed better when no scale reduction was involved. Siegel, Herman, Allen, and Kirasic (1979) also investigated how children translate information across scales by first having kindergartners, second, and fifth graders repeatedly explore a large- or small-scale town and then having them recreate the layout of the town in either a large- or small-scale environment. Accuracy was greatest when children constructed the town in the same-scale environment in which knowledge had been originally acquired and was significantly lower when they were tested in a large-scale setting after being exposed to a small-scale one.

Demonstrating that children may experience difficulty on some scale-coordination problems is only the first step in understanding how children translate information from one scale to another. Scale-translation problems may arise when correspondences within or between scales are not detected, or, put another way, when incorrect assumptions are made about equivalencies that exist within or between scales. In the following discussion, we consider how sources of spatial information within and between scales may not coincide and hence result in scale-translation problems.

Spatial information *between* scales may not be in direct correspondence when representations are used to guide action. Either the person's position is changing without corresponding changes in the relative orientation of the representation and/or the person and representation were never originally aligned. To establish the correspondence, various strategies such as mental rotation (Huttenlocher & Presson, 1973; 1979) or noticing the relative positions of salient landmarks could be employed. However, by simply assuming a spatial equivalency between the two scales, egocentric errors would result. In fact, this is what often happens when young children try to use maps that are not aligned with the space that they represent. Bluestein and Acredolo (1979), for example, gave 3- to 5-year-olds a map-reading task in which they had to infer the location of a hidden object in a room from information contained in the map. The hiding place, midway along one of the four sides of the room, was marked on the map. Although the possible hiding places themselves were not distinctively marked, each corner of the room was—for example, with a red box in one corner, a white triangle in another, and so on. When the map was aligned with the room, even the 3-year-olds were able to go to the correct location. However, when the map was rotated 180° with respect to the room, very few of the 3- or 4-year-olds solved the problem correctly, whereas a high proportion of the 5-year-olds did. To interpret this pattern of results, we would like to suggest that the different age groups related the scales by relying on different spatial correspondences. The younger children appear to have incorrectly assumed an overall spatial equivalency between the two scales. Consistent with this idea is that the majority of the 3- and 4-year-olds' errors were egocentric. That is, they went to the location in the room that would have been correct had no rotation taken place. In contrast, the 5-year-olds may have solved the problem by detecting a topological correspondence between the two scales—for example, the hiding place is on the side of the room between the red box and white triangle. Given the difficulty that children have in mentally changing their points of view (Hardwick, McIntyre, & Pick, 1976), it is unlikely that they would have solved these problems using a mental-rotation strategy.

Presson (1982) has also found that older children may rely on topological correspondences (near/far information) when they relate a rotated map to a space. In Presson's task, kindergartners and second graders had to use a map to locate an object that was hidden in one of four identical containers, each placed in a corner of a room. The map (and room) contained only one landmark that could be used to orient the map. This landmark was situated along one of the sides of the room and was either next to the hidden object or along a different wall. Although the children made errors when the map was not aligned with the room, they tended to preserve the near/far relation of the target to the landmark. Taken together, both of these map-reading studies indicate that children may try to relate information in different scales by detecting or even expecting to find equivalencies that exist across scales. When information in the two scales is not in direct correspondence, young children may nevertheless act as if it is and produce systematic types of spatial errors.

Scale-coordination problems may also arise when different sources of spatial information *within* a scale are not in direct correspondence with one another. Young children, however, may act as if they are and experience difficulty when attempting to relate this information to a different scale. This type of problem is illustrated in a recently completed study on how young children coordinate route and landmark information in maps to guide self-locomotion (Lockman & Glorsky, 1983). Three- and four-year-olds were tested on their ability to follow a route that was depicted on a map of a large room. Children were presented with two map-reading problems: a direct landmark test and an indirect one. In the direct task, landmarks were positioned at the turnpoints along the route. In the indirect task, landmarks were positioned along the routes but not at the turnpoints (see Fig. 1.4). Thus, in this condition landmarks and turnpoints did not coincide. When 3-year-olds attempted to use the map, they generally went straight to the goal, regardless of the route on the map. In contrast, the 4-year-olds apparently understood that the landmarks were related to the turnpoints, but treated them equivalently, as if they were coincident. Thus, in the direct task, the 4-year-olds followed the route correctly, turning at the appropriate points—at the landmarks. However, in the indirect task, the 4-year-olds *also* turned at the landmarks. That is, they generally turned at the wrong points but went from landmark to landmark in the correct sequence. It seems that preschoolers are just beginning to differentiate between the functions of route and landmark information in maps.

In the previous example, we suggested that scale-translation problems can occur when young children treat certain kinds of information within a scale in an equivalent fashion. Scale-coordination problems may also arise if a correspondence is never established between the within-scale sources of information. This may happen when a child registers both types of within-scale information but fails to coordinate them. Or it might happen because one type of within-scale information is never detected at all. Both of these possibilities are illustrated in a study we conducted several years ago on how children construct representations of large-scale environments (Hazen, Lockman, & Pick, 1978). In this experiment, 3- to 6-year-olds were trained to go by a specific route through a series of rooms, each of which contained a distinctive landmark. Once the route and landmarks along it were learned, children were tested on a series of measures designed to test their knowledge of the environment. One such measure was to construct a small-scale model of the environment. To construct a correct model, the children had to coordinate information about the overall shape of the layout with information about the sequence of landmarks in it. Some children appeared to have registered both types of information but failed to coordinate them when constructing the model. That is, at different times in the model-construction task, these children demonstrated knowledge of the correct sequence and correct shape, but never simultaneously (see Fig. 1.5, especially 5B and 5D). Other children, especially the younger ones, appeared to have mainly relied on the sequence information. Their models reflected knowledge of the sequence of landmarks but not knowledge of the overall shape. This latter finding suggests that as some children walked through the space, they registered information about the sequence of landmarks but not about the configuration of the space. Why might this be? As we noted in the previous section, the size or scale of a space may affect the acquisition of spatial information. Walking through a large-

DIRECT TASKS   INDIRECT TASKS

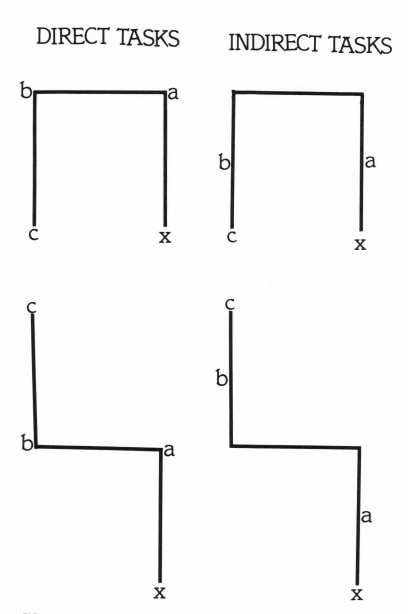

FIG. 1.4.   Schematic representations of the maps used in the study by Lockman and Glorsky (1983). The maps in the left part of the Figure were used in the direct task; the maps in the right part were used in the indirect task. The letters—a, b, and c—indicate the locations of the depicted landmarks in the maps as well as the actual location of the landmarks in the room. X indicates the child's starting position.

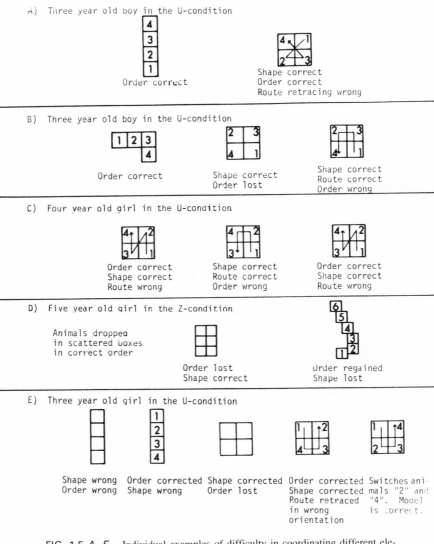

FIG. 1.5 *A—E*. Individual examples of difficulty in coordinating different elements of spatial knowledge during model construction in study by Hazen, Lockman, and Pick (1978). Numbers in the boxes represent the serial position of the landmark contained in that box; arrows represent how the child retraced the route. (From Hazen, Lockman, & Pick, 1978. Reprinted by permission.)

scale space by a specific route may highlight information about landmarks or sequence rather than information about overall layout. When children must demonstrate their knowledge of the space in a different scale, they may not succeed because some of the information was never detected in the original scale. In fact, some of the children seemed to have successfully solved the model-construction task by relying on information about the path to generate the correct shape. With increasing age, children appear to become better at detecting the correspondence between the routes within a space and the overall configuration of that space.

Summary

There has been little work on how children coordinate their spatial behavior with respect to information from different scales. We suggested that this problem might be studied by examining how children construct and use representations, particularly those of large-scale environments. Our strategy was to examine the information and correspondences that are present within and between scales and how children may detect and relate them. This analysis suggested that young children may have difficulty with scale-translation problems when either between- or within-scale sources of information are not in direct correspondence or when some sources of information are not detected at all.

CONCLUSIONS

Our purpose in this chapter has been to examine the role of size or scale in the development of spatially coordinated behavior. We suggested that size or scale factors are implicated in spatial development in three general ways. The most direct way is visuomotor coordination appropriate to the available distance information. Young children will act in a spatially efficient manner, at least when relative magnitude information is perceptually and unambiguously available. Size or scale factors may also affect spatial behavior in an indirect way. Empirical research supports the view that these effects are best understood by considering the processing and response demands entailed by scale differences. Finally, scale factors become important when spatial information must be related across scales. To the extent that information in different scales and the means for detecting it are similar, it should not be difficult for children to relate information across scales.

The present analysis has both theoretical and applied implications. We noted that there has been little work on the processes by which young children arrive at decisions of relative magnitude in problems involving the combination and comparison of several distances. Some of the spatial problems on shortest-route behavior that we considered in the first section appear to be a potentially rich source of information about basic quantitative abilities of infants and toddlers.

One way young children may learn about the consequences of combining different amounts is through spatial problems that they may encounter in their everyday environments. Routes are often blocked and decisions need to be made about alternate ways to get to desired locations. Observations of spatial efficiency in familiar settings with several possible alternatives may be particularly enlightening. Investigations of efficiency of such behavior in cases in which the whole route is visible as opposed to cases in which some portions are occluded would illuminate the relative importance of perception and mental representation.

In the present analysis the question of scale almost automatically focuses attention on optimizing in terms of shortest-route behavior. However, there are other optimization principles that might be relevant to spatial behavior. For example, spatial behavior might be organized to minimize effort or danger—or to maximize simplicity of route. These principles do not necessarily or generally coincide with shortest distance. Situations could easily be established to investigate children's sensitivity to such factors and their interaction with distance.

On the applied side, some of our proposals about the coordination of information across scales may be relevant for constructing representations that will be understood by children. Blind children, for example, are known to have difficulty using tactile maps, but there have been few systematic analyses of the information presented in these representations or of how it is detected. Our proposals suggest that this is an important first step in understanding how representations are used.

ACKNOWLEDGMENT

Preparation of this manuscript was in part supported by Program Project Grant HDO50207 from the National Institute of Child Health and Human Development to the Institute of Child Development, University of Minnesota.

REFERENCES

Acredolo, L. P. Frames of reference used by children for orientation in unfamiliar spaces. In G. Moore & R. Golledge (Eds.), *Environmental knowing*. Stroudsburg, Pa.: Dowden, Hutchinson, & Ross, 1976.

Acredolo, L. P. Small- and large-scale spatial concepts in infancy and childhood. In L. S. Liben, A. H. Patterson, & N. Newcombe (Eds.), *Spatial representation and behavior across the life span: Theory and application*. New York: Academic Press, 1981.

Bluestein, N., & Acredolo, L. P. Developmental changes in map-reading skills. *Child Development*, 1979, *50*, 691–697.

Bower, T. G. R. Discrimination of depth in premotor infants. *Psychonomic Science*, 1964, *1*, 368.

Bruner, J., & Koslowski, B. Visually preadapted constituents of manipulatory action. *Perception*, 1972, *1*, 3–14.

Cornell, E. H., & Heth, C. D. Spatial cognition: Gathering strategies used by preschool children. *Journal of Experimental Child Psychology*, 1983, *35*, 93–110.

Enns, J. T., & Girgus, J. S. *Developmental changes in the perception of impossible figures.* Paper presented at the meetings of the Society for Research in Child Development, Detroit, April 1983.

Field, J. Relation of young infants' reaching behavior to stimulus distance and solidity. *Developmental Psychology,* 1976, *12,* 444–448.

Fox, R., Aslin, R. N., Dumais, S. T., & Shea, S. L. Stereopsis in human infants. *Science,* 1980, *207,* 323–324.

Garfin, D. *Cognitive mapping: Individual differences across the lifespan.* Unpublished doctoral dissertation, University of Minnesota, 1983.

Garfin, D., & Pick, H. L., Jr. *Reaching out for spatial knowledge.* Paper presented at the meetings of the Midwest Psychological Association, Detroit, May 1981.

Gibson, E. J., & Walk, R. D. The "visual cliff." *Scientific American,* 1960, *202,* 2–9.

Gibson, J. J. *The senses considered as perceptual systems.* New York: Houghton-Mifflin, 1966.

Goodnow, J. J. The role of modalities in perceptual and cognitive development. In J. P. Hill (Ed.), *Minnesota symposia on child psychology* (Vol. 5). Minneapolis: University of Minnesota Press, 1971.

Gordon, F. R., & Yonas, A. Sensitivity to binocular depth information in infants. *Journal of Experimental Child Psychology,* 1976, *22,* 413–422.

Hardwick, D. A., McIntyre, C. W., & Pick, H. L., Jr. The content and manipulation of cognitive maps in children and adults. *Monographs of the Society for Research in Child Development,* 1976, *41*(3, Serial No. 166).

Harris, P. L. Development of search and object permanence during infancy. *Psychological Bulletin,* 1975, *82,* 332–344.

Hazen, N. L. Spatial exploration and spatial knowledge: Individual and developmental differences in very young children. *Child Development,* 1982, *53,* 826–833.

Hazen, N. L., Lockman, J. J., & Pick, H. L., Jr. The development of children's representations of large-scale environments. *Child Development,* 1978, *49,* 623–636.

Hazen, N. L., & Volk-Hudson, S. *Children's use of spatial strategies in memory.* Paper presented at the meetings of the Society for Research in Child Development, Detroit, April 1983.

Huttenlocher, J., & Presson, C. C. Mental rotation and the perspective problem. *Cognitive Psychology,* 1973, *4,* 279–299.

Huttenlocher, J., & Presson, C. C. The coding and transformation of spatial information. *Cognitive Psychology,* 1979, *11,* 375–394.

Liben, L. S. Children's large-scale spatial cognition: Is the measure the message? In R. Cohen (Ed.), *Children's conceptions of spatial relationships.* San Francisco: Jossey-Bass, 1982.

Liben, L. S., Moore, M. L., & Golbeck, S. L. Preschoolers' knowledge of their classroom environment: Evidence from small-scale and life-size spatial tasks. *Child Development,* 1982, *53,* 1275–1284.

Lockman, J. J. *Piaget's theory of infant spatial development: A reassessment.* Paper presented at the meeting of the Society for Research in Child Development, Detroit, April 1983.

Lockman, J. J. The development of detour ability during infancy. *Child Development,* in press.

Lockman, J. J., & Ashmead, D. H. Asynchronies in the development of manual behavior. In L. P. Lipsitt (Ed.), *Advances in infancy research* (Vol. 2). Norwood, N.J.: Ablex, 1983.

Lockman, J. J., & Glorsky, R. L. *Young children's use of route and landmark information in maps.* Paper presented at the meeting of the Society for Research in Child Development, Detroit, April 1983.

Lockman, J. J., & Pick, H. L., Jr. *The representation of three-dimensional space.* Manuscript in preparation.

Menzel, E. W. Cognitive mapping in chimpanzees. In S. H. Hulse, H. Fowler, & W. K. Honig (Eds.), *Cognitive aspects of animal behavior.* Hillsdale, N.J.: Lawrence Erlbaum Associates, 1978.

Newcombe, N. Methods for the study of spatial cognition. In R. Cohen (Ed.), *The development of spatial cognition.* Hillsdale, N.J.: Lawrence Erlbaum Associates, in press.

Piaget, J. *The construction of reality in the child.* New York: Basic Books, 1954.

Pick, H. L., Jr., & Lockman, J. J. From frames of reference to spatial representation. In L. Liben, A. H. Patterson, & N. Newcombe (Eds.), *Spatial representation and behavior across the life-span: Theory and application.* New York: Academic Press, 1981.

Presson, C. C. The development of map-reading skills. *Child Development,* 1982, *53,* 196–199.

Rader, N., Bausano, M., & Richards, J. E. On the nature of the visual-cliff avoidance response in human infants. *Child Development,* 1980, *51,* 61–68.

Rieser, J. J., Doxsey, P. A., McCarrell, N. S., & Brooks, P. H. Way-finding and toddlers' use of information from an aerial view of a maze. *Developmental Psychology,* 1982, *18,* 714–720.

Rieser, J. J., & Heiman, M. L. Spatial self-reference systems and shortest-route behavior in toddlers. *Child Development,* 1982, *53,* 524–533.

Siegel, A. W. The externalization of cognitive maps by children and adults: In search of ways to ask better questions. In L. S. Liben, A. H. Patterson, & N. Newcombe (Eds.), *Spatial representation and behavior across the life-span: Theory and application.* New York: Academic Press, 1981.

Siegel, A. W., Herman, J. F., Allen, G. L., & Kirasic, K. C. The development of cognitive maps of large- and small-scale spaces. *Child Development,* 1979, *50,* 582–585.

Weatherford, D. L. Spatial cognition as a function of size and scale of the environment. In R. Cohen (Ed.), *Children's conceptions of spatial relationships.* San Francisco: Jossey-Bass, 1982.

Weatherford, D. L., & Cohen, R. *The influence of locomotor activity on spatial representations of large-scale environments.* Paper presented at the meeting of the Society for Research in Child Development, Boston, April 1981.

Wellman, H. M., & Somerville, S. C. The development of human search ability. In M. E. Lamb & A. L. Brown (Eds.), *Advances in developmental psychology* (Vol. 2). Hillsdale, N.J.: Lawrence Erlbaum Associates, 1982.

Wellman, H. M., Somerville, S. C., Revelle, G., Haake, R. J., & Sophian, C. The development of comprehensive search skills. *Child Development,* in press.

Yonas, A., Cleaves, W., & Petterson, L. Development of sensitivity to pictorial depth. *Science,* 1978, *200,* 77–79.

Yonas, A., Pettersen, L., Lockman, J. J., & Eisenberg, P. *The perception of impending collision in 3-month-old infants.* Paper presented at the International Conference on Infant Studies, New Haven, April 1980.

Yonas, A., & Pick, H. L., Jr. An approach to the study of infant space perception. In L. B. Cohen & P. Salapatek (Eds.), *Infant perception: From sensation to cognition* (Vol. 2). New York: Academic Press, 1975.

2 Developing Search Skills in Infancy and Early Childhood

Catherine Sophian
Carnegie-Mellon University

How does an initial set of competencies become elaborated or expanded into a more fully developed set of skills? This question is fundamental to all of developmental psychology, but it is perhaps nowhere more central than in the study of early cognitive development, for the cognitive skills of infants are the foundation for all of cognitive development. Nevertheless, developmental relationships between infant cognition and later cognitive development have seldom been directly investigated, and their implications for theories of cognitive development remain virtually unexplored. These problems are the focus of the present chapter.

A major influence on research on early cognitive development over the past decade or so has been the recognition that young children have positive competencies and not just cognitive deficits that contrast with later capabilities. The tendency to celebrate early competencies is well reflected in an influential collection of papers on infancy entitled *The Competent Infant* (Stone, Smith, & Murphy, 1973) and in a recent *Annual Review* chapter on cognitive development (Gelman, 1978), as well as in innumerable more specialized sources. Historically, this trend is a reaction to earlier views of the infant and even the preschool child as largely unintelligent. Against this background, the demonstration of many fundamental skills early in development clearly marks an important advance in our knowledge about the infant and the young child. Moreover, from a developmental perspective, this work has been useful in showing that early cognition contains the roots of cognitive skills that continue to be important later in development. At the same time, though, the emphasis on competencies has too often led researchers to be content with demonstrating that some capability is present at a single age rather than looking more broadly at developmental relationships between earlier and later skills.

27

To make further progress in understanding early cognitive development, we need to move beyond questions about whether young children are competent or incompetent to questions about how they perform our tasks and what kinds of changes take place with age. We need to look not just at whether children pass or fail our tasks but at what kinds of errors they make and what conditions facilitate or impede their performance. In addition, of course, we need to look not just at a single age group but at patterns of performance across age groups. These precepts are by now familiar ones in the developmental literature, but they are still only infrequently honored in research on the earliest phases of development.

The need for a broader developmental perspective in research on early cognition becomes especially clear when we try to construct a picture of development from infancy into childhood. Even when studies have included more than one age group, they have seldom encompassed both infancy (roughly, the first 2 years of life) and early childhood (roughly, the next 3 or 4 years). Infants and young children are not only seldom included in the same investigations, but they are typically studied by different investigators, using different procedures, often looking at different aspects of cognitive functioning. For instance, studies of perceptual abilities figure prominently in the infancy literature but account for relatively little work with older children, whereas just the reverse is true for studies of logical operations such as transitive inference or class inclusion. This division is at least in part a natural consequence of differences in what infants and children can do: It is quite difficult to find tasks that can be used appropriately and informatively with both infants and older children. Nevertheless, if we want to achieve a coherent picture of early development we need to find ways of studying comparable skills across a wider range of ages.

At present, our theories of cognitive development show the same lack of integration between infancy and childhood that characterizes empirical work. Most accounts highlight the contrasts between infants and young children and give little consideration to possible commonalities between them. For instance, Piaget's theory, which has certainly been the most influential account of cognitive development to date, characterizes infant intelligence as sensorimotor—that is, restricted to action—in contrast to the representational intelligence—operating at the level of thought rather than action—of older children. Piaget indicates little similarity between the two beyond their common dependence on the twin processes of assimilation and accommodation, which he considers basic to cognition at every level. The same contrast between sensorimotor and representational intelligence also appears in several more recent accounts of cognitive development (e.g., Case, 1980; Fischer, 1980), despite efforts in these accounts to move away from Piaget's strong claims of stage-wise development. In these theories, as in Piaget's, the processes that bring about developmental change are thought to be the same at all ages, but the specific cognitive structures that result, and the kinds of cognitive skills they make possible, are considered to be fundamentally different at different ages.

The conviction that infants are fundamentally different than even 2- or 3-year-old children thus underlies both the design of empirical research and the structure of theoretical accounts of development. Without doubt, this sense of different-ness derives much of its force from the many undeniable behavioral differences between infants and young children. These dramatic differences, however, may be overshadowing similarities in some aspects of behavior that are at least as significant for cognitive development.

Infants and older children do share at least one cognitively significant behavior that might be used to compare them more directly: search for hidden objects. Search is a form of problem solving that is meaningful even to infants and yet can be challenging even for much older children. It has played a central role in the study of infant cognition ever since Piaget's (1954) groundbreaking work on the development of object permanence. In work with preschool and early elementary school children, it has proved a useful tool for studying the development of memory (e.g., DeLoache & Brown, 1983; Horn & Myers, 1978; Wellman & Somerville, 1980) and inferential reasoning skills (e.g., Drozdal & Flavell, 1975; Wellman, Somerville, & Haake, 1979). By building upon both of these lines of research, search tasks can be developed that span infancy and early childhood (e.g., Sophian & Wellman, 1983) and thus can provide a more inte-grated view of cognitive development across the first several years of life.

In the present chapter, I present an account of cognitive development from infancy through early childhood based on research on early search. This account has three main parts. First, I argue that despite the obvious differences between infants and young children, there are important similarities in cognitive function-ing that should be reflected in any cognitive-developmental theory. I present evidence for correspondences both in the skills infants and children bring to search tasks and in the kinds of errors they make. Second, I outline several kinds of age differences that do appear in early search. These involve differences in the robustness and consistency of children's search skills, and in the prevalence of various inappropriate search patterns. Third, and finally, I propose some ideas about the kinds of developmental processes that might account for both the similarities and the differences we see across infancy and early childhood. Two developmental processes I postulate are an increase in the reliability of children's information-processing skills, and an increase in the degree to which children differentiate among different kinds of search problems.

CORRESPONDENCES ACROSS INFANCY AND EARLY CHILDHOOD

Correspondences across infancy and early childhood appear both in the compe-tencies children bring to search tasks and in the kinds of errors they make. Corresponding competencies can be seen not just in basic aspects of search that are achieved during infancy and persist into childhood but also in more complex search skills that are still developing well into childhood but already occur in rudimentary form in infancy. Corresponding error patterns can be seen in several types of systematic errors that occur over a wide age range.

Correspondences in Competencies

Several kinds of cognitive competencies underlie search both in infancy and in early childhood. The most fundamental of these involve understanding the nature of objects and of search: realizing that an object still exists when it is out of sight, that it can be recovered by searching for it, and that information about where it disappeared can be used to guide search. These competencies are generally thought to be acquired sometime in infancy, and it is no surprise that, once they are acquired, they persist into later periods of development. Hence, correspondences in these simple competencies are not a very powerful line of evidence for similarities between infants' and older children's cognition. Other, more complex, competencies, however, present a stronger picture of similarities, because they may still be developing well into childhood and yet already be present in rudimentary form in infants' searches. I consider two such competencies here: the ability to select between conflicting kinds of information about an object's location, and the ability to make inferences about unseen movements of an object.

Selective Information Use.   The ability to select appropriately between conflicting kinds of information becomes important in search whenever there is more than one basis for deciding where to search for a hidden object. For instance, a child who wants to put on a favorite shirt may know where it is usually kept, and ordinarily it would make sense to look there. Suppose, however, that her mother tells her it has just been washed and is still in the laundry room. Clearly, the child should ignore the information she has about its usual location and search instead on the basis of the information her mother provided about its present location. Similarly, imagine a child playing hide-and-seek with his friend. He knows his friend hid in the cellar the last few times, but he heard footsteps going *upstairs* this time while he was hiding his eyes. Again, he has to select between conflicting kinds of information in deciding where to search. Many naturalistic search situations, and many experimental search tasks as well, are like these examples in that more than one kind of information is available, and the effectiveness of a child's search depends on how he or she selects among them.

A number of different considerations may influence which of two or more conflicting sources of information should take precedence. Perhaps the most basic of these, and certainly the key one in studies of selective information use in search, is the immediacy of the information involved. It follows from our most fundamental notions about the nature of objects and of time and space that if an object is in a new location now it will no longer be in its previous location, and hence that information about that previous location ceases to be a useful basis for search when information about a subsequent location is available. Both of the preceding examples of selective information use, and all of the studies of selective information use in search, are based on this principle.

The first evidence that children can select appropriately between conflicting kinds of information about an object's location was obtained in a study of 3-, $4\frac{1}{2}$-, and 7-year-old children (Sophian & Wellman, 1980). In that study, information about an object's location was either communicated explicitly in a verbal statement (e.g., "it will be in the bedroom") or conveyed implicitly by selecting target objects that are strongly associated with particular rooms in a house (e.g., a pillow for the bedroom or a spoon for the kitchen). I refer to the former as verbal information and to the latter as knowledge-based information (because it derives from children's knowledge about the typical locations of objects). Differences in children's use of these two kinds of information were evaluated by looking at their performance when only one kind of information or the other was available. Evaluation of selective information use, however, rested on the extent to which children modified their use of the two kinds of information when they were in conflict, as compared to when each was available separately. Because the verbal information was more immediate, it should have taken precedence over the knowledge-based information when the two conflicted. Hence, if children were appropriately selective, they should have used the verbal information more, relative to the knowledge-based information, on conflict trials than on trials involving each kind of information separately. If they were not selective, however, they would be expected to use the two kinds of information to the same extent, relative to each other, on conflict trials as on the trials involving only one source of information or the other.

The data are shown in Fig. 2.1. The upper panel indicates on what proportion of conflict trials children responded in accordance with each of the two sources of information. (Searches that did not accord with either source of information were possible but quite rare in this study.) The lower panel indicates the corresponding proportions of trials on which children used each kind of information when it was the only information available. At all three ages children were selective in that they relied primarily on the more immediate source of information in the conflict condition, whereas they used the two kinds of information more equally when each was tested separately. At the same time, note that at all three ages there were a fair number of conflict trials on which children did not use the more immediate verbal information but searched in accordance with the knowledge-based information instead. Hence, although children showed some selectivity in their use of the two kinds of information, they were by no means perfectly selective.

A follow-up study confirmed that the selective information use that preschoolers show is in fact based on the immediacy of the information and not on

(A) INFORMATION IN CONFLICT

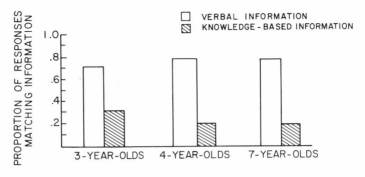

(B)   INFORMATION SEPARATION

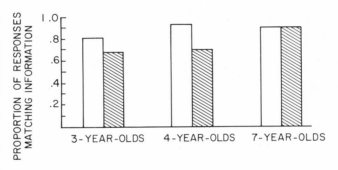

FIG. 2.1. Proportions of searches according with verbal and knowledge-based information on conflict trials (*A*) and on trials testing use of each kind of information separately (*B*). (From Sophian & Wellman, 1980.)

other differences between the conflicting sources of information (Sophian, 1982). In that study, verbal information was pitted against observational information based on watching the object being hidden. On some conflict trials, an object was initially hidden at one place as the child watched; then, it was surreptitiously retrieved and hidden again at a new location in such a way that the child could not see where it went but was told its new location verbally. On these trials, then, the verbal information was more immediate than the observational information and should have taken precedence. On other conflict trials, however, the order of events was reversed so that initially the object was hidden without the child's being able to see where, and its location was indicated verbally; and then it was surreptitiously retrieved and hidden at a new location in such a way that the child could observe the new hiding place. Thus, on these conflict trials it was the observational information that was more immediate and should have taken precedence. Across the two kinds of conflict trials, children tended to use the observational information more than the verbal information, but they also were sensitive to the ordering of the two kinds of information. They used the more immediate information on .76 of the conflict trials overall, and the less immediate information on only .19 of the trials.

To evaluate correspondences between infants' and children's search skills, it is important to consider how early the beginnings of selective information use might be present. Studies of perseveration in infants' searches initially suggested that it might *not* be present early in infancy. In studies of perseveration, an object is first hidden in one place, A, and then is hidden in a new place, B. Reportedly, 8- or 9-month-old infants continue to search at the A location on B trials, generating perseverative errors. These errors have traditionally been attributed to the lack of a mature concept of the object as existing independently of the infant. As long as infants search anywhere for a hidden object, however, it is clear that they have some concept of its continued existence when it is out of sight. Their problem is to determine *where* it is, and on B trials that requires choosing among conflicting sources of information, just as in the studies of selective information use with older children. On the one hand, the infant has current information from watching the object hidden at B; but on the other hand, he or she also has prior information about where the object was on the preceding A trials. The perseverative errors that have been reported seem to indicate that 8- to 9-month-old infants do not select appropriately between these conflicting sources of information. Because perseverative errors have been found to decline after about 9 months of age, that may be when infants first begin using information selectively.

This hypothesis about the development of selective information use was examined directly in several studies using a modification of the perseveration task. The basic method in all these studies was the same. To assess selective information use, measures of infants' use of prior and current information separately were needed, as were data on their responses to conflicts between the two. Three kinds of search trials were used to obtain these measures. First, the initial A trial of each search problem provided a ready measure of infants' use of current information alone. Here infants had no previous experience from which to derive prior information, and watching the object being hidden afforded them current information. Second, a new type of search problem was introduced to measure use of prior information alone. On these problems, the A trials were the same as for traditional perseveration problems but on the B trial the object was hidden in such a way that a screen blocked the infant's view of where the object was being put. Therefore, on these screened B trials, the infant had no current information but could derive prior information from the preceding A trials. Finally, infants' responses to conflicts between prior and current information were measured by looking at their searches on the B trials of traditional perseveration problems. Here, prior information from the preceding A trials pointed to one location, while current information from watching the object hidden at B pointed to a different location.

An initial study (Sophian & Wellman, 1983) produced evidence of selective information use at 16 months but was unable to evaluate it at 9 months. The 16-month-olds' data followed essentially the same pattern that was found in the earlier study with older children. They used both kinds of information to some extent but relied on the current information relatively more, and the prior information relatively less, on conflict trials than when the two kinds of information were independent. Among 9-month-olds, selective information use could not be tested because these infants did not use prior information at all but performed at chance on the screened *B* trials. In the absence of evidence that they used both kinds of information to some extent, their conflict performance could not be meaningfully evaluated.

A second study, therefore, made a special effort to promote 9-month-olds' use of each kind of information separately so that their conflict behavior would be interpretable (Sophian & Sage, 1983b). One variable that was manipulated was the distinctiveness of the locations, because previous work had indicated that 9-month-olds may perform better on the perseveration task when distinctive locations are used (Bremner & Bryant, 1977; Butterworth, Jarrett, & Hicks, 1982). However, in this study, distinctiveness disrupted rather than facilitated infants' use of both prior and current information. Fortunately, a second variable, practice, was more effective in promoting use of the prior information alone. The second half of that study was identical to the first half (except that the distinctiveness of the locations varied in a counterbalanced order), but the practice obtained during the first half helped 9-month-olds to make use of the prior information in the second half. Therefore, in that part of the study, both 9- and 16-month-olds' selective information use could be evaluated. Data for both age groups, for those parts of the study in which they used prior information reliably, can be seen in Fig. 2.2. Again, the data are plotted in terms of the proportion of searches according with each type of information, both in the conflict condition (upper panel) and in conditions testing use of each kind of information separately (lower panel). There is evidence of selective information use at both ages, in that infants used current information more than prior information on conflict trials but used the two kinds of information more equally when each was tested separately. Thus, although it is hard to obtain a good test of selective information use with 9-month-olds, when the necessary conditions are met it turns out even they can be selective.

How does the evidence of selective information use at 9 months fit with the findings of perseveration that initially suggested that selective information use might not emerge until later in infancy? One part of the answer is that infants may be appropriately selective much of the time and yet also make perseverative errors. At the same time, infants may *not* have been selective in some studies that reported high levels of perseveration. We know that 9-month-olds can be selective sometimes, but their early selective information use may be fragile and not evidenced in all conditions and studies.

(A)   INFORMATION IN CONFLICT

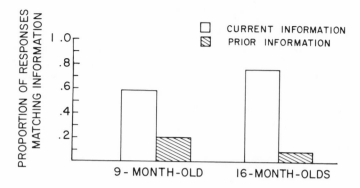

(B)   INFORMATION SEPARATE

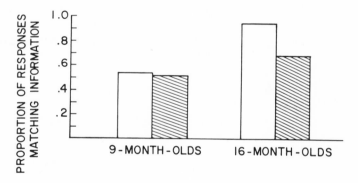

FIG. 2.2.   Proportions of searches according with current hiding information and prior information from previous *A* trials on conflict trials (*A*) and on trials testing use of each kind of information separately (*B*). (From Sophian & Wellman, 1983.)

In the Sophian and Sage (1983b) study of selective information use, 9-month-olds showed both perseveration and selective information use in their searches. When they made errors, they usually searched at the first hiding place, *A,* rather than at the control location. These perseverative errors were not incompatible with selective information use because, even though they were frequent relative to other possible errors, they were still fairly infrequent relative to correct responses. Thus, infants were generally selective even though on some problems they did make perseverative errors.

At the same time, other studies have reported very high levels of perseveration, substantially exceeding correct responding (e.g., Bremner & Bryant, 1977; Butterworth, 1976; Gratch & Landers, 1971; Schuberth, Werner, & Lipsitt, 1978). Although these studies did not test selective information use directly, the level of perseveration they reported does appear to be incompatible with selective information use. The most plausible conclusion would appear to be that 9-month-olds were *not* selective in these studies, even though they have shown selective information use in other research. Unfortunately, we do not yet understand all the factors that influence how selective infants are or how much perseveration they show. We do know, however, that levels of perseveration vary quite a bit across studies, and that selective information use is likely to vary also. Thus, part of the explanation for findings of both perseveration and selective information use in studies of 9-month-olds may be that selective information use is still fairly fragile at that age and may be disrupted under some conditions.

In sum, then, the studies I have been describing have traced a skill first identified as important in work with older children—selective information use—back to the beginnings of search in infancy. Although it is likely to be quite fragile initially, selective information use can be demonstrated even in 9-month-olds. Moreover, limitations on selective information use are by no means confined to infancy; even 7-year-olds may use the less immediate of two conflicting sources of information on some trials, although they show selective information use overall. Thus, the development of selective information use is not complete even well into childhood, yet infants already share this competency with older children.

Inferring Unseen Movements.   The ability to infer unseen movements of an object was considered by Piaget a hallmark of the child's transition from sensorimotor to representational intelligence at the end of infancy. Several recent studies, however, have provided evidence that infants do make various kinds of inferences about unseen movements well before the close of the infancy period. Although some kinds of inferences, such as inferences about the effects of rotational transformations, continue to pose difficulty well into the elementary school years (cf. Huttenlocher & Newcombe, this volume; Huttenlocher & Presson, 1973, 1979; Lasky, Romano, & Wenters, 1980), some can be made as early as 1 year of age. Thus, despite substantial developments in the kinds of inferences children can make, infants do appear to be able to conceive of an object's moving to a different place while it is out of view and to make at least some simple inferences about those movements.

Two lines of research have provided evidence that infants can make inferences about unseen movements of an object. The first is based on a variant of the invisible displacement task Piaget used to assess the advent of representational intelligence at the end of infancy. The second focuses on search on spatial transposition problems.

On Piaget's invisible displacement task, an object is concealed within a container (or the experimenter's hand) that is then moved to several locations in turn. In the traditional Piagetian task, the object is usually left in the last location in the displacement sequence, and a child is considered to pass the task if he or she searches first at that location and then, if the object is not there, continues searching in the reverse order of the displacement sequence. It is not clear, however, why children should show this search pattern, because logically the object could be in any of the displacement locations. Therefore, Sophian and Sage (1983a) focused on a different aspect of invisible displacement performance: the ability to differentiate displacement locations—where the object could have been left—from control locations—where it could not be. Although performance improved with age, even 13-month-old infants showed some success here. They directed an average of .80 of their searches to one of two displacement locations and only .20 to a third, control, location, which represents significantly above-chance performance. The corresponding means for an older group of 21-month-olds were .93 to the displacement locations and .07 to the control location.

On spatial transposition problems, an object is hidden in one of several identical cups and then one or more cups is moved before the child is allowed to search. The object, of course, moves invisibly with its cup when that cup is moved. This task, then, is like the invisible displacement task in that the object moves while it is concealed from view, but it is unlike the invisible displacement task in that the object's location can always be determined from the movements observed. In initial work with a version of this task in which two cups are simultaneously interchanged, 13-month-olds performed at chance (Sophian & Sage, 1983a) and even 3½-year-olds continued to make systematic errors (Sophian, 1984). However, in a subsequent study (Sophian, 1983a), some degree of success was observed at earlier age levels. Although there were still substantial age differences, performance was already significantly above chance at 13 months. Those infants searched the correct one of three locations on an average of .49 of problems on which the cup containing the object was switched with another cup, and on an average of .58 of problems on which the cup containing the object remained stationary while the other two cups were switched. The corresponding proportions at 20 months were .49 and .83, and at 30 months they were .63 and .92.

One reason for children's better performance in this study than in the initial (Sophian & Sage, 1983a) study may have been that it included simpler kinds of transposition problems, on which only one cup was moved, as well as the problems involving the movement of two cups that had been studied earlier. The problems involving moving only one cup proved to be quite easy for infants: The 13-month-olds got .75 of these problems correct when the cup with the object in it was moved, and .60 correct when a different cup was moved so that the object remained in its original position. It may be, then, that experience with these simple problems gave them a better idea of what was going on and so helped them to perform better even on the more complex problems. In any case, it is clear from the results of this study that even at 13 months infants can make some inferences about movements of an object while it is hidden within a cup.

Two different lines of evidence, then, indicate that some ability to make inferences about invisible movements is present as early as 13 months. Although developments in the particular kinds of movements children can comprehend extend well into childhood, the basic ability to consider possible movements of objects while they are hidden from view is one that infants as well as older children possess. This commonality stands in marked contrast to the influential view that the ability to infer unseen movements is a hallmark of the transition from infancy to childhood, and thus it underlines the importance of considering correspondences as well as contrasts between the cognitive skills of different age groups.

Correspondences in Search Errors

The picture of commonalities between infants and young children that emerges from a consideration of their search skills becomes even more striking when we look at error patterns. There may be many ways of achieving partially correct performance, and so the fact that infants as well as older children do so on many tasks does not in itself provide strong assurance that they are doing the same thing on those tasks. If they are alike, however, not only in achieving some degree of correct performance but also in making the same kinds of systematic errors, then there is more reason to believe that common processes underlie performance across ages. In fact, there are marked correspondences in the error patterns of infants and young children.

Three kinds of systematic errors that occur in both infants' and preschoolers' searches are discussed here. The first is the perseverative error pattern we have already discussed in relation to infants' selective information use. Perseverative errors are not restricted to infants but have been observed in older children's searches as well. A second, related, error pattern is the initial-location error children make on transposition problems when two cups are interposed after an object has been hidden in one of them. The initial-location error here consists of searching where the object was hidden initially rather than at the place it ended up after the transposition. Like perseverative errors, these errors persist long after infancy. Finally, a third and quite different error pattern is one based on response biases. Error patterns in which children concentrate their searches at particular places have been observed on a number of different kinds of search tasks with children of widely varying ages.

Perseverative Errors.   Perseverative errors have received most attention in the context of infants' searches, where they have been viewed as an indication of the infant's egocentric conception of objects (e.g., Gratch, 1975; Piaget, 1954). Older childrens' errors too, however, often involve going to the place where the object was found on the preceding trial (e.g., DeLoache & Brown, 1983; Horn & Myers, 1978; Loughlin & Daehler, 1973; Sophian & Wellman, 1980).

A basic methodological issue in the study of perseveration concerns what is an appropriate measure of perseveration. The original studies used infants' relative frequency of searching at the first hiding place, *A*, versus at the correct place, *B*, to index perseveration. A problem with this measure, however, is that there is no way to identify systematic perseveration unless errors to *A* are significantly more frequent than correct responses. If searches at *A* are less frequent, they could reflect merely random responding rather than a systematic return to the prior location. A related problem, from a developmental perspective, is that there is no way to distinguish between decreases in perseveration with age and increases in correct performance that might occur for other reasons.

An alternative measure, characteristic of studies with older children and of a few recent infant studies, is one that measures perseverative errors relative to errors to one or more control locations, which I call *C*. This measure permits the detection of systematic perseveration even when the level of correct performance is quite high, because as long as errors to *A* are more frequent than errors to *C* they cannot be due to random responding. Moreover, because this measure is based solely on the distribution of children's errors, it is independent of changes in their overall level of performance. However, this measure can only be calculated when the search task includes at least one control location in addition to the *A* and *B* locations.

Studies that have included such a control location have produced much less evidence of perseveration in infancy than the original object permanence studies, which did not control for random responses. For instance, Sophian and Wellman (1983) replicated many key findings from earlier, two-location, perseveration studies and yet found no evidence of systematic perseveration when errors to *A* were evaluated relative to errors to a control location. Their data are summarized in Table 2.1.

One finding replicating earlier work on perseveration was that the proportion of infants' searches that were to the *A* location declined with age. In addition, as in many previous studies, 9-month-olds searched about equally often at *A* and at *B*. The proportion of searches at *A* out of those to either *A* or *B* did not differ from the .50 that would be expected by chance. Finally, a third finding replicating earlier work was that when 9-month-olds made errors to the *A* location they tended to repeat them on successive trials in nonrandom error runs. Here, they searched at *A* for an average of 1.8 trials in a row, out of a possible 3, which is significantly above chance.

Despite these findings, however, analyses comparing searches at *A* with searches at the control location did not support the conclusion that 9-month-olds were perseverating. Error runs to *C* were as long as error runs to *A*. Moreover, infants made just as many errors to *C* as errors to *A*. The proportion of errors to *A*, out of those to *A* or *C*, was no greater than would be expected by chance. Thus, comparisons to a control location provided no evidence of perseveration at 9 months although previous findings thought to indicate perseveration were

TABLE 2.1
Measures of Perseveration

Measure	Age Group	
	9-Month-Olds	16-Month-Olds
Proportion of searches at A (chance = .33)	.26	.09
A vs. B $\dfrac{A}{A+B}$ (chance = .50)	.41	.12
Error runs to A (chance = 1.44)	1.80	1.00
Error runs to C (chance = 1.44)	2.04	1.83
A vs. C $\dfrac{A}{A+C}$ (chance = .50)	.52	.77

replicated. Other recent studies have likewise failed to document significant perseveration when controls for random responding were included (Bjork & Cummings, 1979; Sophian, in press).

These negative results clearly indicate the danger of inferring perseveration from two-location studies that do not control for random responses. At the same time, though, it is important to note that not all findings from two-location studies can be attributed to random search. In particular, a few studies have reported errors to A by a large majority of infants (e.g., Bremner & Bryant, 1977; Gratch, Appel, Evens, LeCompte, & Wright, 1974; Landers, 1971), and these above-chance errors clearly do not reflect merely random search. These strong indications of perseveration need somehow to be reconciled with the negative results of recent three-location studies in any complete account of perseveration.

One possibility is that the introduction of a control location in the three-location studies may have disrupted infants' performance and interfered with perseveration they might have shown on a two-location task. Sophian (in press) evaluated this possibility by comparing two- and three-location tasks but found no evidence to support it.

To compare the two tasks, two alternative measures of perseveration were used, because the A versus C measure could not be computed for the two-location task (where there is no C location). One measure was infants' relative frequency of searching at the A versus B locations. As already noted, this measure is problematic for evaluating whether significant perseveration has occurred, but it nevertheless does provide a way of comparing the two tasks. A second measure of perseveration was obtained by comparing traditional B trials, which require infants to choose between the A and B locations, with a control B trial, on which the A location was no longer present so that the only choice was between the correct location and one or more control locations. By definition, perseveration can only occur when the A location is present. Therefore, if infants do perseverate, they should perform less well on the traditional B trials, where perseverative errors are possible, than on the control B trials, where they are not.

The data can be seen in Table 2.2. Neither of the measures of perseveration used to compare the two tasks indicated any difference between them. Moreover, these measures accorded with the measure of errors to the A versus C location on the three-location task in providing no evidence of significant perseveration. Thus, this study reinforces the questions about the prevalence of perseveration that were raised by previous three-location studies and suggests that the negative results cannot be dismissed as due merely to disruptive effects of using a three-location task.

Despite the negative findings regarding perseveration in this and other recent three-location studies, clear evidence of perseveration has been obtained in at least one three-location study (Sophian & Sage, 1983b) as well as in the subset of two-location studies noted earlier. This result corroborates the conclusion that infants' search patterns are not fundamentally different on two- and three-location tasks, although the reasons for the varying results wihin both two- and three-location studies are still not well understood. Whatever the reasons, the variability itself supports the basic point that perseveration is less prevalent than had been thought but nevertheless does play some role in early search.

In addition to being less prevalent among 9-month-olds than initially thought, perseverative errors are not unique to that age group. Data from one study that

TABLE 2.2
Perseveration on Two-versus Three-Location Tasks

	Task	
Measure	*Two-Location*	*Three-Location*
Searches at A vs. B on traditional B trials		
Proportion of searches at A	.47	.31
Proportion of searches at B	.53	.53
A/(A or B) (chance = .50)	.47	.34
Performance on traditional vs. control B trials		
Percent correct on traditional B trials	.53	.53
Percent correct on control B trials	.75	.58
Control–Traditional (chance = 0)	.22	.05
Errors to A vs. C		
Proportion of searches at A	—	.31
Proportion of searches at C	—	.17
A/(A or C) (chance = .50)	—	.69

TABLE 2.3
Perseveration among Preschoolers on Problems Corresponding to
Infant *AB* Task

Age Group	Proportions of Searches at Each Location			
	Correct Location (B)	Prior Location (A)	Control Location (C)	Perseveration A/(A or C)
2-year-olds	.83	.13	.04	.80
2½-year-olds	.90	.07	.03	.83
4-year-olds	.89	.08	.03	.79

extended the perseveration task to preschool children are shown in Table 2.3. In this study, perseverative errors continued to occur as late as $4\frac{1}{2}$ years of age (Sophian & Wellman, 1983). Among these children, perseverative responses are characteristically much less frequent than correct searches, but they still account for a substantial proportion of children's errors.

The combined findings that perseveration is a fairly limited phenomenon in 9-month-olds' searches, and that it continues to occur even through the preschool years, considerably strengthen the picture of continuity between infancy and early childhood that emerged from the findings on search skills. Here is an error pattern that was initially taken to reveal the fundamentally different way in which infants conceptualize objects, and it turns out to be in fact a pattern of searching that infants hold in common with much older children. Other kinds of errors show the same developmental pattern.

Initial-Location Errors.   The initial-location errors children make on transposition problems are analogous to perseverative errors in that they involve returning to a place where the object was hidden earlier without taking into account displacements that have occurred since then. Transposition problems differ from the *AB* task, however, in that information about the object's initial location is in fact relevant to determining its final hiding place, whereas in the *AB* task it is of no value at all. Perhaps for this reason, the transposition task appears to be much more difficult and later to be mastered than the *AB* task.

As in the case of the *AB* task, the earliest studies of transposition problems used a two-location task on which it was difficult to distinguish between systematic errors to the initial location and merely random errors (Bower, 1977; Cornell, 1979; Freeman, Lloyd, & Sinha, 1980; Gratch, 1980). More recent studies, however, added a third location, making it possible to evaluate the systematicity of children's errors by looking at the relative frequency of errors to the initial hiding place and errors to a control location (Sophian, in preparation; Sophian & Sage, 1983a).

The youngest infants in these latter studies were 13-month-olds. These infants showed the same kind of variability in performance noted with 9-month-olds on the *AB* task. In an initial study, they performed at chance and did not make any more errors to the initial hiding place than to a control location (Sophian & Sage, 1983a). In a later study, however, they did make systematic initial-location errors (Sophian, in preparation). The reason for the differing results is not altogether clear, but they probably reflect a general increase in systematicity in the second study, rather than a rise specifically in this error pattern, because correct searches also increased in the second study. As noted earlier in discussing the differences in correct performance (see the previous section, *Inferring Unseen Movements*), the second study included some simpler kinds of problems that were not included in the initial study, and those problems may have helped infants get a better idea of what was going on. At any rate, the key findings are that infants as young as 13 months may make systematic initial-location errors, but there is considerable variability in their performance.

The developmental patterns in initial-location errors provide even stronger evidence of continuity across infancy and early childhood than those obtained in the case of perseveration. In one study, comparing 13-, 20-, and 30-month-olds, the total proportion of searches at the initial hiding place declined with age but the proportion of children's errors that were to the initial hiding place was comparable at all ages (Sophian, in preparation). These data appear in Table 2.4. The same pattern also occurred in another study, shown in Table 2.5, which compared 20-, 30-, and 42-month-olds (Sophian, 1984). Thus, even though children make fewer errors on the transposition task as they get older, the errors they do make continue to be quite systematic and of the same form from 13 months of age until well into the preschool years.

Response-Bias Errors.   A different kind of pattern that has been observed in children's errors in many studies is one in which children search preferentially at particular spatial positions while avoiding others. Numerous studies have shown such asymmetrical search patterns, with children ranging from 9 months (Sophian & Wellman, 1983) to 7 years of age (Sophian & Wellman, 1980).

TABLE 2.4
Patterns of Search on Spatial-Transposition Problems

| Age Group | Search Type | | | % Errors to Initial Location |
	Correct Location	Initial Location	Control Location	
13-month-olds	.49	.38	.13	.71
20-month-olds	.49	.38	.13	.78
30-month-olds	.63	.33	.04	.84

TABLE 2.5
Patterns of Search on Spatial-Transposition Problems

	Search Type			% Errors to Initial Location
Age Group	Correct Location	Initial Location	Control Location	
20-month-olds	.34	.56	.10	.86
30-month-olds	.42	.48	.05	.92
42-month-olds	.71	.26	.04	.88

Even when the searches of a group of children are evenly distributed across the possible locations, individual children may still show position preferences in that they concentrate their searches at particular locations (which may be different for different children). For instance, Sophian and Sage (1983a) found that 13- and 21-month-old infants searched approximately equally often at the left, middle, and right locations as a group, yet individual infants concentrated a large proportion of their searches at a single location. To measure response biases in individual infants' searches, they calculated the standard deviation of each infant's total number of searches at the three locations. This measure will be zero if

TABLE 2.6
Age Differences in Response Bias

Study	Age Group	Bias Score	Age Difference
Sophian and Sage, 1983b	9 months	5.03	$p < .001$
	16 months	2.11	
Sophian and Wellman, 1983			
Experiment 1	9 months	5.71	$p < .001$
	16 months	2.90	
	27 months	4.24	$p < .05$
Experiment 2	33 months	4.15	contrasts: 33 months > 54 months
	54 months	2.86	
Sophian and Sage, 1983a	13 months	3.37	$p < .001$
	21 months	1.18	
Sophian, in press	20 months	2.27	$p < .01$
	30 months	1.94	contrasts: 20 months > 42 months
	42 months	1.26	
Sophian, 1982	23 months	1.86	$p < .05$
	30 months	1.19	
Sophian and Wellman, 1980	40 months	5.95	$p < .001$
	58 months	3.85	contrasts: 40 months > 58 months
	84 months	2.74	40 months > 84 months

infants search equally at the three locations but it will be greater if they search more often at some locations than at others. In fact, it averaged 3.37 at 13 months and 1.17 at 21 months, indicating a decline in response bias with age. Similar evidence of age-related decreases in response biases has been obtained in many other studies with children ranging from 9 months to 7 years of age. Data on response biases from most of the studies discussed in this chapter are summarized in Table 2.6. The specific values obtained vary from study to study, partly because the number of search problems varies and this standard deviation measure of response bias is influenced by the total number of problems involved. Nevertheless, within each study consistent and, in most cases, significant decreases with age appear.

One reason for the widespread age differences may be that as correct performance rises, it leads children to distribute their searches more evenly across locations, because the correct location is characteristically counterbalanced across trials. One way to evaluate this possibility is to look at the degree of response bias children show when they have no information about the correct place to search. Three of the studies in Table 2.6 included such neutral trials (Sophian & Wellman, 1980, 1983). The data from these neutral trials are shown in Table 2.7. Unfortunately, these data cannot be directly compared with data from other trials because of the unequal numbers of trials involved; however, the pattern of age differences does appear to be markedly different. When only neutral trials are considered, many of the age differences fall short of significance, and in one case there is even a reversal of the general downward trend. From these data, it is difficult to be sure whether in fact response biases characteristically decrease or are fairly constant across age when they are measured in a way that is independent of changes in correct performance. Certainly, however, the age groups look much more comparable to each other than the overall measure of response bias suggested.

TABLE 2.7
Response Bias on Neutral Search Trials

Study	Age Group	Bias Score	Age Difference
Sophian and Wellman, 1983			
Experiment 1	9 months	1.11	$p = .07$
	16 months	.95	
	27 months	1.11	$p < .05$
Experiment 2	33 months	1.53	contrasts: 33 months > 54 months
	54 months	.88	
Sophian and Wellman, 1983			
	40 months	1.82	$p = .06$
	58 months	1.55	
	84 months	1.28	

The same picture of fairly comparable response biases across ages emerges from another study that used stochastic modeling to estimate how often children use different kinds of search rules (Sophian, Larkin, & Kadane, in preparation). Not surprisingly, children's use of rules based on information they had about the object and its movements increased with age. However, when children were not using those rules, younger and older children were about equally likely to use a rule based on position preferences. Hence, response biases played a smaller role in children's searches with age as correct responding improved, but when the strength of position preferences was considered independently it was actually quite comparable across age groups.

Summary.   All three of the error patterns we have considered—perseveration, initial-location errors, and response biases—appear to characterize search across a wide age range, spanning infancy and early childhood. Moreover, there is considerable correspondence across age groups in the strength of these error patterns when they are assessed in a way that is independent of correct performance. Thus, error patterns as well as competencies point to strong similarities in search across infancy and early childhood. These similarities need to be taken into account along with age differences as we seek to understand the developmental relations linking infancy with the rest of cognitive development.

WHAT IS DEVELOPING?

Despite the correspondences in many aspects of search at different ages, there is no question but that search performance improves with age. Even in the studies that reveal comparable competencies and/or comparable error patterns across age groups, older children characteristically perform better overall than younger age groups. Three kinds of changes appear to contribute to this developmental improvement: (1) increases in the *robustness* of children's search skills—that is, in the range of conditions under which they can be manifested; (2) increases in the *consistency* with which search skills are utilized within any given condition; and (3) decreases in the prevalence of various *inappropriate* patterns of searching. Although all three of these changes may contribute to findings that search improves with age, they have not been distinguished from each other in most research. Nevertheless, they are empirically distinguishable, and considering them separately may help to illuminate the nature of the developmental processes underlying improvements in search.

The evidence for each of these kinds of changes comes from the same studies we have already looked at in considering correspondences in search across infancy and childhood. Therefore, I only briefly review the aspects of those studies that point to these changes with age.

Robustness

Developmental increases in robustness are reflected in patterns of results in which younger age groups show a specified pattern of search only in a limited subset of conditions whereas older children show the same pattern across a wider range of conditions. Both correct search patterns and systematic error patterns may become more robust with increasing age.

One line of evidence for increasing robustness comes from the measures of infants' use of prior information in studies of selective information use. As noted earlier, one problem in work on selective information use in infancy was the difficulty of finding conditions under which 9-month-olds would use prior information, so that their ability to select between that and current information could be examined. Nine-month-olds did not show any use of prior information in an initial study (Sophian & Wellman, 1983) and did so only in the second half of a second study, after practice (Sophian & Sage, 1983b). Thus, even though they were able to use prior information under some conditions, that competency was clearly quite limited. Unfortunately, the specific nature of the limitations is somewhat unclear, as the reasons for the varying results obtained across studies are still not known. Nevertheless, it does seem clear that the limitations decline with age. Sixteen-month-olds tested in the same studies that produced variable results with 9-month-olds showed reliable use of the prior information throughout. Thus, their ability to use prior information to guide search was more robust than the 9-month-olds'.

Another example of increasing robustness occurred in the research on inferring unseen movements using transposition problems. The youngest children tested on transposition problems—13-month-olds—performed above chance in one study but not in another. Earlier I suggested that this variability might be related to the inclusion of simpler problems in the study in which children were more successful. Twenty- and 30-month-olds, however, performed above chance in both studies. Hence, they showed a more robust ability to infer the object's location from the movements they observed.

Developmental increases in the robustness of search competencies also appear in work with older children. For instance, in a study with preschoolers (Sophian & Wellman, 1983), both 2½-year-olds and 4-year-olds used prior information about where a toy had been hidden and/or found on earlier trials, but only 4-year-olds used another kind of prior information, based on knowledge about the typical locations of objects. On a pretest, 2½-year-olds showed as much knowledge of typical locations as 4-year-olds did, yet they did not use that knowledge to guide search although they did use a more concrete form of prior information based on previous trials. Thus, their ability to use prior information was less robust, across different kinds of prior information, than that of 4-year-olds.

Error patterns as well as correct response patterns may become more robust with increasing age. For instance, I have noted that 9-month-olds made significant perseverative errors in some studies but not in others. Likewise, in studies of error patterns on transposition problems, 13-month-olds have sometimes made significant initial-location errors (Sophian, 1983) and sometimes not (Sophian & Sage, 1983a), whereas older age groups have shown initial-location errors more consistently across studies (Sophian, 1983). Again, the specific nature of the limitations that account for the varying results for younger age groups is not altogether clear, but it is clear that systematic patterns of searching that occur under some conditions are quite easily disrupted at early ages but seem to be more stable later.

Consistency

The second kind of age difference I want to propose is in the consistency of children's searches. Increases in consistency, like increases in robustness, involve a decrease in the variability of children's performance. Consistency, however, reflects variability within a given condition in a given study rather than across conditions or studies. Often, two or more age groups show the same pattern of searching, but older children's searches fit that pattern on a larger proportion of trials than younger children's. For instance, in one study (Sophian, 1982) both 23-month-olds and 30-month-olds used verbal information to guide search, but the 30-month-olds did so more consistently. Likewise, at a younger age level, both 9- and 16-month-olds use information about where a toy was just hidden to guide search, but older infants do so more consistently (Sophian & Sage, 1983b; Sophian & Wellman, 1983).

Inappropriate Response Tendencies

A third recurrent developmental pattern, noted earlier in discussing error patterns, is a decrease in the role of inappropriate response tendencies, such as response bias and perseveration, in children's searches. These inappropriate tendencies continue to appear in children's error patterns well into childhood, but the total number of searches they account for clearly drops with age.

An important characteristic of these inappropriate response tendencies is that they are only inappropriate relative to certain kinds of search problems. In particular, they are inappropriate when other kinds of information are available that the child could use to identify the object's location. In the absence of such information, it would not be at all unreasonable to search at a preferred location or at a location where the object had been found before. This observation suggests that the systematic errors that have been noted in children's searches may be due to children's continuing to use search patterns that are sometimes effective under circumstances in which they are no longer appropriate.

CONCLUSION: DEVELOPMENTAL PROCESSES IN
EARLY SEARCH

The developmental patterns we have found in looking closely at children's search across infancy and early childhood may be summarized fairly succinctly. Both in competencies, like selectivity and the ability to infer unseen movements, and in error patterns, such as perseveration and response bias, we find marked correspondences across infancy and early childhood. At the same time, however, there are clearly age differences in several aspects of performance: in the robustness of children's search skills, in the consistency with which they are used, and in the impact of various inappropriate search patterns on children's performance.

The presence of marked correspondences across age groups, on the one hand, but also of substantial age differences, on the other, places an interesting set of constraints on theoretical accounts of early cognitive development. Many theoretical approaches can account readily for either correspondences or age differences but have trouble providing a principled explanation for both together.

Theoretical Implications

One prominent class of developmental theories consists of stage theories. Stage theories have often been proposed to account for age differences in search— particularly in perseveration. They can explain age differences readily, but characteristically they do so by postulating that particular abilities—in the case of perseveration, the ability to represent an object independently of one's actions— do not emerge until fixed points in development. This kind of claim does not fit well with the evidence for correspondences in search skills across a wide range. Indeed, both the research on selectivity and that on inferring unseen movements fit a common pattern in developmental research, in which an ability initially considered characteristic of a later period of development is demonstrated with younger children. Findings of this kind have often been used to challenge stage theories, and they have occurred often enough to justify wariness about any claim that some ability of interest is necessarily beyond the reach of certain age groups.

A contrasting theoretical position is one that claims that basic cognitive abilities are either innate or are acquired in essentially their full form within the first months of life. This might be called the early-competence model. It fits quite well with the correspondences we have observed in search but in itself offers little insight into the age differences. Indeed, a pure early-competence theory will almost always be incomplete at best, because the abilities demonstrated at younger ages typically do differ from those found with older children, if only in being more limited in the conditions under which they can be carried out.

At root, both stage theories and early-competence theories run into difficulties for the same reason. There is no clear demarcation between earlier and later skills, no definite beginning point at which a skill appears for the first time, nor any clear transition point at which one skill is replaced by another. As a result, neither claims that a skill is present from birth, on the one hand, nor claims that that skill does not emerge until some later point, on the other, can be fully correct. Both stage theories and early-competence theories presuppose that cognitive skills are more discrete, more dichotomously present or absent, than close inspection of children's performance can justify.

A more viable alternative is to view cognitive development as a relatively continuous process in which skills gradually evolve into more powerful forms. From this perspective, it is less important *when* various cognitive skills emerge than *how* early skills develop into more advanced ones.

Proposed Developmental Processes

I would like to propose two kinds of continuous changes to account for the developmental patterns we have seen in early search. Because of their continuous and ongoing nature, I refer to these changes as ''developmental processes.'' One developmental process I propose is an increase in the reliability of children's information-processing skills, which enables children to carry out both correct and incorrect search patterns more regularly. The other is an increase in the extent to which children differentiate between different kinds of search problems in applying those skills.

Children's information-processing skills are important in the development of search because all systematic search patterns involve using some kind of information about the object and its movements, and /or about the possible locations, to guide search. If children have trouble keeping track of that information, or completing the processing needed to infer from it where to search, then their search patterns will be correspondingly unsystematic. With improvements in the reliability of information-processing skills, then, this kind of difficulty will occur less frequently and children's search patterns will become more robust and more consistent.

Differentiation among different problem types is important in the development of search because the same search pattern may be effective on some kinds of search problems but quite counterproductive on others. Indeed, we have already noted that the various inappropriate search patterns children show seem to involve the use of a search pattern that would be useful on some types of problems on other problem types to which it is not well suited. One thing that children need to do, then, in developing their search skills is to differentiate more effectively between classes of search problems that call for the use of different search skills. As they do so, they will make systematic errors less frequently and search correctly more often.

Both changes in information-processing skills and changes in differentiation have long been considered important factors in cognitive development. Changes in information-processing skills have been invoked in many contemporary theories, which postulate changes either in cognitive capacity (e.g., Halford & Wilson, 1980; Pascual-Leone, 1970) or in operating efficiency (e.g., Case, 1980) to explain development on Piagetian tasks. Differentiation has likewise played an important role in developmental theorizing, at least since Werner's (1948) classic work.

In combination, the changes in processing reliability and in differentiation among search problems proposed here can account for both the correspondences across age groups and the age differences we have seen in early search. The correspondences are a natural consequence of any account based on continuous developmental processes, but the age differences need to be explained by the specific kinds of processes proposed.

Essentially, in postulating continuous developmental processes, I am claiming that children do not abandon early skills or search patterns for more effective ones as they develop, but rather they gradually modify their original skills and search patterns so that they function more effectively. As in early-competence theories, then, correspondences across age groups are seen as arising because different age groups are using essentially the same skills.

Age differences are attributed to changes in *how* children use these skills, specifically to changes in how reliably they use them and in how much they differentiate among different search problems. These two kinds of changes combine in different ways to account for developments in correct performance and in error patterns. Both contribute to increases in correct performance, but they have differing effects on error patterns. Improvements in processing reliability lead to increases in the proportions of children's errors that fit a specific error pattern (like perseveration) because they enable children to carry out erroneous search patterns as well as correct search patterns more regularly. Increases in differentiation, in contrast, lead to decreases in systematic errors because they enable children to choose more effectively between appropriate and inappropriate skills to use in a given situation. These contrasting effects explain why increases in correct performance are so consistently observed but developmental trends in error patterns are more variable. Correct performance will increase as long as either developmental process is operating, but systematic errors may increase or decrease depending on the balance between the two processes.

Direct evidence of developmental changes in processing reliability can be found by looking at how often children search at control locations that are not consistent with any information in a problem. These searches provide a fairly direct indication of processing reliability, because they should occur only when systematic search patterns based on problem information have given way to random search. Accordingly, they would be expected to decrease with age, as the reliability of children's information processing improves.

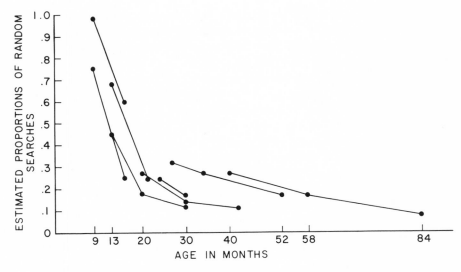

FIG. 2.3.   Estimated proportions of random searches in eight studies of early search, based on frequencies of searches at control locations.

In fact, they do characteristically decrease with age. Fig. 2.3 summarizes data on control errors from many of the studies discussed in this chapter.[1] Each line in the Figure represents a separate study. In spite of the variations across studies in the kinds of search problems used and in the levels of random search observed, all of the studies show a decline in random search with age. The biggest drop seems to take place by 20 or 21 months. On the average comparisons between age groups under 21 months involve an age difference of 7 months and a drop in the probability of random searching of about .40, whereas adjacent age groups over 20 months are on the average 14 months apart in age but differ by only .08 in the probability of random searching. Moreover, this difference is not due only to there being less room for further declines at the older age levels (i.e., because random search is already infrequent by then). The same pattern appears even when the drops are measured relative to the amount of random search present at the younger age level in each comparison (which corresponds to the maximum possible decline in random search for that comparison). In comparisons of age groups under 21 months, the older group has declined on the average to 42% of

---

[1]The estimated proportions of random searches depicted in Fig. 2.3 take into account the differing chance probabilities of search at control locations in different studies that result from variations in the number of control locations and/or the number of other locations that are present on the various search problems in those studies. The estimates are based on the following calculation:

$$\text{estimated proportion} = \text{proportion of control searches} \times \frac{\text{total \# locations}}{\text{\# control locations}}$$

the random search shown by the younger group (and thus has dropped by 58%). In contrast, in comparisons of age groups over 20 months, the older group still shows on the average 69% of the random search that the younger group showed (and thus has dropped by only 31%).

There is also evidence to support the postulated changes in differentiation with age. One reason for proposing an increase in differentiation, of course, is to account for declines in the proportion of children's errors that reflect the use of an inappropriate search pattern (Sophian & Sage, 1983b). These declines cannot be explained by changes in processing reliability, because more reliable use of inappropriate sources of information would lead to more systematic error patterns rather than less systematic ones. Because the systematic errors children make seem to result from the use of quite reasonable search strategies, but in inappropriate contexts, a natural explanation for their decline is that children get better at adapting their searches to specific types of problems.

Further evidence for changes in differentiation with age comes from the research on selective information use described at the beginning of this chapter. Selective information use is a form of differentiation in that it involves children's adjusting their use of a given search pattern according to what alternative bases of responding are available on a given problem. We have seen that there is some evidence of selective information use as early as 9 months of age, but it increases with age.

One further line of research provides concurrent evidence for both the changes in processing reliability and the changes in differentiation I have proposed here. In this work, stochastic modeling was used to estimate the prevalence of different kinds of rules in children's search (Sophian et al., in preparation). Search rules that take into account at least part of the information children have about an object and its movements were distinguished from rules that do not make use of that information but involve responding on the basis of position preferences or other extraneous considerations. One finding was that children's use of rules based on the relevant information increased with age, which fits well with the increase in processing reliability postulated here. A second finding was that there were changes with age in the kinds of rules children used when they were basing their searches on relevant information. These changes correspond to the increase in differentiation I have postulated. Younger children's rules most often focused on one kind of information, which was used in the same way across all problem types. In contrast, older children's rules tended to take into account more than one aspect of the relevant information and to use that information in different ways on different types of problems.

In sum, I have suggested that the commonalities and age differences found in early search are best captured by postulating continuous developmental processes that enable children to use skills they have had since infancy more effectively. Two hypothesized developmental processes were: (1) an increase in the reliability of children's information-processing skills; and (2) an increase in the degree to which children differentiate appropriately among different search problems. In combination, these processes account for increases in correct performance, decreases in errors to control locations, decreases in systematic errors, increases in selective information use, and changes in the kinds of search rules children use.

Search and Cognitive Development

I have focused on search here because it affords a unique opportunity for directly comparing infants and children. The issue of continuity in development is obviously much more general than search, however. Unfortunately, the kinds of closely comparable data about a wide range of age groups that have informed this account of the development of search are simply not available for most other domains of cognitive development. One possible exception is language, where again there is more evidence for continuity than one might expect. For example, many of the errors that have been considered characteristic of early stages of language development actually continue to occur (albeit infrequently) even in adults (see, e.g., Bybee & Slobin, 1982; MacWhinney, 1978). Kaplan and Kaplan (1970) argue for continuity in psycholinguistic development even between the cries of the young infant and the subsequent course of language acquisition.

Nevertheless, it remains the case that there is not a strong empirical basis for evaluating the generality of the conclusions drawn here across other domains of cognitive development. Still, there are at least two reasons to expect some generality. First, the basic conceptual point that there are no clear boundaries at which a cognitive skill begins or ends is clearly as applicable to other cognitive domains as it is to search. Second, the kinds of skills we have focused on in characterizing early search—skills for encoding and selecting among various kinds of information—are unlikely to be unique to search but should play a role in many areas of cognitive development. Indeed, there is already some evidence to support this supposition. Developments in selective information use like those described here for search have also been found in work on early causal reasoning (Sophian & Huber, in press). These considerations, together with the evidence of continuity in the development of search, are surely sufficient reason for at least taking seriously the possibility of continuity—and collecting the kinds of data that could enable us to begin evaluating continuity—throughout cognitive development. In doing so, perhaps we will manage to reunite infants with the children they become.

ACKNOWLEDGMENTS

This work was supported by NICHHD grant #1 RO1 HD1695–01. The author would like to thank Jill Larkin, Margaret Clark, Robert Siegler, and David Klahr for helpful comments on earlier drafts of this chapter.

REFERENCES

Bower, T. G. *A primer of infant development*. San Francisco: Freeman, 1977.

Bjork, E. L., & Cummings, E. M. *The "A, not B" search error in Piaget's theory of object permanence: "Fact or artifact?"* Paper presented at the meeting of the Psychonomic Society, Phoenix, Arizona, 1979.

Bremner, J. G., & Bryant, P. E. Place versus response as the basis of spatial errors made by young infants. *Journal of Experimental Child Psychology*, 1977, *23*, 162–171.

Butterworth, G. E. Asymmetrical search errors in infancy. *Child Development*, 1976, *47*, 846–867.

Butterworth, G. E., Jarrett, N., & Hicks, L. Spatio-temporal identity in infancy: Perceptual competence or conceptual deficit? *Developmental Psychology*, 1982, *18*, 435–449.

Bybee, J. L., & Slobin, D. I. Rules and schemas in the development and use of the English past. *Language*, 1982, *58*, 265–289.

Case, R. Intellectual development: A systematic reinterpretation. In F. H. Farley & N. J. Gordon (Eds.), *New perspectives in educational psychology*. Canada: National Society for the Study of Education, 1980.

Cornell, E. H. The effects of cue reliability on infants' manual search. *Journal of Experimental Child Psychology*, 1979, *28*, 81–91.

DeLoache, J. S., & Brown, A. L. Very young children's memory for the location of objects in a large scale environment. *Child Development*, 1983, *54*, 888–897.

Drozdal, J. G., & Flavell, J. H. A developmental study of logical search behavior. *Child Development*, 1975, *46*, 389–393.

Fischer, K. W. A theory of cognitive development: The control and construction of hierarchies of skills. *Psychological Review*, 1980, *87*, 477–531.

Freeman, N. H., Lloyd, S., & Sinha, C. G. Infant search tasks reveal early concepts of containment and canonical usage of objects. *Cognition*, 1980, *8*, 243–262.

Gelman, R. Cognitive development. *Annual Review of Psychology*, 1978, *29*, 297–332.

Gratch, G. Recent studies based on Piaget's view of object concept development. In L. B. Cohen & P. Salapatek (Eds.), *Infant perception: From sensation to cognition*. New York: Academic Press, 1975.

Gratch, G. Some thoughts on cognitive development and language development. In A. P. Reilly (Ed.), *The communication game: Perspectives on the development of speech, language, and nonverbal communication skills*. New Brunswick, N.J.: Johnson & Johnson Baby Products Company, 1980.

Gratch, G., Appel, K. J., Evans, W. F., LeCompte, G. K., & Wright, N. A. Piaget's Stage IV object concept error: Evidence of forgetting or object conceptualization? *Child Development*, 1974, *45*, 71–77.

Gratch, G., & Landers, W. F. Stage IV of Piaget's theory of infant object concepts: A longitudinal study. *Child Development*, 1971, *42*, 359–372.

Halford, G. S., & Wilson, W. H. A category theory approach to cognitive development. *Cognitive Psychology*, 1980, *12*, 356–411.

Horn, H. A., & Myers, N. A. Memory for location and picture cues at ages two and three. *Child Development*, 1978, *49*, 845–856.

Huttenlocher, J., & Presson, C. C. Mental rotation and the perspective problem. *Cognitive Psychology*, 1973, *4*, 279–299.

Huttenlocher, J., & Presson, C. C. The coding and transformation of spatial information. *Cognitive Psychology*, 1979, *11*, 375–394.

Kaplan, E. L., & Kaplan, G. A. Is there any such thing as a pre-linguistic child? In J. Eliot (Ed.), *Human development and cognitive processes*. New York: Holt, Rinehart & Winston, 1970.

Landers, W. F. The effect of differential experience on infants' performance in a Piagetian Stage IV object-concept task. *Developmental Psychology*, 1971, *5*, 48–54.

Lasky, R. E., Romano, N., & Wenters, J. Spatial localization in children after changes in position. *Journal of Experimental Child Psychology,* 1980, *29,* 225–248.

Loughlin, K. A., & Daehler, M. W. The effects of distraction and added perceptual cues on the delayed reaction of very young children. *Child Development,* 1973, *44,* 384–388.

MacWhinney, B. The acquisition of morphophonology. *Monographs of the Society for Research in Child Development,* 1978, *43*(1–2), (Serial No. 174).

Pascual-Leone, J. A mathematical model for the transition rule in Piaget's developmental stages. *Acta Psychologica,* 1970, *32,* 301–345.

Piaget, J. *The construction of reality in the child.* New York: Basic Books, 1954.

Schuberth, R. E., Werner, J. S., & Lipsitt, L. P. The Stage IV error in Piaget's theory of object concept development: A reconstruction of the spatial localization hypothesis. *Child Development,* 1978, *49,* 744–748.

Sophian, C. Selectivity and strategy in early search. *Journal of Experimental Child Psychology,* 1982, *34,* 342–349.

Sophian, C. Perseveration and infants' search: A comparison of two- and three-location tasks. *Developmental Psychology,* in press.

Sophian, C. Spatial transpositions and the early development of search. *Developmental Psychology,* in press.

Sophian, C. *Inferring unseen movements: Early developments in search for objects moved within containers,* in preparation.

Sophian, C., & Huber, A. Early developments in children's causal judgments. *Child Development,* in press.

Sophian, C., Larkin, J. H., & Kadane, J. B. A developmental model of children's search. In H. M. Wellman (Ed.), *Development of search ability.* Hillsdale, N.J.: Lawrence Erlbaum Associates, in preparation.

Sophian, C., & Sage, S. Developments in infants' search for displaced objects. *Journal of Experimental Child Psychology,* 1983, *35,* 143–160. (a)

Sophian, C., & Sage, S. *The development of selectivity in infants' search.* Unpublished manuscript, 1983. (b)

Sophian, C., & Wellman, H. M. Selective information use in the development of search behavior. *Developmental Psychology,* 1980, *16,* 323–331.

Sophian, C., & Wellman, H. M. Selective information use and perseveration in the search behavior of infants and young children. *Journal of Experimental Child Psychology,* 1983, *35,* 369–390.

Stone, L. J., Smith, H. T., & Murphy, L. B. (Eds.). *The competent infant.* New York: Basic Books, 1973.

Wellman, H. M., & Somerville, S. Quasi-naturalistic tasks in the study of cognition: The memory-related skills of toddlers. In M. Perlmutter (Ed.), *Naturalistic approaches to children's memory.* San Francisco: Jossey-Bass, 1980.

Wellman, H. M., Somerville, S. C., & Haake, R. J. Development of search procedures in real-life spatial environments. *Developmental Psychology,* 1979, *5,* 530–542.

Werner, H. *The comparative psychology of mental development.* New York: International Universities Press, 1948.

3 Oh Where, Oh Where: Memory-Based Searching by Very Young Children

Judy S. DeLoache
University of Illinois

One important type of spatial skill that emerges early yet undergoes considerable further development is memory for the location of objects. The extensive literature on object permanence (Gratch, 1975; Harris, 1975, 1983) has amply documented the emergence at around 8 months and the refinement over the next several months of the ability to remember not only the existence but also the location of a hidden object. Recent naturalistic studies have testified to the salience of location in a variety of early mnemonic activities. Parental diary records indicate that nearly a quarter of all identified memory episodes of 7- to 11-month-old infants involve remembering the location of an object or a person (Ashmead & Perlmutter, 1980). Location also seems to be a highly salient cue for recall memory; Nelson and Ross (1980) reported that half the recall episodes in the diary records of mothers of 20- to 30-month-olds were stimulated or cued by the location where the remembered object or event had been experienced. And Ratner (1980) found that one of the most frequent categories of memory demands placed on young children by their parents is for the recall of location information ("Where did you leave your shoes?").

Spatial cognition is thus implicated in early memory, and the interface between the two early skills is worthy of study. In addition, tasks that require the young child to remember the location of an object in the environment provide a window on early signs of mnemonic regulation. Very young children are cooperative and competent in such situations earlier than in memory tasks requiring verbal recall (Perlmutter & Myers, 1979); children who are unable or unwilling to retrieve verbal information from memory will readily retrieve objects from the environment (Brown & DeLoache, 1978; Wellman & Somerville, 1980). Because regulatory skills are more likely to be used in planning and executing tasks that subjects can comprehend and are motivated to perform (DeLoache, 1980; Shatz, 1978), such skills should be exercised relatively early in object-retrieval tasks.

In this chapter, we consider the questions of how, and how well, the very young child remembers where in space he or she last saw a given object. The answer to the quantitative question—"*How well* does the young child remember spatial location?"—is clear, as I illustrate shortly. The answer to the qualitative question—"*How* does the young child go about remembering?"—is less clear, and most of this chapter is devoted to it.

For the ensuing discussion, we must distinguish between natural memory and mediated memory. Natural memory refers to memory that occurs as a consequence of meaningful activity; no deliberate or conscious effort is required. In mediated memory, the person engages in some activity in the service of remembering. What a person remembers is a product of deliberate mnemonic activity. Similar distinctions have often been made in the memory literature, including voluntary versus involuntary, intentional versus incidental, and effortful versus noneffortful or automatic memory. In this chapter I first discuss natural memory with respect to very young children's remembering in what spatial location an object has been hidden. Second, I discuss evidence of mediated memory in very young children, evidence that suggests that even children below the age of 2 may in some situations engage in very simple forms of explicit mnemonic activity.

NATURAL MEMORY FOR LOCATION

With respect to the question of "how well" young children remember location, the answer is, "Very well indeed." From at least 18 months of age, memory for the location of a hidden object is extremely good, especially when the object is hidden in the natural large-scale environment. This assertion is based on several studies investigating the abilities of children between 18 and 30 months of age to remember the spatial location of a hidden object (DeLoache & Brown, 1979, 1983, 1984; DeLoache, Cassidy, & Brown, 1983).

The memory task that we have used in this research is presented to the child as a game of hide-and-seek to be played with a small stuffed animal. The child is told that Big Bird is going to hide and the he or she should remember where Big Bird is in order to find him later. The child then watches while the toy is hidden in some natural location in the large-scale environment, often in the child's own home. The hiding locations consist of places common to almost any living room, such as under a couch or chair cushion, behind a door, inside a cabinet, and so forth. A timer is set for a specified interval, and the child is told that when the bell rings, he can go find the toy. During the interval, the child is usually engaged in talking or playing with the experimenter. Young children readily apprehend the goal and the rules of the game, and most of them greatly enjoy playing it.

In several studies using the basic task, our young subjects have exhibited excellent memory for the location of an object hidden in the large-scale environment. The level of performance across the studies is quite high, averaging well over 80% errorless retrievals. (Errorless retrieval is defined as the child's searching *first* at the correct location.) We have, in fact, often obtained ceiling memory performance from 2-year-old children.

The robustness of young children's memory for spatial location is also reflected by the fact that the rate of errorless retrievals is only minimally affected by a number of variables that one might a priori assume would affect it. For one thing, the age of the children has not been consistently related to memory performance. In some studies we have found significant age differences, with subjects between 24 and 30 months outperforming 18- to 24-month-olds, but in others no age effects appeared. Thus, there may be a small degree of developmental change in memory for spatial location over this age period, but even $1\frac{1}{2}$-year-olds generally perform quite competently in the basic task.

Memory for the location of an object also seems to be relatively impervious to the length of time the child must remember; we have found little change in performance over intervals ranging from a few minutes to several hours. Amount of experience with the hide-and-seek game does not affect the rate of errorless retrievals; children given pretraining on the task do not do better than children participating in it for the first time, and performance generally remains stable over days. It does not make any difference whether the children are verbally instructed to remember the toy's location or not; subjects told to "be sure to remember where Big Bird is so you can find him" do not do better than children who are given no memory orientation. It also does not matter whether the task is embedded in a familiar or unfamiliar environment; errorless retrievals are equivalent whether children are observed in their own homes or in an unfamiliar laboratory playroom.

In other words, it seems to be fairly difficult to degrade young children's memory for where an attractive toy is hidden within a natural, large-scale environment. Performance is often near ceiling, and it remains near ceiling through the various manipulations just described. Young children generally remember the location of a hidden toy, and they do so with no obvious mnemonic effort. Thus, with respect to the basic task, the answer to the "how" question seems to be, "naturally." Memory for location emerges as a consequence of the meaningful activity of a hiding and finding game in which young children readily engage.

MEDIATED MEMORY FOR LOCATION

But, what about other situations? What if more than natural memory is required for success? Are young children in any way sensitive to memory demands or capable of any deliberate mnemonic effort? This question is the primary focus of the research described in this chapter, in which we consider the emergence and early development of self-regulatory skills. These skills are the various processes by which people organize their thoughts and actions (Brown, 1978; Brown & DeLoache, 1978), including activities such as planning ahead, predicting the outcome of some action (what will happen if?), monitoring ongoing activity (how am I doing?), checking on the results of actions (did that work, did it achieve my goal?), correcting errors or inadequacies (because what I just did didn't work, what would be a reasonable thing to try now?). These general skills are the basic characteristics of efficient thought throughout life.

What is the origin of these important cognitive skills? We assume they do not spring full-blown from the brow of the young child, and yet, the general picture that is painted in the memory-development literature is more like an all-or-none phenomenon. Older children are known to be (or at least capable of being) strategic and planful. Younger children—that is, preschool children—are *not* those same things. They are assumed to be incapable of being strategic or planful, and, indeed, most of the evidence supports this negative view of the young child as nonstrategic (Brown & DeLoache, 1978).

The research presented here disputes this view. A new picture is drawn of the young child, who in some situations does seem to behave strategically, albeit in limited and primitive ways. We have used the hide-and-seek task, but we have varied it to go beyond the simple assessment of natural memory and to look for evidence of very early self-regulation—that is, of strategic activity in very young children. We have obtained evidence of three types of primitive regulation in the behavior of $1\frac{1}{2}$- to $2\frac{1}{2}$-year-old children in the hide-and-seek and related memory tasks. In each case, I first describe very briefly the mature form of the regulatory behavior typically observed in older individuals' performance, and then I describe our analogous findings with respect to very young children's memory for the spatial location of a hidden object.

Exploitation of Stimulus Information

The first issue discussed here concerns children's use of information to encode the location of a hidden object and to retrieve it later. With older subjects, the general pattern of results has been that developmental differences are found when cues are available to be strategically exploited, but no age differences appear when mnemonic strategies are not applicable. For example, in a recognition memory task requiring recency judgments, Brown (1975) and Brown, Campione, and Gilliard (1974) found no age differences between second- and fourth-grade subjects when no supplementary cues were available. When contextual, spatial, or color background cues were provided, the older children outperformed the younger ones, who failed to take advantage of the additional cues. Training the younger children to use these cues eliminated the developmental differences. This pattern of results was interpreted in terms of mnemonic strategy development. Older children strategically exploited the available cues to enhance memory, and they did so spontaneously. Less mature children needed training to use the cues effectively.

An analogous experiment was designed for very young children (DeLoache & Brown, 1983). Each child participated in three conditions that differed in terms of the type of cues available. In two of the conditions, there were no special cues for identifying the correct hiding place. The first condition (Natural) was the basic hide-and-seek task, in which a toy was hidden in natural locations in the large-scale environment (the child's own home) The toy was always hidden in, under, or behind pieces of furniture. In the second condition (No Landmark), the toy was placed inside one of four small boxes arranged in the center of the room. The boxes were identical, so their relative position was the only cue to the correct one. In the third condition (Landmark), contextual cues were provided that could be used to retrieve the toy, if the child thought to use them. The toy was again hidden in one of four identical boxes, but this time each of the boxes was placed on or near a piece of furniture. Thus, the furniture was a potential cue, a landmark denoting the correct one of the four boxes.

Notice that the relevant information was the same in both the Natural and the Landmark conditions; what differed was whether the subject merely had to notice the item of furniture itself or had to recognize its relation to the box with the toy. In the Natural condition the child only had to notice that the toy was hidden in the armchair, while in the Landmark condition he or she had to notice that the box in which the toy was hidden was the one on the armchair. Thus, in the Natural condition the information was intrinsic to the hiding place, whereas in the Landmark condition, the child him- or herself had to link or integrate the information with the actual hiding place.

We compared the rate of errorless retrievals in these three conditions for a younger group of subjects whose mean age was 21 months and an older group with a mean age of 26 months. As shown in Fig. 3.1, a clear interaction occurred, with an age difference in the children's performance in the Landmark condition, but not in the other two conditions. In the No Landmark condition, in which the toy was hidden in one of four boxes in the center of the room, the old and young groups were at the same level. (Their performance is equivalent to that generally reported for similar delayed-response tasks—for example, Blair, Perlmutter, & Myers, 1978; Horn & Myers, 1978.) Both age groups did substantially better in the Natural condition, the standard hide-and-seek task, and again there was no difference between them. (The general level of performance in the Natural condition is comparable to results we have obtained in other studies with the hide-and-seek task—DeLoache & Brown, 1979.) The large difference in the performance of the two age groups in the Landmark condition indicated that the older children exploited the available landmarks, but the younger ones did not.

The pattern of results for the three conditions combined thus reveals an absence of developmental differences in searching for a hidden object when no supplementary cues are available (No Landmark) and when distinctive cues are

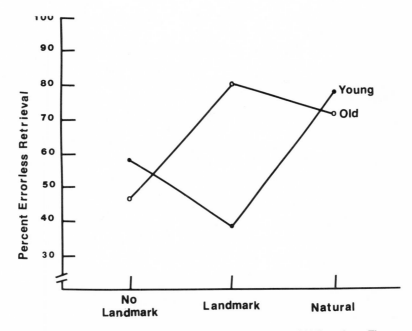

FIG. 3.1.   Errorless retrievals as a function of the type of hiding place. The apparent age × condition interaction is significant. (DeLoache & Brown, 1983.)

intrinsically associated with the hiding location (Natural). When potential cues are available, but have no inherent relation to the hiding place (Landmark), clear developmental differences emerge, with older children capitalizing on their presence and younger children failing to do so. These data may reflect an early form of mnemonic regulation. The older subjects may have done so well in the Landmark condition because they actively integrated the landmark cue with the relevant box. That is, at the time of hiding they noticed and encoded the relationship between the baited box and the nearby piece of furniture and then at retrieval used that information to direct their search. The younger subjects may have failed to encode the relationship in the first place or they may have neglected to draw on that information for retrieval.

In a subsequent study (DeLoache, 1983), we obtained further evidence of early progress in children's ability to exploit arbitrary cues (i.e., cues that are not intrinsic to the hiding place itself). Two of the conditions in this experiment were direct analogues of the Natural and Landmark conditions of the previous study. In one (Container = Location), four visually distinctive containers (a small box, a tin can, a basket, an overturned flower pot) served as the hiding locations, and the object (a piece of candy) was hidden in one of them on each trial. In another condition (Container = Cue), the same containers were again used, but this time they were simply potential cues to the location of the hidden candy. Each of the containers was attached to the top of one of four identical wooden boxes, and the candy was hidden in one of the boxes. Thus, in the first condition the four containers were themselves the hiding places; in the second condition the same containers were potential cues to indicate which box held the candy. In the third condition, color photographs of the containers were affixed to the tops of the boxes and served as potential visual cues (Picture = Cue). For half the subjects in each of the three conditions, the relative positions of the containers were switched after the cnady had been hidden (Move condition), thus eliminating spatial position as a cue and leaving the visual information as the only reliable cue to the current location of the cany. For the other half of the subjects, the boxes were never moved (Stationary).

The results, which are shown in Fig. 3.2, parallel those from the preceding study. In the condition in which the container was itself the hiding place for the object (Container = Location), both old and young subjects did equally well, regardless of whether or not the boxes were moved. In the second condition (Container = Cue), in which the container was simply a cue designating the correct box, an interesting pattern of results emerged. The older children's performance in this condition was equivalent to their performance in the Container = Location condition; they did very well, and it did not matter whether the boxes were moved or not. Thus, the older subjects used the visual distinctiveness of a

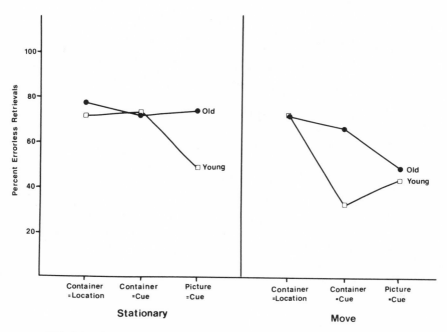

FIG. 3.2. Errorless retrievals as a function of different kinds of cues. (De-Loache, 1983.)

container equally well whether the container was the actual location of the object or was merely a cue to the correct location. In contrast, the younger children were not able to perform effectively when the same container was the only cue to the correct box (Container = Cue/Move), although when the container cue was combined with spatial-location information (Container = Cue/Stationary), the younger children did as well as in the Container = Location condition. Finally, in the Picture = Cue condition, the results were essentially what one would expect, given the existing literature with delayed response tasks. The pictures, which were probably not highly attractive or familiar to young children, substantially assisted the retrieval efforts of the older subjects when they were combined with stable spatial position (Picture = Cue/Stationary), but they were of limited use to the other three groups.

This experiment thus replicates and extends the finding of the landmark study concerning developmental differences in very young children's use of visual information to guide search. In both studies, both age groups searched quite competently for objects hidden in distinctive locations. To put it another way, there were no age differences when there was a direct relationship between the hidden object and a distinctive hiding place. Age differences did appear when the relation between the object and the information specifying its current location was less direct, so that the child had to provide the link between them (as in the Landmark and Container = Cue conditions). The older, but not the younger, child seemed to actively exploit the available cue, transforming it through his or her own mental activity from a potential to a functional cue.

One particularly interesting and informative aspect of these data concerns the performance of the younger children in the Container = Cue/Stationary condition. Their performance was the same as that of the older children in this condition, and they did much better than the other younger groups in the Picture = Cue conditions. This indicates that the younger children were not oblivious to the container cues—they did perform better when the containers were added to consistent spatial-position information than when only the relatively nonsalient picture cues were available. This finding suggests that the age difference found in both studies for the use of arbitrary or indirect cues is probably a retrieval, rather than an encoding, effect. The younger children do notice the arbitrary cues, but they do not actively exploit them to guide search, as the older children do. These data lend further support to our interpretation of the age difference as having to do with the development of early, simple strategies for exploiting information.

When the results of these studies are combined with other research on memory for the location of a hidden object, the following developmental progression is clear in very young children's use of available cues; By 24 months or even before, children are capable of using perceptual information that is intrinsic to the hiding place itself, such as the distinctive hiding locations used in the hide-and-seek game and the container study or differences in the size of a set of containers (Daehler, Bukatko, Benson, & Myers, 1976). Young subjects can also utilize a matching picture cue, one that bears a preexisting, nonarbitrary relation to the hidden object (Ratner & Myers, 1980). A highly salient cue that is associated with a reliable spatial cue (as in the Container = Cue condition) may improve their performance but they are unable to use the same cue in isolation. Slightly older children are able to use previously unrelated information; for example, they can exploit a nearby landmark or object as a cue to the relevant location or associate an unrelated picture with the correct box (Blair et al., 1978; Horn & Myers, 1978; Perlmutter, Hazen, Mitchell, Grady, Cavanaugh, & Flook, 1981). Even later, preschool children become capable of planning ahead to make sure a cue will be available in the future (Ryan, Hegion, & Flavell, 1970). Thus, the relevant developmental dimension seems to be the extent to which the young child must actively integrate existing stimulus information or impose his or her own organization in order to search successfully.

As was discussed earlier, inferences regarding the development of strategic intervention in older children have been based on findings of developmental differences when strategic intervention is possible, and an absence of age differences when it is not. One could argue, then, that the landmark and container studies reveal an early form of deliberate remembering, but such an interpretation should obviously not be accepted prematurely. Additional evidence is needed, such as direct observation of deliberate actions undertaken in the service of remembering. Convergent evidence of this sort greatly strengthened the claims that young grade-school children were capable of strategic action, and such evidence is certainly no less needed to support any claim for strategic behavior by much younger children.

Precursors of Mnemonic Strategies

So far, I have described one aspect of the behavior of 2-year-old children in a memory for location task that is reminiscent of the strategic behavior of older subjects. Are there other such parallels between early and later mnemonic functioning? One of the simplest mnemonic strategies is rehearsal. When we have some information that we want to be sure to be able to retrieve at some future time, we repeatedly check to make sure that we do still recall it and repeat it to make its later retrieval more probably. Everyone is overly familiar with the well-worn example of rehearsing telephone numbers, and we all rehearse other information from time to time, including talks about our research.

In a famous experiment, Flavell and his colleagues reported that children as young as 5 rehearsed words they were supposed to memorize. The children were observed silently mouthing the words to themselves as they waited for a recall test. Istomina (1975) made similar observations of older preschool children spontaneously rehearsing lists of items they were supposed to remember to "purchase" at a pretend store.

Even earlier evidence of simple mnemonic strategies was reported by Wellman, Ritter, and Flavell (1975) in a memory for location task. Three- and 4-year-old children watched while an experimenter hid a toy dog in one of three cups. The experimenter then left the room for 40 seconds, instructing the children either to "remember where the dog is" (remember condition) or simply to "wait here with the dog" (wait condition). The children in the remember condition engaged in several simple behaviors that appeared to serve a mnemonic function. They looked at, pointed to, and touched the baited cup more often during the delay period than did the subjects in the wait condition.

Wellman et al. (1975) also reported a few dramatic examples of behaviors whose sole function seemed to be in the service of remembering. One was visual rehearsal, best exemplified by one subject who looked at the baited cup and nodded her head yes, looked at the unbaited cups and shook her head no, then again looked at the correct cup and nodded affirmatively. Another strategy was to make the baited cup distinctive; for example, one boy kept his hand on the relevant cup during the entire delay interval. Wellman et al. have thus shown behavioral analogues in preschool children of the more complex strategies of rehearsal and elaboration present in older subjects. Furthermore, the use of these simple strategies correlated positively with memory performance; children who exhibited the strategic behaviors tended to achieve higher memory scores.

A group of 2-year-olds observed by Wellman et al. (1975) in the same task gave no evidence of any of the deliberate behaviors exhibited by the 3- and 4-year-olds. However, this negative result is inconclusive because, as the authors point out, the task was not really appropriate for 2-year-olds. Fully a third of them failed to complete even three trials, often because they were unwilling to remain alone in the testing room. Also, they may not have fully comprehended the verbal instructions. The question remains whether children younger than 3 years of age might be capable of engaging in some kind of mnemonic activity.

Our initial two attempts to find evidence of deliberate mnemonic effort of the sort observed by Wellman et al. were unsuccessful. In one case, we compared the rate of errorless retrievals when children received explicit memory instructions with their performance in what was ostensibly a nonmemory condition. The memory condition was the standard hide-and-seek task, in which the children were told at the time of hiding to "try to remember where Big Bird is hiding so you can get him when the bell rings." In the nonmemory situation, the children were told, "Big Bird is tired and needs to take a nap." The toy was then concealed in the same manner as in the regular task, but no mention was made that the subject would be expected to retrieve the toy. The experimenter merely said that she was "setting the alarm clock so Big Bird will know when to wake up." Just one nap trial was administered, and it always preceded the regular hide-and-seek trials, because the memory demands actually being placed on the children would immediately become apparent. The results were unambiguous: Every one of the 16 2-year-olds (22 to 29 months) retrieved the toy in the nap task. Thus, advance warning that a memory demand will be made is not required for young children to remember the location of a hidden toy. As long as the hiding of the toy is a meaningful activity to them, they generally remember its location with no special effort.

In the second unsuccessful attempt, we compared errorless retrievals as a function of whether the children spent the delay interval in the same room in which the toy was hidden or in a different room. Our reasoning was that if a child did the sort of things that facilitated the performance of the Wellman et al. subjects, he or she would do better when the hiding place remained in view throughout the interval—that is, when it was possible to engage in those behaviors. However, there was no difference in errorless retrievals whether the children waited in the same room as the hiding place, and thus had visual access to it during the delay interval, or in a different room.

In both of the just-described studies, we had looked for an effect on the rate of errorless retrievals, and had found none. This may be in part attributable to ceiling effects in the children's performance: Subjects in the hide-and-seek task often achieve perfect or near-perfect scores for errorless retrievals. Our first positive evidence that children younger than 2 years of age do exhibit some of the behaviors observed in the Wellman et al. (1975) study came from a pilot study that had been designed for another purpose, and from a measure other than errorless retrievals. In that study (Cassidy, 1980), 22-month-old children's performance in the hide-and-seek task was compared for two different settings: their own homes and a laboratory playroom. Our original motivation was to see if the excellent performance we had obtained in previous work with the hide-and-seek game (DeLoache & Brown, 1979, 1983, 1984) might be in part attributable to the fact that the children had always been tested in a very familiar environment. We thought that a well-formed schema for his or her own livingroom might make it easier for a child to remember where within that environment a toy has been hidden. The laboratory playroom was furnished like a regular living room, but was unfamiliar to the children. Cassidy (1980) found that errorless retrievals did not differ as a function of the environment in which the hide-and-seek task was embedded, but she informally (and alertly) observed that the children did engage in several behaviors reminiscent of those reported by Wellman et al. (1975) Furthermore, they seemed to do so more often in the unfamiliar laboratory than in their own homes. We have since conducted two additional experiments investigating this phenomenon.

In those experiments (DeLoache et al., 1983), two observers carefully recorded the behavior of 20-month-old children (18 to 24 months in age) during the interval between when they saw the toy hidden and when they were allowed to search for it. We found that the children often interrupted their play with a set of attractive toys to return their attention to the ongoing memory task, engaging in a variety of target behaviors that indicated they were still preoccupied with the memory task. One such target behavior was relevant vocalization. The children frequently talked about the toy "Big Bird"), the fact that it was hidden ("Big Bird hiding"), where it was hidden ("Big Bird chair"), or about their plan to retrieve it later ("Me find Big Bird"). Other target behaviors included looking or pointing at the hiding place, hovering near it, and peeking at the toy or attempting to retrieve it early. These behaviors resemble the mature mnemonic strategies of rehearsal and monitoring, and they could function to keep alive the information to be remembered—that is, to remind the children of the toy and its location. The data thus suggest that children younger than 2 years of age may in some rudimentary way be sensitive to the memory demands of the task.

But do these target behaviors qualify as mnemonic strategies, or even as precursors of strategies? On the one hand, there was no relationship between the occurrence of the target behaviors and memory performance—that is, children who exhibited more of the target behaviors were not necessarily more successful at retrieving their toy. Thus, we did not find the facilitative effect one would normally expect from mnemonic strategies (although the fact that most children's performance was at or near ceiling makes interpretation somewhat problematic). On the other hand, some additional data that we have show that the target behaviors are in many other ways analogous to later, more sophisticated strategies.

For one thing, the children performed the target behaviors differentially as a function of the familiarity of the environment in which the task was embedded, and the familiarity of the task itself. In both studies we compared the behavior of children playing the hide-and-seek game in their own homes versus in a laboratory playroom. One study used a within-subjects design in which each child was observed in both settings, with the order of the settings counterbalanced. As Fig. 3.3 shows, in both experiments, significantly more target behaviors occurred in the laboratory setting than in the home.

Why should very young children be more oriented to a hidden object in an unfamiliar laboratory than in their own homes, especially given that there was no difference in their rate of errorless retrievals in the two settings? One possibility is that when playing the memory game in an unfamiliar setting the children may have less confidence in their ability to remember where the toy is hidden, so they do things to keep alive their memory for its location until they are permitted to retrieve it.

This supposition is strengthened by the fact that in the within-subjects study significantly more target behaviors occurred on the first day of observation, during the children's initial exposure to the memory task, than on the second. The overall mean number of target behaviors for the lab–home and home–lab groups dropped substantially and significantly from Day 1 to Day 2, as shown in Fig. 3.4. The days' effect was especially clear in an additional group of subjects who were tested only in the laboratory on two successive days (the lab–lab group). Thus, in two different situations in which very young children might be expected to feel less confident—being tested in an unfamiliar setting or par-

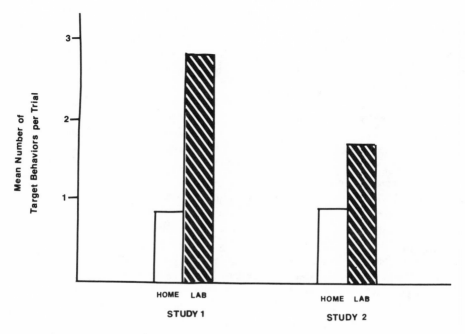

FIG. 3.3. The incidence of target behaviors as a function of setting. Significantly more occurred in the laboratory setting in both studies. (Study 1 used a between-subjects design, and Study 2 was within subjects.) (DeLoache et al., 1983.)

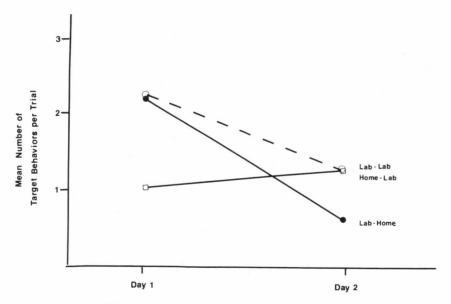

FIG. 3.4. The incidence of target behaviors over days.

ticipating in an unfamiliar task—they actively monitor the situation and them-selves. These two familiarity effects combine so that the condition that produced by far the most target behaviors was when the children's first exposure to the hide-and-seek game was in the laboratory, and the least occurred when the familiar game was played in the children's own homes on the second day.

The question remains whether these target behaviors are specifically in the service of memory. To address this issue we tested two more groups of 20-month-old children in variations of the hide-and-seek game that removed the memory requirement. We wanted to see if the children would still exhibit the target behaviors even if they were not required to remember the toy's location. For one group the main modification to the task was that the toy remained visible throughout the interval. At the time of hiding, the experimenter said to the child, "Big Bird needs to take a nap now, and when the bell rings, you can go and get him up." The toy was then placed so that it remained visible (e.g., instead of hiding the toy under a cushion, the experimenter placed it on top of the cushion). For the second group, the memory burden was removed from the children in a different way. This time, everything was the same as in the standard hide-and-seek game except that instead of the children's retrieving the toy at the end of the interval, the experimenter retrieved it. In both those situations, in which there was no necessity for the children to remember where the toy was in order to retrieve it later, very few target behaviors appeared, significantly fewer than in the standard memory task (see Fig. 3.5). Thus, when the children did not bear the responsibility for retrieving the toy themselves, they seemed unconcerned with its whereabouts. When the toy was visible during the interval, the children ignored it; when the toy was invisible, so they had to retain its location in memory, they remained preoccupied with it. To rephrase a familiar term used for the pre-object permanence child, we might characterize the behavior of our subjects as, "in sight, out of mind."

It seems reasonable, then, to interpret the target behavios as reflecting a very early natural propensity to keep alive what must be remembered. The behaviors we observed arise spontaneously in the course of the memory task as a function of the children's uncertainty about the outcome of the task. Later, more elaborate mnemonic strategies may harness and build upon such simple, spontaneous activities, transforming them into increasingly deliberate and planful actions in the service of memory.

As a footnote to this discussion, I would like to mention one especially interesting behavior that we observed a few times in the regular hide-and-seek task (too seldom to analyze). After watching the experimenter hide the toy, sometimes a child would briefly check a hiding place used on a previous trial (most often the immediately preceding trial). Although this behavior was fairly rare (only six or seven subjects ever did it), it is intriguing in light of the fact that the most common error made by young children in memory for location tasks is searching a location that was correct on an earlier trial. It is as though our

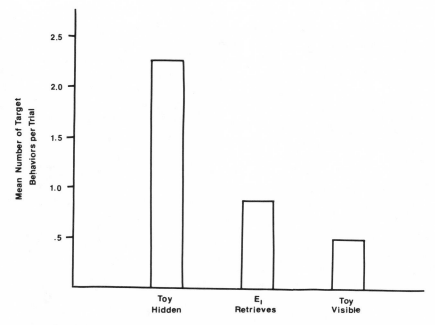

FIG. 3.5. Comparison of the level of target behaviors as a function of whether the children must remember the toy's location (Toy Hidden) or not (*E* Retrieves and Toy Visible).

subjects were reassuring themselves of the irrelevance of the old location, eliminating it as a potential distractor, and it is difficult not to interpret this behavior as reflecting deliberate mnemonic intent.

Organization of Memory-Based Searching

In the last study discussed here (DeLoache & Brown, 1984), we examined the organization of spatial search. We asked whether very young children are capable of assessing the current states of their own memories and then using those assessments to organize their subsequent behavior. We know that older subjects can. In internal memory tasks, children as young as kindergarten age allocate retrieval effort based on subjective certainty or feeling of knowing judgments: The more certain they are that they know something that they cannot immediately retrieve, the more extensive and persistent are their efforts to retrieve it (Posnansky, 1978; Wellman, 1977).

To see if subjective certainty influences how young children search for an object in the environment, we employed a surprise procedure, a technique frequently used in object-permanence research to illuminate infants' understanding and expectations about objects (e.g., Charlesworth, 1969; Gelman, 1972;

LeCompte & Gratch, 1972; Ramsay & Campos, 1978). On two of six hide-and-seek trials, the experimenter hid the toy as usual, but then surreptitiously moved it without the child's knowing it. After the first Surprise trial, the child was always informed that the experimenter had moved the toy and that she had put it in a shopping bag she had brought with her. She explained that, "Big Bird wanted to play a trick on you so I helped him hide in my bag."

We expected that the length or persistence of the child's search of the correct location would reflect his or her level of certainty: The more certain the child is of the correct location, the longer he or she should continue searching there after failing to find the toy right away. We compared the length of each child's first search on Surprise trials with all Error trials that occurred—that is, all the times the child mistakenly went to the wrong place first. Note that in both cases, the child's initial search had failed to retrieve the toy. On Surprise trials the child was in fact at the correct location so he or she should have been fairly confident. On Error trials the child was wrong—he or she may have forgotten the correct location or may have become confused—so the level of certainty should have been considerably lower.

Two age groups of children participated in this study, an older group whose mean age was 27 months (25 to 30 months) and a younger group with a mean age of 21 months (18 to 24 months). For both age groups, the first search was significantly longer on Surprise trials, when they were in fact correct, than on Error trials, when they were mistaken. There was also a tendency to re-search the correct location on Surprise trials. A good example of a persistent search was the Surprise trial behavior of a 23-month-old boy: He looked under the couch cushion where his toy had been hidden, then pulled the cushion completely off the couch and examined the area, turned around to say "No!" to his mother, and then turned back and briefly checked the correct hiding place one more time. Thus, for both the younger and older children, their subjective certainty determined how persistently they searched.

These results, which concern the retrieval of an object from the external environment, are analogous to those obtained with adults and older children (Posnansky, 1978; Wellman, 1977) for the retrieval of internally stored information. In both cases, children's retrieval efforts are based on their assessments of their own memory states—how much they think they know or how well they think they know it. That children are capable of this form of metamemory earlier in an external memory task such as the hide-and-seek game is consistent with other research showing that metamemory skills are generally exercised earlier with respect to external variables (Gordon & Flavell, 1977; Yussen & Levy, 1977).

We also examined the subsequent searching that the children did on Surprise and Error trials. An intelligent response to the surprising absence of an object at its remembered location is to search plausible alternative locations. Imagine an adult who remembers leaving his or her car keys on the coffee table, but fails to find them there. This person would probably search all around the table surface in case he or she had misremembered the precise spot, possibly checking to see if the keys had been brushed off the table onto the floor. Or the person might find out if someone else moved the keys. Thus, this hypothetical adult selects from all the potential locations in the room those places that are near or in some way related to where he or she remembers the keys should be. In other words, searching is confined to places that would be plausible locations of the keys if the adult's memory for where he or she left them is essentially correct.

After their initial unsuccessful searches on Surprise and Error trials, the children usually (71% of the trials) went on to search one or more additional locations. We examined all additional searches on Surprise and Error trials to see if the children's behavior was like that of the intelligent adult. A search was scored as intelligent, or "related," if it fell into one or more of the following three categories: (1) the child searched a place that was *near* to the correct location (for example, if the toy had been hidden under one couch cushion, the child went on to look under the next cushion or behind the couch); (2) the child searched an *analogous* location (if the toy had been hidden under a pillow at one end of the couch, the subject looked under a different pillow at the other end of the couch or on a chair); (3) the subject sometimes looked in the bag to which the experimenter had moved the toy on the first Surprise trial.

We had expected differential searching on Surprise and Error trials, and in particular, more related searching on Surprise trials. If a person is sure that an object was hidden in a given place, and it is not there, then it makes sense to search other places related to it. If a person is not really certain of the original location of the object, then it is not so clear where to search next (unless he or she happens to suddenly remember the correct location). As shown in Fig. 3.6, this pattern was observed for the older subjects, but not for the younger ones. When the younger children failed to find their toy, regardless of whether it was a Surprise or an Error trial, they tended to search in places where it had been hidden before, reminiscent of the typical error in delayed-response tasks of searching for an object where one has previously found it (Daehler et al., 1976; Horn & Myers, 1978; Loughlin & Daehler, 1973; Perlmutter et al., 1981; Webb, Massar, & Nadolny, 1972), as well as the Stage IV error in object-permanence research (Harris, 1975).

The older children displayed qualitatively different searching on Surprise and Error trials. On Surprise trials the old subjects almost always (95%) began their additional searching at locations that were in some way related either to the correct location or to their previous Surprise trial experience, and three-fourths of their total Surprise trial searches were so related. In contrast, less than one-fourth of their Error trial searches were related. Thus, the older, but not the younger, children used their own senses of certainty to organize how they searched for a missing object.

The related Surprise trial searching of the older children suggests that they (like the hypothetical adult with the lost car keys) may have generated plausible hypotheses to explain the toy's absence, which then guided their subsequent

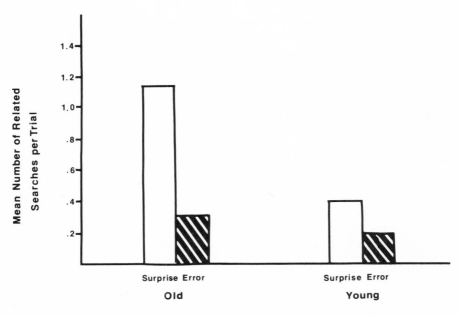

FIG. 3.6.   Comparison of related searching on Surprise and Error trials. Only the difference for the older subjects was significant. (DeLoache & Brown, 1984.)

search efforts. For example, their frequent searches of locations that were analogous to the correct location suggests that they sometimes assumed that they must have misremembered a detail about the toy's location, such as which specific one of a category of spatial locations it was. Supporting examples include a child's going from the couch pillow under which the toy was hidden to a different pillow at the other end of the couch or to a pillow on a chair.

The older subjects occasionally seemed to consider the possibility that some intervening event had spatially displaced the toy. A 30-month-old searched both under and beside the couch in which his toy had been hidden. Another subject explicitly verbalized this hypothesis: He looked in the desk drawer in which his toy had been hidden, said ''Did Mickey Mouse fall out?'' and then proceeded to search behind the desk.

Some children also realized that a social agent might be responsible for the toy's absence. On the second Surprise trial, several subjects inferred (correctly) that the experimenter had again moved their toy; they went directly from their initial searches to the experimenter's bag, the place to which the toy had been moved on the first Surprise trial. A 29-month-old girl whirled around from her initial search of the correct location, yelling to the experimenter, ''In your bag!'' She then ran immediately to look in the bag, saying, ''Jackie, *you* took him.''

Additional evidence for the assertion that the older children were trying to figure out where their toy was likely to be is the fact that many of their Surprise trial searches were of completely new locations (i.e., ones that had never been used as hiding places), and most of these new locations were related to the correct one. This tendency to search new, related locations on Surprise trials indicates that the older children are able to conceive of several possible locations, and that they select potential locations to search on the basis of their relation to the original hiding place. Whereas the younger subjects tended to search locations that had been previously associated with the object, the older children did something much more active than simply searching at the location with the strongest memory trace. They ignored past associations and selected places to search because they were plausible alternative locations for the toy. This age difference in related searching signals an increase in the flexibility with which children reorganize their search behavior. When confronted with failure, the younger subjects simply reiterate previously successful responses, but the older children try new solutions, based on their construal of the present situation.

PRIMITIVE SELF-REGULATORY SKILLS

Let me summarize and integrate the research I have described. Our investigation of very young children's memory performances has revealed surprising competence, both in terms of the level of performance and the processes underlying it. Two-year-old and even younger children are very good at remembering spatial locations; in fact, their performance is often virtually perfect. They are sensitive to memory demands placed on them in some circumstances, and they exhibit a propensity to keep alive information to be remembered, even though such behaviors do not seem functional in the particular context in which we observed them.

When mediated memory is essential for good performance, developmental differences appear in the period between $1\frac{1}{2}$ and $2\frac{1}{2}$ years of age, suggesting the emergence of simple forms of self-regulation. For one thing, the scope of information that can be exploited expands as the child becomes capable of integrating arbitrarily related information, exerting cognitive effort to transform potential cues into functional ones. The flexibility of young children's problem-solving efforts also increases. If their initial effort fails, 2-year-olds are able to initiate a creative solution (e.g., search a new but related location), whereas younger subjects fall back on responses that were successful at a previous time.

The mnemonic achievements I have described for very young children are fairly impressive, but not awesome. Two-year-old children may be better mnemonists than we had suspected or given them credit for, but they are still novices. Thus, we have a sort of "doughnut-hole" phenomenon: We can either be impressed by the unsuspected sophistication that young children are capable of displaying in some situations, or we can emphasize the limited domain of these primitive skills. I should like to avoid either of these extremes; I want to have my doughnut and eat it too. It is important that those of us who tend to be impressed by what we are discovering about young children's capacities are not blind to the holes in their competence. And it is equally important that those who tend to see the toddler as so much unrisen dough also recognize the extensive array of ingredients already present. We will make progress only if we neither exaggerate nor belittle the cognitive achievements of very young children.

What, then, are the limitations on the simple forms of early self-regulation that we have observed, and how do young children overcome them? In terms of limits, the abilities I have described are almost certainly restricted to external memory tasks in which the environment assists the novice mnemonist. However young children represent a hidden object and its spatial location (which is an interesting question itself), there are abundant cues present to help them retrieve both their representation and the actual object. The children have to recall the existence of the hidden object, but they only have to recognize its location. Scanning around the room is a simple and effective way of reminding themselves of the toy's location, and young children often do this. What I am suggesting, then, is that young children's fledgling regulatory efforts occur when the organization present in the external environment minimizes the amount of internal organization that the children themselves must produce.

Another limitation on young children's mnemonic activities is the extent to which they have conscious control over them. I seriously doubt that average 2-year-olds query themselves, "What can I do to help me remember?" Rather, early regulation emerges in the context of ongoing activity in which the children have adopted the goal of retrieving objects at a slightly later time. The fact that the target behaviors occur almost exclusively when there are memory demands placed on the children indicates some sensitivity to the need for future retrieval.

Young children do seem to assess their own momentary sense of confidence or certainty, and that self-assessment influences their immediate behavior. When they are uncertain or insecure, they repeatedly return their attention to the task demands. When they are very confident of their judgment, they are highly persistent in the face of failure. However, only the older children we observed (i.e., those over 2) were able to use their own feeling of knowing as a basis for organizing their subsequent behavior.

Young children also seem to make some assessment of the difficulty of the task they face; our subjects engaged in the strategylike target behaviors more often in one setting (the laboratory) than in the other (the home). However, the data also reveal that their task analyses are imperfect. There is no evidence that the hide-and-seek game is actually any more or less difficult in one setting or the other. It may be that the children mistakenly use a general sense of insecurity aroused by being in an unfamiliar setting as information relevant to the task. Children have to learn to judge when such behaviors are actually necessary to improve performance and when they are irrelevant.

This brings us to a final way in which the target behaviors we observed in our 2-year-old subjects differ from mature strategies. Although these target behaviors were similar in form to the deliberate mnemonic behaviors reported by Wellman et al. (1975) for older children, there was no evidence that they served the same function of improving memory performance.

There are various explanations for why the strategylike target behaviors did not relate to memory performance. One is purely artifactual: The ceiling effect present for the memory-performance measure may have obscured a true relationship. If this is so, then a more difficult version of the hide-and-seek task, in which ceiling performance is not so common, might yield a correlation between target behaviors and memory performance. In Siegler and Shrager's (this volume) work on addition, strategy use was correlated with performance only for more difficult problems. Additional research is needed to resolve this matter. We are planning to use a multiple-object hide-and-seek task, in which three toys are hidden per trial and in which the overall performance will be poorer (DeLoache & Brown, 1979), to see if engaging in the target behaviors might facilitate retrieving the objects.

We would not be surprised to obtain such a result. However, we would also not be surprised if we again found no correlation between the occurrence of the target behaviors and young children's memory performance. It seems to us perfectly reasonable that there may in fact not be a very direct relation between incipient strategies and performance. These behaviors may arise spontaneously in the midst of goal-directed activity, but only gradually become harnessed in the service of the goal. Thus, even though the target behaviors that our very young subjects spontaneously exhibited were not adaptive for the task in which the children were involved at the time, they may be adaptive in the long run. That is, they may provide a basis for the evolution of later, more deliberate, finely tuned, and instrumental mnemonic strategies.

From what has been presented here, we can summarize what we might generally expect precursors or immature forms of self-regulatory skills to look like. First, they will almost certainly not be perfect versions of the mature strategies; they will resemble them in some ways, but not in others. Nascent skills are probably exercised in limited domains, appearing only when there is a near-ideal match between a child's current skills and the amount of organization demanded by the task at hand. The fragile skills probably first appear within the context of immediate, ongoing activity, rather than in a planful or self-conscious way. The means/end distinction may at the outset be fairly fuzzy, with the strategy only gradually coming to serve as an explicit means subordinated to the achievement of a given goal.

In conclusion, I have argued that we have evidence for the existence of rudimentary forms of self-regulation in very young children. We have learned something about what very early manifestations or precursors of later skills are like. We know what the mature forms are like: The vast literature on mnemonic strategies leaves us quite well informed in that regard. What we need now is a better understanding of the refinement of these primitive, limited mechanisms into the complex, adaptive skills that older people possess. How does a young child who repeatedly looks at the place her toy is hidden turn into an adult who nervously rehearses for her research presentation to a group of distinguished colleagues?

ACKNOWLEDGMENTS

The research reported in this chapter was supported by USPHS grants HD–05951 and HD–06864, an award from the University of Illinois Research Board, and a Hatch grant from the Agricultural Experiment Station at the University of Illinois. I wish to thank Deborah Kresser, Pamela Buccitelli, and Jacqueline Gramann for their assistance in carrying out the research. I also thank Ann Brown, Gerald Clore, Elissa Newport, and Susan Sugarman for their helpful support and suggestions.

REFERENCES

Ashmead, D. H., & Perlmutter, M. Infant memory in everyday life. In M. Perlmutter (Ed.), *New directions for child development: Children's memory* (No. 10). San Francisco: Jossey-Bass, 1980.

Blair, R., Perlmutter, M., & Myers, N. A. The effects of unlabeled and labeled picture cues on very young children's memory for location. *Bulletin of the Psychonomics Society,* 1978, *11,* 46–48.

Brown, A. L. The development of memory: Knowing, knowing about knowing, and knowing how to know. In H. W. Reese (Ed.), *Advances in child development and behavior* (Vol. 10). New York: Academic Press, 1975.

Brown, A. L. Knowing when, where, and how to remember: A problem of metacognition. In R. Glaser (Ed.), *Advances in instructional psychology* (Vol. 1). Hillsdale, N.J.: Lawrence Erlbaum Associates, 1978.

Brown, A. L., Campione, J. C., & Gilliard, D. M. Recency judgments in children: A production deficiency in the use of redundant background cues. *Developmental Psychology,* 1974, *10,* 303.

Brown, A. L., & DeLoache, J. S. Skills, plans, and self-regulation. In R. Siegler (Ed.), *Children's thinking: What develops?* Hillsdale, N.J.: Lawrence Erlbaum Associates, 1978.

Cassidy, D. J. *The effects of environmental familiarity on very young children's memory for object location.* Unpublished Master's thesis, University of Illinois at Urbana-Champaign, 1980.

Charlesworth, W. R. Surprise and cognitive development. In D. Elkind & J. H. Flavell (Eds.), *Studies in cognitive development: Essays in honor of Jean Piaget.* New York: Oxford University Press, 1969.

Daehler, M., Bukatko, D., Benson, K., & Myers, M. The effects of size and color cues on the delayed response of very young children. *Bulletin of the Psychonomic Society,* 1976, 7, 65–68.

DeLoache, J. S. Naturalistic studies of memory for object location in very young children. *New Directions for Child Development,* 1980, *10,* 17–32.

DeLoache, J. S. *Simple mnemonic regulation in the memory-based searching of toddlers.* Paper presented at the meeting of the Society for Research in Child Development, Detroit, April 1983.

DeLoache, J. S., & Brown, A. L. Looking for Big Bird: Studies of memory in very young children. *The Quarterly Newsletter of the Laboratory of Comparative Human Cognition,* 1979, *1,* 53–57.

DeLoache, J. S., & Brown, A. L. Very young children's memory for the location of objects in a large-scale environment. *Child Development*, 1983, *54*, 888–897.

DeLoache, J. S., & Brown, A. L. Intelligent searching by very young children. *Developmental Psychology*, 1984, *20*, 37–44.

DeLoache, J. S., Cassidy, D. J., & Brown, A. L. *Precursors of mnemonic strategies in very young children's memory*. Unpublished manuscript, 1983.

Gelman, R. Logical capacity of very young children: Number invariance rules. *Child Development*, 1972, *43*, 75–90.

Gordon, F. R., & Flavell, J. H. The development of intuitions about cognitive cueing. *Child Development*, 1977, *48*, 1027–1033.

Gratch, G. Recent studies based on Piaget's view of object concept development. In L. B. Cohen & P. Salapatek (Eds.), *Infant perception: From sensation to cognition* (Vol. 2). New York: Academic Press, 1975.

Harris, P. H. Infant cognition. In M. M. Haith & J. J. Campos (Eds.), *Infancy and development psychobiology*. New York: Wiley, 1983.

Harris, P. L. Development of search and object permanence during infancy. *Psychological Bulletin*, 1975, *82*, 332–344.

Horn, H., & Myers, N. A. Memory for location and picture cues at ages two and three. *Child Development*, 1978, *49*, 845–856.

Istomina, Z. M. The development of voluntary memory in preschool-age children. *Soviet Psychology*, Summer 1975, *13*, 5–64.

LeCompte, G. K., & Gratch, G. Violation of a rule as a method of diagnosing infants' levels of object concept. *Child Development*, 1972, *43*, 385–396.

Loughlin, K. A., & Daehler, M. A. The effects of distraction and added perceptual cues on the delayed reaction of very young children. *Child Development*, 1973, *44*, 384–388.

Nelson, K., & Ross, G. The generalities and specifics of long-term memory in infants and young children. In M. Perlmutter (Ed.), *New directions for child development: Children's memory* (No. 10). San Francisco: Jossey-Bass, 1980.

Perlmutter, M., Hazen, N., Mitchell, D. B., Grady, J. C., Cavanaugh, J. C., & Flook, J. P. Picture cues and exhaustive search facilitate very young children's memory for location. *Developmental Psychology*, 1981, *17*, 109–110.

Perlmutter, M., & Myers, N. A. Development of recall in two- to four-year-old children. *Developmental Psychology*, 1979, *15*, 73–83.

Posnansky, C. J. Age- and task-related differences in the use of category size information for retrieval of categorized items. *Journal of Experimental Child Psychology*, 1978, *26*, 373–382.

Ramsay, D. S., & Campos, J. J. The onset of representation and entry into Stage 6 of object permanence development. *Developmental Psychology*, 1978, *14*, 79–86.

Ratner, H. H. The role of social context in memory development. In M. Perlmutter (Ed.), *New directions for child development: Children's memory* (No. 10). San Francisco: Jossey-Bass, 1980.

Ratner, H. H., & Myers, N. A. Related picture cues and memory for hidden-object location at age two. *Child Development*, 1980, *51*, 561–564.

Ryan, S. M., Hegion, A. G., & Flavell, J. H. Nonverbal mnemonic mediation in preschool children. *Child Development*, 1970, *41*, 539–550.

Shatz, M. The relationship between cognitive processes and the development of communication skills. In B. Keasey (Ed.), *Nebraska symposium on motivation* Lincoln: University of Nebraska Press, 1978.

Webb, R. A., Massar, B., & Nadolny, T. Information and strategy in the young child's search for hidden objects. *Child Development*, 1972, *43*, 91–104.

Wellman, H. M. The early development of intentional memory behavior. *Human Development*, 1977, *20*, 86–101.

Wellman, H. M., Ritter, R., & Flavell, J. H. Deliberate memory behavior in the delayed reactions of very young children. *Developmental Psychology,* 1975, *11,* 780–787.

Wellman, H. M., & Somerville, S. C. Quasi-naturalistic tasks in the study of cognition: The memory-related skills of toddlers. In M. Perlmutter (Ed.), *New directions for child development: Children's memory* (No. 10). San Francisco: Jossey-Bass, 1980.

Yussen, S. R., & Levy, V. M., Jr. Developmental changes in knowledge about different retrieval problems. *Developmental Psychology,* 1977, *13,* 114–120.

4 The Child's Representation of Information about Location

Janellen Huttenlocher
University of Chicago

Nora Newcombe
Temple University

This chapter presents an analysis of how people represent one aspect of spatial information—namely, the locations of objects and geographic features, and the locations of observers relative to these. We examine two issues. The first is how people encode information about location and how this may change with development. The second is how people infer the outcomes of transformations in the relation of an observer to a set of items, and how this may change with development. While the issue of encoding and the issue of transformation have generally been dealt with separately, transformations of location information are carried out on initial encodings of that location information. We consider how apparent developmental change in the ability to transform spatial information may depend on how the information is encoded—both how it is initially encoded and how it is encoded as a person attempts to solve a particular problem.

The analysis of the encoding and transformation of information about location presented here is applied across the full range of situations in which location information is involved. That is, we are concerned with understanding how people deal with location in large-scale as well as small-scale contexts, and in situations in which they move around the world as well as in situations in which one or several objects move in relation to them. The starting point for our theorizing and research has been the mystery surrounding a classic finding in developmental psychology—namely, Piaget's finding that children have difficulty with perspective taking.

Piaget and Inhelder (1948/1967) showed children an array of three mountains and asked them to imagine how it would look to an observer in a different location. Children responded by building models or by selecting one of a set of pictures that showed the array from various perspectives: rotated 90°, 180°, 270°, or shown at 0° rotation. Until 9 or 10 years of age, children tended to respond incorrectly, often by selecting the view which showed the array from their own perspective. Piaget and Inhelder made several claims on the basis of these findings. One claim was that children cannot coordinate their own perspective with that of an observer in another spatial position. A further claim was that, in choosing a picture representing their own point of view, children show egocentrism, or a lack of understanding that other people see things differently. Finally, the task was taken as an index of the acquisition of a particular sort of representational system, projective space, which was held to be related to but distinct from another representational system, Euclidean space. We turn to this matter later in the chapter.

Piaget and Inhelder's finding concerning performance on the three-mountains problem has been replicated many times (e.g., Flavell, Botkin, Fry, Wright, & Jarvis, 1968; Laurendeau & Pinard, 1970). However, several elements of their interpretation of these findings can be questioned, and their theoretical claims need to be further elaborated. First, the notion that children's difficulty with the perspective task arises from an inability to appreciate that people in other positions see things differently does not appear to be correct. Lempers, Flavell, and Flavell (1977) have found, for instance, that 2 year olds displayed a box with a picture glued to one side nonegocentrically, turning it away from themselves, and that even $1\frac{1}{2}$ year olds held it so both they and the other person could see it. Clearly, then, children have no difficulty realizing that other people have different views than they do.

In an attempt to explain Piaget's findings, Flavell and his associates proposed a distinction between two aspects of understanding of visual perspective taking (Masangkay, McCluskey, McIntyre, Sims-Knight, Vaughn, & Flavell, 1974; Salatas & Flavell, 1976). The first is the understanding that other people see something different if they are in a different position. While this is exhibited at an early age, working out the particulars concerning what the observer sees can be done at first only for very simple problems—for example, whether or not the other person has a clear line of sight. The second aspect of visual perspective-taking tasks is the computational ability to work out what the other person sees for situations involving complex objects or arrays of several objects. It is this component that Flavell suggests improves with age, accounting for why children have difficulty with the three mountains task. What exactly changes developmentally about the computation process is not specified in these papers.

Even the claim that children have difficulty with computational aspects of perspective taking seems somewhat paradoxical. People are mobile creatures, and move about in relation to a stable environment. The ability to represent that stable world and to infer the locations of stationary entities when they are not currently perceptible seems important to adaptation—to finding the way back to a home location, to returning to important objects found earlier, such as sources of food or water, and so on. Thus, the finding that children, who by the age of 8 or 9 years can find their way effectively in the world, seem unable to make inferences in Piaget's perspective-taking task, might reflect the particular task used rather than a fundamental cognitive difficulty.

Indeed, children can easily do certain problems involving computational aspects of spatial transformation. Huttenlocher and Presson (1973) introduced a different spatial transformation problem where children were asked to imagine an array rotating about its own axis, and to select a picture showing how the array would look to them after the rotation. This array-rotation problem is logically equivalent to the perspective taking problem (henceforth called the observer-movement problem). That is, both problems require subjects to infer a new relation between an observer and an array; they differ only with respect to whether it is the observer or the array that is moved. The difficulty of this array-rotation problem was compared to the difficulty of the observer-movement problem with the same materials. The study confirmed that children indeed had considerable difficulty with observer-movement problems and showed that the array-rotation problem was far easier. Further, egocentrism was found only with observer-movement problems. Children evidently approached the problems differently, and some aspect of imagining observer movement was harder than imagining array movement.

In fact, children could even deal with computational aspects of perspective taking itself in a new task introduced by Huttenlocher and Presson (1979). In this task, children were asked to consider an observer in another position, and to identify the item in an array which would be nearest to that observer, or farthest, or on the observer's left or right (henceforth this will be called the item-question task). Observer-movement problems were *much* easier than they were with Piaget's picture-selection task, indicating that children can compute the relation of an array of objects to another observer under certain conditions. The difficulty of observer-movement problems was compared to the difficulty of array-rotation problems with the same materials on this item-question task. Answering item questions about array rotation was more difficult than selecting a picture, showing that these tasks are not simply easier than the picture-selection task. This pattern of results is shown in Table 4.1.

In interpreting the observed interaction between transformation and task, Huttenlocher and Presson (1979) noted that transformations operate on initial

TABLE 4.1
Pattern of Results in Huttenlocher and Presson
(1973, 1979)

	Observer Movement	*Array Rotation*
Picture selection	Hard	Easy
Item question	Easy	Hard

encodings of location information. They showed that the observed pattern of results could be explained by positing that children used a particular sort of initial encoding. An examination of the literature on spatial coding suggests the existence of striking developmental changes, and it seems possible that one factor in the development of transformation ability might be age-related changes in the way location information is encoded. This issue is explored in the present chapter. First, we analyze the ways that location information can be encoded in principle. Then we consider the literature on location coding and its development. Next, we analyze how transformation processes may operate with various encodings, and review the Huttenlocher and Presson studies in the light of this discussion.

To anticipate the discussion, when our analysis of location coding is applied to the existing literature on spatial transformation, it is possible to explain the various findings, including the interaction shown in Table 4.1. In contrast, when our analysis is applied to the existing literature on the development of location coding in preschool children, certain critical information is found to be lacking. In particular, most studies have assessed location coding in tasks where children are provided with a small set of locations (a set of boxes or dots) where objects are to be placed. Yet to choose among a small set of alternative locations, only a simple form of location coding is required, namely coding in relation to single landmarks. In the absence of prespecified locations, a more complex form of location coding is required, namely coding in relation to a spatial framework.

At the end of this chapter, two studies of coding in young children are presented. The studies reveal a startling phenomenon. In particular, children under 3 years can successfully place a set of objects in a set of specified locations after moving to a new position. However, they place objects randomly after movement when no such specified locations are provided. Thus children under 3 years can code items independently of themselves in relation to single landmarks, but not in relation to spatial frameworks. Our analysis of location coding, together with the review of the existing literature and the present findings, thus provide a more complete picture of the child's developing representation of information about location.

Before beginning, we should note two limitations on the scope of the chapter. First, in focusing on how people represent the locations of items relative to one another in a plane, we generally treat the individual items simply as space occupying units. In reality, they are typically internally complex, with particular shapes and component parts, and hence not only occupy positions relative to one another as units, but also are oriented in particular ways relative to one another (e.g., an object may have its back toward one object and face toward another). However, in treating the representation of location information, we ignore these internal properties and treat objects simply as units with distinct identities (as balls, trees, houses, etc.). The major exception is the observer, for whom orientation is important, since observers may use egocentric schemes to locate objects, treating themselves as differentiated entities with objects located to their left, right, front, or back. A second limitation on the scope of our discussion is a focus on findings that directly bear on the encoding and transformation of location information. For a more exhaustive review of the literature on the Piagetian perspective-taking task, see Fehr (1978).

ENCODING LOCATION

Single Targets

Spatial coding involves a relation between two entities that can be treated as being of two distinct sorts: targets and landmarks. Targets are coded in relation to landmarks, which are treated as fixed. A prototypical target is one that is found in varying locations—a small inanimate object that is moved around by people, or an animate creature that moves itself. A prototypical landmark is a large immovable object like a building, or a distinctive place like a lake. Of course, anything can be treated as either a target or landmark, simply by locating the one relative to the other. For example, a newly discovered lake may be encoded relative to a familiar but less obviously locational entity like a campsite.

Probably the simplest form of spatial coding is egocentric, such that a target is coded in relation to the observer's own left, right, and so on. Such representations are simple in the sense that they are based on the way object locations are actually perceived. However, such encodings are of limited usefulness: They will not withstand movements through space. That is, with such coding, if the observer moved and were asked to place the target in its original position, he would mistakenly place it in the same relative position to himself as it had been earlier. For an observer to be able to locate an object after he moves, it must be coded independently of himself, relative to fixed landmarks.

Locating a target in relation to a fixed outside landmark is an advance over egocentric coding, since the general area in which a target belongs will remain consistent after movement. However, one landmark, treated as a unit, is only sufficient to establish a unique location of a target under special conditions, namely, where the target is immediately adjacent to a distinctive landmark. For example, a cover placed on a target locates that target, as does a distinctive feature against which that target stands, such as the front of a car or the window at the edge of a room. The reason the target and landmark must be adjacent is that there is no way to specify the direction of the target in relation to a single unitary landmark, and with increasing distance, the circular path around that landmark quickly becomes very large. Two unit landmarks are not usually sufficient to locate a target either. They define a line, but the target might be on either side of it. That is, distance of a target from each landmark establishes two circular paths, but unless these paths are just tangent to each other, they intersect at two locations. Three unit landmarks not on a line can be used to establish a unique location, since only one point of intersection will exist for the three circular paths.

A set of landmarks that is sufficient to establish a unique location of a target in a plane will be called a local framework. A set of landmarks used to locate all the elements under consideration will be called an overall framework. (The elements may include a set of targets and an observer.) An overall framework permits inferences about the relations of the elements to one another. While coding of a target in terms of a local framework is all that is needed to place a target correctly after movement, there are many cases where coding in terms of an overall framework is needed. Thus, we will see later in this chapter that in transformation problems, where subjects must infer a hypothetical relation between an observer and a set of targets after movement, the locations of the observer and the targets must be represented in relation to a common overall framework.

The frameworks used to locate targets are perhaps typically composed of visible or relatively proximal landmarks. However, frameworks may also include distant landmarks. Thus, the locations of buildings in a city, or mountains in a larger area, may form parts of extended frameworks, as may geographic entities such as oceans or continents on the Earth's surface. Thus an overall framework for one area may in turn be related to a still larger framework, or "framework of frameworks". In short, the coding of spatial location may well be hierarchical (cf. Stevens & Coupe, 1978). Such coding permits inferences about the relations among targets in different frameworks that are often treated separately.

Rather than using actual landmarks in forming an overall framework, subjects can also establish a coordinate system, either a Cartesian system, with an origin and X and Y axes, or polar coordinates, with an origin and distance and angle information. Such a coordinate system must itself be anchored in space in some way. One method would be to utilize actual landmarks, or even the observer himself, in establishing the coordinate system. For example, the Y axis could be considered to extend out toward the door of a room and the X axis to a window. Alternatively, the observer could establish a coordinate system using his own present position as the origin, his line of sight to establish the Y axis, and an imaginary line drawn through his arms to set the X axis. Note that this coding is not egocentric; the established origin maintains its location even when the observer later moves. Indeed, in transformation problems requiring explicit representation of an observer, use of such a coordinate system with initial observer position as the origin is highly efficient.

The development of a coordinate system was discussed by Piaget and Inhelder (1948/1967). Such a system, which they called "Euclidean space", was distinguished from "projective space," although the two were held to be closely related. "Projective space" was postulated as the ability required to solve Piagetian perspective problems. Whether or not such a coordinate reference system is actually used in the literal sense outlined above has never been directly assessed, but has rather been contrasted with a postulated earlier form of representation, called topological space, in which only relations of touching, enclosure and neighborhood are encoded. What we have called overall frameworks may be functionally equivalent to coordinate systems; certainly, much further work would be needed to distinguish empirically between these two coding possibilities.

Sets of Targets

There are alternative ways to code the locations of a set of targets correctly. An array of targets may be coded as a unitary array of a particular sort independent of outside landmarks (e.g., four targets might be coded as the four points of a pattern such as a diamond, or a cross). Then the unitary array may be coded in the framework. A particular array can be coded as different patterns (e.g., as a diamond, not a cross) which, though geometrically equivalent, may have different psychological consequences (Hinton, 1979; Rock, 1973). When the array involves distinctive entities, the coding must include the identities of the targets in particular positions—for example, an array might be coded as a diamond with sides $A-B$, $B-C$, $C-D$, and $D-A$, or alternatively, as a cross with lines $A-C$ and $B-D$.

To preserve information about the locations in space of each of the separate targets in an internally coded array, that array must be treated as consisting of distinctive elements in different positions. Hence the set of targets in an array cannot be located with respect to a single landmark like a cover. To orient an internally encoded rigid array in a spatial framework, thus establishing unique locations for each of the individual targets, requires fixing two of those targets with respect to the framework. Then, unless flips of the figure are allowed, the other points fall into place.

Rather than being coded as units of particular types, sets of targets may also be encoded one by one in relation to a framework. That is, the internal relations among targets may not be explicitly coded at all. If all targets are coded relative to the same framework (common framework), the relation of the targets to one another can be inferred; that is, it should be possible, at least in principle, to answer questions about array shape. However, if each target is coded in relation to a different framework (local framework), the relations of the targets to each other cannot be inferred. They could only be determined by placement of the individual objects in the actual physical space and observation of the relation between them. That is, by actually placing each target relative to a proximal landmark or local framework, the internal relations among the set of targets (as well as their relation to the observer) can be seen directly, without any necessity for inference.

In summary, there are alternative forms of representation which, for certain purposes, can serve equally well to represent planar location information. A single target can always be correctly located with respect to a framework consisting of at least three landmarks, or with respect to a coordinate system. When a landmark is directly coincident with the target, the target can also be located correctly with reference to that single landmark. Finally, a target can be correctly located egocentrically, in relation to a person's own left, right, front, back, but only when the observer does not move. Arrays of targets can be coded as a unit, which is then coded in relation to a framework by fixing two points. Alternatively, arrays of targets can also be coded by locating each target individually. For individually coded targets it is only possible to infer the shape of the array (i.e., the location of targets with respect to each other) if those targets are coded in relation to a common framework.

Encoding with Specified Locations

The discussion thus far has concerned the ways that targets are located in a space within which they could be placed in any position. That is, if one had not previously observed the targets, there would be no reason to place them in any particular locations rather than others. By contrast, many psychological studies do not examine such a free-placement situation, but instead provide a set of possible locations designated by spots or covers or the like; the problem for the child is just to determine in which of the prespecified locations the target or targets belong. In such cases, it is not generally necessary to use a framework consisting of three unit landmarks to correctly locate an item. In fact, it will frequently be sufficient to relate a target in relation to one outside landmark, if there is a landmark that is nearer to one of the prespecified locations than to other locations.

Empirical Evidence about Encoding with Specified Locations

Single Targets.   Piaget's (1937/1954) studies of object permanence provided the first evidence about the origins of location coding. In these studies he examined the behavior of infants to an object that is hidden under a cover. The earliest evidence of spatial coding occurs when the infant seeks an object under a single such cover, because this indicates that he has associated the object to the cover. This occurs by about 9 months of age. Piaget then introduced two covers and hid a target under one of them. In these tasks, the two covers may be distinctive, in which case an association of the object to the cover still can serve to locate the target. Often, the covers are not distinctive; in these cases the two covers constitute prespecified locations and other landmarks must be used to locate the target. Alternative systems can be used to retain information about which of two indistinguishable covers hid the target. Coding could be egocentric, since the infant remains stationary while watching the object disappear and searching for it. On the other hand, coding could be allocentric, involving landmarks present in the room (e.g., doors, furniture).

Egocentric and allocentric coding can only be distinguished if the infant's position is changed before he searches for the object, in which case success would indicate that coding was allocentric, independent of the child. Piaget reported anecdotal evidence suggesting that by the second year of life, infants begin to note that objects remain fixed relative to landmarks even as they move. For example, an infant may look to a particular study window for the father who often appears there. This may result in error, however, as when Lucienne at 15 months looked for her father in the study window even though he was clearly visible in the garden.

In recent studies, child movement has been varied more systematically, and evidence obtained that when there is a single distinctive and coincident landmark 9-month-old infants can change position and still locate objects. Thus Bremner and Bryant (1977) tested 9-month-olds by hiding an object under one of two covers and then moving the infant to the opposite side of the display before allowing him to search. If the covers were similar, the infant approached the wrong cover, even when there were distinctive landmarks in the room (Bremner, 1978a; Bremner & Bryant, 1977). That is, the target was not coded in relation to an outside landmark when that landmark was not coincident with the target. When the covers were distinctive, however, correct searches were above chance (Bremner, 1978a,b). Hence coding in relation to a salient coincidental landmark does occur. Similar results have been obtained by Acredolo and Evans (1980).

It should be noted that while errors on two choice tasks have been taken to show that egocentric coding occurred, this is not necessarily the case. If performance is at chance, the child cannot be said to be using an egocentric system, but rather is failing to code the location of the object. When there are only two choices, egocentric encoding, as opposed to failure to code the relation of the target to the framework at all, can only be inferred if performance is consistently below chance after the child moved. That is, the child must consistently choose the egocentric target, not simply make errors. In Acredolo's and Bremner's infant work, consistent egocentric choice has only appeared in infants younger than 1 year.

There is evidence that children use only single landmarks that are coincident with the target until considerably later than infancy. Using a four-choice search task, DeLoache (this volume) has found that 18- to 22-month-olds are only successful in finding a hidden object when a coincident local landmark marks the target. Features of the larger spatial context are not effective until the child is 24 to 29 months of age.

Braine and Eder (1983) used a multilocation search task as well as a two-choice one with 2-year-old children (22–29 months and 30–35 months). The children learned the location of a reward, either with two identical boxes, or with nine identical boxes in a three × three array, and then had to find the reward after moving to the opposite side of the table. The entire array was hidden before the children moved so they could not keep watching the correct box while moving. Surprisingly, performance was above chance for the nine-box array, showing that outside landmarks were used in coding, whereas performance was at chance for the two-box array in most cases, and consistently egocentric for younger children on some problems. Braine and Eder argue that the nine-box array somehow stimulated the encoding of the target's location in relation to other boxes and outside landmarks. However, the experiment does not provide a strong test of this possibility.

The findings we have reviewed suggest that while infants can associate a small object to a single coincident landmark, they do not associate targets to a more distal landmark until the age of 2. Since these studies involve prespecified locations, the question of whether or not toddlers can use local frameworks to locate a target in space has not been explored. When visible landmarks are lacking, correct responding after movement may appear late. Acredolo (1977) found that children as old as 3 or 4 years sometimes fail in a two choice task after going to the opposite side of a specially constructed small room free of landmarks, although 5-year-olds succeeded. In the featureless environment, responding was at chance for the younger children (as it was for 16-month-olds in Acredolo's (1978) infant study using a no-landmark environment). To succeed in the no-landmark situation, children must use their own remembered position as a landmark. In fact, when 4-year-olds were reminded that they had moved, their performance improved. With just one target and only two possible locations for the target, it would be sufficient that they treat their initial position as a point in space; that is, there is no necessity to develop a framework of remembered locations.

These findings of Acredolo (1977) suggest that dependence on the actual presence of visible landmarks decreases slowly in the preschool years, and that, by 5, children can use a remembered location as a landmark. However, Acredolo, Adams, and Goodwyn (1983) report very different results, in particular that 18-month-olds can do a two-choice task after reversing positions in a no-landmark environment. The discrepancy between these two findings remains to be explained.

Arrays of Targets.   Studies of infants and preschoolers have often focused on memory for a single target which may be located in one of two possible locations. DeLoache used four possible locations and Braine and Eder nine, but no study discussed to this point used more than a single target. But the development of the ability to encode the locations of a set of targets is obviously an interesting question in terms of the present analysis of location coding, as well as important for analysis of transformation problems involving several objects.

Mandler, Seegmiller, and Day (1977) found that 5-year-old children, at least when they remain in one place, can encode and retain the locations of a surprising number of targets. Mandler et al. presented kindergartners with 16 different familiar objects, each on a spot drawn on a table, and then removed those objects. These kindergartners could replace six or seven of these objects (about 40%) on the correct spot. In fact, the authors note that the reason they used 16 objects was because their pilot work showed that some children could place an entire set of 12 objects correctly. Similarly, in a room-size space, Newcombe and Liben (1982) found that over 75% of first graders could correctly place a set of 10 objects on 10 prespecified locations, after a single learning trial.

Consider what these data suggest about how location information may be encoded. It seems unlikely that each separate target is coded in relation to landmarks, or to the observer, because the targets are close enough to each other that their locations do not seem sufficiently distinctive for success using single landmarks. It also seems unlikely that large sets of irregularly arranged targets would be coded internally as a complex array of a particular sort. Perhaps the most likely possibility is that certain targets are coded as being at the edge of the array near a particular fixed landmark, and other targets are coded relative to these. The child himself may be a landmark, since children remained in their original position. Since location is prespecified, there is no need to suppose that coding was in relation to frameworks sufficient to locate the object in space.

Empirical Evidence about Encoding without Specified Locations

The studies discussed thus far involve prespecified locations. What has been assessed is the child's ability to assign one or more targets to particular positions, and this may well involve encoding the proximity of the targets to single landmarks. No information is provided about whether the child can use local frameworks for encoding the location of a target in space, or whether sets of targets can be internally coded as a certain shape. Preservation of shape would seem to be nontrivial, at least under movement transformations; even for adults, predicting the correct relative locations of a set of points in space after a transformation can pose problems. Hinton (1979) found that people have difficulty predicting the locations of the corners of a cube after movement of the cube to an unfamiliar position such as standing on a corner. They even "lose" corners, identifying only six locations rather than eight.

Evidence about children's encoding of array shape, and about their use of local frameworks as well as single landmarks, is found in studies in which children reconstruct models of toy towns (e.g., Herman & Siegel, 1978; Siegel, Herman, Allen, & Kirasic, 1979), their classrooms (e.g., Liben, Moore, & Golbeck, 1982), or arrays of unrelated objects (e.g., Cohen, Weatherford, Lomenick, & Koeller, 1979) without possible locations being specified. While children improve with age on some reconstruction tasks, the reason for the improvements is not yet clear. One clue as to how elementary-school–aged children change in their reconstruction of arrays is suggested by the results of Herman and Siegel (1978). These investigators found a large age-related interaction in the ability to reconstruct a model town depending on whether children were in a classroom or in a large gymnasium. In a classroom, kindergartners reconstructed a model village as accurately as second and fifth graders after three exposures, but in the gym, they were much inferior, even after three trials.

Herman and Siegel suggested that the kindergarten children required local landmarks for accurate reconstruction and hence had difficulty in the "unbounded space" of the gymnasium. This suggests the possiblity that their coding of location might be only of targets in relation to single proximal landmarks, not in relation to local frameworks that could accurately locate each object in space (much less common frameworks that include all the targets and the child himself). If the coding were dependent on single proximal landmarks in this way, severe problems with spatial-transformation problems like perspective taking might be expected (see below).

However, one uncertainty in interpreting the Herman and Siegel study is that the measure of accuracy was the percentage of objects placed within a foot of their correct location. Using this measure, only 22% of the kindergartners' first trial placements in the unbounded space were "correct." This suggests very inadequate performance, but from this measure, one cannot tell whether arrays lack the correct shape and size, with many reversals of relative position of targets, or, instead, if younger children preserve shape, size, and relative position, even without local landmarks, but simply make larger random errors (i.e., are messier), or indeed err by overregularizing shapes to create good Gestalten. Thus, it is not clear if kindergartners have a fundamental difficulty in coding location when the framework involves an unbounded space, and the question of the nature of developmental changes in location coding past 6 years of age must be explored further. Study 1, reported below, bears on this issue.

In summary, encoding studies to date suggest that true egocentric coding is most common in the first year of life, although Braine and Eder observed it into the third year. Initially, salient and physically coincident landmarks seem necessary for allocentric coding. Later, landmarks need not be coincident. However, there is no evidence that landmarks form even local frameworks, because the studies have provided prespecified locations. In tasks involving reconstruction of multiple target arrays without prespecified locations, Herman and Siegel's

(1978) data provide tentative evidence that even at 5 years of age, children may be dependent on proximal landmarks, suggesting that they are not yet able to form local frameworks sufficient for locating a target in space. In the encoding literature, investigators have not discussed the extent to which children use common frameworks for sets of targets and observer position. However, we will see below that information about those issues emerges from studies of children's ability to solve various transformation problems.

TRANSFORMATION

We now turn to the ability to infer the outcomes of transformation involving observers or arrays. Subjects are either asked to infer the relation between an array and an observer who is in another position, or between an observer and an array that has been rotated. To draw such inferences about the location of an observer to a set of target items requires that the observer and targets be coded in relation to a common framework. Hence we must be concerned with the way subjects initially encode location information. In principle, all possible codings that include the observer and targets in a common framework should be sufficient for inferring the effects of transformations. However, transformation processes may interact with the problem representation in determining the difficulty of drawing inferences, so that certain logically sufficient encodings may not be psychologically sufficient for inference. We turn first to certain findings concerning the nature of transformation processes. Then we examine transformation problems involving the relations between observers and sets of targets, and the interaction of problem difficulty with encoding.

Judging the Identity of Forms

There is considerable evidence about the transformation processes used by adults in solving certain problems involving complex visual forms. In these problems subjects are asked whether two similar visual forms shown in different orientations are actually identical or mirror images. Subjects report that they first imagine rotating one of the forms until its orientation matches that of the other, and then compare their corresponding parts. Consistent with these reports, people's reaction times increase linearly with the angle of separation between the figures. The transformation process is described by some investigators as a continuous rotation process (e.g., Shepard & Metzler, 1971) and by others as a series of discrete steps (e.g., Carpenter & Just, 1978).

Consider what it is that the subject mentally rotates in these tasks. Cooper and Podgorny (1976) posed the question of whether the entire form (or array) is treated as a unit during the transformation process, or whether the different portions of the form are treated as separate features. If various features were treated separately, they argued, the speed of rotating a form should vary inversely with its complexity. They familiarized subjects with randomly shaped polygons of varying complexity, and then gave them figure comparison tasks. Complexity did not affect speed of rotation, and the authors concluded that the forms were rotated as units. However, Yuille and Steiger (1982) did find effects of complexity using variations of figures like those used by Shepard and Metzler. In addition, these authors noted that in many tasks, only a distinctive feature of a form must be transformed. When Yuille and Steiger told subjects to rotate just a distinctive feature, the complexity effects they had obtained were reduced considerably.

Yuille and Steiger's findings suggest that at least in some cases, subjects do not treat complex forms as units, but rather rotate sections in a piecemeal fashion. Familiarity may allow subjects to treat a form as a unit, or else to find distinctive features which eliminate the need for having to rotate the entire form. Further evidence that features are rotated separately is reported by Carpenter and Just (1978; Just & Carpenter, 1983) who studied subjects' eye movements in tasks involving comparisons of two figures. They found that subjects examined each of the critical portions of the two figures, taking an equal amount of time in examining each portion. Taken together, the findings of Yuille and Steiger and of Carpenter and Just suggest that there may be severe constraints on the number of elements that can be transformed at one time.

In summary, the transformation processes involved in judgments as to whether two similar complex forms are identical preserve certain aspects of the actual physical operations used with real physical forms. That is, the transformation process involves not only reorientation of a form, but a series of intermediate recodings such as would occur in turning a real object through space. The transformation process seems to involve mentally moving one portion of a form at a time, which is not possible with a real solid object. However, the mental operation of rotating one distinctive feature is like the physical operation of taking hold of an object at one end to pivot it around its axis. Contrary to actual physical rotation, which inevitably preserves the internal relationships among parts of a rigid object, mental rotation does not preserve that information. Either the subject must have internally coded the set of targets as a unitary array of a particular sort and then regenerate the positions of all the targets after rotating a distinctive feature, or must keep track of all the critical features, rotating them either simultaneously or one at a time. The fact that subjects often rotate one portion of the form at a time may well reflect a constraint on the way information about complex figures is coded, or what can be retained during the transformation process.

Tasks involving figure comparison do not require subjects to calculate where in space the critical parts of a figure would be located, but rather to check whether the distinctive features are in corresponding locations on the transformed figure and the comparison figure. There is evidence that when location is not prespecified by providing a comparison figure, transformation tasks may be difficult even for adults. As we have noted, when Hinton (1979) asked subjects to imagine rotating a cube so that it stands on a point, subjects were inaccurate about where the corners of the cube would be located, and sometimes even failed to preserve the number of corners. In this problem, subjects are dealing with an unfamiliar position of the cube, and rather than simply remembering cubes in such positions, must actually infer the locations in space of the corners. Either their initial encoding does not explicitly represent all corners, or they are lost during transformation. In any case, inferring the locations in space of a set of eight elements is difficult, again suggesting constraints on the amount of information that can be transformed.

Transformation of Observers and of Arrays

Huttenlocher and Presson (1973) found that Piagetian observer-movement problems are much more difficult than array-rotation problems with a picture selection task. Further, even at age 10, children in observer-movement problems exhibited an ''egocentric'' tendency to choose the array in its original orientation, a tendency which did not occur in array-rotation problems. In explaining these findings, Huttenlocher and Presson (1973) proposed that the transformation processes used in these problems preserve certain aspects of the actual operations involved in real movement. That is, they proposed that, although array-rotation and observer-movement problems are logically equivalent geometric problems, subjects treat them literally, as problems where the observer moves or where the array moves, respectively. We describe below the implications of this hypothetical literalness for performance on various tasks.

Not only the transformation process but also array encoding may differ for observer-movement and array-rotation problems, because of differences in people's prototypical experiences in the two cases. When people move with respect to a set of separate objects, they do not usually move around the perimeter, looking at the objects as if they were a unitary rigid array. Rather, they often move among the objects, as with objects in a room. Thus they do not usually see the apparent relations among objects changing in a continuous and simultaneous fashion, and may be predisposed to code location as involving separate objects in distinct locations with respect to a framework. In contrast, when people move single objects with respect to themselves—for example, a cup or a cube, the object is seen to change in a continuous way. Thus, when the problem is to rotate a set of targets, subjects may be predisposed to represent those targets as a single, rigid, internally-coded array independent of the outside framework, as they do with single objects. We return to this issue below.

Picture Selection Tasks.   There is a special feature of picture selection tasks which should be noted at the outset: they do not require relocation of all the targets. We have seen that there are severe limitations on the process of mentally relocating targets. We have also seen that tasks vary in whether all targets or just one distinctive target must be relocated. For picture selection tasks, because the pictures from which the subject selects preserve the relative positions of the items, it is necessary to compute the new position of just one target (which constitutes a distinctive feature) to select the correct picture.[1]

Insofar as the transformation process is treated literally, as involving either movement of the observer or movement of the target array, picture-selection tasks will be more complex for observer-movement problems than for array-rotation problems. For observer-movement problems, the subject must first mentally locate a hypothetical observer vis-a-vis the array. Then the array, or an item from it, together with the hypothetical observer, must be mentally relocated so that the hypothetical observer's view coincides with that of the actual viewer. Only then does the imagined array correspond to the correct picture. In contrast, for array-rotation problems it is only necessary to mentally relocate the array or an item from it vis a vis the actual observer. Once this is done, the imagined array corresponds to the correct picture. Note that on this account, the fact that observer movement is more difficult than array rotation is not because of having to imagine an observer in a different position, but because the problem involves a greater number of mental operations.

While observer-movement problems should be more difficult than array-rotation problems for all encodings on picture selection tasks, the extent of the difference in difficulty between these problems should be greater with item by item coding in relation to the outside framework than with unitary array coding in relation to the observer. The necessity for locating a hypothetical observer and transforming that observer together with one of the targets contributes to the difficulty of observer-movement problems for all codings. However, with item by item coding further difficulty is contributed by the fact that the hypothetical observer and target both must be transformed for observer movement, whereas only the target must be transformed for array rotation. If the items and the observer are coded individually in relation to the framework, they are not directly related to each other and hence must be transformed separately. In contrast, with unitary array coding in direct relation to the observer, the target and observer can be transformed together. Thus the difference in difficulty between observer movement and array rotation should be greater with item by item coding in relation to the framework than with unitary array coding in relation to the observer.

We suggested above that coding may differ for these two problems; for observer-movement problems, item and observer may be coded into an outside

---

[1]Of course, if pictures showing the items scrambled were included, then computation of the positions of all the targets would be required. If arrays were internally coded, then rotation of one target would allow regeneration of the positions of the other targets and then subjects could do even scrambled picture tasks, but this is not necessary on the classic picture selection task.

framework, and for array-rotation problems, targets may be coded as an array, independent of the framework, and oriented directly with respect to the observer. Given the processes involved in picture selection tasks, described above, the difference in the difficulty of the two problems with such an encoding difference would be equal in magnitude to that for item by item coding relative to an outside framework on both problems.

Finally, unless the observer and targets are coded in terms of a common framework, neither array-rotation nor observer movement problems can be solved. Lacking a common framework, as indicated more fully below, the effects of movement on the relation between observer and targets could only be determined when the observer was actually in the required physical position relative to the landmarks that had been used in encoding target locations.

The Issue of Task Demands.   We have seen that there are certain peculiarities to picture selection tasks when transformations are treated literally, as involving observer movement or array rotation. In one way, these tasks artificially increase the difficulty of observer-movement problems because subjects must not only represent a hypothetical observer in relation to fixed targets, but must also relocate the targets and hypothetical observer relative to the actual observer. In another way, picture selection tasks artificially decrease task difficulty because, by preserving the relative locations of the targets, they require transformation of just one target.

Before discussing other tasks, let us stress the critical difference between transformation problems where an observer is imagined to be in another viewing position, and ''encoding'' problems where an observer actually moves relative to a covered array. (Recall that encoding problems are used to show that coding is allocentric not egocentric in infants.) The critical difference is that when a subject physically moves to a new position, it actually transforms the relation between the observer and the external landmarks that remain visible. Therefore, if targets are coded in relation to landmarks, no computation is needed to determine their relations to the observer at the new point. Indeed, there is no need to mentally represent an observer at all. In contrast, transformation problems ask about the relation of a hypothetical observer to an array when that relation is *not* directly available. Hence subjects must explicitly represent the hypothetical observer in a common framework with the array, and compute the new relation between observer and array. Consistent with this, in a direct comparison of these two types of problems with identical arrays, picture selection tasks were indeed much easier when subjects physically moved with respect to a hidden array than when they imagined such movement (Huttenlocher & Presson, 1973).

In summary, the Piagetian perspective task may pose special difficulties because of the following features: While the problem is to determine the effects of observer movement with respect to a fixed array, answering the question requires relocating the array or an item from it with respect to its framework. Related to this aspect of the Piagetian task is the necessity to represent both the hypothetical and the actual observer, and to bring the two into correspondence. Thus, failure on the Piagetian task does not necessarily imply either inability to represent the location of a hypothetical observer, or to compute the locations of targets relative to that observer.

Item Question Tasks.   Huttenlocher and Presson (1979) developed an item question task to test just the ability to work out the relation of targets to an observer without the extra demands created by a picture selection task for the observer-movement problem, and without the help provided by the fact that pictures show the correct relative positions of the objects. For observer-movement problems, children were asked what object would be farthest from a hypothetical observer, or nearest, or to the observer's left or right. Array-rotation problems were also presented using the same sort of question: If an array were rotated by some amount, what would then be farthest from you, or nearest, or to your left or right?

For observer-movement problems, answering item questions involves imagining the location of a hypothetical observer and computing his relation to the targets, but not a step of bringing that hypothetical observer into correspondence with the actual observer. For this reason, observer-movement problems should be easier with item questions than with picture selection tasks regardless of whether coding is of a unitary array in relation to the observer or item-by-item in relation to the framework. In fact, for observer-movement problems, the form of encoding is irrelevant, because the targets need not be relocated relative to the framework. In contrast, for array-rotation problems, the form of encoding is critical for the difficulty of item questions. With internal coding, the difficulty of item questions would be no greater than that of picture selection tasks unless array coding were incomplete. However, with item by item coding, all of the targets must be relocated separately to answer the questions, since there is no way to anticipate which target will be in the queried position without carrying out the transformation.

Consider now the effects of coding on the relative difficulty of array-rotation problems and observer-movement problems. If arrays are coded internally, the problems should be roughly equal in difficulty, because each problem involves just one step. While the item question might concern any target, with unitary array coding, relocation of a single target permits regeneration of the locations of the others. With item by item coding, however, array-rotation problems should be more difficult than observer-movement problems because all the targets must be relocated separately. Finally, if there were item-by-item coding in relation to the framework for observer movement problems and unitary array coding for array rotation problems, the two problems should be about equal in difficulty because the difference between them is only whether the observer or the unitary array must be transformed.

Table 4.1 shows the pattern of results obtained by Huttenlocher and Presson (1979). Observer-movement problems were far easier with item question tasks than with picture selection tasks for eight year olds, suggesting that these problems indeed involve less complex mental operations. These results also show that, by age 8, children can easily compute the position of the observer vis a vis a set of targets, when this is the only step required for problem solution. Array-rotation problems were far harder with item questions than with picture selection tasks; further, they were also harder than observer-movement problems with item questions. These are the results expected if targets were individually coded in relation to an outside framework for both sorts of transformation problems (or, alternatively, if the targets were internally coded in relation to the observer for array-rotation, but this coding were incomplete). If targets had been successfully internally coded, rotation of one target would have allowed for regeneration of the array.[2]

Presson (1980) obtained further data supporting the hypothesis that coding in relation to outside landmarks occurs in Piagetian perspective tasks. He showed children a model of the room they were in, with landmarks on each of the four walls. The room model was placed with respect to the child so as to show the required relation of the framework to the hypothetical observer. Children then chose a picture showing what the array would look like to that observer. In these circumstances, performance improved and egocentric errors diminished, relative to a standard condition, at least for 90° and 270° movement. This was true at all three ages tested, including 7, 9, and 11 years.

Presson's task has some of the features of actual physical movement; the child had to choose the picture showing array items in the same relation to the model that actual array items had to the actual room. Hence, to make the correct choice, the child must code the targets in relation to landmarks and be able to map actual features on to modeled features. However, none of the other features of transformation tasks we have discussed, such as explicit coding of position of actual and hypothetical observer, is necessary. The fact that having the room model present was helpful even in 11-year-olds suggests that coding in observer-movement problems is relative to the framework, at least until that age. In addition to Presson's study, studies of large-scale spatial encoding with older children suggest that developmental improvement continues past the age of 11 years (Anoo-

---

[2]Recently, Olson and Bialystock (1983) have argued that the pattern of performance shown in Table 4.1 can be predicted using a representation "which individually links each display component to the child's own initial position with respect to that display. There is no need to implicate other external features of the environment, nor is there any need to relate display components to each other" (p. 154). However, Olson and Bialystock's discussion reveals that they depart from their stated principles at several crucial points. First, they claim that the items in a diamond-shaped array are coded as "front", "back", "left" or "right". But for "front" and "back" this individual linkage of items to the subject clearly does not work. An item can only be a "back" item if some other item is in front of it. Second, Olson and Bialystock use Euclidean axes in their explanation of transformation. They speak, for instance, of projecting a dimension from front to back, or applying a rotational transformation to an axis. Thus, their discussion of transformation does not operate on the propositions they list (p. 154).

shian & Young, 1981; Cousins, Siegel & Maxwell, 1983; Curtis, Siegel & Furlong, 1981). The exact nature of this change has not been specified, but it may well involve the formation of overall configurations of a set of locations and ability to manipulate this configuration. Thus, forming an internal coding and using it in a transformation task may, possibly, be a late-appearing skill.

Other Tasks.   So far, we have considered how people deal with picture selection tasks and with questions about which item will occupy a specified position after a transformation. There are certainly other tasks which might be used. As we have noted, Piaget and Inhelder used a model-building task, and found similar results to those obtained with picture selection. Presson (1982) found the same pattern of performance in adults' model building that Huttenlocher and Presson found with picture-selection tasks: observer-movement problems are more difficult than array-rotation problems, and errors are more likely to be egocentric. In model building, like picture selection, observer-movement problems require an extra step of bringing about a correspondence between the hypothetical and actual observer. This is because the model must be built from the actual observer's perspective. Model building is unlike picture selection, however, in that it requires determination of where all targets would be. However, since each target can be physically placed after its position is computed, processing constraints should be less important than for item questions. The fact that adults continue to have difficulty with observer-movement problems on this task suggests, at least, that the fact that these problems require two steps continues to contribute to task difficulty. It may also indicate that at least some adults continue to code targets in terms of an outside framework, rather than internally.

Harris and Bassett (1976) examined the order of placement of items in a model-building task. Children were presented with arrays of three blocks in a line on a board with a landmark. Contrary to other studies, the display remained visible and children copied it on their own board. For this task, it is not clear that the observer need be represented; encoding instead may have been in relation to the landmark. This task was indeed considerably easier than ordinary picture selection or model-building tasks; even six-year-olds did moderately well. Children tended to place first that block which would be closest to themselves (and to the landmark) after the required transformation, which would be consistent with coding in relation to the landmark. Harris and Bassett argued that their result indicated that the child transformed the whole array as a unit. However, they did not then have available results indicating that even adults do not transform complex arrays as units.

A second task we have not yet considered is the complement of the item-question task. Instead of being given a position and asked what item will occupy it following a transformation, the subject is given an item, and asked what position it will occupy. For such position questions, contrary to item questions, array-rotation problems should be very easy because the subject can simply compute the new location of the target being questioned. Again, contrary to item questions, position questions should be difficult for observer-movement problems. For a person to indicate in terms of his present location where a particular item would be located with respect to an observer, the target being questioned must be mentally relocated together with the hypothetical observer. Thus, this task, like picture selection tasks, requires two steps. It also requires transformation of a target-observer-framework representation, when coding is of targets in relation to a framework. This pattern of performance (observer movement harder than array rotation for position questions) has been found by Presson (1982) using adults, and presumably would be found even more strongly with children.

In summary, transformation tasks ask about a hypothetical relation between an observer and a set of targets. To draw such inferences requires that both the observer and the array be represented in a common framework. There is evidence that common frameworks are used by age 8, since transformation problems involving observer movement with item questions are easily done by this age. However, coding using a common framework may not be sufficient for solving Piagetian perspective tasks, which also require establishing a correspondence between the hypothetical and actual observer to enable picture selection. Codings which abstract away from the actual framework, representing the array just in relation to the observer, would be better suited to handling these problems, and are clearly adequate for other inference tasks as well. However, they may arise only later, perhaps not always even in adults.

STUDY 1

It is not clear how children who cannot yet solve transformation problems (i.e., younger than 8) encode location information. It is possible that until then, they encode single items in relation to local frameworks rather than using common frameworks for several items. In fact, it even seems possible that 6-year-old children may rely on single proximal landmarks. This possibility is suggested by Herman and Siegel's (1978) study. Their 6-year-old subjects had difficulty in reconstructing arrays in a task without prespecified locations, even from the point of origin, unless proximal landmarks were available. In contrast, their 8-year-old subjects did well in the absence of such landmarks, and this is the age at which Huttenlocher and Presson found that children could do observer movement problems with item questions.

However, while Herman and Siegel found a large age-related effect of the nature of the framework in a reconstruction task, their measures showed that metric accuracy was reduced in this case, but did not permit a determination of whether or not children preserved array shape, size, or relative position of items without local landmarks. If their kindergarten subjects did lose such vital information, it would suggest that children of this age still lack the ability to use local frameworks, since these would be sufficient for preserving information about the locations of targets in space. It would indicate that local frameworks, let alone overall frameworks, are developed late. Since local frameworks, we postulate, arise prior to overall frameworks or coordinate systems, difficulty with reconstruction tasks like that of Herman and Siegel even at 6 years would certainly explain why success on Piagetian perspective tasks emerges so late.

To examine the subject's reconstructions in more detail, and in particular, to determine how well children preserve the locations of targets with and without local landmarks, we replicated the Herman and Siegel study, with one important change: we varied the presence versus absence of nearby landmarks in the same large space, namely a church basement that our subjects had only occasionally visited earlier, rather than using two different spaces. This allowed us to separate out two factors that were confounded in the Herman and Siegel study—namely, the presence of local landmarks and the familiarity of the classroom versus the gymnasium. This seemed important because of the possibility that kindergarten

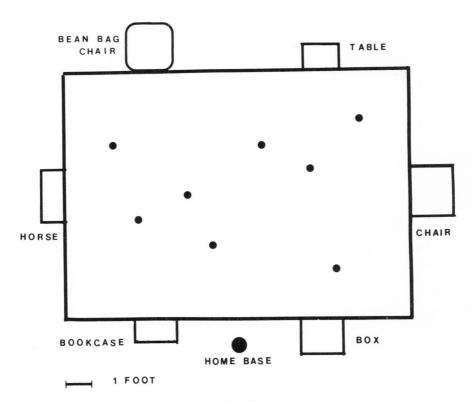

FIG. 4.1.

children performed especially poorly in the gym because they were unfamiliar with it, and perhaps were even frightened by its size.

We used an experimental space delineated by a 10 × 14 foot rug, with distant perimeter landmarks such as doors, windows and bulletin boards always present. Six landmarks were present on the perimeter of the rug for children in the landmark-present group. The targets were eight toys laid out in two random configurations, one presented to half the children and the other to the other half (see Fig 4.1 and 4.2). We tested 40 kindergartners and 40 fourth graders, half boys and half girls. Each child stood at "home base" while the experimenter pointed out the eight toys and labeled each one. The toys were then collected, and each child was asked to place the toys where they had been. After the placements were recorded, the entire process was repeated twice, for a total of three trials.

When the data were scored using Herman and Siegel's within-a-foot criterion, we, too, found a significant interaction of grade with landmarks. Fourth graders were unaffected by landmarks; 65% of the placements were correct with land-

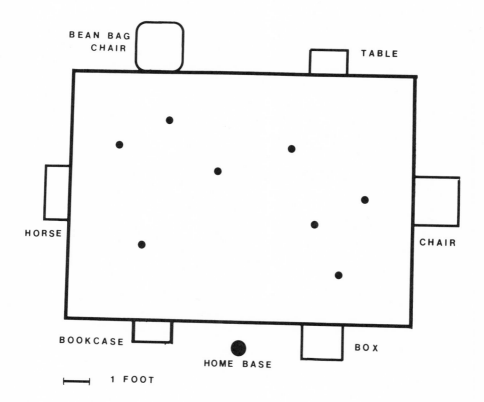

FIG. 4.2.

marks and 63% without. For kindergartners, 41% of the placements were correct with landmarks but only 24% correct without. This seems to confirm the dependence of younger children on local landmarks, in a situation in which performance of the older children was not constrained by ceiling effects. (This interaction was embedded in a higher-order interaction of grade × landmark × sex × configuration × trial, but since examination of the interaction proved theoretically uninterpretable, we are not concerned that it qualifies the main result, pending replication of such a pattern.)

However, the most interesting aspect of the data was that placements were accurate in relative position and overall shape, even among kindergartners without local landmarks. An example of this is seen in Fig. 4.3, in which no placement is within a foot of its correct location, and yet the relationships of the items to one another are quite well preserved. We examined accuracy of relative position information more formally by connecting each pair of points and determining if the remaining points fell on the proper side of that line. With eight points, there are 28 possible lines, and for each, the six remaining points were examined. Chance responding would be 50%, because on the average, half the

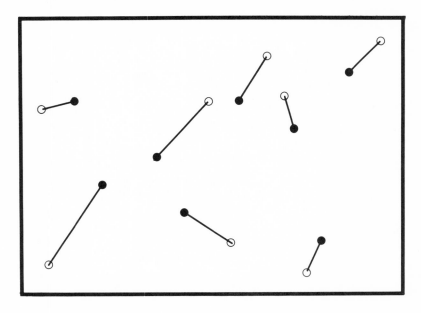

|———| 1 FOOT

●   CORRECT LOCATION

○   CHILD'S PLACEMENTS

FIG. 4.3.

points would fall on the correct side of the line by chance. Children scored 91% overall. An analysis of variance involving these configuration scores showed no main effect of landmarks, nor a grade × landmark interaction. Even main effects of grade were significant for only one of the two configurations.

In short, although metric accuracy improves with age, kindergartners, even without proximal landmarks, do retain the overall shape of an array and correctly assign the proper objects to the proper locations. Thus this study indicates that kindergarten children do not encode location only in relation to local landmarks. The children must, at a minimum, have used local frameworks to encode the location of each object separately. However, they need not be credited with use of an overall framework or a coordinate system, although it is possible they did use such systems.

In replicating the Herman and Siegel study, we, like they, did not have children move vis-a-vis the array, so we obtained no evidence as to whether the locations of the objects are preserved under observer movement. Herman, Roth, Miranda, and Getz (1982), however, have examined reconstructions by kindergarten and third-grade children after movement to the opposite side of experimental spaces that had only distal, but no proximal, landmarks. Even kindergartners preserved shape and relative position in reconstructions after moving to the opposite side. This further supports the conclusion that kindergarten children at least use local frameworks to encode the locations of single targets in space, while leaving open the issue of when children use overall frameworks or coordinate systems.

STUDY 2

By 5 or 6 years of age, children can code targets in relation to local frameworks. This is evident in their ability to reconstruct an array without prespecified locations in the absence of proximal landmarks even after they physically move to another location. Our second study was designed to provide information as to the age at which such local frameworks arise, by examining children's ability to reconstruct arrays, both from their original vantage point, and when they move to a new vantage point. Previous studies with very young children have always involved prespecified locations such as boxes, covers, and so on. In such cases, success may only indicate the use of single-landmark coding; such coding cannot be distinguished from the use of local frameworks. In the present study, we contrasted performance of children between 2 and 3 years of age under two conditions: with spots to indicate the locations of targets, and with free placement.

Children of average age 2 years 6 months were tested using an experimental space defined by a circular board 2 feet in diameter. Children were randomly assigned to one of two groups: free placement or specified location. Half the trials involved remembering the location of two toys, placed either vertically in front of the child, one near and one far, or horizontally, one to the child's left and one to the child's right. The other half of the trials involved remembering the location of four toys, one placed in each of the four positions: near, far, left, and right. Four-toy arrays thus delineate a definite shape, which could be coded as, for instance, a diamond or a cross. Two-toy arrays do not similarly define a shape, but only a straight line that can vary in length and orientation.

The experiment consisted of two sessions. The first examined placements at the starting position, and the second placements after the child moved to the opposite side of the space. At each session, for both groups of subjects, there were practice trials in which the experimental space was covered with a plastic overlay to which two circles or four circles were attached to indicate the locations of the toys. Examples were given of remembering two toys—one toy at the left and one at the right, and one toy at the top and one at the bottom—and four toys—one toy in each of the four compass positions. For 21 of the children, overlays with spots continued to be used during the experimental trials, and for the other 19 children, the overlay was removed, and children simply placed the objects where they belonged on the board. For these free-placement subjects, responses were counted as correct for four-toy trials if they were anywhere within the correct quadrant, and for two-toy trials if they were anywhere within the correct half of the board. Each trial involved a different set of two or four toys to prevent the buildup of interference.

The results are shown in Table 4.2. For two-item arrays, children in both conditions performed excellently at a fixed vantage point. Following movement to the opposite side, performance varied for the two conditions, declining for free-placement subjects following movement, but not for subjects tested with spots. Similar results were found for four-item arrays. Movement again significantly reduced accuracy, but the spots helped the children perform better. The interaction of condition and movement was significant; spots led to better performance when the child had to move to the opposite side. Children in the spot condition were above chance after moving, whereas children in free placement were not.

Consider the nature of the errors in the free-placement task. Children typically did *not* preserve shape or size of arrays after moving. The most common error was to place the toys in front of them, often putting more than one toy in the same quadrant, and rarely preserving the diamond shape of the array. We also evaluated the extent to which the original relative positions of the toys were preserved in the free-placement reconstructions. We scored preservation of relative position along the horizontal and vertical axes separately. With these measures, too, performance was at chance. Thus, without location prespecified, children performed very poorly indeed. They seemed not to have internally coded the array as a particular shape, nor to have encoded individual targets

TABLE 4.2
Percentage Correct in Study 2

	Two Objects		Four Objects	
	No Movement	Opposite Side	No Movement	Opposite Side
Spots (n = 21)	85%[a]	82%*	80%*	63%*
Free placement (n = 19)	93%*	69%*	78%*	40%

[a]Note: Chance performance is 50% for the two-object task and 25% for the four-object task. Asterisks throughout indicate above-chance performance by binomial test.

using local frameworks such that they could place the items correctly after moving.

One possible reason for poor performance on free placement after moving is that children might fail to keep track of how far they move; another reason is that movement itself might distract them and impair memory. However, subjects with specified locations moved too. Further, preliminary evidence from pilot studies with free placement indicates these factors are not very important, since when children move completely around the array, they perform comparably to the 0° condition.

What do these results indicate about location coding in children under 3 years of age? First, the fact that the children can succeed after movement, when given prespecified locations, indicates that they must at least code targets allocentrically in relation to single landmarks. This is consistent with earlier studies with prespecified locations. The fact that their performance is at chance after movement in the four-toy free-placement tasks, and that performance declines to a very low level after movement in the two-toy free placement tasks, further indicates that they do not yet possess local frameworks, independent of themselves, for accurately placing targets in space. The lack of preservation of shape for four-target arrays after movement clearly shows that they do not code the array internally.

It is also clear, however, that 2-year-olds' performance cannot be explained simply as due to their encoding of location only in relation to single landmarks, since this would not explain how they succeed in coding the locations of the targets in free placement at the point of origin. Nor can we assume that in this case they simply code the targets egocentrically, since they do not systematically misplace targets as if in their original viewing position after movement in the free placement task. Perhaps they used themselves as one point in a local framework, but like the 3-year-olds in Acredolo (1977), did not maintain that spot's existence after they left it, leaving them unable to locate targets accurately after movement. Thus the crucial change in spatial coding between ages 3 and 5 or 6 could involve beginning to use local frameworks independent of the child, including frameworks using their own remembered position as a point.

CONCLUSIONS

We have examined the representation of location information and its development. We have examined both coding and transformation, and have considered what sort of coding is involved in various transformation tasks where subjects must infer the relation between an observer and a set of targets after movement. In fact, examining the ability to solve various sorts of transformation tasks provides evidence about the development of encoding.

It seems that children slowly develop the ability to encode the locations of objects in a plane. The process begins before one year with associations of single targets to coincident landmarks. Before 3 years, children can associate each of a set of targets to a distal landmark, as seen in Study 2 where children can place four targets in prespecified locations after movement by the age of $2\frac{1}{2}$ years. However, they do not yet have local frameworks independent of themselves for locating targets; they fail to preserve target location after movement when location is not prespecified. By age 5 or 6, they have local frameworks independent of themselves as seen in their ability to locate targets after movement without prespecified location. By age 8, children use overall frameworks including the observer, as seen in their ability to succeed at transformation problems. However, observer-movement problems have not been used with younger children, so such overall frameworks may in fact be established earlier.

Elementary school children have difficulty with Piagetian perspective problems, but not because they are "egocentric" in the sense of not knowing that things look different to others. They know this by 2 years. Their lack of egocentrism is also seen in encoding tasks with prespecified locations, where they actually move and then find hidden targets or place objects, showing coding with respect to landmarks by 2 to 3 years. Inference problems involving a hypothetical observer are easy for children by 8 years when they are asked item questions concerning the relations of the targets to the imagined observer, which do not require reassignment of the positions of the targets and imagined viewer vis a vis the framework. Array-rotation problems where only one target must be relocated in relation to landmarks are also easy by this age. Success on these problems requires an overall framework that includes the targets and observer.

Certain inference problems are still difficult for children at 9 or 10 years. They have difficulty with array-rotation problems where several targets must be relocated, suggesting lack of complete representation of the array during rotation. They have difficulty with the Piagetian perspective problem, suggesting that target location may be encoded with respect to an outside framework. We do not yet know the extent to which the developmental changes that underlie the emerging ability to solve these problems involve an increasing tendency towards internal coding of arrays, the establishment of coordinate systems that serve in place of actual spatial frameworks, or both. It is also important that adults continue to have problems with these tasks, so representational change, if it occurs in early adolescence, may not be universal or complete.

In conclusion, let us consider the relation of the current discussion to the general position laid out by Piaget and Inhelder in 1948. They argued that children progress from topological coding of spatial location in terms of relationships of touching, enclosure, and neighborhood, to understanding of projective and coordinate space at about the age of 9 or 10 years. We too have argued that changes in spatial encoding underlie changes in ability to solve transformation tasks. We propose that children progress from coding in terms of a coincident outside landmark, to coding in terms of local frameworks which allow them to locate targets in space, and finally to overall frameworks that include themselves as well as sets of targets.

There are certain key differences from Piaget's position. We do not propose that children use fundamentally different geometries at different stages of development. First, with respect to Piaget's concept of topological space, we attribute the early dependence on landmarks, not to the lack of even an elementary notion of distance, but, rather, to the fact that the ability to relate items to distal landmarks or sets of distal landmarks forming a framework only gradually increases. This makes less mysterious the idea that young children remember targets ''in the neighborhood'' of certain landmarks; ''neighborhood'' is a concept which involves some understanding of distance, and which is not essentially topological. Second, with respect to Piaget's distinction between projective space and Euclidean space, we attribute the ability to solve a set of transformation problems (observer movement with item questions and array rotation with picture selection) to encoding location using an overall framework, which seems close to Euclidean space. The Piagetian perspective-taking task remains difficult since it may require coding arrays internally, independently of the framework, and this may not be the usual way of representing location information in dealing with observer movement. This account of development thus does not imply a distinction between ''projective'' and ''Euclidean'' space, but rather an increasing ability to abstract location information from particular concrete situations, forming efficient representations for solving transformation problems.

ACKNOWLEDGMENTS

The preparation of this chapter was supported in part by a grant from The Spencer Foundation to Janellen Huttenlocher, and in part by a Grant-in-Aid from Temple University to Nora Newcombe. We thank Sister Patricia and the parents, teachers, and students of Our Lady of Sorrows, Mercerville, N.J. for their help with Study 1; Temple Daycare, the Whiteside Taylor Center, Campus Daycare, YMHA Playgroup, Trinity Playgroup, LaSalle Daycare, University City Montessori School, Parent-Infant Center, YWCA Chestnut House Nursery, and the Learning Center for help with Study 2; Judith Dubas,

William Dundon, Wendy Haight, Lorraine Kubicek and Carolyn Spies for running subjects and scoring data; Zalman Usiskin for suggesting the measure of relative position used in Study 1; Robert W. Weisberg for writing a computer program to score relative position; and Judith Goodman, Lynn S. Liben, Herbert L. Pick, Mary C. Potter, Catherine Sophian, and Robert W. Weisberg for critical comments on the manuscript.

REFERENCES

Acredolo, L. P. Developmental changes in the ability to coordinate perspectives of a large-scale space. *Developmental Psychology*, 1977, *13*, 1–8.

Acredolo, L. P. The development of spatial orientation in infancy. *Developmental Psychology*, 1978, *14*, 224–234.

Acredolo, L. P., Adams, A., & Goodwyn, S. W. *The role of self-produced movement and visual tracking in infant spatial orientation*. University of California, Davis, 1983.

Acredolo, L. P., & Evans, D. Developmental changes in the effect of landmarks on infant spatial behavior. *Developmental Psychology*, 1980, *16*, 312–318.

Anooshian, L. J., & Young, D. Developmental changes in cognitive maps of a familiar neighborhood. *Child Development*, 1981, *52*, 341–348.

Braine, L. G., & Eder, R. A. Left-right memory in 2-year-old children: A new look at search tasks. *Developmental Psychology*, 1983, *19*, 45–55.

Bremner, J. G. Egocentric versus allocentric spatial coding in 9-month-old infants: Factors influencing the choice of code. *Developmental Psychology*, 1978, *14*, 346–355. (a)

Bremner, J. G. Spatial errors made by infants: Inadequate spatial cues or evidence of egocentricism? *British Journal of Psychology*, 1978, *69*, 77–84. (b)

Bremner, J. G., & Bryant, P. E. Place versus response as the basis of spatial errors made by young infants. *Journal of Experimental Child Psychology*, 1977, *23*, 162–171.

Carpenter, P. A., & Just, M. A. Eye fixations during mental rotation. In J. W. Senders, D. F. Fisher, & R. A. Monty (Eds.), *Eye movements and the higher psychological functions*. Hillsdale, NJ: Lawrence Erlbaum Associates, 1978.

Cohen, R., Weatherford, D. L., Lomenick, T., & Koeller, K. Development of spatial representations: Role of task demands and familiarity with the environment. *Child Development*, 1979, *50*, 1257–1260.

Cooper, L. A., & Podgorny, P. Mental transformations and visual comparison processes: Effects of complexity and similarity. *Journal of Experimental Psychology: Human Perception and Performance*, 1976, *2*, 503–514.

Cousins, J. H., Siegel, A. W., & Maxwell, S. E. Wayfinding and cognitive mapping in large scale environments: A test of a developmental model. *Journal of Experimental Child Psychology*, 1983, *35*, 1–20.

Curtis, L. E., Siegel, A. W., & Furlong, N. E. Developmental differences in cognitive mapping: Configurational knowledge of familiar large-scale environments. *Journal of Experimental Child Psychology*, 1981, *31*, 456–469.

Fehr, L. A. Methodological inconsistencies in the measurement of spatial perspective taking ability: A cause for concern. *Human Development*, 1978, *21*, 302–315.

Flavell, J. H., Botkin, P. T., Fry, C. L., Wright, J. W., & Jarvis, P. E. *The development of role-taking and communication skills in children*. New York: Wiley, 1968.

Harris, P. L., & Bassett, E. Reconstruction from the mental image. *Journal of Experimental Child Psychology*, 1976, *21*, 514–523.

Herman, J. F., & Siegel, A. W. The development of cognitive mapping of the large-scale environment. *Journal of Experimental Child Psychology*, 1978, *26*, 389–406.

Herman, J. F., Roth, S. F., Miranda, C., & Getz, M. Children's memory for spatial locations: The influence of recall perspective and type of environment. *Journal of Experimental Child Psychology*, 1982, *34*, 257–273.

Hinton, G. Some demonstrations of the effects of structural descriptions in mental imagery. *Cognitive Science*, 1979, *3*, 231–250.

Huttenlocher, J., & Presson, C. C. Mental rotation and the perspective problem. *Cognitive Psychology*, 1973, *4*, 277–299.

Huttenlocher, J., & Presson, C. C. The coding and transformation of spatial information. *Cognitive Psychology*, 1979, *11*, 375–394.

Just, M. A., & Carpenter, P. A. *Individual differences in spatial ability.* Unpublished manuscript, Carnegie-Mellon University, 1983.

Laurendeau, M., & Pinard, A. *The development of the concept of space in the child.* New York: International Universities Press, 1970.

Lempers, J. D., Flavell, E. R., & Flavell, J. H. The development in very young children of tacit knowledge concerning visual perception. *Genetic Psychology Monographs*, 1977, *95*, 3–53.

Liben, L. S., Moore, M. L., & Golbeck, S. L. Preschoolers' knowledge of their classroom environment: Evidence from small-scale and life-size spatial tasks. *Child Development*, 1982, *53*, 1275–1284.

Mandler, J. M., Seegmiller, D., & Day, J. On the coding of spatial information. *Memory and Cognition*, 1977, *5*, 10–16.

Masangkay, Z. S., McCluskey, K. A., McIntyre, C. W., Sims-Knight, J., Vaughn, B. E., & Flavell, J. H. The early development of inferences about the visual percepts of others. *Child Development*, 1974, *45*, 357–366.

Newcombe, N., & Liben, L. S. Barrier effects in the cognitive maps of children and adults. *Journal of Experimental Child Psychology*, 1982, *34*, 46–58.

Olson, D. R., & Bialystock, E. *Spatial cognition: The structure and development of mental representations of spatial relations.* Hillsdale, NJ: Lawrence Erlbaum Associates, 1983.

Piaget, J. *The construction of reality in the child.* New York: Basic Books, 1954. (Originally published, 1937.)

Piaget, J., & Inhelder, B. *The child's conception of space.* New York: W. W. Norton, 1967. (Originally published, 1948.)

Presson, C. C. Spatial egocentricism and the effect of an alternate frame of reference. *Journal of Experimental Child Psychology*, 1980, *29*, 391–402.

Presson, C. C. Strategies in spatial reasoning. *Journal of Experimental Psychology: Learning, Memory, and Cognition*, 1982, *8*, 243–251.

Rock, I. *Orientation and form.* New York: Academic Press, 1973.

Salatas, H., & Flavell, J. H. Perspective taking: The development of two components of knowledge. *Child Development*, 1976, *47*, 103–109.

Shepard, R., & Metzler, J. Mental rotation of three-dimensional objects. *Science*, 1971, *171*, 701–703.

Siegel, A. W., Herman, J. F., Allen, G. L., & Kirasic, K. C. The development of cognitive maps of large- and small-scale spaces. *Child Development*, 1979, *50*, 582–585.

Stevens, A., & Coupe, P. Distortions in judged spatial relations. *Cognitive Psychology*, 1978, *10*, 422–437.

Yuille, J. C., & Steiger, J. H. Nonholistic processing in mental rotation: Some suggestive evidence. *Perception and Psychophysics*, 1982, *31*, 201–209.

5 Commentary: Landmarks and Movement

Paul L. Harris
Oxford University

The four chapters on spatial development addressed quite disparate issues: the development of search, the emergence of mediated memory, the sensitivity to size and scale, and the ability to imagine spatial transformations. Accordingly, most of my comments are directed at each chapter individually. Nevertheless, I hope to conclude by picking out certain themes that echo across the four chapters.

SOPHIAN

Catherine Sophian's chapter impressed me for several reasons. First, she presented experiments spanning age groups that developmental psychologists have typically kept firmly apart, both theoretically and empirically. Second, she presented data that make a very strong case for continuity alongside gradual development across a wide age range. Third, she presented an intriguing developmental account in terms of both processing ability and the ability to differentiate one task from another.

I first comment on one important finding and then discuss Sophian's developmental account. Sophian argued that perseveration in search for a hidden object among 9-month-old infants is a fragile phenomenon. Rather than go back to *A* where the object was originally hidden, infants divide their errors apparently at random between *A* and *C*. If Sophian's interpretation is correct, this is a very important finding because it undermines a claim that has kept a whole generation of developmental psychologists, myself included, very busy—the claim that infants have a systematic misconception about the nature of objects or their hiding places.

However, I do not think it is correct to say that infants are responding randomly. Location C is admittedly a different location where the object has never been hidden, but it is still identical in appearance to A. In other words, the baby may be perseverating to containers of a particular description. This is very consistent with a good deal of evidence suggesting that 9-month-old infants do use distinctive landmarks to define the location of an object (Harris, 1983). I would predict that if another type of container were substituted for C, one obviously distinct in shape and size from A, the baby would not perseverate to it. We already have implicit confirmation of this. No one has observed babies on B trials who search under the table or in the experimenter's pocket. If infants who approach A or C when they are identical are perseverating to a given container type, they are not behaving randomly, and we can hold on to our belief that there is a systematic misconception about the nature of objects among young infants.

In accounting for developmental change, Sophian postulates two types of improvement: increased differentiation among tasks and more efficient information processing. Although I think that both of these improvements probably do play a part in the improvement of search, I do not think that Sophian has provided us with a clean way of separating their respective contributions. As evidence for improvement in information processing, she focuses on so-called random responses. Her argument is that children will tend to search at a location that is consistent with some or all of the information that they have been given, provided they can encode and retain that information. If not, they will search randomly. For example, given three locations, A, B, and C, and hiding at A and B, infants should confine their search to A or B, if they are searching in a way that is consistent with given information. If they cannot encode or retain such given information, they may search at C.

In an analysis of a wide range of experiments, Sophian (see Fig. 2.3) demonstrates that such random responses do drop with age, especially in infants between 9 and 20 months of age. She concludes that information-processing reliability is improving, so that infants can make systematic responses that are consistent with given information, thereby leading to a reduction in random responding.

However, it is possible to argue, as I suggested earlier, that responses to C locations are not random. They are systematic in so far as they reflect search at a hiding place whose appearance is identical to a hiding place where the object has previously been found (i.e., A or B). The decline in responding to C might therefore reflect the emergence of new strategies, or what Sophian calls increased differentiation among problem types. Specifically, infants might adopt the following four increasingly differentiated strategies when faced with a three-place (A, B, and C) search task in which the object is hidden at A or B but not C, and the container is moved or remains stationary:

1. Search at a container that resembles a previously correct container (permits no differentiation among *A, B,* and *C* locations).
2. Search at a container located in a previous hiding place (permits differentiation of *A* and *B* from *C* locations).
3. Search at a container located in the most recent hiding place (permits differentiation of *B* from *A* and *C* locations).
4. Search at the container that was located in the most recent hiding place, even if it is now in a new position (permits differentiation of *B* container from *B* location on unseen movement tasks).

The apparent drop in random responding would, on this account, reflect the increasing adoption of strategy 2 instead of 1. Thus, it is possible to construct an account in which developmental change is wholly attributable to the adoption of increased task differentiation rather than increasingly efficient information processing.

As further evidence for an improvement with age of information-processing ability, Sophian notes that in some studies (Sophian & Sage, 1983; Sophian & Wellman, 1983) certain types of error have tended to increase with age. Specifically, Sophian and Sage (1983) observed that as compared to 13-month-old infants, 21-month-old infants made a greater proportion of errors to so-called relevant locations (locations involved in the hiding procedure) rather than irrelevant control locations. Similarly, Sophian and Wellman (1983) observed that as compared to 9-month-old infants, 16-month-old infants made a greater proportion of errors to a previous hiding place rather than control locations. Sophian concludes that such increases in error rate with age are best explained by supposing that infants' information processing is becoming more reliable, so that any given strategy, correct or incorrect, is adopted more consistently. However, it is again possible to put forward a different account based upon task differentiation. The increased tendency to err at relevant locations as opposed to control locations may reflect the adoption of strategy 2 in favor of strategy 1.

Is it possible to demonstrate improvement in information-processing capacity more convincingly? One approach is to manipulate information-processing variables directly and to observe their effects. In an early investigation into the $A\bar{B}$ error, I compared search at *A* and *B* with and without delay. Infants of 9 and 10 months searched correctly at *B* with no delay but perseverated to *A* with a delay (Harris, 1973). These results were subsequently replicated in a more systematic study of delay length carried out by Gratch and his colleagues (Gratch, Appel, Evans, LeCompte, & Wright, 1974). The implication seemed to be that infants could not withstand delays of 1 sec or more.

More recently, however, Diamond (1983) has followed this up with a titration procedure. Diamond uses a wider age range and a wider range of delays. She finds that for any given delay length, older infants are less likely to perseverate than younger infants. Nevertheless, older infants can be made to perseverate by increasing the length of delay. These results are obviously difficult to explain in terms of task differentiation. The visible displacement task used by Diamond is essentially the same task whether a short or a long delay is used. Thus, a more plausible interpretation is that the choice between strategies 2 and 3 is governed by two factors: the growing insight that movement to a new container deletes a previous container as a likely hiding place and an age change in the ability to remember information about which container is the more recent hiding place. Neither factor considered alone appears sufficient to explain the pattern of error. Cognitive explanations couched solely in terms of a growing insight into deletion rules (e.g., Harris, 1975) cannot explain how delay tolerance increases gradually with age. On the other hand, explanations couched solely in terms of an age change in memory (e.g., Harris, 1973) cannot explain error in the face of a visible object (Butterworth, 1977; Harris, 1974).

Thus, I am by no means unsympathetic to Sophian's claim that age changes in search can be explained by improvements in both task differentiation and infor- mation-processing efficiency. Nevertheless, I would argue that she has not of- fered a clear way of distinguishing between these two types of improvement, that the age changes she reports probably reflect increased task differentiation, and that there are more satisfactory ways of demonstrating the impact of information- processing variables.

A more general comment concerns the issue of developmental continuity. In my view, Sophian underplays the discontinuities in development by using two strategems. First, she subsumes quite disparate phenomena under the same su- perordinate term. One glaring example of this occurs early in the chapter. Older children can select between verbal information and typical location information, whereas younger infants can select between more and less recent hiding informa- tion. To simply call each of these abilities an example of selectivity and hence a demonstration of continuity is to ignore some of the important differences be- tween the two types of selectivity. Second, Sophian ignores all developments in search that occur before 9 months of age. Compare an infant of 6 months, who is unable to retrieve an object completely hidden by a cloth, with an infant of 18 months, who is able to keep track of an object carried to several places in the experimenter's hand and deposited invisibly at one of them. The qualitative difference is enormous. However, if we look at the description of development offered by Sophian and at the mechanisms of change that she proposes, there is no room for the emergence of such qualitative change. She describes three types of developmental improvement: increasing robustness, increasing consistency, and decreasing inappropriateness. Increased robustness is simply an extenstion of what one does already. Increased consistency is simply a more reliable tenden- cy to do what one does already. And decreased inappropriateness of responses is an increased tendency to avoid responses that would not work. None of these changes include the emergence of novel behavior. The same criticism applies to the mechanisms of change proposed by Sophian. Increased processing reliability permits only the more effective application of a strategy, correct or incorrect. Differentiation enables ''children to choose more effectively between appropriate and inappropriate skills to use in a given situation.'' Thus differentiation involves a more refined selection from the strategies already possessed but not the creation of new strategies.

Finally, I would like to suggest that to the extent that continuity does exist, and that the three processes of change described by Sophian can capture those continuities, it would be interesting to study the process of change more directly. All the studies reported by Sophian involve cross-sectional comparisons. However, the types of change that she describes in robustness, consistency, and appropriateness could well be studied in a training experiment. My guess is that short-term training studies will improve infants' abilities to differentiate among tasks, but will have little impact on information-processing skills. So, it should be possible to encourage infants to attend to, say, the most recent hiding, but only within a fixed delay length.

DELOACHE

De Loache also looked at search but with her eye on a different question from Sophian. The children were given the task of retrieving a hidden object from one of several hiding places in a large-scale environment, often the child's own home. Because of the age of the children—21 months and upward—and because of the simplicity of the hiding, the children's performances were typically very accurate. When errors did arise, they could be attributed to faulty retention of the hiding information rather than to any inability to grasp where or how the object had been hidden. Accordingly, DeLoache asked questions about the development of memory, specifically mediated memory, rather than about the emergence of accurate search per se. She defines mediated memory as follows: ''In mediated memory, the person engages in some activity in the service of remembering. What a person remembers is a product of deliberate mnemonic activity.'' Despite the general assumption that mediated memory usually emerges in mid-childhood, DeLoache presents provocative evidence suggesting that it can be found—at least in the context of search tasks—among 2 year olds. I argue that the experiments DeLoache has described point the way toward a demonstration of mediated memory, but do not in themselves provide such a demonstration.

The main evidence offered by DeLoache comes from studies in which the subject's behavior was observed during the delay period. A record was kept of so-called target behaviors: vocalizations about the hidden object, glances toward its hiding place, pointing toward it, or hovering near it. The frequency of such behaviors was greater if the environment or task was unfamiliar. DeLoache concludes that ''in an unfamiliar setting the children may have less confidence in their ability to remember where the toy is hidden, so they do things to keep alive their memory for its location until they are permitted to retrieve it.''

Unfortunately, other aspects of the data undermine this conclusion. There was no indication that children who exhibited more of the target behaviors were more successful at retrieving the toy; there was no indication that retrieval accuracy varied as a function of the familiarity of the environment; and there was no indication that accuracy was reduced if the children were made to wait in a different room so that target behaviors were disrupted. In short, there was no evidence that the strategies being used by the children were actually improving retention.

Nevertheless, one could reasonably argue that children did intend to improve retention even if they did not succeed in exhibiting such an improvement. One study does lend support to this argument. It involved three different groups of 20-month-olds. One group had to retrieve Big Bird from his hiding place when he woke up. The second group had to retrieve Big Bird when he woke up, but he took his nap in a spot fully visible to the subjects. The third group saw Big Bird hidden but knew that the experimenter was going to retrieve him. The results showed that the first group, who had to remember Big Bird's whereabouts and retrieve him, engaged in more target behaviors than the other two groups.

The differential incidence of target behaviors certainly encourages the notion that they were produced with the aim of trying to remember the toy's whereabouts. However, I think it is important to keep clear the distinction between two types of mnemonic strategy. First, one could argue that target behaviors occur as a by-product of the child's plan of action or knowledge state. They do not reflect any awareness on the part of the infant of his or her mnemonic limitations, and they are not intended to compensate for those limitations. The fact that they either succeed or fail in helping the infant remember better is an accidental and unintended outcome. Alternatively, one could argue that such target behaviors do reflect a minimal self-awareness. The infant deliberately engages in such behaviors with the expectation that they will aid memory, whether they eventually do or not. DeLoache is clearly adopting the second hypothesis, whereas I would favor the first.

How could one explain the occurrence of target behaviors according to the first hypothesis? During the waiting period, the children in all three groups are likely to think about what will happen when the bell rings to mark the end of the waiting period, and such thoughts may trigger the overt execution of various components of the actions and outcomes that are envisaged.

The incidence of such target behaviors, or ''terminal responses'' as they are called, has also been studied in the rat and the pigeon during fixed-interval schedules of reinforcement (Staddon, 1977). The general finding is that the incidence of target behaviors, such as approaching the reward box or pecking at the key, increases as the time for reward approaches. If rats and pigeons exhibit target behaviors analogous to those exhibited by young children, we should obviously be cautious about invoking the deliberate use of mnemonic strategies.

Nevertheless, in apparent support of DeLoache's interpretation, the incidence of target behaviors varied across the three conditions. Can the alternative hypothesis that I have proposed explain such variation? I think it can: The target behaviors that are observed for the three groups will differ because the infants will do different things when the bell rings. Infants who will only witness the experimenter search for the hidden object have no goal or action of their own—other than passive observation—to execute ahead of time. Infants who will retrieve Big Bird from his visible location need not envisage the uncovering of Big Bird, nor his place of hiding; they have only to envisage the act of crossing the room and picking up Big Bird. Only the group who will retrieve Big Bird from his hiding place will be thinking about his invisible whereabouts, and enacting their search and uncovering of Big Bird by pointing or looking.

In summary, the target behaviors observed by DeLoache might be akin to terminal responses exhibited by rats and pigeons when the time for reward approaches: the anticipation of a future behavior by engaging in a subcomponent of that behavior such as orienting in the direction of the goal or approaching the goal. The incidence of target behaviors will vary among the three groups because the future behavior in which they are to engage when the bell rings is different for the three groups. This account does not involve any assessment by the infants of their own mnemonic capacities, nor any attempt to overcome the limits of those capacities.

Can this interpretation be extended to the twin findings that target behaviors were more frequent if the task and the environment were unfamiliar? Staddon and Simmelhag (1971) observed that target behavior in the pigeon decreased over trials in that it became concentrated into the few seconds prior to reward as opposed to being spread out over the entire waiting period. Thus, pigeons appear to reduce their target behaviors following increased familiarity with the task environment.

Finally, I believe it is possible to offer a much simpler interpretation of the difference between Surprise and Error trials. DeLoache notes that on Surprise trials, when the object had been surreptitiously removed by the experimenter, the first search was significantly longer than on Error trials, when the infant had mistakenly approached an empty hiding place. Her interpretation of this difference in persistence is that "for both younger and older children, their subjective certainty determined how persistently they searched. . . . children's retrieval efforts are based on their assessments of their own memory states—how much they think they know or how well they think they know it." I think it is more parsimonious to assume that on Surprise trials an infant has no alternative hiding place registered in memory because he or she has been tricked by the experimenter. Hence, the infant searches persistently at the location of the initial search. In contrast, on Error trials, in which the location was empty but due to the infant's mistake, rather than the experimenter's intervention, the infant would be likely to have registered the correct hiding at some point, and would be likely to notice it and to search there after an error. Once the infant has checked hiding places that have been registered in memory, he or she may go on to explore alternative hiding places based on plausible inferences about the displacement of the hidden object, as DeLoache reported.

In summary, the data presented by DeLoache are open to alternative interpretations that do not invoke deliberate mnemonic strategies or subjective assessments of memory states. These interpretations are admittedly a good deal more pedestrian than those offered by DeLoache but they appear to be just as plausible.

It is possible to design an experiment in which these alternative interpretations can be ruled out? DeLoache showed that error rates were higher for four identical boxes than for four distinct boxes. If children were able to assess their fragile memories accurately and to take appropriate remedial action, it should be possible to demonstrate that: (1) target behavior is more frequent when the boxes are identical than when they are distinct; and (2) if target behavior is possible (i.e., the child waits in the same room as the hiding place) the difference between the two conditions is attenuated. This experimental procedure involves two advantages. First, it involves a task—the identical-boxes task—in which target behaviors might conceivably improve accuracy. Second, the response that the child must make to the hiding place in the two conditions is identical: All that need be varied is the appearance of the empty hiding places. Thus, whereas it was possible to argue that the differential incidence of target behaviors observed by DeLoache was due to variation in the eventual response to be made by the child, such an argument is ruled out when the response to be made is held constant. Obviously, if target behaviors are not related to memory demands, but are a by-product of the impending execution of some future act, just as they are in the rat and the pigeon, they should be equally frequent in the two conditions, or conceivably more frequent with distinct boxes, because that condition eventually produces a higher frequency of successful search.

My concern over the difference between these two alternative interpretations is motivated in part by puzzlement about the origins of children's insights into their own psychological processes. If children who exhibit certain target behaviors do so right from the start in order to aid their memories, we are stuck with the question of how they ever discovered that such behaviors would help, in the absence of any experience of the memory deficits that occur in their absence. If, on the other hand, we suppose that there is an initial period when these target behaviors are not adopted in order to help memory but simply as a by-product of some other process, we can envisage a learning period in which the child gradually discovers that under certain circumstances, these incidental behaviors serve to increase the probability of successful search, and can be deliberately used to improve performance. From the evidence that DeLoache has presented so far, it seems safer to assume that the infants she studies were still in the initial period and were not yet adopting deliberate mnemonic strategies. I am hopeful, however, that the clever experimental techniques that DeLoache has devised can be adapted to prove me far too cautious in my estimate of young children's mnemonic awareness.

LOCKMAN AND PICK

Jeff Lockman and Herb Pick covered a lot of territory in a short space of time. Their chapter fell into three sections and I comment on each. In the first section, they discussed the infant's sensitivity to relative distance. Do infants reach for objects that are within reach, and do they select the shortest route to reach an object? They concluded that infants show a sensitivity to distance information but "during the infancy and toddler periods, certain stimulus and response constraints are overcome." They noted in particular that efficient use of distance information may be impaired if it is not perceptually available, if it conflicts with other information, or if it is masked by perseverative tendencies.

Even though I do not quarrel with their summary, I doubt that it is precise enough to allow predictions about future studies. In my view, Lockman and Pick chose a set of tasks that were too disparate to permit any clear generalizations to emerge, and for that reason I focus more narrowly on two very intriguing studies that they report.

The first study focused on the toddler period: Children had to go around a barrier to get to their parent, who was visible on the other side of the barrier. To reach their parent by the shortest route, the children aged 12 and 18 months had to alternate going to the left and the right on successive trials. Although both age groups tended to use the shortest route on the initial trial, the 12 month olds were prone to perseveration on later trials. Lockman and Pick note the similarity of these perseverative errors to those observed in manual search tasks. However, I would like to stress a procedural difference between the two tasks that is important when we try to develop an explanation that covers perseverative error in both tasks. In the search task, the target is invisible. In Lockman and Pick's detour task, the parent remains fully visible behind the low barrier. To the extent that we try to offer a common explanation for both types of perseveration, we are led to think about how the infant codes and updates an object's position, visible or invisible (Harris, 1983, in press). Explanations in terms of the infant's limited conception of an invisible object (Piaget, 1954), on the other hand, will only frustrate the search for a common explanation of locomotor and manual-search errors.

Lockman and Pick report a second study involving a detour situation but with younger infants. Infants either watched an object go over and behind a tall upright barrier, or go around it. Infants could retrieve the object in both cases by making a detour reach around the screen. This ability emerged between 8 and 12 months of age. I found this study fascinating for two reasons. First, it suggests that infants appreciate that the same point in space can be reached by two different trajectories—the trajectory followed by the object and the trajectory followed by the hand. Second, it illustrates an early appreciation that an object can move invisibly from one place to another. To my knowledge, this is one of the earliest demonstrations of an ability that standard Piagetian studies place much later—at around 18 months.

Of course, there are data on infant tracking that suggest that babies can learn to look toward the end of a screen where an object will reemerge (Nelson, 1971). Lockman and Pick's data, however, are much more powerful because the infant is not searching at the point of reappearance but is interpolating an invisible point along the trajectory.

It is interesting to ask how the infants were so successful. Did the sound of the object striking the table behind the barrier help them (Bigelow, 1983)? Were they able to use the movements of the experimenter's arm as a cue? Alternatively, do they have an appreciation that objects cannot suspend themselves in the air but must rest upon a surface? If so, they should be able to reach around the screen to the point where its path intersects the table surface, even when the surface of the table is raised or lowered relative to the screen and also relative to their own bodies. For what it is worth, my guess is that invisible trajectories that are governed by gravity are understood quite easily because they are so regular. Piaget (1954) notes that his three infants began to search systematically on the floor for a falling object between 6 and 9 months of age. If vertical, gravity-induced trajectories are understood at such a young age, we may have overestimated the difficulties of invisible trajectories for young infants by forcing them to infer where the object is moving by keeping track of the container in which it moves.

In the second section of their chapter, Lockman and Pick claim that: "size or scale factors may also affect spatial behavior in an indirect way." By this, they mean that variation in size or scale is correlated with a variation in a variety of other processing or response demands that may be directly responsible for the variation in spatial behavior that is observed. For example, variation in size is often correlated with variation in the distinctiveness of the loci to be remembered, the number of vantage points needed to obtain a complete picture of the layout, and the responses that must be made to the target (reaching versus walking).

In reading Lockman and Pick's analysis, I came to the view that they were being too generous. The difficulty is not that variations in size and scale are often correlated with several other types of variation, but that they are confounded. To put it less generously, Lockman and Pick's own careful analysis suggests that whereas one might be tempted to look for clear-cut generalizations across studies in which size is manipulated, the confounding variation that is introduced in a motley collection of other variables make such generalizations very unlikely.

Indeed, the conclusion that I draw from this section of Lockman and Pick's chapter is that size and scale manipulations that involve such indirect effects are deceptively complex, and one might well abandon them as a useful framework for establishing developmental regularities.

In the final section of their chapter, Lockman and Pick discussed the difficulties that young children face when moving between two different scales, especially if the two are not aligned one with another. They point out that the ability to see the relationship between a map and a space is similar to a cross-modal problem, because difficulties could arise in either of the two modalities or in coordinating the two. There is by now a sizable literature on the pitfalls in designing cross-modal experiments (Bryant, 1968; Milner & Bryant, 1970). Any developmental change can be attributed either to developments in within-modal processing or to developments in cross-modal processing. The only way to resolve which type of development is taking place is to include within-modal controls. For example, in the case of visual–tactual tasks, one also needs estimates of visual–visual abilities and tactual–tactual abilities.

One of the experiments described by Lockman and Pick did include the appropriate controls: Siegel, Herman, Allen, and Kirasic (1979) asked kindergarten, second-, and fifth-grade children to explore a large- or small-scale town and then to reconstruct it in either a large- or small-scale environment. This experiment includes the crucial control conditions in which no translation was required (explore large–reconstruct large; explore small–reconstruct small). The authors did find, as Lockman and Pick report, that one of the two translation tasks (explore small–reconstruct large) was especially difficult. However, there is a further important point. This relative difficulty with the translation task did not vary with age. In other words, the evidence that we have so far does not indicate that translation across scales is a difficulty that affects young children in particular. For all we know at present, the difficulty persists across development.

The ability to translate between two spaces that are not in alignment is probably a stronger candidate for developmental change. This problem was taken up toward the end of Lockman and Pick's chapter. It is, however, the principal burden of the chapter contributed by Huttenlocher and Newcombe and I now turn to that chapter.

HUTTENLOCHER AND NEWCOMBE

Janellen Huttenlocher and Nora Newcombe have looked at children's abilities to imagine transformations of a set of objects produced by either movement of the observer or movement of the array. Their hypothesis is that an important factor underlying the ability to imagine such transformations is the way in which the spatial relationships of the objects are encoded in the first place. More specifically, they argue that some earlier findings (Huttenlocher & Presson, 1979), as well as the findings from ongoing research, can be best understood by supposing that children do not encode an array of four objects into a single gestalt shaped like a cross or diamond. Instead, children note the position of each object in relation to adjacent landmarks.

Huttenlocher and Newcombe use this hypothesis to explain the intriguing cross-over in difficulty illustrated in Table 4.1 of their chapter. For tasks involving movement of the observer, picture selection is hard, but item questions are easy. Huttenlocher and Presson (1979) explain this as follows: When asked to imagine which item would occupy a given position relative to a moving observer (i.e., the item questions), a single mental step is required. Subjects need only imagine a hypothetical observer moving to the designated position around a set of items that stays stationary relative to the wider framework. The item that would be, for example, nearest this hypothetical observer can then be identified. In contrast, to visualize how the entire array would look to this hypothetical observer and to pick out an appropriate picture (i.e., the picture-selection questions), the hypothetical observer and the subject must be reunited. Hence, a second mental step is needed. The array plus hypothetical observer must be rotated back until the subject and observer are colocated. Then, the subject can "see" how the entire array would look were he or she to adopt the hypothetical observer's stance relative to the array.

I am happy to endorse this interpretation of the difficulties involved in the observer-move task. In fact, together with Elizabeth Bassett (Harris & Bassett, 1976), I put forward a similar interpretation. Our data convinced us (contrary to an earlier claim of Huttenlocher & Presson, 1973) that children could imagine themselves in the position of a hypothetical observer—for example, on the far side of the array. What they found difficult was the second step: the rotation of array plus hypothetical observer relative to the wider framework. An examination of various spatial tasks suggested that young children appreciate that when they move, array–framework relationships remain invariant (Harris, 1977). Accordingly, they run into difficulties in executing the second step required by the picture-selection task, because it requires that they mentally destroy that invariance by rotating the array relative to the wider framework.

The interpretation of the observer-move task proposed by Huttenlocher and Newcombe and by Harris and Bassett (1976) does not rest upon the supposition that items are coded on an individualized basis relative to various landmarks. This is a central claim in Huttenlocher and Newcombe's chapter, and it figures prominently in the account of array-rotation tasks that Huttenlocher and Newcombe propose.

When asked to imagine a rotation of the set of objects, picture-selection tasks are easy because a mental transformation of any one of the separately coded objects to its new position is sufficient to select the appropriate picture. The pictures either displayed every object in the wrong position, or every object in the right position; because no picture was partially wrong and partially right, an exhaustive mental repositioning of each object was unnecessary. The item questions, in contrast (e.g., "Which object would end up nearest you?"), do typically demand the successive mental repositioning of several objects. There is no way for the subject to know which object will end up in the target position except by mentally moving successive objects until they find the one that ends up in that position.

I find this account strained for two reasons. First, it does not explain why Presson (1982) also found that overall-appearance questions were relatively easy for an array-rotation task. Presson (1982, Experiment 1) asked subjects to build a model of the rotated array rather than select a picture. Obviously, reconstruction of the entire array demands just as exhaustive a transformation of the visible array as a position question because all objects are involved. Hence, one would have expected the appearance task to be harder when reconstruction of the entire array was demanded. The second problem goes back to the observations made by Harris and Bassett (1976). They looked at the order in which children placed blocks during a reconstruction task similar to that used by Presson (1982) and found it quite revealing. Consider a subject faced with a "horizontal" array: three blocks—red, white, and blue—in the left, middle, and right positions, respectively. The subject is asked to imagine a clock-wise rotation of 90°, so that the blocks end up in a "vertical" alignment: the red block in the far position, the white block remaining in the middle, and the blue block in the near position. Harris and Bassett (1976) observed that subjects typically reconstructed this array in a fixed order: They picked up a blue block and placed it in the near position, and then moved on to position the white and red blocks. The implication of this result is that subjects imagined rotation of the entire array as a single unit and then read off, beginning with the most salient near position, the identity of the three blocks.

Consider instead the hypothesis favored by Huttenlocher and Newcombe. The subject focuses on one item, moves it through 90°, and then goes on to another item, and then the third. According to this hypothesis, there is no reason to suppose that subjects will concentrate first on the blue block; they are just as likely to focus on the red or white block. Accordingly, we can only explain the finding of Harris and Bassett (1976) that most subjects begin by positioning the blue block if we are prepared to suppose that subjects successively imagine a repositioning of all the items in mental space before they place a single block in position on the model layout. Had subjects actually adopted the successive repositioning strategy, one would surely expect them to position each block on the model layout as soon as its position had been determined, thereby easing the load on working memory.

Nevertheless, it is important to underline the fact that Huttenlocher and Presson (1979) used four-item arrays arranged in a cross or diamond shape, whereas Harris and Bassett (1976) used three-item arrays arranged in a line, either "horizontally" from left to right, or "vertically" from near to far. It is quite possible that children find it much easier to treat items arranged in a line as a single unidimensional whole, but have difficulty in coping with two-dimensional shapes. Accordingly, the wholistic rotation strategy favored by Harris and Bassett (1976) may be deployed for linear arrangements, and the successive strategy favored by Huttenlocher and Newcombe may be deployed for two-dimensional arrangements.

This last point brings me to my final comment. Huttenlocher and Newcombe (Study 2) report on 2- and 3-year-olds' abilities to retain the shape of an array after they have moved to new positions relative to that array. The dramatic impairment on the four-object task with free placement, and the relatively good performance on the two-object task with free placement, goes some way to supporting the distinction I have made between linear and two-dimensional arrangements. There is, of course, a confounding with number of items, but this can be easily removed in future studies by using three- and four-item arrays in both linear and two-dimensional arrangements. I would also hope that Huttenlocher and Newcombe will keep track not just of the final configuration that children produce, but of the order in which the individual blocks are positioned. According to their hypothesis of piecemeal encoding, very little systematic ordering need occur in the reconstruction task, whether the subject remains stationary or moves to the opposite side. Because we observed consistent ordering among 4 year olds (Harris & Bassett, 1976, Experiment 3), I would expect ordering among younger children, at least for linear arrays. The same technique would also be informative for the larger arrays employed in Study 1. Do young children behave like the chess players in Chase and Simon's experiments (Chase & Simon, 1973), ordering their placement of items in terms of the local configurations that they can detect, or do they order their placements in an unpredictable fashion, reflecting the piecemeal encoding of each separate item, as proposed by Huttenlocher and Newcombe?

CONCLUSIONS

Despite their diversity, two common themes emerged among these chapters. First, the role that landmarks play in spatial encoding was taken up in several chapters. One of the only manipulations that DeLoache found to reduce the accuracy of search in her subjects was to introduce identical as opposed to distinctive containers to mark the hiding place of the object. I argued that distinctive containers were playing a covert role in Sophian's data: Although infants appeared to be approaching each of the identical containers at random, they were at least distinguishing those containers from other potential hiding places, such as the experimenter's pocket or the underside of the table. Finally, Huttenlocher and Newcombe claimed that encoding in terms of adjacent landmarks emerges very early and is often more accessible to young children than the configurational encoding of which older children and adults make use.

A second theme that emerged concerned the encoding of movement, that of a hidden or imagined object relative to the subject or that of the subject relative to a static array. Lockman and Pick reported that infants could interpolate an invisible trajectory well before 1 year of age. As I pointed out, this striking precocity conflicts with standard assumptions about the infant's insight into visible displacement and deserves close experimental analysis. The more typical pattern regarding invisible displacement was described by Sophian: error-prone search well into the second year. Especially noteworthy was the regular pattern of error that she reported, a response to the container occupying the place where the object originally disappeared, even though the correct container had moved away from that location. Finally, Huttenlocher and Newcombe report that children have difficulty in coping with a different type of invisible displacement, one that leaves the target object(s) stationary relative to the wider framework but that introduces an invisible displacement of the subject relative to the array.

In hearing these two themes echo through the chapters, I began to think about one obvious but unanswered question: What exactly is the developmental relationship between the two themes? Let me frame my question more precisely. The first theme emphasizes that infants readily code the fact that one object is adjacent to a larger landmark. The second theme emphasizes the way in which infants do or do not keep track of the invariant or changing relationships between an object and the wider framework when the object is moved alone, when the object is moved inside a container, or when the subject moves relative to the object and framework. At first sight, it is natural to suppose that the infant begins to work on the first theme, the encoding of static adjacency relationships, and only later begins to cope with the updating of those relationships as required by relative displacement. To put it another way, the infant begins to imagine a mobile world composed of snapshots of the static world. Stated in this fashion, I wonder whether we are using the right metaphor. It seems equally plausible to claim that the infant's perception of the static world is itself a product of the relative displacements that he or she knows to be possible. Thus, objects are encoded in relation to static landmarks because infants know that an object can be displaced relative to such static landmarks. Conversely, separate objects that form a cross or diamond are not encoded configurationally because they are perceived to be four distinct objects, each capable of independent motion. I am confident that research on early space perception and cognition will enable us to be more precise on these issues in the next few years.

Meantime, I would like to note one other common characteristic of the four chapters that I have discussed. They have all introduced provocative experimental observations. As is clear from my comments, I have sometimes doubted the interpretation proposed by the authors, or I have found other interpretations equally plausible. Nevertheless, as I have tried to show, experimental techniques exist for testing these alternative interpretations. In fact, I am reassured to find two vital features of a healthy science: the availability of alternative interpretations and the experimental tools for choosing between those alternatives.

REFERENCES

Bigelow, A. E. Development of the use of sound in the search behavior of infants. *Developmental Psychology*, 1983, *19*, 317–321.

Bryant, P. E. Comments on the design of developmental studies of cross-modal matching and cross-modal transfer. *Cortex*, 1968, *4*, 127–137.

Butterworth, G. Object disappearance and error in Piaget's stage IV task. *Journal of Experimental Child Psychology*, 1977, *23*, 391–401.

Chase, W. G., & Simon, H. A. Perception in chess. *Cognitive Psychology*, 1973, *4*, 55–81.

Diamond, A. *The development of recall memory.* Paper given at Society for Research in Child Development meeting, Detroit, 1983.

Gratch, G., Appel, K. J., Evans, W. F., LeCompte, G. K., & Wright, N. A. Piaget's stage IV object concept error: Evidence of forgetting or object conception? *Child Development*, 1974, *45*, 71–77.

Harris, P. L. Perseverative errors in search by young infants. *Child Development*, 1973, *44*, 28–33.

Harris, P. L. Perseverative search at a visibly empty location. *Journal of Experimental Child Psychology*, 1974, *18*, 535–542.

Harris, P. L. Development of search and object permanence during infancy. *Psychological Bulletin*, 1975, *82*, 332–344.

Harris, P. L. The child's representation of space. In G. Butterworth (Ed.), *The child's representation of the world.* New York: Plenum, 1977.

Harris, P. L. Infant cognition. In J. J. Campos & M. M. Haith (Eds.), *Handbook of child psychology* (Vol. 2, Gen. Ed. P. Mussen). New York: Wiley, 1983.

Harris, P. L. Object perception and object permanence. In P. Salapatek & L. B. Cohen (Eds.), *Handbook of infant perception.* New York: Academic Press, in press.

Harris, P. L., & Bassett, E. Reconstruction from the mental image. *Journal of Experimental Child Psychology*, 1976, *21*, 514–523.

Huttenlocher, J., & Presson, C. C. Mental rotation and the perspective problem. *Cognitive Psychology*, 1973, *4*, 279–299.

Huttenlocher, J., & Presson, C. C. The coding and transformation of spatial information. *Cognitive Psychology*, 1979, *11*, 375–394.

Milner, A. D., & Bryant, P. E. Cross-modal matching by young children. *Journal of Comparative and Physiological Psychology*, 1970, *71*, 453–458.

Nelson, K. E. Accommodation of visual-tracking patterns to object movement patterns. *Journal of Experimental Child Psychology*, 1971, *12*, 182–196.

Piaget, J., *The construction of reality in the child.* New York: Basic, 1954.

Presson, C. C. Strategies in spatial reasoning. *Journal of Experimental Psychology: Learning, Memory and Cognition*, 1982, *8*, 243–251.

Siegel, A. W., Herman, J. F., Allen, G. L., & Kirasic, K. C. The development of cognitive maps of large and small scale spaces. *Child Development*, 1979, *50*, 582–585.

Sophian, C., & Sage, S. Developments in infants' search for displaced objects. *Journal of Experimental Child Psychology*, 1983, *35*, 143–160.

Sophian, C., & Wellman, H. Selective information use and perseveration in the search behavior of infants and young children. *Journal of Experimental Child Psychology*, 1983, *35*, 369–390.

Staddon, J. E. R. Schedule-induced behaviour . In W. K. Honig & J. E. R. Staddon (Eds.), *Handbook of operant behaviour.* London: Prentice-Hall, 1977.

Staddon, J. E. R., & Simmelhag, V. L. The ''superstition'' experiment: A reexamination of its implications for the principles of adaptive behavior. *Psychological Review*, 1971, *78*, 3–43.

ORIGINS OF NUMBER SKILLS

6 Development of Numerical Concepts in Infancy

Mark S. Strauss and Lynne E. Curtis
University of Pittsburgh

Research on the development of quantitative abilities of young children has a long history. As early as 60 years ago, Douglass (1925) published one of the first American studies on "The Development of Number Concept in Children of Preschool and Kindergarten Ages" in the *Journal of Experimental Psychology*. In that report, Douglass raised a question that continues to confront researchers in the field today—that is, what are we willing to accept as evidence of possession of number concept? Douglass (1925) wrote:

> What then is the standard by which we shall judge possession of concept? This problem, encountered early in any quantitative study of concept possession or development, is even more prominent in the study of number concept because of the counting phenomenon. Is it necessary that a child recognize a group of four objects, let us say dots on a piece of paper, before he may be said to "know" four? . . . Must we insist that the "knowing" of four depends upon perceiving four *without counting?* or adding? Does a child really "know" four until he is able to assemble a group of four objects, to select four from a large number? Must he be able to distinguish four from three, from five, and all other numbers? Can he be said to have a "true" concept of four if he is not aware of all of its properties, e.g., that it is half of eight or a third of twelve, that it is twice two and the sum of three and one, and that it is the difference between ten and six and between five and nine? Must one not know that it is the square of two and the square root of sixteen, and that it is the logarithm of 10,000? Can a child be said to possess the concept of the number four until he can identify tactile, auditory, kinaesthetic, or gustatory experience of four in all the possible variations and situations? It is clear that there is no limit which may be set to the extension or perfection of concept. It is never complete, and the bounds of its development are limitless. Those who have ap-

131

proached concept studies have recognized this complication. What we find is varying degrees of "conceptness"—that is, varying degrees of attainment to a theoretically perfect concept [pp. 444–445].

This diversity is reflected by the numerous criteria that researchers have used over the past 60 years to define possession of a number concept. In this particular case, Douglass chose to use three different ways of estimating the quantity of a group of identical objects: How many dots did you see? Which picture has X dots? How many marbles do I have in may hand? Through children's performance on these tasks, Douglass found that 5-year-olds can readily "know and recognize" one-, two-, and three-item arrays, but have inaccurate number concepts of four and above.

Subsequently, the investigation of other quantitative skills in preschool children has confirmed and extended these early findings. For example, young children are able to make linear and nonlinear magnitude discriminations between small numerosities that differ by at least three (Siegel, 1971). They are also skilled at recognizing one-to-one correspondence between both identical and spatially dissimilar numerical arrays (Siegel, 1971; Wohlwill, 1960).

Rochel Gelman and her colleagues have summarized most of this work (Gelman & Gallistel, 1978) and have extensively studied the young child's conception of number (Gelman, 1972, 1977, 1978). Through clever studies of children's counting and understanding of the effect of various numerical and nonnumerical transformations of small arrays, Gelman has demonstrated that preschool-age children possess a range of fairly sophisticated quantitative abilities that reflect underlying number-abstraction and numerical-reasoning principles. The use of a variety of methods to assess a variety of abilities leads to the conclusion that preschoolers as young as 2 years of age possess some numerical abilities.

Within the past 5 years, researchers have become interested in investigating whether still younger infants and children are able to demonstrate quantitative or numerical concepts. Although this is an interesting question in its own right, such efforts are conceptually motivated by the notion that the acquisition of numerical abilities may represent a natural domain of competence, just as the acquisition of language abilities does (e.g., Gelman, 1982).

It is clear that quantitative and numerical concepts are pervasive in the everyday lives of infants and young children, as they are for adults. Herbert Ginsburg (1977) has:

(considered) how thoroughly quantity fills the world of infants. They lie in cribes with a certain number of bars. The walls in their rooms display repetitions of bricks or wooden boards or regularity in the pattern of the wallpaper. Their parents go into the room and out of it over and over again. Some of their toys are bigger than others; some are identical and others are equivalent in size. If they push a toy, it moves; and the harder they push, the harder it moves. Infants thus have ample opportunity to learn about number, repetition, regularity, differences in magnitude, equivalence, causality, and correlation [p. 30].

Even though we recognize the presence of numerous quantitative features in an infant's environment, whether infants and young children are aware of, can make use of, or learn about these features is a question that has only recently been asked. Is numerosity a salient dimension for infants? If so, what quantitative information do infants abstract from their environments?

The study of numerical concepts in infancy is a recent endeavor. Only within the past 5 years has the development of appropriate methods allowed infant researchers to assess the origins and development of numerical concepts in preverbal infants. The purpose of this chapter is to present and discuss current research that has been conducted in the past 5 years.

In the first section, we review the current research literature. This research has focused on four primary issues: (1) whether infants can discriminate between visual arrays that differ only in numerosity; (2) whether infants possess any understanding of ordinal concepts that would allow them to make judgments with respect to relative numerosities (e.g., whether one quantity is greater or lesser than a second quantity); (3) whether infants are able to match intermodally equivalent quantities across both visual and auditory modalities; and (4) whether there are any developmental trends with respect to the just-described abilities over the first year and a half of life.

In the second section, we critically review the extant research. The quantitative skills that infants demonstrate are placed in the perspective of other concurrent perceptual and cognitive developments in infancy as an aid to interpret the results of these studies. To presage the discussion, it is argued that, despite evidence that infants are able to make both cardinal and ordinal discriminations with respect to visual quantity, research thus far has not demonstrated that infants actually have a cognitive understanding of exact quantities. The abilities demonstrated by the infant research to date are best considered to be "protonumerical" abilities that form a foundation upon which the formal number system can be built.

Finally, the last section of this chapter presents some initial "theoretical" ideas on the origins of these protonumerical abilities. Also discussed is speculation on a plausible developmental sequence of number.

EMPIRICAL RESULTS

Research studies of number concepts of preschool-age children have repeatedly revealed that, even before children enter school, they possess a range of quantitative abilities. These include such skills as magnitude discrimination, counting, invariance and conservation of small quantities, and estimation of numerosities.

One way in which these number concepts themselves are typically characterized is in terms of two related notions (e.g., Brainerd, 1973, 1979; Klahr, in press; Piaget, 1952): cardinality and ordinality. Cardinality refers to that property of number represented as a class of arrays containing an equal number of items; this would be demonstrated in the ability to recognize that two arrays are equivalent in terms of numerosity. Ordinality refers to that property of number represented as an ordered relation between two unequal quantities; this is demonstrated in the ability to recognize that one array is larger or smaller than another array.

This distinction serves well to organize the research to date on infant quantitative abilities. The initial question asked simply whether infants could discriminate between two arrays containing different small numerosities. In order to discriminate between two different arrays, infants must be able to abstract the cardinality of an array containing a particular numerosity over numerous exposures to or experiences with it.

However, as Klahr (in press) has pointed out, infants' sensitivity to the cardinal feature of numerical arrays is only half of the story. In order to speak of mature representation in this domain, the internal symbol must have numerical properties—that is, both cardinality and ordinality. Habituation to a particular numerosity, when all other perceptual dimensions are varying, could only result from repeated encoding of the cardinality of the set. Several studies have begun to assess whether infants and young children are able to make relational judgments based on the ordinal property of number.

A third set of studies has examined a more diverse collection of preverbal number abilities. These can be characterized as studies of the abstractness and/or flexibility of infants' and young children's notions of numerical correspondence and numerical change. One study has asked whether infants are able to match intermodally equivalent quantities across visual and auditory presentations. A second study investigated whether young children are aware of the effect upon a small group of items of adding or subtracting one item.

Finally, whether there are any developmental trends with respect to the just-described abilities over the first year and a half of life has begun to be investigated in several studies.

Discrimination of Numerosities: A Cardinal Task

Are infants able to discriminate between precise small numerosities? The answer to this simple question is unequivocally affirmative. This conclusion is based on one of those infrequent occurrences in infancy research: concurrent, converging findings by at least two different groups of researchers (e.g., Starkey & Cooper, 1980; Starkey, Spelke, & Gelman, 1980; Strauss & Curtis, 1981). These results indicate that, by 10 months of age, infants are able to discriminate between arrays of two and three items (Starkey & Cooper, 1980; Starkey et al., 1980; Strauss & Curtis, 1981); can sometimes discriminate between three and four items (Strauss & Curtis, 1981); and are not able to discriminate between four and five items (Strauss & Curtis, 1981) or between four and six items (Starkey & Cooper, 1980). (Evidence of neonatal perception of numerosity [Antell & Keating, 1983] is discussed in a subsequent section.) That this phenomenon is a general and robust one is confirmed by consistent results across a variety of stimulus conditions with both identical stimuli or stimuli in which the items vary both within and between arrays.

All of the discrimination studies to date are based on variants of the habituation paradigm. The details unique to each of these procedures are discussed later in this chapter, but there are common invariant features that do emerge across studies.

Because numerosity covaries in the natural world with a number of other physical dimensions (such as surface area, contour density, configuration, brightness, and so on), procedures had to be designed that would assure that infants' discriminations could be made solely on the basis of numerosity and not on the basis of any other correlated attribute. This became possible with the adaptation of the multiple-habituation technique, which had previously been used to study the development of perceptual categories in infants (e.g., Caron, Caron, & Carlson, 1979; Cohen & Strauss, 1979; Strauss, 1979). Typically, an infant is presented with several members of a category until habituation occurs. During a test phase, the infant is presented with two types of instances of the familiar, invariant category (old and new instances) as well as with instances of a new category. The infant's ability to categorize is inferred from his or her generalization (continued habituation) to new instances of the invariant category and dishabituation to instances from a new category. Recent studies have shown precisely this pattern of results, from which it can be concluded that infants are able to abstract the relevant categorical information that is invariant across stimuli.

As applied to number abstraction, a category would consist of arrangements of an invariant number of items presented with items varying along all or a subset of the following dimensions: length of the array, density of items in the array, item type, item size, item position. These manipulations are designed to focus the infant's attention on the only invariant feature across arrays and to control for all nonnumerical bases of discrimination. If an infant who had been habituated to a category of a certain number (N) generalized to a new instance of the same invariant category and dishabituated to an instance of a novel category (quantity $N + 1$ or $N - 1$), then number-abstraction ability would be inferred. Conversely, if the infant generalized to the novel category, then it would be inferred that infants are not capable of abstracting numerosity of arrays.

Indeed, as we have seen, young infants are able to discriminate between some precise small numerosities that differ from each other by only one item.

In the first published study, Starkey and Cooper (1980) used an experimental method that employed duration of first fixation in a standard habituation–dishabituation-of-looking procedure. Four- to 7-month-old infants were habituated to two different arrays of equal-sized dots. The two habituation arrays contained an invariant numerosity, but length and density of the arrays varied. Infants were tested in either a small-number (two versus three) discrimination or a large-number (four versus six) discrimination. In each of these number conditions, half of the infants were habituated to the smaller quantity and were tested with the larger, and the other half of the infants were habituated to the larger quantity and were tested with the smaller to control for the possibility that infants might prefer complexity.

In the small-number condition (two versus three), infants' fixations showed dishabituation to the novel numerosity, whereas in the large condition (four versus six), infants' fixations generalized to the novel numerosity. In other words, infants are able to abstract the invariant numerosity of small arrays that vary in length and density and to discriminate between the abstracted numerosity and a novel $(N + 1)$ one, but only when the numerosities involved are small.

The construction of the multiple-habituation set effectively rules out discrimination on the basis of length, density, configuration, and complexity. Because the stimuli were constructed of identical, equal-sized dots, however, discrimination on the basis of background brightness, contour area, or background area remains a possibility not ruled out by this study. Several studies have demonstrated that young infants are sensitive both to brightness and contour differences (Hershenson, 1967; Karmel & Maisel, 1975). Although the data were certainly suggestive and provocative, firm conclusions had to await additional studies that controlled for all nonnumerical cues.

These controls were provided in two subsequent studies that support more strongly the notion that infants are skilled abstractors of numerical invariance and can discriminate between small numerosities (Starkey et al., 1980; Strauss & Curtis, 1981).

Strauss and Curtis (1981) investigated two major questions: (1) Can preverbal infants discriminate between small numerosities when all nonnumerical features, which tend to cc 'ary with number, are controlled?; and (2) Does item heterogeneity across arrays have any effect on these abilities?

Infants were assigned to one of three numerosity conditions: two versus three, three versus four, and four versus five. Within each of these, half of the infants were habituated to the smaller numerosity and were tested with the larger one, and the remaining infants were habituated to the converse.

In order to ensure that numerosity was the only cue for discrimination and to rule out all other explanations as the basis for discrimination (such as configuration, figure area, brightness, density, length, background area, contour), during habituation the size and position of the items in each array were randomly varied in both experimental conditions. In order to vary position, each of the appropriate number of items was placed randomly on a 4 × 4 matrix of possible placements. Size was varied in two ways. First, the items themselves varied in size. Second, the arrays were photographed from one of six randomly determined distances. This resulted in a series of arrays that precluded discrimination on the basis of any simple configurational similarity among the slides and a wide range of visual angles between 2° and 7°.

In addition to the major question of whether infants would be able to discriminate between arrays containing different numerosities, this study assessed whether the type of array (whether the items were homogeneous or heterogeneous across arrays) used might have any effect on discrimination ability. Therefore, half of the infants were assigned to a homogeneous condition in which the item type and number remained invariant while the size and position of the stimuli varied. The remaining half were assigned to a heterogeneous condition in which only number remained invariant while item type, size, and position varied. We were unsure what effect array type might have. With infants, it could be argued that the heterogeneous condition contains more potentially distracting features (varying item type as well as size and position) and, as a result, may be more difficult. On the other hand, it is known that infants over 7 months of age are very skilled at abstracting invariant perceptual information. It could be argued, therefore, that the heterogeneous condition would be easier because the infants' attention was being directly focused toward the only invariant information—that is, numerosity.

As it turned out, array heterogeneity had little effect on infants' discrimination abilities in two of the numerosity conditions. Ten to 12 month olds could discriminate between arrays of two items and those of three items (and vice versa) regardless of the heterogeneity of the arrays, and they were unable to discriminate between arrays of four items and those of five items. Where array heterogeneity seemed to have an affect was in the three versus four discrimination. Females were able to discriminate arrays of three and four items in the homogeneous condition, whereas males were able to discriminate in the heterogeneous condition. It may be that as the discrimination task becomes more difficult, and infants have to attend carefully to the stimuli, as in the case of three versus four, the stimuli may prove to be differentially attractive to males versus females. At any rate, the results of this numerosity-discrimination study are clear: Infants can discriminate between two versus three, sometimes between three versus four, and not between four versus five. This is true even though stimuli vary widely to control for all nonnumerical bases of discrimination.

Confirming evidence was provided by a study by Starkey et al. (1980) that investigated whether infants could enumerate objects that were complex and different from one another. These authors tested the abilities of 6 to 10 month olds to discriminate between arrays of two versus three items that were both heterogeneous arrays of common household objects containing a variety of colors, shapes, sizes, and surface textures. These were arranged randomly on an imaginary 3 × 3 matrix. As in earlier studies, half of the infants were habituated to the smaller quantity and were tested with the larger, and the remaining half were habituated and tested conversely.

These infants also were able to discriminate between heterogeneous arrays of two and three different items. After being habituated to a particular numerosity, infants looked reliably longer at the novel numerosity. Starkey et al. (1980) concluded that infants could abstract precise, small numerosities across arrays of discrete objects. Infants seemed to be responding to the number of objects in these arrays by abstracting a numeric invariant over changes in the displays.

Thus, the ability to abstract the numerosity of an array of a small number of items seems to be a fairly general, robust, and abstract ability. The control of nonnumerical cues to discrimination by these two studies allows us to conclude with some confidence that by 10 to 12 months of age infants can indeed discriminate between small numerosities.

Relative Numerosity Judgments: An Ordinal Task

It now seems clear that infants can discriminate between precise small numerosities, a task that is presumed to rely on the cardinal property of number. Whether infants can learn to make judgments on the basis of relative numerosity, a task that is presumed to rely on the ordinal property of number, is a topic that has only recently come under investigation. In order to respond on the basis of relative numerosity (that is, to the larger or smaller of two small arrays), a child must abstract the appropriate relation or order (that is, more or less) between two numerosities. More specifically, the N and $N + 1$ $(N - 1)$ numerosities must be responded to as members of an ordered series.

Several studies suggest that by 3 years of age children may be able to make use of ordinal information in some tasks. Siegel (1971, 1972, 1974) has reported a series of studies that show that young children are sensitive to the ordinal properties of quantity—that is, to the ordering relation that holds between any two unequal properties. The weight of the evidence (Bullock & Gelman, 1977; Estes, 1976; but see Brainerd & Siegel, 1978, reported in Greenberg, 1981) seems to suggest that 3- and 4-year-old children are able to learn to respond on the basis of the ordinal property of number in a variety of contexts (discrimination learning and transfer, "magic" paradigm and transfer).

A discrimination learning and transfer paradigm was designed for use with 16 month olds (Curtis & Strauss, 1982, 1983). In addition to requiring an ordinal understanding of number, the task is designed to demonstrate a more advanced understanding of small numerosities and the relationship between them. This results from the nature of the transfer trials, which require the generalization of a leraned relational response to novel, perceptually different numerosities than those used in the training trials.

In this task, infants were conditioned to touch the side of a panel that contains the greater or smaller of two simultaneously presented arrays of dots (e.g., two versus one). The stimuli in this study were constructed of red-filled circles, chosen randomly from a set of circles with five different diameters, that were placed randomly on an imaginary 3×4 matrix. These manipulations precluded discrimination on any basis other than numerosity. When a child responded successfully, he or she was rewarded by an animated toy puppy dog and bright lights. After a criterion of five successive correct responses had been reached, the child was given two types of transfer trials that varied his or her prior exposure during training to specific numerosities. One type pitted the previously rewarded numerosity with a novel, larger or smaller numerosity (e.g., two versus three). The second type presented two novel, perceptually different, larger or smaller numerosities (e.g., three versus four).

The design of the relative numerosity study allowed the investigation of multiple, related aspects of numerosity. First, the study was designed to investigate whether infants could demonstrate an ordinal understanding of numerosity. In particular, the study was designed to answer the question: Are infants capable to making relative numerosity judgments? Second, the study explored some of the parameters influencing the strength of the infants' abilities to respond relationally using the dimension of numerosity (i.e., testing whether it is easier for the infants to learn to respond to the larger or the smaller of the arrays, and varying prior experiences with the transfer numerosities). Finally, the assessment of which numerosity discriminations the infants were able to learn supplemented existing knowledge of infants' abilities to discriminate between discrete, small numerosities.

Sixty-four 16-18-month-olds have been tested. Results are shown in Tables 6.1 and 6.2: *Proportion of Children Reaching Criterion* and *Proportion of Relational Responses during Transfer Trials.* Based on preliminary findings, 16-month-olds seem to demonstrate the ability to make use of the ordinal property of number to solve a relative numerosity problem, at least in some numerosity conditions. For example, in the one–two condition, in the transfer in which the previously reinforced numerosity is pitted against a novel, larger numerosity,

TABLE 6.1
Relative Numerosity Judgments: Proportion of Children Reaching
Criterion[a]

	More			*Less*	
1 –②[b]	8/9	(.89)	①– 2	8/9	(.89)
2 –③	8/9	(.89)	②– 3	8/11	(.73)
3 –④	8/11	(.73)	③– 4	8/9	(.89)

[a]Criterion = five successive correct responses or 30 trials.
[b]Circled numbers represent positive numerosity.

TABLE 6.2
Relative Numerosity Judgments: Proportion of
Relational Responses during Transfer Trials

Training Numerosity	Transfer Trials		
1–②ᵃ	2–3	3–4	1–2
N = 8	.750	.750	.688
①– 2	2–3	3–4	
N = 8	.500	.250	.438
2 –③	3–4	4–5	
N = 8	.625	.687	.786
②– 3	3–4	4–5	
N = 8	.375	.562	.438
3 –④	2–3	1–2	
N = 8	.312	.500	.562
③– 4	2–3	1–2	
N = 8	.312	.500	.500

ᵃCircled numbers represent positive numerosity.

over 80% of the responses were relational. In the transfer in which two novel, perceptually different numerosities were pitted, over 60% of the responses were also relational. These preliminary results seem to suggest also that both discrimination learning and relational responding are impaired when the response to the smaller numerosity is rewarded.

That infants are able to make relative numerosity judgments is consistent with a study reported by Cooper in his chapter of this volume. Using an habituation paradigm in which infants were presented successively with two numerosities that differed by one and were tested with the same or novel relation, Cooper also found that 14- to 16-month-old infants could detect and remember less-than and greater-than relationships.

Abstractness and Flexibility of Number Skills: Numerical Correspondence and Numerical Change

Starkey, Spelke, and Gelman (1982) have studied the ability of 6- to 8-month-old infants to detect intermodal numerical correspondences between a visible arrangement and an audible sequence of sounds. Infants were presented with a choice of looking at a picture containing either two or three objects while they heard either two or three drumbeats from a centrally located speaker. Babies came to look longer at the visual display with the number of items that matched the number of drumbeats. To do this, the authors concluded, infants must be able to abstract away from the modality of presentation (visual or auditory) and the type of items to be enumerated (objects or events).

That these data support the notion of the abstractness of this ability is unquestioned. However, a controversy exists whether intermodal perception in general is best thought of as a basic, innate capacity or as a more sophisticated matching ability that requires experience with the multimodal properties of objects and events to develop (e.g., Butterworth, 1981; Sullivan & Horowitz, 1983). Some form of coordination of the visual and auditory modalities exists shortly after birth. That neonates turn their eyes in response to auditory stimuli is evidence for an inherent connection between auditory and visual systems. As Butterworth noted, this more or less reflexive connection does not in any sense imply reflective knowledge. In fact, it seems reasonable to suspect that this reflexive connection may be the basis for the subsequent development of reflective knowledge and voluntary behavior.

In a somewhat different line of research, Starkey (1983) has presented some preliminary data with older (24- to 35-month-old) infants on their ability to assess and remember the effects of numerical change. Starkey used a variant of a search paradigm, in which he placed two to four items into a container that obstructed the items from the children's view and touch. The experimenter then added or subtracted one item and the children were instructed to remove all of the objects from the container. Based on the number of times the children reached into the container to retrieve items, Starkey found that young children are sensitive to numerical change when the set size (either initial or final) is small. When the number of items was small (<4), children were correct 73% of the time; when the number of items was larger (>4), accuracy dropped to 24% correct.

In order to solve this task, young children must be able to retrieve, modify, and remember numerical information that was previously perceived but no longer present. Thus, by 2 to $2\frac{1}{2}$ years of age, young children's number abilities are fairly abstract and flexible.

Development of Number Abilities: A Beginning

As the preceding review suggests, by 18 months of age infants demonstrate a range of number abilities. Unfortunately, the early development of these abilities remains unclear because of the paucity of developmental studies.

Two recent efforts have been undertaken to begin to address the issue of the developmental course of one of these abilities—that is, the ability to discriminate between precise, small numerosities. Although it is true that infants of different ages had been studied (from 4 to 12 months), no single set of experimental parameters had been applied to different ages. Curtis and Strauss (1983) extended their procedures, used originally with 10- to 12-month-olds (Strauss & Curtis, 1981), to 5-month-olds. Additionally, Antell and Keating (1983) extended the procedures of Starkey and Cooper (1980) to even younger infants—that is, to newborns.

Curtis and Strauss (1983) made use of the multiple-habituation paradigm to assess whether 5-month-olds could abstract the numerosity of small arrays and discriminate between them. Infants were again assigned to either a heterogeneous or a homogeneous condition within either a two versus three or a three versus four discrimination. The four versus five numerosity discrimination was not tested, due to the inability of older infants to make the discrimination. Regardless of the heterogeneity of the stimuli and the numerosity presented, infants were able to discriminate between the novel and familiar test numerosities.

An inspection of the means reveals that there may be a trend in the ability to discriminate between these small numerosities. Regardless of condition, infants are able to discriminate between arrays of two and three items, and in some conditions may be able to discriminate larger arrays of three and four items. That similar results were obtained for 10- to 12-month-olds leads us to question whether there is a developmental trend in the ability of infants to discriminate between larger arrays as they get older. The results of another study currently under way with 7- to 8-month-olds will help to clarify this trend. In the meantime, it is interesting to note that these data converge with those obtained by Starkey and his colleagues.

Somewhat discrepant data are provided by a study by Antell and Keating (1983). These authors reasoned that if number represents a "natural domain of competence," then it may not be unreasonable to suspect that even very young infants may be able to discriminate between small numerosities. Using the two-versus-three and the four-versus-six dot stimuli of Starkey and Cooper (1980), Antell and Keating found that even neonates could discriminate between two versus three but not between four versus six. This pattern of results was similar to that obtained by Starkey for 4 to 7 month olds. On the basis of these results, the authors suggest that the ability to abstract numerical invariance in the small sets is present in human newborns.

Based on only one study's findings that newborns possess this ability, it is important to view these results with caution until they are replicated. As the authors themselves have suggested, the results may be confounded by brightness or contrast-density differences between habituation and test numerosities. Given the stimuli, this is certainly a possibility, and it is particularly important to evaluate alternative explanations for newborns for several reasons. It is well known that infants "lock onto" central features, rather than actively scan entire figures (Salapatek, 1975). In addition, differences in brightness or contrast density are quite salient dimensions for newborns (Hershenson, 1964; Karmel & Maisel, 1975). Finally, the range of individual differences for newborn acuity typically varies between 20/400 and 20/800 (Banks & Salapatek, in press). Given poor acuity and these other factors, it is questionable what the functional stimuli are for newborns in this case. Until these issues are resolved, judgment of the developmental invariance of numerosity-discrimination abilities should be reserved.

Data on the development of relative numerosity judgments remain sketchy. A study by Cooper (this volume) suggests that infants may not be sensitive to the relation between small quantities until they are 14 to 16 months of age. Using a habituation paradigm, Cooper was unable to demonstrate relational responding in 10- to 12-month-olds. These data are consistent with a pilot study reported by Curtis and Strauss (1982). Using a discrimination-learning paradigm to train the concept of "larger quantity," only 46% of the 12-month-old infants reached the criterion of five successive correct responses, whereas 71% of the 16-month-olds were able to do so. Thus, although not confirmed by definitive study, it seems likely that the ability to make relative numerosity judgments is not demonstrated until 14 to 16 months of age.

Noticeably lacking from this review thus far has been speculation on the mechanisms underlying infant numerosity skills. This issue is particularly important and controversial and is raised in the following section.

WHAT INFANTS MAY NOT BE DOING

It is not uncommon in infant research to discover behavioral skills that, on the surface, appear to be quite similar to behaviors that are demonstrated in either older children or adults. For example, it has been argued that cognitive processes, such as recognition memory (e.g., Olson, 1976) or certain types of perceptual abilities such as categorical color perception (e.g., Bornstein, this volume), may be developmentally invariant from at least early infancy through adulthood. Even though this may be true, unfortunately most infancy researchers have been satisfied with demonstrating commonalities among infants and children or adults; little effort has been made to explore rigorously how these processes may be different or how they may change with development. Although such demonstrations of possible commonalities between infants and the more mature organisms are certainly very important, we believe that it is just as important to follow up such research with critical analyses of how such abilities may also differ as the infants develop into childhood.

If one considers the present research on infant numerical concepts, it is certainly impressive that even young infants appear to possess some type of cardinal and ordinal knowledge with respect to small, discrete quantities. Yet the nature of this knowledge may in fact be quite different from the numerical skills demonstrated by older children. Indeed, at this point in time, we prefer to call the infant numerical abilities *protonumerical* skills, so that it is clearly recognized that the nature and internal representation of these abilities may in fact be quite different from their counterparts in older children.

With the preceding in mind, we have entitled this section *What Infants May Not Be Doing*. As this title suggests, we believe that a careful exploration of the processes that underlie infants' numerical abilities may reveal some very important immaturities in infants' understanding of numerical concepts. To a large extent, our discussion of the issues raised in both this and the following section—*What Infants May Be Doing*—is highly speculative in nature, and conclusions should be considered quite tentative at this point in time. The previously reviewed empirical base upon which this discussion rests is still very limited. However, such speculative discussions are considered as critical both to a better understanding of the nature of infant numerical concepts and to the design of future research.

Are Infants Counting?

Although, in general, counting is considered a verbal labeling process, it has been suggested by some (e.g., Gelman, 1982; Starkey, Spelke, & Gelman, 1980) that infants may possess some type of rudimentary counting ability. It is important to consider what is implied by this suggestion. At a minimum, counting implies that there is some type of iterative process that: (1) is sequential in nature; (2) allows for a continual differentiation of tagged and untagged items; and (3) assigns some type of special priority to the final "tag" in the sequence (e.g., a number in verbal counting).

For the following reasons, we believe that it is unlikely that infants possess any counting strategies. First, infants presented with a visual array are most probably not scanning these arrays in any systemic order or sequence. Although there exist no eye-movement data on how infants scan these arrays, we find it unlikely that they are treated any differently than visual patterns, which are usually scanned in a more or less random fashion (e.g., Salapatek, 1975). Additionally, if infants were relying on some type of counting process, one would expect a significant difference between the infants' abilities to abstract number when the presented arrays are either linear or random. Thus far, this does not appear to be true. For example, in the study by Starkey and Cooper (1980), infants were presented with linear arrays. In the study by Starkey et al. (1980), infants of the same age were habituated with arrays that varied randomly with respect to arrangement. Yet, despite these differences, the results of the two studies were virtually identical. Naturally, stronger conclusions on this point require more systematic research that specifically explores the effects of array arrangement on infants' abilities to abstract number.

Second, we find it unlikely that infants are keeping track of tagged versus untagged items. Gelman and Gallistel (1978) have shown that such an internal tagging process is difficult even for young children, who typically will aid themselves by literally touching or regrouping items during the counting process. In our research thus far, we see no indications that infants attempt to physically touch or tag presented visual arrays. Thus, it is implausible that a totally internal tagging routine exists in infants, given the difficulty of this task for older children.

Third, we are hard pressed to imagine what type of final tag that is not verbal in nature could be given to a sequence and then generalized to other numerically equal arrays.

Finally, there is no evidence that infants can abstract numerosities larger than about three or four. Logically, there is no reason why a counting strategy should have such a limitation. Thus, unless someone proposes a type of counting strategy whose nature is very different from that demonstrated by older children, we believe it is most logical to conclude that infants are not counting.

Do Infants Immediately Perceptually Apperceive Visual Quantities?

An almost opposite viewpoint from counting is the suggestion that infants' abilities to abstract quantity is a type of pure perceptual process that is essentially automatic in nature. For example, von Glasersfeld (1981, 1982) has suggested that, even though the perception of quantity may not be identical to the perception of features such as color or warmth, there may exist an innate physiological system that automatically codes rhythms and quantity.

We tend to agree with Klahr (in press) that infants' abilities to abstract exact quantities may be more perceptual than conceptual in nature, but that they probably should not be conceived as "pure perceptual processes (that) are typically characterized as highly parallel," but rather as "partially controlled by higher order cognitive processes that determine the *target* of the quantification effort (e.g., dots, cubes, red things), and some inherent limitation on rapid segmentation of the visual field into three or four perceptual chunks [p. 8]."

Our reason for believing this has to do with the lack of evidence that infants are able to quickly or immediately abstract quantity information. Whereas previous research has demonstrated that other types of perceptual dimensions, such as form or color, can be abstracted by infants after only very few brief exposure (Fagan, 1974; Olson, 1979), our own research suggests that this is not true with respect to quantity information. For example, in our first habituation study on quantity (Strauss & Curtis, 1981) we found that the ability of 12 month olds to abstract a three-versus-four discrimination was to some extent a function of how much attention the infants had given to the stimuli (female infants gave more attention to the homogeneous stimuli and males gave more attention to the heterogeneous stimuli). Similarly, our research with 5 month olds (Curtis & Strauss, 1982) has demonstrated that infants could make a two-versus-three discrimination only in conditions in which their looking times during the habituation phase were relatively long.

Our research on ordinal concepts (Curtis & Strauss, 1983) has suggested a similar conclusion. During the training period, in which infants are required to "learn" to touch the greater or lesser quantity, infants typically require an average of 25 or more trials to reach criterial performance. Typically, the infants begin by responding to a number of irrelevant dimensions, such as side, size, and so on, before they come to realize that quantity is being reinforced. In other words, our research suggests that the abstraction of quantity does not appear to be an immediate, automatic process. In contrast to our results, Cooper (this volume) has presented some initial results that indicate that by 12 months of age, infants can abstract quantity after *repeated* exposures to a brief (700-msec) stimulus. Such demonstrations with younger infants may lend support to the notion that infants' abilities to abstract quantity are in fact the result of some type of automatic perceptual quantifier, although a firmer conclusion awaits further research that specifically varies the length and number of trials needed in order for infants to abstract quantity.

Are Infants Naturally Abstracting Quantity Information from Their Environments?

A question that arises from the research conducted with infants thus far is whether the experiments themselves *teach* the infants to abstract quantity information, or whether they provide an opportunity for the infants to manifest quantitative knowledge they bring to the experiments? Most likely, infants come into the number-concept experiments with some preexisting knowledge of quantity that they have derived from an extended, long-term learning process rather than from the "relatively" small number of trials they encounter in the laboratory situation. However, nothing in the research conducted thus far provides evidence to support this supposition. One way to study this question might be to study carefully infants' abilities to make cardinal or ordinal judgments after varying numbers of training trials. Similarly, this question may be answerable through natural observational studies. For example, is there any evidence that infants in their natural environments spontaneously sort objects into equal-numbered groups, and, if so, does the size of these sorted groups increase as the infants develop?

Are Infants Capable of Coordinating Cardinal and Ordinal Quantitative Information?

As Brainerd (1979) has stated:

> Whenever a collection of terms forms a progression, there is an important isomorphism between ordinal and cardinal numbers; that is, the ordinal number of any such collection automatically gives that cardinal number of the collection. Moreover, the ordinal number of any specific term in the collection automatically gives the cardinal number of the terms up to and including that point in the progression [p. 46].

Recognition of the isomorphism between ordinal and cardinal numbers is basic to any true understanding of numerical concepts. Has the research to date on infant quantitative abilities demonstrated that infants can coordinate cardinal and ordinal quantitative information? We believe not, and, indeed, we argue in the next section that one of the major transitions that must occur with respect to young children's knowledge of number is an understanding of the relationship between cardinal and ordinal quantities.

First, consider the evidence from the infant-habituation research. This research has demonstrated that infants can represent exact small quantities (e.g., two) and that they can discriminate these quantities from different quantities (e.g., three). Although this can be considered a demonstration of cardinal knowledge, there is no evidence that, in discriminating the novel quantity from the original or habituated quantity, infants recognize the novel quantity to be either larger or smaller than the original number (e.g., its ordinal relationship). In other words, infants presented with the novel quantity may recognize a *difference* between the two numbers, but they may not represent any relational or ordinal information about the two quantities. That infants respond identically to the novel quantity whether it is either larger or smaller than the original suggests that perhaps they would also respond equivalently to *any* new quantity, regardless of the magnitude of the difference. Cooper (this volume) agrees with this conclusion, and indeed provides empirical evidence that, until at least 3 months of age, infants are merely discriminating the relationships of equality and nonequality.

With respect to the conditioning studies (Curtis & Strauss, 1982, 1983), infants learn to respond to the greater or lesser of two quantities and then to generalize this response to novel quantities. Although this demonstrates that they are abstracting relational information, it does not demonstrate that they are also aware of the exact cardinal information in the displays. Even though they may be, it is also possible that they are merely encoding the concepts of more or less and not attending to either the exact quantities or the magnitude of the difference (which would imply some interval scale knowledge). Future research that carefully compares the infants' rates of learning in conditions in which the quantities are constant (as was done in Curtis & Strauss) to conditions in which the quantities vary (e.g., one versus two, one versus three, two versus four) could perhaps be used to explicate this point. One would expect differences in infants' abilities to generalize to new quantities that were either identical to or differed from the training stimuli in the *magnitude* of the difference between the two stimuli.

Thus far, however, the infant research has not, in fact, demonstrated that infants do coordinate cardinal and ordinal quantitative information, and as mentioned previously, we argue later that this may represent one of the important developmental transitions in children's understanding of number.

It should also be noted that, to date, the existing research has also not demonstrated whether infants have any knowledge that quantities can be represented on an interval scale. Knowledge of the isomorphism between cardinal and ordinal information is a prerequisite for interval knowledge, and thus we do not believe that interval knowledge is a part of infants' representations of quantity. As previously reviewed, Starkey (1983) has recently presented some preliminary data using a search paradigm that suggested that 24- to 36-month-old infants can add and subtract small quantities. This research would indicate that, by 2 to 3 years of age, children can coordinate cardinal and ordinal information and do have some type of interval knowledge. Whether this type of paradigm could be used for younger, preverbal infants remains to be seen; however, it does represent a new and interesting possible future direction for the infant numerical research.

Do Infants Have Classificatory Concepts of Quantity?

In addition to defining a concept of number by its underlying cardinal and ordinal properties, it is important to recognize that a fully developed concept of number also includes an understanding that a number represents a classificatory concept. As Russell (from Brainerd, 1979) stated: "Returning now to the definition of number, it is clear that number is a way of bringing together certain collections, namely, those that have a given number of terms [p. 64]." In other words, infants or children must eventually come to understand that a particular quantity (e.g., two) is a concept in and of itself, and that there is a conceptual equivalence among pairs of any item.

In many ways, this view of number makes it very similar to other research that has been conducted on infants' understanding of natural categories such as dogs, people, and so on (see, for example, Olson & Strauss, in press); Strauss, 1979). In this research, infants are typically presented with a variety of stimuli, drawn from some class or category (e.g, male faces) that is specified by the experimenter. The recognition test is a test for generalization; test trials consist of presenting novel instances from the category used during familiarization and novel instances from a different category (e.g., female faces).

In commenting upon these studies, Olson and Strauss (in press) cautioned that the perceptual knowledge displayed in a typical infant-categorization experiment should not be thought of as concept knowledge. Concepts embody many types of knowledge, of which perceptual knowledge is only one. For instance, the concept of a face or person is not exhausted by the perceptual knowledge that underlies the abilities infants have to notice categorization built into experimental designs in recent studies. The perceptual knowledge is an important constituent of *some* concepts. Yet, these studies should properly be thought of as studies of the use of knowledge about perceptual categories. Otherwise misleading claims about infant abilities can result when terms like *concept* are used too loosely.

With respect to number, we would also caution that the ability to recognize a common quantity across, for example, slides of various items, is only one aspect of the number concept. A true cognitive or semantic understanding of ordinality and cardinality, interval scales, and counting are just a few of many aspects that we would require before we would want to claim that a child has a "concept" of number.

Even with respect to the simple ability of being able to generalize a particular quantity across different examplars, we expect that there would be significant developmental changes past the infancy period. Current infant research has demonstrated that infants recognize a common, small quantity despite changes in size, arrangement, and even different types of items when the items are all photographs. Yet this ability may still be quite limited in infants. For example, would infants, like older children, recognize that pairs of pictures, objects, or sounds all represent the quantity of two, even when the comparisons must be made across very different contexts and modalities (e.g., vision, audition, touch, etc.)? Very likely, this degree of generalizability will not be evident in infants, and will emerge only as numerical abilities progress from what can be considered knowledge that is more perceptual in nature to an internal knowledge base that is more conceptual in nature.

In summary, even though the research on infant numerical abilities has begun to answer a number of interesting and important issues, many more issues must be carefully studied. Caution must be taken to assess both the maturity of infants' knowledge about number and the extent to which this knowledge is similar to that of older, verbal children. Indeed, we believe that it is the exploration of how infants and verbal children differ that will ultimately lead to an understanding of the origins of numerical concepts.

WHAT INFANTS MAY BE DOING

Although there is still a limited empirical data base with respect to infant numerical skills, it is possible to present some conclusions and some speculation as to what is developing during the infancy period. Following are some of these speculations.

With respect to cardinal abilities, we know that even young infants (by at least 5 months of age) can abstract exact quantities when they are small numerosities (less than four or five). Most likely, this is not done through the use of a counting process, but is rather more perceptual in nature. Very possibly this represents an innate ability, although it is as yet unclear whether there are developmental changes with respect to size of the quantities that can be abstracted. Results of our own initial research with 5-month-olds does, in fact, suggest that there is a gradual increase in the numerosities that can be abstracted, but these results are still quite preliminary.

With respect to ordinal abilities, we know that by at least 14 to 16 months of age, infants can make ordinal judgments with small, discrete quantities. Again, whether or not this can be done by younger infants is as yet unknown. However, it appears that this is a relatively difficult task even for 14- and 16-month-old infants, and both our results and Cooper's suggest that until 14 to 16 months of age, infants are not encoding discrete ordinal information.

To be a bit more speculative, we believe that ordinal quantity judgments probably do not develop until later infancy and that the ability to coordinate cardinal and ordinal information may not develop until 2 to 3 years of age.

However, even the young infant may be able to make ordinal judgments with *nondiscrete* quantities, and indeed infants' abilities to make such judgments with continuous quantities may serve as the foundations for both their eventual knowledge of discrete ordinal concepts and their knowledge of how discrete cardinal and ordinal properties are related.

To be more specific, it is known that even young infants can discriminate certain quantitative differences, such as size (e.g., Strauss & Cohen, 1980) or intensity (e.g., Cohen, DeLoache, & Struass, 1979). In comparison to variations of discrete quantities, variations of continuous quantities such as size, length, area, and so on, should be much more perceptually salient to infants. It is thus conceivable that at an early age (e.g., 4 to 5 months) infants are able to make ordinal judgments with respect to continuous quantities, such as size or length, and that the ability to detect such magnitude differences may be innate. In the natural environment, differences in discrete quantities natually covary with differences in continuous quantities. For example, infants will commonly encounter large versus small piles of cookies or blocks with the larger piles containing a greater number of items. Or, in early number books, pictures of two, three, or four items will take up progressively larger amounts of surface area. Consequently, there are many opportunities for infants to observe both how discrete quantities vary with changes in continuous dimensions (assuming that the discrete quantities are small quantities and thus abstractable) and how the cardinal and ordinal aspects of discrete quantities covary.

Thus, we are suggesting that infants begin with two primary abilities: (1) the ability to abstract and make cardinal judgments with respect to small discrete quantities; and (2) the ability to make magnitude or ordinal judgments with respect to continuous quantities. During their environmental interactions, infants should have many opportunities to observe how cardinal and ordinal properties interact. For example, they can observe how "a pile of cookies decreases in size as they are eaten" or "how a pile of many blocks is larger than a pile of a few blocks." As they continue to have such interactions, infants might eventually learn through an incidental process the ability to make ordinal judgments with discrete quantities and finally they might come to understand the relationship between the cardinality and ordinality of discrete quantities. Indeed, this would explain why older children must eventually "learn" to disassociate discrete quantity from continuous dimensions, as is typically tested in Piagetian number-conservation tasks.

In order to test these ideas, we are just beginning a series of studies that will compare developmentally infants' abilities to make ordinal judgments and to generalize this knowledge when the stimuli are either totally continuous (e.g., long versus short lines), totally discrete (e.g., dots varying in size and arrangement as in Curtis & Strauss [1983]), or a combination of both (e.g., long or short lines composed of discrete dots). We predict that the youngest infants will make ordinal judgments with only continuous quantities and that they will not benefit from conditions in which both continuous and discrete dimensions covary. In contrast, slightly older infants, though not able to benefit from the covariation of continuous and discrete quantity, may be able to generalize their knowledge to discrete quantities when the covarying continuous information is taken away. However, such judgments may not be possible when the infants are trained and tested with only discrete information.

Unfortunately, this research is just beginning and we must limit our conclusions to these speculations.

CONCLUSIONS

The goal of most developmental research is to understand mechanisms of transition. We assume that infants are born with certain innate abilities and information-abstracting mechanisms; through interactions with their environments, children build upon these early abilities to approach gradually the adult knowledge state. Although this represents a noble goal, in fact most infancy research has not been very developmental in nature. The infancy research literature is replete with demonstration studies of how even very young infants appear to possess what, on the surface, appear to be very impressive information-processing skills. Unfortunately, this research rarely goes beyond this "demonstration" stage, and careful explorations of what processes underlie these abilities or how these processes mature are rare.

To a large extent, this chapter has been an attempt to illustrate how, in one specific domain, the development of quantitative knowledge, one must go beyond demonstrations of a particular competence to consider carefully and explore what developing processes may underlie this competence. We have suggested that infants may be born with the ability to extract small, discrete cardinal quantities and with the ability to make ordinal-magnitude judgments with respect to basic perceptual dimensions, such as size, brightness, distance, or length. With these beginnings, during the first year and a half of life, infants gradually develop the ability to make ordinal judgments with discrete quantities and perhaps come to coordinate cardinal and ordinal information with respect to discrete quantities. We believe that these developments are "driven" by infants' early abilities to understand and make magnitude judgments with respect to continuous quantities and their environmental experiences of observing how discrete and continuous quantities covary.

Sixteen- or 17-month-old infants, however, still have limited understandings of quantity. For example, we believe that they do not have an interval knowledge of quantity, that they do not have any true counting mechanisms, and that they do not have a true concept of number in the sense that they understand the equivalence of a particular quantity across all contexts. Naturally, with the development of language and formal counting, such concepts will develop, but we leave it to others to research these later transitions.

What, then, is the significance of the early quantitative skills that are demonstrated by infants during the first 2 years of life? The answer to this question revolves around the basic issue of what are numbers. As Brainerd (1979) has discussed:

> In its most basic psychological sense, number appears to be a quality of sensible objects. For example, the numerousness of a set of objects is just as much a perceptible quality of reality as color, flavor, odor, height, and so on. Before number can begin its evolution as a *concept*, however, an apparently simple assumption must be made. Explicitly, it is necessary to assume that *number is a property that is independent of sensible objects*. In other words, number refers to the sensible world but it is somehow more that this; this is what will be called the abstract attitude toward numbers. The importance of the abstract attitude is very great because it permits us to use numbers and to invent computational systems such as arithmetic and algebra without having to ground what we do in direct experience or observation [p. 4].

Even though it is true that the abstract knowledge of mathematics goes beyond our "real world, sensory-based" knowledge, and it is also true that one need not have experienced 10,000 items multiplied by 5 to solve this type of mathematical problem, we believe that the *development* of such abstract thinking must be based originally on some type of sensory, real-world knowledge. Piaget referred to this type of knowledge as a "practical intelligence," and in *Genetic Epistemology* (1970) Piaget recognized that in the sensorimotor period, there exists a practical intelligence that has its own logic—a logic of actions—and that it is upon this world of actions that higher levels of abstract thinking are based.

Indeed, it could be argued that this type of practical or sensory-based knowledge is a vital aspect of all cognition. Although most adult experimental research does not focus on this type of knowledge, it is, nevertheless, a major aspect of adult thinking in most, if not all, domains of cognition.

What adult does not occasionally add or count by using his or her fingers? Or, similarly, consider spatial knowledge. Even though it is true that adults have many abstract abilities, such as reading maps, performing mental rotations, and so on, what happens when one becomes disoriented or lost in his or her spatial environment? Usually one reverts to a very sensory-based form of behavior and attempts to orient his or her body to landmarks in the environment, or to internally "feel" from what directions he or she has just walked.

In general, we believe that the infancy period is critical, because it provides the child with real-world, sensory knowledge upon which all later forms of abstract cognition are based. The types of quantitative knowledge that develop during this period reflect one, clear example of this general developmental process, from sensory-based to abstract thought.

ACKNOWLEDGMENTS

Preparation of this chapter was supported in part by research grants to the first author from The Buhl Foundation and The National Science Foundation. Reprint requests should be mailed to Mark S. Strauss, Department of Psychology, University of Pittsburgh, Pittsburgh, Pennsylvania, 15260.

REFERENCES

Antell, S. E., & Keating, D. P. Perception of numerical invariance in neonates. *Child Development*, 1983, *54*, 695–701.

Banks, M., & Salapatek, P. Infant perception. In M. Haith & J. Campos (Eds.), *Infancy and biological development*. Vol. 1 of P. Mussen (Ed.), *Manual of child psychology*. New York: Wiley, in press.

Brainerd, C. J. The origins of number concepts. *Scientific American*, 1973, *228*, 101–109.

Brainerd, C. J. *The origins of the number concept*. New York: Praeger, 1979.

Brainerd, C. J., & Siegel, L. S. *How do we know that two things have the same number?* Research Bulletin No. 469, University of Western Ontario, 1978.

Bullock, M., & Gelman, R. Numerical reasoning in young children: The ordering principle. *Child Development*, 1977, *48*, 427–434.

Butterworth, G. The origins of auditory–visual perception and visual proprioception in human development. In R. D. Walk & H. L. Pick, Jr. (Eds.), *Intersensory perception and sensory integration*. New York: Plenum Press, 1981.

Caron, A. J., Caron, R. F., & Carlson, V. R. Infant perception of the invariant shape of objects varying in slant. *Child Development*, 1979, *50*, 716–721.

Cohen, L. B., DeLoache, J., & Strauss, M. S. Infant visual perception. In J. Osofsky (Ed.), *Handbook of infancy*. New York: Wiley, 1979.

Cohen, L. B., & Strauss, M. S. Concept acquisition in the human infant. *Child Development*, 1979, *50*, 419–424.

Curtis, L. E., & Strauss, M. S. *Development of numerosity discrimination abilities*. Paper presented at the meetings of the International Conference of Infant Studies, Austin, Texas, 1982.

Curtis, L. E., & Strauss, M. S. *Infant numerosity abilities: Discrimination and relative numerosity*. Paper presented at the meetings of the Society for Research in Child Development, Detroit, 1983.

Douglass, H. R. The development of number concept in children of preschool and kindergarten ages. *Journal of Experimental Psychology*, 1925, *8*, 443–470.

Estes, K. W. Nonverbal discrimination of more and fewer elements by children. *Journal of Experimental Child Psychology*, 1976, *21*, 393–405.

Fagan, J. F., III. Infant recognition memory: The effects of length of familiarization and type of discrimination task. *Child Development*, 1974, *45*, 351–356.

Gelman, R. The nature and development of early number concepts. In H. W. Reese (Ed.), *Advances in child development and behavior* (Vol. 7). New York: Academic Press, 1972.

Gelman, R. How young children reason about small numbers. In N. J. Castellan, Jr., D. B. Pisoni, & G. R. Potts (Eds.), *Cognitive theory* (Vol. 2). Hillsdale, N.J.: Lawrence Erlbaum Associates, 1977.

Gelman, R. Counting in the preschooler: What does and does not develop. In R. S. Siegler (Ed.), *Children's thinking: What develops?* Hillsdale, N.J.: Lawrence Erlbaum Associates, 1978.

Gelman, R. Basic numerical abilities. In R. J. Sternberg (Ed.), *Advances in the psychology of human intelligence* (Vol. 1). Hillsdale, N.J.: Lawrence Erlbaum Associates, 1982.

Gelman, R., & Gallistel, C. R. *The child's understanding of number.* Cambridge, Mass.: Harvard University Press, 1978.

Ginsburg, H. *Children's arithmetic: The learning process.* New York: Van Nostrand, 1977.

Greenberg, N. A. Young children's perceptual judgments of non-redundant cardinal number equivalence. Doctoral dissertation, University of Western Ontario, 1981.

Hershenson, M. Visual discrimination in the human newborn. *Journal of Comparative and Physiological Psychology,* 1964, *58,* 270–276.

Hershenson, M. Development of the perception of form. *Psychological Bulletin,* 1967, *67,* 326–336.

Karmel, B. Z., & Maisel, E. B. A neuronal activity model for infant visual attention. In L. B. Cohen & P. Salapatek (Eds.), *Infant perception: From sensation to cognition* (Vol. 1, *Basic visual processes*). New York: Academic Press, 1975.

Klahr, D. Transition processes in quantitative development. In R. Sternberg (Ed.), *Mechanisms of cognitive development.* San Francisco: W. H. Freeman, in press.

Olson, G. M. An information processing analysis of visual memory and habituation in infants. In T. J. Tighe & R. N. Leaton (Eds.), *Habituation: Perspectives from child development, animal behavior, and neurophysiology.* Hillsdale, N.J.: Lawrence Erlbaum Associates, 1976.

Olson, G. M. Infant recognition memory for briefly presented visual stimuli. *Infant Behavior and Development,* 1979, *2,* 123–134.

Olson, G. M., & Strauss, M. S. The development of infant memory. In M. Moscovitch (Ed.), *Infant memory.* New York: Plenum, in press.

Piaget, J. *The child's conception of number.* New York: Norton, 1952.

Piaget, J. *Genetic epistemology.* New York: Norton, 1970.

Salapatek, P. Pattern perception in early infancy. In L. B. Cohen & P. Salapatek (Eds.), *Infant perception: From sensation to cognition* (Vol. 1, *Basic visual processes*). New York: Academic Press, 1975.

Siegel, L. S. The sequence of development of certain number concepts in preschool children. *Developmental Psychology,* 1971, *5,* 357–361.

Siegel, L. S. The development of concepts of numerical magnitude. *Psychonomic Science,* 1972, *28,* 245–246.

Siegel, L. S. Development of number concepts: Ordering and correspondence operations and the role of length cues. *Developmental Psychology,* 1974, *45,* 693–699.

Starkey, P. *Some precursors of early arithmetic competencies.* Paper presented at the meetings of the Society for Research in Child Development, Detroit, 1983.

Starkey, P., & Cooper, R. S. Perception of numbers by human infants. *Science,* 1980, *210,* 1033–1035.

Starkey, P., Spelke, E., & Gelman, R. *Number competence in infants: Sensitivity to numeric invariance and numeric change.* Paper presented at the meetings of the International Conference of Infant Studies, New Haven, Connecticut, 1980.

Starkey, P., Spelke, E., & Gelman, R. *Detection of intermodal numerical correspondences by human infants.* Paper presented at the meetings of the International Conference of Infant Studies, Austin, Texas, 1982.

Strauss, M. S. The abstraction of prototypical information by adults and 10-month-old infants. *Journal of Experimental Psychology: Human Learning and Memory,* 1979, *5,* 618–635.

Strauss, M. S., & Cohen, L. B. *Infant immediate and delayed memory for perceptual dimensions.* Paper presented at the International Conference of Infant Studies, New Haven, Connecticut, April 1980.

Strauss, M. S., & Curtis, L. E. Infant perception of numerosity. *Child Development,* 1981, *52,* 1146–1152.

Sullivan, J. W., & Horowitz, F. D. Infant intermodal perception and maternal multimodal stimulation: Implications for language development. In L. P. Lipsitt & C. K. Rovee-Collier (Eds.), *Advances in Infancy Research* (Vol. 2). Norwood, N.J.: Ablex, 1983.

von Glaserfeld, E. An attentional model for the conceptual construction of units and numbers. *Journal for Research in Mathematics Education,* 1981, *12,* 83–94.

von Glaserfeld, E. *Sensory-motor sources of numerosity.* Paper presented at the meetings of the Jean Piaget Society, Philadelphia, 1982.

Wohlwill, J. F. A study of the development of the number concept by scalogram analysis. *Journal of Genetic Psychology,* 1960, *97,* 345–377.

7

Early Number Development: Discovering Number Space with Addition and Subtraction

Robert G. Cooper, Jr.
Southwest Texas State University

This chapter outlines several important acquisitions in early number development, proposes an organizing framework that highlights important aspects of these acquisitions, and discusses some of the necessary features of a theory for explaining them. The particular number concepts discussed are acquired between infancy and approximately 8 years of age without formal instruction. Piaget argued strongly for the importance of such informally learned concepts (e.g., Piaget, 1953):

> It is a great mistake to suppose that a child acquires the notion of number and other mathematical concepts just from teaching. On the contrary, to a remarkable degree he develops them himself, independently and spontaneously [p. 74].

Although this chapter is faithful to this general thesis in Piaget's work and to the notion that the child actively constructs number concepts, in many other ways it departs from Piaget's theories of number development. An account of a more extended course of number development in which conservation plays a less central role is presented.

Brainerd (1979) has classified theories of number development by reducing them to one of three theory types: *cardinal theory, ordinal theory,* or *Piaget's cardinal–ordinal theory.* The classification depends on the types of skills claimed as precursors by the theories. Thus, a cardinal theory would focus on the perception of ''manyness,'' whereas an ordinal theory would focus on ''less-than'' and ''greater-than'' relations as precursors to number concepts. The orientation proposed here is primarily ordinal, as is Brainerd's own theory. However, unlike Brainerd's approach, the one here proposes that a small number of cardinal categories corresponding to small numerosities have a central role in the origin of number concepts.

Several of the other chapters in this volume are concerned with the development of spatial concepts, and an analogy to space may help introduce the current orientation. Consider number development as learning about the space of number. In this space one must learn where things are, and how to get from one place to another. For purposes of the analogy, the locations are specific numerosities and the actions (transformations) to get from one place to another are additions and subtractions. How do you get from two to five? You must start in a particular direction (increasing numerosity), and go past certain landmarks (three and four) until you arrive at five (having gone a certain distance). Points in this space capture the cardinal characteristics of number; direction and landmarks, their ordinal properties; and distance, their interval properties. The developmental component in the analogy is that children learn about this space of numbers by traveling in it. It is through experiences of moving in the space (by addition and subtraction) that children learn its ordinal structure, which is the primary content of early number development.

Throughout this chapter the role of additions and subtractions as transformations that provide crucial information for number development is emphasized. The system within which this information is used is based in part on a model of cognitive development proposed by Klahr and Wallace (1973, 1976), which Klahr has continued to develop (e.g., Klahr, 1983). This model provides a touchstone throughout this chapter and hence is outlined briefly here. The model deals with the relation between states and transformations. Within the realm of number the states are initially established by *quantifiers* (e.g., subitizing, counting, and so on, which Gelman (1972) has called estimators). The transformations can be quantity preserving (e.g., spreading out a group of objects) or quantity changing (e.g., addition or subtraction). Gelman (1972) referred to knowledge about transformations as *operators,* and I follow that convention. Klahr proposes that children can store in a "time line" sequences of states and transformations. Generalization from these stored data allows the forming of "common consistent sequences." Klahr proposes a mechanism of "redundancy elimination" that increases the efficiency of the system by eliminating unnecessary steps. For example, quantification before and after a quantity-preserving transformation always leads to the same quantity, and hence the second quantification can be eliminated. This presentation is far too brief to capture the refinement of Klahr's current formulation, but it does capture the part most relevant to this chapter: It is a model that describes learning as based on generalization and redundancy elimination from a sequence of state–transition–state episodes stored in memory.

The presentation in this chapter is particularly close to Klahr's model with respect to the focus on state–transition–state episodes—that is, quantification of absolute or relative numerosity—number changing or preserving transformation—re-quantification. It deviates most from Klahr's model with respect to the role of the child's current level of understanding in determining what can be learned from such episodes. Thus, rather than claiming that Klahr's model is wrong, this deviation is a claim that Klahr's model is incomplete or under-emphasizes certain important features of development. In addition, however, this chapter claims that Klahr's focus on redundancy elimination and efficiency is incorrect as the local goal governing the course of development. Rather, I argue, it is the detecting of consistent interrelationships between states and transitions that is the goal. Knowing the interrelationships allows for efficient use of skills but in a much more flexible way than Klahr's mechanism.

The first section of this chapter characterizes what is currently known about the development of number concepts during the first $1\frac{1}{2}$ years of life. The process of change proposed to account for these early acquisitions is the same that is used to account for more advanced developments described later in this chapter. Two central claims are made in this section. The first is that infants' abilities to perceive small numerosities gives them only cardinal information, and the use of this information is initially limited to discriminations of "same" or "different" numerosity. The second is that the ordinal organization of numerosities is dis-covered by observing the transition rules among numerosities as a function of additions and subtractions. The information in this section is directly related to the chapter by Strauss and Curtis in this volume.

The second and third sections of this chapter describe the results of recent studies concerning knowledge of the effects of additions and subtractions on the relative numerosity of two arrays. The course of development is described in terms of a developmental sequence of rules for predicting the effects of additions and subtractions. The process of development is characterized in terms of a "bootstrap" operation involving changes in quantification (how relative numer-osity is represented) and operator knowledge. The third section demonstrates that even when initial and final states are accurately represented and the transforma-tion reliably coded, the underlying regularity may not be discovered. This dem-onstration is used to argue for the role of the child's current understanding of a problem in directing the course of development—that is, that the child is an active constructor of knowledge.

The fourth section of the chapter presents data on children's abilities to infer intervening transformations when they have been given information about initial and final numerosities. Although this appears to be merely the other side of the abilities presented in sections two and three, the developmental course is some-what different. The difference in patterns of development for small- and large-numerosity tasks is particularly informative on this point. It is argued that the difference provides support for the "time-line" concept in Klahr's theory, al-though the acquisition of inference per se requires a modification of the control mechanism of the theory.

The last section of the chapter reviews and expands the general themes that have appeared throughout the previous four sections. The emphasis is on transi-tions in number development. These transitions are discussed in terms of what children know about numerosity, relationships among numerosities, and the effects of additions and subtractions on numerosity. The differences in performance produced by the use of small (one to four) versus large (greater than four) numerosities are used to illustrate the impact of type of numeric representation. In summary, it is argued that with development children's underlying concepts of number change, not just their skills for using number; that these changes are the result of an active, complex, concept-driven process; and that incrementing and decrementing operations play an important role in this process.

DETECTION BY INFANTS OF NUMERICAL INFORMATION

There is a growing body of evidence that demonstrates that infants can detect and use some numerical information about small numerosities (e.g., Starkey & Cooper, 1980; Strauss & Curtis, 1981). Recently it has been demonstrated that some of these abilities are present in very young infants (Antell & Keating, 1983). In another chapter in this book Strauss and Curtis describe a substantial body of research that explores infant number skills and how they change during the first 2 years of life. Some of our own work is directed toward similar questions. In particular, we have been asking questions such as, "Do infants detect the relative numerosity relationships between two arrays?" Habituation studies of infant number-detection skills have been successful because infants can notice when a currently presented array differs in numerosity from those presented earlier. However, we are now investigating what infants understand about equality and inequality independent of particular numerosity.

In this chapter the mechanism that extracts numerosity information is described as a *numerosity detector* although this detection is not meant to be attributed to some low-level process. In this section of the chapter it is argued that we do know some of the characteristics of the process, such as what the process is *not* (e.g., conventional counting, perception of canonical forms), and that the process extracts only some limited numerical information. Further, the characteristics of the process make it reasonable to refer to it as *subitizing* because, as is the case for adult subitizing, the numerosity range is limited and the process is relatively rapid. However, we do not know what the process is. Detector is meant to be a neutral term, referring to the mechanism that performs this process.

Rapid Numerosity Perception

Our recent infant number studies use a modification of the habituation procedures we have used in the past. The details of our former procedure are discussed by Strauss and Curtis in this volume. In our current procedure, two arrays are presented sequentially, and the measure of interest is looking time to

TABLE 7.1
Two-Array Infant Subitizing Experiment: Design
and Mean Looking Time

Condition	Numerosity of Array 1	Numerosity of Array 2	Looking Time in Seconds
Numerosity = 3			
Habituation	3	3	3.43
Test	3	3	3.67
	2	3	4.59
	3	2	5.23
	2	2	5.17
Numerosity = 2			
Habituation	2	2	2.13
Test	3	3	6.14
	2	3	4.34
	3	2	3.29
	2	2	2.47

the second array. The arrays consist of linear displays of colored squares that differ in size and spatial arrangement between the first and second arrays, and from trial to trial. As in the past, we present the habituation trials until a criterion is met: a decrease of 50% in looking time averaged over three successive trials. When the criterion is met, the test trials are presented.

This procedure can be illustrated with a study that was designed to determine if infant numerosity detection is a rapidly acting process like adult subitizing. During habituation the first and second arrays had the same numerosity, two or three. Size and linear interobject distance varied from trial to trial, but numerosity did not. The first array was presented for 700 msec, and the second array until the infant looked away. After the habituation criterion was met, the test trials were given. These involved changing the first array, the second array, changing both, or changing neither. A summary of the data is presented in Table 7.1. The important result, from our point of view, is that changing only the first array (the 700-msec array) led to an increase in looking time relative to no change. This discrimination demonstrates that infants can perceive the numerosity of briefly presented arrays. This is consistent with our finding that 3-year-olds are as accurate detecting two and three with 200-msec exposures as with unlimited exposure (Cooper & Starkey, 1977).

These results are inconsistent with the model of adult subitizing advanced by Mandler and Shebo (1982), which proposes, "a response to arrays of 1 to 3 that is fast and accurate and is based on acquired canonical patterns [p. 1]." Canonical patterns cannot be the basis fo the infants' success because all the arrays are linear. In addition, the performance that we have observed in adults with linear arrays for numerosities up to four reveals flat RTs that provide a further challenge to theories based on learned canonical patterns. Because Antell and Keating (1983) have demonstrated numerosity perception in very young infants, and because this study demonstrates that it occurs rapidly for linear arrays with somewhat older infants, it seems safe to conclude that it is not based on learned canonical patterns.

Equality and Inequality Relationships

In our current studies we have been varying the relationship between the first and second array to look at what might be more advanced number skills in infants. The types of relationships used are illustrated in Table 7.2. In this work we have been addressing many of the same questions as Curtis and Strauss (1983)—for example, questions about infants' understanding of cardinal and ordinal properties of number. In one experiment, we have presented habituation trials in which

TABLE 7.2
Design for Experiment on Infants' Perceptions of
Relative Numerosity

Condition	Numerosity of Array 1	Numerosity of Array 2	Trial Type
Less than			
Habituation	3	4	
	2	4	
	1	2	
Test	3	4	Old
	2	3	New
	4	3	Reversed
	2	2	Equal
Greater than			
Habituation	4	2	
	4	3	
	2	1	
Test	4	3	Old
	3	2	New
	3	4	Reversed
	2	2	Equal
Equal			
Habituation	4	4	
	2	2	
	1	1	
Test	4	4	Old
	3	3	New
	2	4	Less than
	4	2	Greater than

the numerosity of the first array is always less than the numerosity of the second array, as is illustrated in the top third of Table 7.2. Then, for the test trials we present: (1) a trial that was actually part of the habituation series; (2) a novel trial with the same relationship—for example, first array less than second; (3) a novel trial with the relationship reversed—for example, first array greater than second; and (4) a novel trial in which the two arrays are equal. Alternatively, we have presented greater-than relationships, as illustrated in the middle section of Table 7.2. Our results with 14- to 16-month-old infants are consistent with those of Strauss and Curtis (Curtis & Strauss, 1983; Strauss & Curtis, this volume); these infants do seem to detect and remember less-than and greater-than relationships. The 10- to 12-month-old group shows a different pattern. During the test trials they only increase their looking time on the trials in which the two arrays are equal. It is as if they code the relationship as "different than" for both less-than and greater-than conditions.

In a similar study, we presented two arrays that were equal on each trial and varied the numerosity and spatial arrangement from trial to trial. Test trials included old and new equality trials, and less-than and greater-than inequality trials. The type of stimuli used in this experiment are illustrated at the bottom of Table 7.2. Ten- to 12-month-olds increased their looking time to both less-than and greater-than test trials, indicating that they discriminated inequality from equality. Six- to 7-month-olds were slow to habituate and did not show a consistent pattern of dishabituation.

Thus, the data that we have gathered, like those of Curtis and Strauss, suggest either that young infants do not "know" that one is less than two is less than three, and so on, or that they do not make use of this information. Further, the earlier emergence of use of numerosity-independent "equality" relations suggests that the subitizing states are initially unordered. We infer this because infants' competence with the equality relationship shows that they can make use of this relative numerosity relationship by 12 months of age. Thus, the difficulty of 12-month-olds is not with relative numerosity per se, but rather with failing to detect as different less-than and greater-than relationships. From this it is reasonable to conclude that subitizing is not the product of a serial enumerative process of the sort that constitutes conventional counting. The process of putting objects, events, or sounds in one-to-one correspondence with an ordered list or set of states inherently provides an ordered set of number states. Although infants do not have access to such an ordered set of states, this does not preclude a serial enumerative process as the basis for numerosity detection by infants, but if that is the process it must be one of which the infant has no direct cognitive knowledge.

This provides us with two alternatives in trying to understand the development that allows infants to make use of less-than and greater-than relationships. One is that we must propose a mechanism by which infants order the previously unordered subitized states. The other is that we must propose a mechanism by which infants become aware of or at least able to use the information implicit in their subitizing process.

Ordering Numerosity Detectors

The hypothesis proposed here is that infants learn the order of subitized states. As becomes clear in this chapter, this alternative was chosen in part because it is consistent with the type of numerical development that we believe occurs later in development. However, it is also consistent with our data on adult subitizing, which show that numerosity detection for small numerosity is a parallel, not serial, process. Because our recent studies show that infant numerosity detection has many of the properties of adult subitizing, we suspect that the infant process is also parallel.

The situation that we believe is crucial for infants' learning to order the outputs of numerosity detectors that constitute subitizing is the act of incrementing (adding to) and decrementing (taking from) sets of objects. The knowledge that we propose the infant has initially is the ability to detect numerosity and to classify transformations as either incrementing, decrementing, or other—that is, to code initial state, transformation, and final state. With this starting point we propose that infants learn to order their numerosity detectors and acquire some understanding of equality and inequality relations.

First, note that incrementing transforms arrays such that numerosity detectors are activated in sequence—for example, one is transformed into two, is transformed into three. Likewise, decrementing transforms in the opposite direction, three into two into one. However, the infant may not keep these two alternatives separate. Both incrementing and decrementing may be first classified simply as number changing. If this were the case, then we might expect infants to be able to conceive of equality relations as our 10- to 12-month-old infants were before they could conceive of the two inequality relations, for which neither our study nor that of Curtis and Strauss (1983) found evidence in 12-month-olds.

Before going on to discuss inequality relations, it is instructive to ask why 6- to 7-month-old infants were not able to make use of numerosity-independent equality relations. The past work on infant numerosity perception demonstrates that young infants respond implicitly to equality—that is, they habituate as long as numerosity remains the same and dishabituate when it changes (e.g., Starkey & Cooper, 1980), or in cross-modal studies they prefer to look at arrays that have the same numerosity as a sequence of clicks they have just heard (Starkey, Spelke, & Gelman, 1982). If they can detect equality, why do they not use it as the invariant in our studies—that is, if they know that $1 = 1$, $2 = 2$, and $3 = 3$, why do they not know that 1 is to 1 as 2 is to 2 as 3 is to 3? The explanation proposed here is that the invariant must have some meaning before infants seek to investigate the world with respect to it. This point is not new; it might be rephrased as the claim that children are active in directing their development or in terms of development being goal directed.

The goal-directed component in development can perhaps be best illustrated by analogy. When were the observation skills developed that allowed humans to discover that dropped objects fall at the same rate independent of weight? Alternatively, how many college students know where the sun is when the full moon is rising? This knowledge is quite rare. Further, knowledge of these two easily observed phenomena is highly correlated with knowledge of the relevant principles. It is not being suggested that knowledge of the principles is required prior to the observations. On the contrary, I believe in Klahr's proposal that the principles are discovered. However, I want to reemphasize the long-standing notion that, in general, new principles are discovered when they fit into some prior system of understanding. More explicitly, I would argue that they are differentiated from past knowledge. Thus, I would argue that we will understand the nature of number development by understanding how new knowledge is differentiated from past knowledge.

Applying this argument to infant number development, we might ask, "Given unordered subitized states, what is the next step that would add an interesting (from the infant's point of view) capability to the system?" There seem to be two plausible steps that might occur early in infant number development. The first is that infants would come to realize that oneness and twoness are information about the same kind of thing. Using the spatial analogy again, infants discover that one, two, and three are part of the same space because moves can be made among them by additions and subtractions. It is by virtue of addition and subtraction transformations that infants acquire the concept of numerosity. Thus, the relationship of one and one, or three and three, become relationships of the same type, equality of number, and are not like other kinds of equality relationships—for example, blue and blue.

The second step is that by observing the effects of additions and subtractions, infants might come to recognize not only that oneness and twoness are related to one another, but also that they can be ordered. Older infants can detect inequality relations and make use of them, as was shown in Curtis and Strauss' experiment to choose the greater (or lesser) of two arrays, and in our experiment to dishabituate when a less-than relation is changed to a greater-than relation, or vice versa. We would argue that these capabilities depend on ordered subitized states, and that this ordering depends on experience with the effects of incrementing or decrementing transformations on subitized states. This is different from the hypothesis proposed by Strauss and Curtis in this volume. They propose that infants learn about numerical inequality relationships by generalization from inequality relationships among "more perceptual" dimensions like length. This proposal is quite similar to that offered by Brainerd (1979). There are basic differences in theoretical orientation underlying this position and the one proposed in this chapter, but the current data do not discriminate between them. Without exploring these differences, it can still be argued that an advantage of the mechanism proposed here is that it accounts for several other features of early number development in addition to the acquisition of relative numerosity—for example, "counting-on" solutions to addition and "counting-off" solutions to subtraction problems.

Thus, it is argued here that to some degree young infants treat cardinal numerosity as an independent characteristic of stimuli. Changing cardinality by incrementing or decrementing transformations provides the experience that "tells" infants that twoness (the type of information provided by their "two detector") is related to threeness (the type of information provided by their "three detector"). This provides the basis for generalizing the concept "equality of number" from one small numerosity to another. It also provides the basis for ordering the subitized states. Having ordered subitized states then provides the basis for understanding inequality relations.

The failure of 6- and 7-month-olds to make use of a general equality relation can be analyzed within this framework. From the child's perspective, there are numerous relationships that might be attended to in this experiment, including those having to do with size, color, and spatial arrangement. The procedure is designed to focus the child on equality of numerosity as the invariant across trials. However, to detect this invariant the child must consider "2 = 2" to be the same kind of equality relationship as "3 = 3," and different from "blue = blue" or "big = big." If our previous analysis of subitizing as a set of independent numerosity detectors is correct, then learning will need to occur before this generalized notion of numerical equality (at least generalized within the subitizing range) can take place. Once again the kind of experience that informs the child that twoness and threeness can be considered as the same class of information is the experience provided by addition and subtraction operations that map one into the other.

In summary, then, what is proposed in this part of the chapter is that infant subitizing initially functions as a set of independent numerosity detectors, and that the process of organizing the detectors is accomplished by observing the effects of additions and subtractions. This leads to ordering of the subitized states, the concept of numerosity-independent equality of number, and the concept of inequality of number. It is the relationship between the numerosity detector states and the effects of addition and subtraction that give rise to the notions of more and less. From the child's point of view "more" is invented in this process. It is not an independent concept that a child learns to apply to numerosity; it is a property that emerges from the interrelationship of numerosity and addition/subtraction. Thus, at the end of this process the child has the knowledge that adding makes more and subtracting makes less. This knowledge of addition/subtraction is what we have characterized as the primitive level and is the starting point for the number-development phenomena considered in the next section.

ADDITION/SUBTRACTION

This section of the chapter first briefly reviews the major results from a number of our studies on preschool children's understanding of the effect of addition and subtraction. Then, one recent study is described in detail to highlight certain features of the developmental course of informal addition/subtraction knowledge. Several general claims are made based on the studies reviewed: (1) there is a reliable developmental sequence in acquiring an understanding of addition and subtraction during the preschool years; (2) this sequence can be described as a sequence of rules for predicting the effects of additions and subtractions on the relative numerosity of two arrays; (3) each new rule makes use of and elaborates the previous rule; (4) in part, the development of new rules depends on discovering the limitations of current rules; (5) the development also depends on increasingly elaborate quantification of relative numerosity.

The basis for much of the work discussed in this section can be traced to a study by Brush (1972, 1978) demonstrating that some preschool children will assert that an array that has had an object added to it has more than another array even if the incremented array has many fewer objects. Thus, Brush's young preschoolers seem to be using the knowledge of the effect of incrementing and decrementing that we just discussed for infants—for example, that adding to an array increases its numerosity. However, the effect of adding or subtracting on the relative numerosity of two arrays is a much more complex question. If two arrays are initially equal, then adding to one makes it have more or subtracting makes it have less. However, if they are unequal, adding one to the smaller may still leave it the smaller or may make the two arrays equal, but it never makes the smaller array into the larger one.

We now examine the results from several studies that assess children's growing understanding of this kind of transformation. In all of these studies children viewed two arrays of objects constructed in one-to-one correspondence. Objects were added to one of the arrays if the initial numerosities were to be unequal. Then one or more objects were added to one of the arrays, and the children were questioned about the relative numerosity of the two arrays. These experiments have provided substantial support for a four-step sequence in children's understanding of addition/subtraction: primitive, qualitative, superqualitative, and quantitative. As illustrated in Table 7.3, these steps differ with respect to the rules children use to interpret the effects of addition or subtraction on relative numerosity.

TABLE 7.3
Trial Type and Pattern of Performance for Addition/Subtraction
Experiments

Trial Type	Predicted Performance[a]			
	Primitive	Qualitative	Superqualitative	Quantitative
Initially Equal				
$\begin{array}{cc} n & n \\ & +1 \\ \hline n & n+1 \end{array}$	more (C)	more (C)	more (C)	more (C)
$\begin{array}{cc} & +1 \\ \hline n & n+2 \end{array}$	more (C)	more (C)	more (C)	more (C)
$\begin{array}{cc} n & n \\ & -1 \\ \hline n & n-1 \end{array}$	less (C)	less (C)	less (C)	less (C)
$\begin{array}{cc} & -1 \\ \hline n & n-1 \end{array}$	less (C)	less (C)	less (C)	less (C)
Differ by 1				
$\begin{array}{cc} n & n-1 \\ & +1 \\ \hline n & n \end{array}$	more (I)	equal (C)	equal (C)	equal (C)
$\begin{array}{cc} & +1 \\ \hline n & n+1 \end{array}$	more (C)	more (C)	more (C)	more (C)
$\begin{array}{cc} n & n+1 \\ & -1 \\ \hline n & n \end{array}$	less (I)	equal (C)	equal (C)	equal (C)
$\begin{array}{cc} & -1 \\ \hline n & n-1 \end{array}$	less (C)	less (C)	less (C)	less (C)
Differ by 2				
$\begin{array}{cc} n & n-2 \\ & +1 \\ \hline n & n-1 \end{array}$	more (I)	equal (I)	less (C)	less (C)
$\begin{array}{cc} & +1 \\ \hline n & n \end{array}$	more (I)	more (I)	equal (C)	equal (C)
$\begin{array}{cc} n & n+2 \\ & -1 \\ \hline n & n+1 \end{array}$	less (I)	equal (I)	more (C)	more (C)
$\begin{array}{cc} & -1 \\ \hline n & n \end{array}$	less (I)	less (I)	equal (C)	equal (C)
Differ by 3				
$\begin{array}{cc} n & n-3 \\ & +1 \\ \hline n & n-2 \end{array}$	more (I)	equal (I)	less (C)	less (C)
$\begin{array}{cc} & +1 \\ \hline n & n-1 \end{array}$	more (I)	more (I)	equal (I)	less (C)

TABLE 7.3 *(Continued)*

	Predicted Performance[a]			
Trial Type	*Primitive*	*Qualitative*	*Superqualitative*	*Quantitative*
$\begin{array}{cc} n & n+3 \\ & -1 \\ \hline n & n+2 \end{array}$	<u>less</u> *(I)*	<u>equal</u> *(I)*	more *(C)*	more *(C)*
$\begin{array}{cc} & -1 \\ \hline n & n+1 \end{array}$	<u>less</u> *(I)*	<u>less</u> *(I)*	<u>equal</u> *(I)*	more *(C)*

[a]Note: Predicted responses are for the transformed array. Correct responses are indicated by *(C)* and incorrect responses are indicated by *(I)* and are underlined.

The four rules illustrated in Table 7.3 can be more explicitly described with a decision tree. Such descriptions are provided for each of the four rules in Figs. 7.1 to 7.4. The role ascribed to these decision trees is limited; for each rule the final node reached in the decision tree is the same as the judgment reached by a child using that rule. The claim is not that the process used by children corresponds to the sequence of decisions in the decision tree. However, later in the chapter it is argued that the relationship among these four decision trees illustrates two important characteristics to be accounted for in a developmental model. For the present they are used only to clarify each of the four rules as they are described.

Primitive understanding does not differentiate "more than before" from "more than the other." The child asserts that an array added to has more, or one

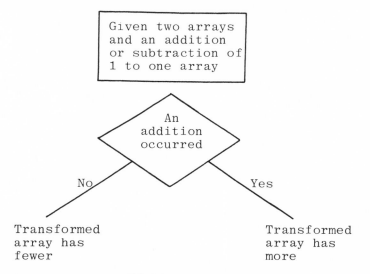

FIG. 7.1. Primitive Rule.

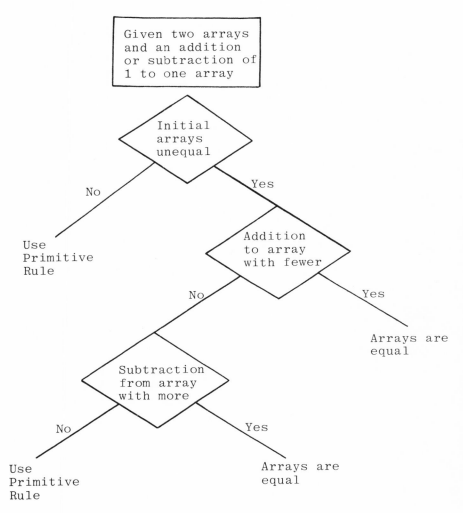

FIG. 7.2. Qualitative Rule.

subtracted from has less. Thus the primitive level includes no understanding that initial relative numerosity is an important consideration in predicting the effect of a transformation. As illustrated in Fig. 7.1, the primitive rule only leads to correct predictions when the initial arrays are equal.

Qualitative understanding makes the differentiation between "more than before" and "more than another." As is illustrated in Fig. 7.2, the qualitative rule differs from the primitive rule because it takes into account initial relative numerosity, but does not quantify differences. One array is coded as being less than, equal to, or greater than another. An addition changes a less-than relationship to equal regardless of the initial differences. Likewise, a subtraction changes a greater-than relationship into equal. If the initial numerosities are equal, then, just as for the primitive level, an addition is interpreted as making the array added to have more, and a subtraction as making the array have less. Thus at this level children's judgments are correct if the initial arrays are equal or differ by one.

Superqualitative understanding entails further progress in making use of relative numerosity, but still does not fully quantify it. At this level the child differentiates between differences of one and greater than one, but fails to quan-

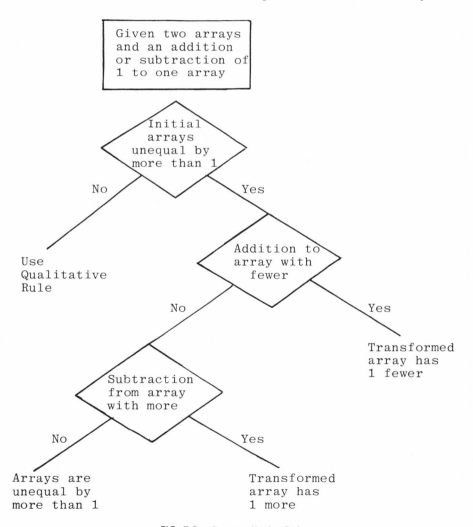

FIG. 7.3. Superqualitative Rule.

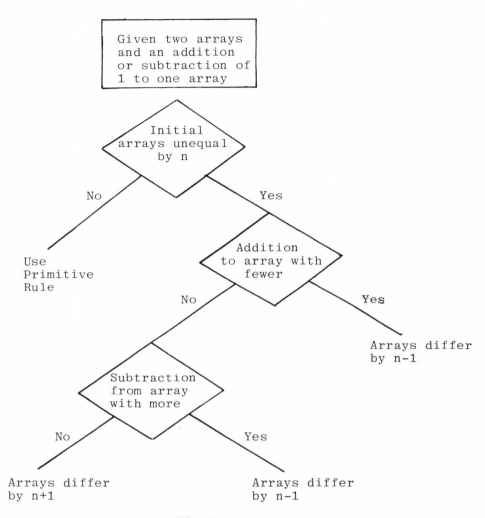

FIG. 7.4. Quantitative rule.

tify these greater differences. In one of our experiments a child who solved problems with the superqualitative rule labeled arrays with one more as having the "most" and arrays with more than one more as having the "mostest." The children using the superqualitative rule are limited to a five-category system for coding relative numerosity: much less than, less than, equal to, greater than, and much greater than. In general, additions of one move the child's judgment through the sequence so that, after four additions, an array that was initially judged to be much less than another would then be judged as much greater. The important addition to the qualitative rule that is apparent in the decision tree for the superqualitative rule (Fig. 7.3) is the decision that differentiates between arrays that differ by one and arrays that differ by more than one. An exception to the general rule occurs if the arrays differ greatly in numerosity. If, after an addition, the array added to is still clearly much less than the other, the second addition will not lead to a judgment of equality. (This is an example of a quantifier rather than operator solution.) Despite this more sensible integration of quantifier information at the superqualitative level, it is still the case that the child's understanding of addition and subtraction only provides correct "operator" solutions when the initial arrays are equal or differ by one or two.

Finally, *quantitative* understanding involves quantifying the initial differences between arrays and quantifying the amount added (for example, by counting on solutions) to arrive at fully accurate performance. An examination of the decision tree for the quantitative rule in Fig. 7.4 reveals that it differs from the superquantitative rule in the type of quantification used for relative numerosity.

Summary of Past Addition/Subtraction Results

Five experiments, with children from the age of 2 to 7 years, have been conducted with the types of problems listed in Table 7.3. For illustrative purposes Table 7.4 summarizes data across these studies. Two patterns are of particular importance for this chapter. The first is the general pattern of developmental change in understanding addition and subtraction for large numerosities. Two-

TABLE 7.4
Percentage of Children at Each Level of Addition/Subtraction
Understanding for Small and Large Numerosities

Age	Small-Numerosity Tasks				Large-Numerosity Tasks			
	PR	QL	SQL	QN[a]	PR	QL	SQL	QN
2-year-olds (n = 16)	68.8	18.7	—	—	62.5	12.5	—	—
3-year-olds (n = 18)	16.7	22.2	5.6	55.5	22.2	55.5	11.1	0.0
4-year-olds (n = 30)	12.8	16.2	6.4	61.3	36.6	56.7	0.0	0.0
5-year-olds (n = 40)	2.5	5.0	2.5	87.5	15.0	25.0	10.0	50.0
6-year-olds (n = 53)	0.0	0.0	0.0	100.0	17.0	13.2	13.2	56.6
7-year-olds (n = 14)	0.0	0.0	0.0	100.0	7.2	14.2	7.2	71.4

[a]Note: PR is primitive, QL is qualitative, SQL is superqualitative, and QN is quantitative. When the percentages do not add up to 100% it is because some children could not be classified at a single level. No superqualitative or quantitative trials were given to 2-year-olds.

year-olds are primarily at the primitive level, 3- and 4-year-olds at the qualitative level, and 7-year-olds primarily at the quantitative level, indicating an orderly improvement with age. The second important pattern is the strikingly better performance on small-numerosity tasks. This could be explained in one of two ways: Either the stage of development is more advanced for small number or the children are employing a quantifier solution for these problems.

The problem of quantifier solutions to addition/subtraction problems parallels the problem of such solutions to conservation problems (see Cowan, 1979; Klahr, 1983; Siegler, 1981). Young children show superior performance for small-numerosity number-conservation tasks, and the numerosities for which they succeed increase during the preschool years (e.g., Cooper, Starkey, Blevins, Goth, & Leitner, 1978). It has been shown that when children can give correct explanations the numerosity effect goes away—that is, explicit knowledge of the conservation principle eliminates the numerosity effect (Starkey & Cooper, 1977; Tollefsrud, 1981). In a set of unpublished studies (Tollefsrud, Campbell, Starkey, & Cooper, in preparation) it has been demonstrated that children who perform better on conservation tasks with small numerosity than large have longer response times for correct responses with large numerosities and are likely to show some overt quantification behaviors. From these data one can conclude that conservation problems are initially solved using quantifiers, and that operator solutions develop later.

For addition/subtraction problems we have also tried to establish the basis for precocious performance on small-numerosity problems. Two types of evidence suggest that superior performance for these problems is also based on quantifier solutions. First, we conducted an experiment in which the arrays were not visible after the addition or subtraction. Performance on small-numerosity trials was much poorer than when the final arrays were visible and was indistinguishable from that on the large-numerosity trials. In particular, children predominantly responded to all problems using the primitive rule. Second, when larger-numerosity arrays were constructed so as to be difficult to count, performance declined on qualitative and quantitative problems for those children just beginning to show some success with this type of larger-numerosity task. Both of these findings suggest that early success with small-numerosity addition/subtraction problems and initial success on larger-numerosity problems are based on quantifier solutions except for those problems that can be solved using the primitive rule.

Superqualitative Experiment

We have recently conducted an experiment with a group of kindergarten children to observe the transition from the qualitative to quantitative approach to interpreting the effects of additions and subtractions on relative numerosity. The experiment was a short-term longitudinal study in which repeated assessments of addition/subtraction were conducted over a 9-month period.

The subjects were a group of 12 boys and 12 girls selected from a group of 85 kindergarten children. The selection was based on performance on qualitative, superqualitative, and quantitative large-numerosity addition and subtraction problems. Initial selection was based on 75% or greater success on problems requiring at least qualitative knowledge, and 25% performance or poorer on problems requiring superqualitative or quantitative knowledge. Thirty-seven children met these criteria, and 31 of these continued to do so on a retest 2 weeks later. From this group, 12 children of each gender were chosen at random.

At the beginning of the study all the children were tested to see if they could accurately count randomly arrayed sets of objects containing six, seven, nine, and 10 objects. All but one of the children were correct on three of the four arrays; this child made mistakes on seven and nine. In addition all the children were given a conservation of equality and a conservation of inequality task (see Cooper, Campbell, & Blevins, 1983, for details of these tasks). Seven of the children passed a judgment-only criterion, and two passed with correct explanation. Finally, every child was given a six-trial addition/subtraction assessment at intervals averaging every 3 weeks for a period of 7 months.

The trials used for assessment of level of addition/subtraction understanding are illustrated in Table 7.5. The size and color of the objects in the arrays and the numerosities of the arrays varied from trial to trial and from assessment to assessment; however, the n indicating numerosity in the table was always in the range six to 10. Trial type 1 can be solved correctly with a qualitative approach, trial types 2 and 4 require at least a superqualitative approach for correct solution, and trial types 3 and 5 require a quantitative approach. Trial type 6 can be solved either by using a quantitative approach or by ignoring the "operator" solution and using a "quantifier" solution in its place.

TABLE 7.5
Trials for Longitudinal Study of the Qualitative to Quantitative
Transition in Addition/Subtraction Knowledge

Trial Type	Initial Array	Transformations and Resulting Arrays					
		1		2		3	
1	n	$+1$	$n+1$	$+1$	$n+2$	$+1$	$n+3$
	$n+1$		$n+1$		$n+1$		$n+1$
2	n	$+1$	$n+1$	$+1$	$n+2$	$+1$	$n+3$
	$n+2$		$n+2$		$n+2$		$n+2$
3	n	$+1$	$n+1$	$+1$	$n+2$	$+1$	$n+3$
	$n+3$		$n+3$		$n+3$		$n+3$
4	n		n		n		n
	$n+2$	-1	$n+1$	-1	n	-1	$n-1$
5	n		n		n		n
	$n+3$	-1	$n+2$	-1	$n+1$	-1	n
6	n	$+1$	$n+1$	$+1$	$n+2$	$+1$	$n+3$
	$n+10$		$n+10$		$n+10$		$n+10$

Of the 24 children, 17 were classified as quantitative by the end of the study, and two as superqualitative. Of the 17 who became quantitative, 10 were never classified as superqualitative: Either they went through that type of solution very rapidly, or they never employed the superqualitative solution strategy. Of the seven who were at least once classified as superqualitative and who reached the quantitative level, the average amount of time at the superqualitative level was 8.3 weeks. Because this average excludes the two children who did not attain the quantitative step, this average may underestimate the length of time that children who acquire the superqualitative rule usually employ it. Further, our repeated testing may have sped development. Therefore, using our data to make strong claims about rate of progress from one level to another is probably inappropriate. However, of the children detected as using superqualitative reasoning, only one was measured fewer than three successive times at this level, and she was measured at this level for two successive times. Thus, it seems safe to assume that the children who were never measured to be at the superqualitative level never use this type of solution.

These results demonstrate an interesting variation in the pattern of development of intuitive addition/subtraction knowledge, with some children going through the superqualitative level and others not. They are important for two reasons. First, they add further support to the notion that children initially code the difference in numerosity between arrays in a qualitative way. Second, the superqualitative rule is apparently not a very stable solution. For children who use it, one can predict that they will acquire the quantitative rule relatively quickly.

Why is the superqualitative rule a relatively unstable solution to these problems? In answering this question it is interesting to note that children operating at this level do not use it exclusively. For example, for trial type 6 they abandon the operator solution for a quantifier solution—that is, they requantify after the transformation using an approximate quantifier (not counting or subitizing). Thus, they are potentially confronted with the fact that they are using a system that does not always work. Second, note that implicit in the superqualitative level is a consideration of the amount that one array is more or less than another—for example, "much more" versus "one more." One could imagine a more elaborate system going from "much much less," through "much less," and so on, to "much much more." Although we have no reason to suspect this kind of coding on our task by young children, there are situations in which adults use this kind of elaborate qualitative scale for coding differences when they lack specific quantitative information about magnitude of difference. The situations in which adults use these kinds of coding schemes suggest a possible reason for children's using them: lack of information about the absolute magnitude of the difference between two arrays. In the experimental task, the children have a procedure for quantifying the difference between the two arrays, counting the number of objects added to one array that are not matched by objects being added to the other array. Why do children at the qualitative level not use this strategy? Alternatively, why do they not weigh them? Most children and adults would not weigh the arrays because the information gained is not relevant to the task. Children do not quantify the difference between the two arrays for one of two reasons: Either they do not know that the information is relevant or, if they do, they do not know how to use it. In either case the children do not have solutions that involve quantifying the difference between the two arrays.

How do children come to use these procedures at the quantitative level? For the moment we assume the competence of the qualitative level; the children have discovered that initial relative numerosity is relevant to predictions about the impact of additions or subtractions on relative numerosity. Gelman (1977) reports that when preschool children are returning a small-numerosity array to its previous numerosity after a surreptitious subtraction, if the difference is one they directly add one back. If the difference is more than one, then they are unsure exactly how many to add back. So in Gelman's research we see early emergence of the superqualitative approach for small number using only one array. This appears to be a reasonable extension of a capacity we have already attributed to infants, the knowledge that an addition or subtraction changes an array to the next higher or lower integer numerosity. We can now imagine preschool children learning the same thing about relative numerosity between two arrays; if they differ by just one, they can be made equal by adding one to the lesser.

What is particularly significant for our purposes is how rapidly movement to the quantitative level follows the superqualitative level, and that this is apparently not the only route to the quantitative level. In this light it is interesting that having attained the qualitative level seems to be necessary for large-number conservation, and that the quantitative level is sufficient. What we would like to suggest occurs is that the children discover point prediction with respect to additions or subtractions of other than one. These might be additions of two or three, or they might be additions of zero, the prototypic conservation problem. Our investigation of the superqualitative level gives us a glimpse of part of this development from qualitative to quantitative coding of differences.

Conclusions from Addition/Subtraction Studies

In this section several studies are summarized that document a systematic pattern of development in preschoolers' understanding of the effects of additions and subtractions on the relative numerosity of two arrays. Just as development in infancy was described as learning about movement in the space of small numerosities as a function of additions and subtractions, the development described in this section can be conceived of as learning about movement in the space of relative numerosity as a function of additions and subtractions. This learning involves detecting the relationship between a start point (initial relative numerosity), a transformation (addition or subtraction), and an end point (final relative numerosity). Given this model of learning, why do preschoolers not immediately arrive at the quantitative rule that would assure correct responding? The answer seems to be that at first they do not use the correct information about relative numerosity in the initial and final states. To clarify how this changes, the course of development from primitive to quantitative understanding is reviewed.

The primitive rule ignores initial numerosity and predicts final numerosity based on the transformation that occurs. This rule provides correct answers only when the initial numerosities are equal. For small numerosities children do not need the rule, because quantifier solutions are just as rapid, so it is unlikely that children discover the failure of the rule using quantification by subitizing. As children begin to quantify larger numerosities (e.g., by counting), they acquire new information about a range of numerosities to which they have been applying the primitive rule, and hence acquire information about its limitations. The qualitative rule takes this into consideration. As illustrated in Fig. 7.2, a test is made to see if the conditions that make the primitive rule accurate obtain (initial equality). If they do not, then a new basis for judgment is executed. However, the newly constructed part of the qualitative rule may be limited for two reasons. First, the system that has been used for coding relative numerosity is only a three-state qualitative system. Second, if they make use of the small-numerosity range in which subitizing works, the three-state qualitative rule usually works within such a restricted range.

The move from the qualitative rule to the superqualitative rule can be viewed in the same way: determining the conditions under which the rule is correct, and constructing a new rule for the conditions in which the qualitative rule leads to errors. Part of the change in coding relative numerosity in the superqualitative rule may be supported by the increase in the subitizing range that occurs in the later preschool years (Cooper & Starkey, 1977). The move to the quantitative rule provides a further elaboration of the process just outlined.

In this developmental process one can see the interweaving of the development of quantifiers and transformation operators. New forms of quantification allow for new operators to be discovered. Uncovering the limitation of an operator leads to new forms of quantifying relative numerosity. Although at the beginning of this section it was asserted that the decision trees used to describe the rules did not model psychological process, an interesting relation among the rules can be discerned by comparing the four Figures. Each more-advanced rule makes some use of previous rules, integrating them into a more complex structure. In addition, the test that is added to construct the more complex structure is an increasingly more complex test about initial relative numerosity. A number of alternative decision-tree models of these rules can be constructed, all of which exhibit these two characteristics. Thus, although the rules themselves do not model psychological process, these two characteristics may be related to the underlying psychological processes.

TRANSFER EXPERIMENT

This section of the chapter focuses on a more difficult type of task that is not usually fully solved until 9 or 10 years of age, but that can be considered an informal concept because the solution is almost never taught to children. In this task the child is presented with two equal numerosity arrays in one-to-one correspondence. One is then screened and one or more objects are transferred from the visible to the screened array. The child's task is then to predict how many objects must be added to the visible array to make it equal to the screened array. Piaget (Piaget, 1974/1980; Piaget, Grize, Szeminska, & Vinh-Bang, 1977) considered this task to be theoretically interesting because the transfer of n objects produces a difference of $2n$ because both a subtraction and an addition of n are being performed by the act of transferring the objects.

This task is relevant to the issues discussed in the previous section because, although it involves a slightly different rule than the ones discussed previously, the task situation is similar. In particular, there is an initial numerosity relationship, a transformation, and a final numerosity relationship. Moreover, the initial numerosities for this task are always equal, so the complexity of the task should be simpler, as was the case for the primitive level of addition/subtraction. For the transfer task this means that the child need only consider the final relative numerosity (i.e., the child does not have to compare initial to final relative numerosity to determine the effect of the transformation). However, in the transfer task the child is asked to quantify the relative numerosity difference produced by the transformation, so some of the skills involved may be the same as those used with the quantitative addition/subtraction rule.

Despite some similarity of this task to primitive addition trials, and the similarity of the skills required for solution to the quantitative rule, Piaget found substantially slower development on this task. He reported that preschool-age children expect the difference to be n. Somewhat older children learn by example that a transfer of one produces a difference of two but they do not generalize this rule to large arrays that they cannot count. By 8 years of age, children correctly predict the difference for all transfers of n objects, and by 9 or 10 they can explain the principle. Our own results (see Table 7.6) have generally been consistent with those of Piaget (Campbell, Cooper, & Blevins, 1983; Cooper et al., 1983). An examination of the pattern of development we have observed provides some support for the position being advanced by Klahr (1983), and again points to some aspects missing in his perspective.

There are two dimensions of expanding understanding in the transfer problem. One is the increase in the numerosities of the arrays to which inferences can be made. Children initially restrict their inferences to numerosities they can count, they then extend them to larger numerosities, and ultimately to more abstract quantities. This type of expansion of understanding can be illustrated by

TABLE 7.6
Proportion Correct on Transfer Task

	Transfer of One		Transfer of Two		
Grade	Prediction	Generalization	Prediction	Generalization	Rule
Preschool	.36	.00	.19	.00	.00
$n = 16$					
Kindergarten	.66	.13	.22	.06	.00
$n = 16$					
First	.53	.20	.47	.21	.13
$n = 37$					
Second	.73	.41	.70	.26	.31
$n = 40$					

a child who first knew that with four objects in each array, a transfer of one required that two objects be added to the lesser array, and then generalized this to arrays of 100 objects, and ultimately to equal arrays of unspecified numerosity (i.e., "a whole bunch"). This type of development is what Klahr (1983) has referred to as "data generalization" and Newman, Reil, and Martin (1982) have labeled as "specific to general," describing the range of application of the knowledge.

The second dimension of development on the transfer problem concerns the completeness of the rule acquired. This is the dimension that Klahr (1983) has called "rule formation" and Newman et al. (1982) have called "concrete to abstract." Children may first be able to respond correctly for transfers of one but not of other numerosities. Later, they may be able to respond correctly for transfer of any specific numerosity with which they have had recent experience. Ultimately, children can respond correctly for transfer of any numerosity because they are using the abstract rule that for a transfer of n objects, the resulting difference will be $2n$.

Our findings with 4- to 8-year-olds illustrate both dimensions of development just described. As is indicated in Table 7.6, two measures of performance were obtained for transfers of one and two. The prediction measure was the proportion of correct responses on two trials for which the numerosity transferred remained the same, and the numerosities of the arrays were small (three or five). For transfers of one and two, children frequently missed the first trial and succeeded on the second. For the generalization measure children were then asked to make the prediction to a larger numerosity. Successful performance on this task would be indicative of "data generalization" in Klahr's terminology. Note that there is improvement with age on this task, but even second graders do not demonstrate high levels of performance. Finally, the children were reminded that transferring one produced a difference of two, and that transferring two produced a difference of four. They were then asked to make a prediction for a transfer of four and to explain why they made that prediction. Successful performance is indicative of what Klahr has called "rule formation" and is tabulated in the last column under "rule." Note that less than a third of the second graders succeeded in this prediction. Further, only two children were able to explain adequately the underlying $2n$ regularity. Interestingly, however, among the inadequate explanations were many that suggested that the difference was $n + 1$ or $n + 2$. Either of these explanations is correct for only 50% of the trials the children experienced.

The performance on this task is substantially poorer for a given age level than the addition/subtraction tasks discussed previously. Why? The answer that the task is harder, which is consistent with most people's intuition, does not suffice; it is just a restatement of the problem. The process of solution development needs to be specified so the locus of difficulty can be identified. First, it is surely the case that quantifying relative numerosity before and after the transformation is relevant to developing solutions on the transfer task. Even the youngest children in the study benefit from this experience. However, generalization to larger numerosities was nonexistent for the preschoolers and quite low even for the first graders. Does generalization of new numerical facts depend on extensive experience, even after simpler operations like those involved in conservation and addition/subtraction have been generalized throughout the range of integers at a much younger age? We think not. Rather, the difficulty on this problem is that the empirical regularity is not only not understood but, if you will, counterintuitive to young children. It is not consistent with their way of thinking about the problem. Given that they do not understand the phenomenon, they have no way to know its limits—that is, the range for which data generalization is appropriate.

The problem that children have in making use of a counterintuitive result is illustrated in a protocol we have translated from a study of Piaget's (Piaget, Kaufmann, & Bourquin, 1977) that involved a task that provides another perspective on children's understanding of addition. In this task a child was asked to construct two arrays by adding chips two at a time to one pile and three at a time to the other. The following protocol is a $5\frac{1}{2}$-year-old who was astonished when she ended up with two equal arrays of six (Piaget et al., 1977):

C: They're both the same!
E: How does that work?
C: I don't know.
E: Could you do it again?
C: No, I don't think so.
E: Let's try (same procedure).
C: Again they're both the same!
E: How did you do that?
C: I counted 6 there and 6 there. (pure imagination!)
E: For your pile, what did you do?
C: I took 2 (at a time).
E: And for mine?

C: I took 3.
E: How many times did you take 3?
C: I don't remember any more.
E: And 2?
C: I don't remember either [p. 33].

The difficulties that children have on the inference task and the similar difficulties just illustrated indicate that tasks need to be analyzed to determine two characteristics: the prerequisite skills required for success, and the task characteristics to which the children must attend to know what part of their past knowledge is relevant to task understanding. Turning first to prerequisite skills, transfer is an addition and subtraction task. The two arrays are equal at the beginning of the task. The removal of an object or objects makes them unequal. The addition of this object or objects to the other array makes the inequality greater. For a transfer of one, a superqualitative level on the addition/subtraction task would be sufficient to code the inequality produced. For the transfer of any numerosity more than one, a quantitative level would be required to keep track of the differences produced. Analyses that have been conducted on the relationship between the two tasks reveal that, in fact, having attained the superqualitative level is necessary for correct performance on generalization of transfer of one— that is, generalizing from transfers of one with small arrays to transfers of one with larger arrays. Further, having attained the quantitative level is necessary for correct performance on transfer of two, and for generalizing to transfers of four (Campbell et al., 1983).

Many children attain the quantitative level of addition/subtraction skill substantially before they succeed on the transfer task. What is it that keeps children from employing these addition/subtraction skills effectively? Piaget (e.g., 1974/1980) has suggested that it is the difficulty of differentiating the transfer into its two components, an addition and subtraction, which from the child's point of view seem to happen at the same time. In fact, the Geneavans describe this as a "double compensation" problem because the subtraction from one array and the addition to the other must both be compensated for to restore the equality relationship. At the present time there is little that we can add to this description of the problem. The incorrect explanations described previously that the difference was $n + 1$ or $n + 2$ are indicative of children's trying to find a pattern in the data. If the data-generalization component of learning to solve the task were just a matter of detecting the change in numerosity and keeping track of the transformation, then it should be easily accomplished with the same skills that support the quantitative level on addition and subtraction problems. However, for addition/subtraction the magnitude of the difference is the same as the number of objects in the transformation. It is the fact that this is not true for the transfer problem that makes the solution counterintuitive to young children.

Although we do not have a solution to the overall problem to propose, we do feel that a simple tabulation of initial state, transformation, and final state implicit in Klahr's model will not suffice. It seems certain that the failure of the initial hypotheses that children generate is important in motivating them to look for alternative rules. The later emergence of explanations suggests that analyzing the problem as including both an addition and a subtraction in a single transformation may occur after the underlying regularity is discovered, which would be consistent with Piaget's later theorizing (1978).

INFERRING ADDITION AND SUBTRACTION TRANSFORMATIONS

The child's developing understanding of the relationship between initial and final numerosity and the intervening transformation can be investigated in ways other than the addition/subtraction tasks discussed in the last two sections. One procedure that we have used over the last several years is to ask the child to infer an intervening operation from information about initial and final numerosity. In one of these experiments (Blevins, Campbell, & Cooper, 1983) the child was presented with two arrays in spatial one-to-one correspondence. The experimenter ascertained that the child correctly identified whether the arrays were equal or unequal. If one of the arrays had more, the experimenter stated how many more it contained. Then both of the arrays were covered. The child was told that something was being done to one group: Either one object was being added, one subtracted, the group was being stretched out, or the group was being pushed together. After the transformation, the arrays were uncovered. The child was told the final relative numerosities by the experimenter, reminded of the initial relative numerosities, and told which array had been transformed. The child was then asked what had been done: addition, subtraction, stretching, or "squashing."

The same system for classifying trials as primitive, qualitative, or quantitative as was used for the addition/subtraction task was employed for this inference experiment. For example, if the initial numerosities were equal and an addition was performed, that trial could be solved at the primitive level. Likewise, if the arrays initially differed by one and an addition was performed to the array with fewer objects, that trial could be solved at the qualitative level. No trials were included to differentiate between superqualitative and quantitative solutions. To keep the present discussion consistent with our previous writing on the topic, trials on which the initial numerosities differed by two are called quantitative. Children's performance was classified as primitive, qualitative, or quantitative according to the highest level for which they answered three out for four trials correctly. If their response did not meet this criterion, no level was assigned.

TABLE 7.7
Distribution of Performance on the Inference Task as a Function of
Numerosity and Grade[a]

Numerosity	Grade			
	Preschool	Kindergarten	First	Second
Small				
None	1	1	0	0
Primitive	2	1	2	0
Qualitative	1	4	10	2
Quantitative	6	9	16	16
Large				
None	2	6	6	1
Primitive	5	1	6	1
Qualitative	1	3	5	4
Quantitative	2	5	10	12

[a]Note: These are the same data as those presented by Blevins, et al. (1983) with data from three additional subjects included.

Developmental Patterns on the Inference Task

The general developmental pattern on the inference task is depicted in Table 7.7. Two general patterns are of interest. One is the general improvement with increasing age in the age range $4\frac{1}{2}$- to 8-years-old. The other is the superior performance on the small numerosity trials with most of the children even in the two youngest groups succeeding on the quantitative trials. For large numerosity only the second-grade children were predominantly at the quantitative level. The "no-level" categorization was much more frequent for large numerosity. Those who were scored as "no level" did not make random errors. They failed to distinguish number transformations from length transformations, confusing addition with expansion and subtraction with contraction. An analysis of the errors of all the children revealed that the majority of errors involved this type of confusion.

We have conducted a variety of other experiments with variations on the procedures just described. In one (Cooper et al., 1978) we varied the amount and kind of information the children had about numerosity before and after the transformation. Three conditions in which the experimenter provided no verbal information were included: one in which there were two arrays both screened, another in which there were two arrays but only the transformed array was screened during the transformation, and a third in which there was only one array. The large effect of numerosity remained, but the different conditions influenced performance only slightly. These manipulations varied the kind of numerosity information available. Therefore, it appears that by the time children know enough to use the information, they can get the numerosity information they need to solve inference problems.

Finally, we have examined inference performance in $2\frac{1}{2}$- to 3-year-old children. These children perform well on small-numerosity primitive trials (22 of 24 meeting or exceeding the 75% criterion) and they perform quite well on the other small-number trials (17 meeting the criterion for qualitative and 15 for quantitative classification). However, they performed poorly on all large-number trials (four of 24 passing large-number primitive).

Large-Numerosity Inference

In addition to the difference in time of emergence, the course of development seems to be quite different for small- and large-numerosity–inference performance. It is, therefore, worth examining in more detail the underlying process involved in success on this task. This is done first for large numerosity because it fits the pattern already presented in previous sections of this chapter. If one knew absolute numerosity before and after a transformation, and if one knew the rules governing transformations, then one could determine which transformation had occurred. Suppose one did not know some of the rules governing transformations. For example, suppose one did not know the conservation rule and instead believed that spreading out an array could increase numerosity. If this were the case and one knew that absolute numerosity had increased, how could one decide whether an addition or an expansion had occurred? In fact, these are the kinds of errors we have observed: confusion between addition and expansion and between subtraction and contraction. Further, contingency analyses reveal a largely consistent pattern of relationships of performance on the large-numerosity–inference task and performance on addition/subtraction and conservation tasks. For large numerosity, qualitative addition/subtraction is necessary for qualitative inference, and quantitative addition/subtraction is necessary for quantitative inference. In addition, conservation judgment with adequate explanation is necessary for qualitative and hence quantitative inference. However, primitive inference is necessary for correct conservation judgment, which is inconsistent with the preceding analysis. Perhaps this is additional evidence for the types of theories that discuss the acquisition of conservation in terms of differentiation of number-changing from number-preserving transformations. The relationship of performance on the small-number–inference trials to conservation performance also does not fit the preceding analysis and is discussed in more detail next.

Small-Numerosity Inference

It appears that the same analysis of the problem should obtain for small numerosity as for large. One must know what can change numerosity and what cannot in order to infer the correct transformation. One could argue that this is the case for very young preschoolers; they understand conservation and addition/subtraction but only for small numerosity, and thus can only succeed on small-numerosity–inference problems. However, it was argued earlier that the apparent precocious development of number conservation for small number is really just an application of quantifier solutions to the problem. Further, data from several sources suggest that children younger than 3 years of age can make inferences before they reliably solve small-number conservation problems (e.g., Cooper et al., 1983; Gelman, 1972; Starkey, 1981, 1983).

Despite the quantifier explanation for conservation, this cannot be the explanation for early small-numerosity–inference performance. On the inference task it is not relative or absolute numerosity that is in doubt; it is the intervening transformation that the child must establish. Neither counting nor subitizing can directly give that information to the child. If the precocious development for small numerosity on the inference task is not based on precocious subitizing, what is its basis? That is, how are the inferences possible without a belief in number invariance?

At this point it is instructive to review some of the arguments that were made about infant subitizing. The subitized states were seen as ordered on the basis of observing the effect of additions and subtractions—for example, an addition of one maps two into three, and a subtraction maps two into one. Although for adults these facts are intimately tied to conservation, they may not be for young children. A child may know that an addition maps two into three and that if a change from two to three has occurred then an addition must have taken place, without knowing that changing spatial arrangement is irrelevant to number. If inference for small numerosity is based on knowing the mapping rules among the subitized states, then there should be no difference in difficulty among the types of inference (primitive, qualitative, and quantitative). The child infers the transformation that has occurred directly from change in absolute numeric representation. This approximates the pattern we found, although the primitive trials do appear to be somewhat easier.

This analysis can be applied to Gelman's (1972, 1977) magic task. Gelman found that children were able to detect when a surreptitious addition or subtraction had occurred even though they failed a standard number-conservation task. Children can succeed on the magic task by learning that the one with two is correct, and then being able to tell that neither has two any more. If both arrays now have three, the child can infer that an addition took place because that is what is required to turn two into three. It might even be that the child knows that changing spatial arrangement cannot change two into three, but such knowledge does not guarantee that such changes leave number unchanged.

A similar argument can be constructed with respect to some of Siegler's work (Siegler, 1981; Siegler & Robinson, 1982). Siegler's Rule 1 for conservation-type problems with small numerosity differentiates between those trials on which a "quantitatively relevant transformation" occurs—that is, addition or subtraction trials—and those on which some other transformation occurs—that is, con-servation trials. When children are using Rule 1, the former are solved correctly and the latter are frequently in error because judgments are based on length. Again, children seem to have learned about some specific kinds of changes in numerosity without acquiring conservation.

Now let us return to the perplexing fact from the large-numerosity–inference task—that is, that primitive inference is a necessary condition for acquiring conservation and not vice versa. Remember that on the primitive inference trials the initial numerosities are equal, and therefore the final numerosities are un-equal. Moreover, they are unequal based on number name, and based on one-to-one correspondence. Just as in the small-number range the child can discover that the only way to get from two to three (as subitized states) is an addition of one, the child could discover that the only way to get from equality to inequality based on number names or one-to-one correspondence is an addition or subtraction. For example, if two arrays are initially counted to have seven each, the child could learn that the only transformation that can cause a new count to produce number names that differ from one another is an addition or subtraction. That having acquired conservation ensures success on large-number primitive-inference trials suggests that this knowledge about making things unequal might be important for further differentiating the concept of equal in a way that is a component part of the acquisition of conservation.

The Course of Inference Development

That inference skills develop at all is a challenge to Klahr's theory. In Klahr's theory, transformation operators are learned to provide efficiency in a system whose implicit goal is to keep track of numerosity. There is no added efficiency in inferring a transformation, if one must already know numerosity to make the inference. Hence, the theory must be broadened to include new goals, or in-ference must be treated as an epiphenomenon. We would argue that it is the goal structure in the theory that needs changing, that it is the development of a predictable system of interrelations that the child is seeking, not simply an efficient system for determining numerosity.

The pattern of inference development is consistent with Klahr's theory in other ways, and with the general thesis of this chapter about learning about number space from experience with additions and subtractions. Initially, children learn the transformations required for particular moves in the small-numerosity range of the number space—for example, a move from three to two is accom-plished with a subtraction. This specific knowledge is acquired very early. Large-numerosity primitive inference is the first example of rule formation in the development of inference. This is a rule about the transformations required for movement from equality to inequality. The next is qualitative inference, which is a rule about movement from inequality to equality. The last is quantitative inference, which is a rule about the transformations involved in movements between inequality states.

SUMMARY AND CONCLUSION

In this chapter, several themes recur across the discussions of the specific features of the three areas of number development addressed. First and foremost, it has been argued that the child's concept of number changes dramatically in the first 7 years of life; development does not consist merely of learning to use already-present skills. Second, this change is not the product of a simple empirical-discovery procedure. Third, incrementing and decrementing transformations (addition and subtraction) play a crucial role in the child's construction of number concepts. Finally, the course of development is controlled in part by the presence or absence of important precursor abilities and in part by the child's structuring of problems that may or may not bring the relevant abilities into play.

Several different parts of the preceding discussion could be highlighted as evidence that early number development consists of substantive change in underlying capabilities. The alternative position being refuted here is the type that Bryant (e.g., 1974) has taken with respect to number, Trabasso (e.g., 1975) with respect to transitivity, and Shatz (1978) with respect to communication. In infancy, we have argued, the initial numerosity detectors provide only cardinality information. During the first $1\frac{1}{2}$ years of life these detector states are ordered through the actions of incrementing and decrementing. Further development occurs in the construction of a numerosity-independent concept of equality and inequality. Finally, the integration of the ordered numerosity detectors and addition and subtraction give rise to the concept of more, less, and the knowledge implicit in primitive addition and subtraction. In the preschool years, the course of understanding the effect of addition/subtraction transformations provides further evidence of substantive change. In this case we saw that the way in which children code relative numerosity is intimately intertwined with their understanding of addition and subtraction. Development of solutions to the inference task shows a similar pattern, although delayed by approximately a year.

We can look at this substantive change in a different way. Performance of preschoolers on the tasks we have described differs substantially for small and large numerosity. Children apparently do not treat information about numerosity from subitizing in the same way as information from counting or one-to-one correspondence. Klahr (1983) has also suggested that this might be the case. A child who does not understand that subitized numerosity and counting are information about the same thing—that is, numerosity—and that it behaves the same way regardless of magnitude has a very different picture of number than does an adult. Part of the task of number development in the preschool years is to discover that subitizing and counting yield information about the same thing.

Number development is not the product of a simple empirical discovery procedure. Klahr and Wallace's (1976) model provides an example of such a simple procedure, although Klahr's (1983) revision may not. With such a procedure conservation might be learned by counting before and after the transformation and discovering equivalent cardinality. Piaget's initial observation that some children would deny equivalence despite accurate counting continues to be confirmed by other researchers (e.g., Coburn & Saxe, 1983). One directly relevant result from the present chapter concerns the sequence of incorrect solutions to the addition/subtraction problems. Perhaps most interesting is the super-qualitative level because it is so sophisticated and yet to an adult so obviously inadequate. Another relevant result is the developmental delay in discovering the transfer rule even after the correct system for coding the initial state, transformation, and final state is present.

The point is not that number development is a magical process, but rather that it depends on experience in a complex way. A simple empirical procedure is a specific form of rote learning. The framework for rote learning cannot be learned or changed by rote learning, yet the framework within which children learn from their experiences clearly changes. Hence, they learn different things from the same type of experience at different points in development. A particular example of this is the difference between small- and large-numerosity performance. At least in the tasks discussed in this chapter, the principles for solving small- and large-numerosity problems are the same. If one had an automatic procedure that tabulated subitized state before and after a transformation for small numerosity, and cardinal value arrived at by counting before and after a transformation for larger numerosities, it would find that exactly the same regularities obtained. However, even after counting is quite reliable, numerosity differences remain, thus demonstrating that such a simple procedure is an incomplete model.

Incrementing and decrementing operations play a crucial role in early number development. Their role for infant development has already been outlined; an examination of their role in preschoolers' understanding of equality and inequality yields a similar picture. Addition and subtraction allow children to discover the interrelations among absolute and relative codings of number. We can see in the primitive, qualitative, and quantitative levels of addition and subtraction knowledge what a Piagetian might call a vertical decalage in relation to the development of infant number skills described in this chapter. In the case of the preschool child larger numerosities are involved, and the numerosities that are affected by addition and subtraction are the relative numerosities between two arrays.

It has been argued that both prerequisite skills and problem structuring are important in directing the course of number development. The role of prerequisites is seen in the relationship of some skills as either necessary or sufficient conditions for others. The role of task structuring can be seen in the lack of effect of kind of numerosity information available on solutions to large-numerosity–inference problems. As soon as children develop an appropriate strategy for approaching this problem, they can use a variety of different kinds of numerosity information. For the children who fail it is the correct approach that is missing, not access to the relevant numerical facts. Because this point has important implications for studying number development, it is developed here.

From the point of view presented in this chapter, it is not surprising (at least in retrospect) that children can be taught some skills substantially before those skills would be naturally acquired. For example, Gelman (1982) has been able to teach young preschoolers number conservation. Problem structuring determines the kinds of hypotheses that children entertain in discovering regularities in their environment. Knowledge builds on other knowledge, not merely by providing prerequisite skills that are differentiated into more complex ones, but also by providing a richer system within which to discover questions and construct hypotheses. If adults take over this latter job by teaching, then the only limit on what children can acquire involves the availability of prerequisite skills. If children have the ability to quantify two arrays (counting), quantify the difference between them (counting), and classify transformations, then they have the prerequisite knowledge to solve both conservation and the types of addition/subtraction problems discussed in this chapter. However, it may be a significant challenge even for a clever teacher to get them to deploy these skills effectively. This is not meant to denigrate this kind of research on teaching. On the one hand, how many of us would have learned calculus if we had waited for it to be the next logical step in our development of mathematical techniques as it was for Archimedes, 1900 years before Newton and Leibniz codified it in a form that could be relatively easily learned by most of us? Clearly the teaching of useful skills can be valuable in its own right. Further, discovering when things can be taught may help determine what types of skills are prerequisite to the taught skill. However, two caveats are in order. First, unless the teaching per se is analyzed carefully, the results from such studies may mislead us about the process of development. Second, the learning produced may be of limited use and may perhaps be unstable if it is not part of a more general integrated system.

In summary, we have tried to present informal number development as an active, concept-driven process. The processes of quantification and transformation classification are crucial to this process. Some of the unusual and ''incorrect'' solution strategies developed by children illustrate the ''bootstrap'' nature of the process. Ernst Mach wrote (in Bell 1937): ''. . . the power of mathematics rests on its evasion of all unnecessary thought and on its wonderful saving of mental operations [p. xx].'' This may be true about its power, but we would argue that this is not a primary force in the learning of mathematical concepts by young children, as some have suggested. In general we have found that the easiest children to test in our studies are those who are just acquiring the concept under investigation. Many of the children in our transfer study began to discover the principle part way through the procedure. There seemed to be an inherent joy in discovering how things interrelate, and it is the interrelations among quantifies and transformations that constitute the concepts of informal mathematical knowledge.

ACKNOWLEDGMENTS

This research was supported by a National Institute of Education grant (NIE–G–80–0143) and by a National Institute of Mental Health grant HD 15035. I wish to thank several people who have worked on research projects and have participated in seminars and informal discussions that helped develop the framework for this chapter: Belinda Blevins, Robert Campbell, Patricia Mace, and Prentice Starkey. I wish also to thank Mark Bickhard for his comments on the conceptual framework used in the chapter and Catherine Cooper for her comments, suggestions, and editorial expertise.

REFERENCES

Antell, S. E., & Keating, D. P. Perception of numerical invariance in neonates. *Child Development*, 1983, *54*, 695–701.

Bell, E. T. *Men of mathematics*. New York: Simon & Schuster, 1937.

Blevins, B., Campbell, R., & Cooper, R. G. *Children's inferences about addition and subtraction transformations*. Paper presented at the Society for Research in Child Development meetings, Detroit, 1983.

Brainerd, C. J. *The origins of the number concept*. New York: Praeger, 1979.

Bryant, P. E. Perception and understanding in young children: An experimental approach. New York: Basic Books, 1974.

Brush, L. R. *Children's conception of addition and subtraction: The relation of formal and informal notions*. Unpublished doctoral dissertation, Cornell University, 1972.

Brush, L. R. Preschool children's knowledge of addition and subtraction. *Journal for Research in Mathematics Education*, 1978, *9*, 44–54.

Campbell, R., Cooper, R. G., & Blevins, B. *Development of extensions of addition/subtraction reasoning in elementary school children: Infinity, transfer, and connexity*. Paper presented at the Jean Piaget Society meetings, Philadelphia, 1983.

Coburn, M., & Saxe, G. *Factors influencing children's use of counting to form number conservation concepts*. Paper presented at the Society for Research in Child Development meetings, Detroit, 1983.

Cowan, R. A reappraisal of the relation between performance of quantitative identity and quantitative equivalence conservation tasks. *Journal of Experimental Child Psychology*, 1979, *28*, 68–80.

Cooper, R. G., Campbell, R., & Blevins, B. *Numerical representation from infancy to middle childhood: What develops?* In D. R. Rogers & J. A. Sloboda (Eds.), *The acquisition of symbolic skills*. New York: Plenum Press, 1983.

Cooper, R. G., & Starkey, P. *What preschoolers know about number: Does subitizing develop?* Paper presented at the American Psychological Association meetings, San Francisco, 1977.

Cooper, R. G., Starkey, P., Blevins, B., Goth, P., & Leitner, E. *Number development: Addition and subtraction*. Paper presented at the Jean Piaget Society meetings, Philadelphia, 1978.

Curtis, L. E., & Strauss, M. S. *Infant numerosity abilities: Discrimination and relative numerosity*. Paper presented at the Society for Research in Child Development meetings, Detroit, 1983.

Gelman, R. The nature and development of early number concepts. In H. W. Reese (Ed.), *Advances in child development and behavior* (Vol. 7). New York: Academic Press, 1972.

Gelman, R. How young children reason about small numbers. In N. J. Castellan, D. B. Pisoni, & G. R. Potts (Eds.), *Cognitive Theory* (Vol. 2). Hillsdale, N.J.: Lawrence Erlbaum Associates, 1977.

Gelman, R. Accessing one-to-one correspondence: Still another paper about conservation. *British Journal of Psychology*, 1982, *73*, 209–220.

Klahr, D. Transition processes in quantitative development. In R. Sternberg, (Ed.), *Mechanisms of cognitive development*. San Francisco: Freeman, 1983.

Klahr, D., & Wallace, J. G. The role of quantification operators in the development of conservation of quantity. *Cognitive Psychology*, 1973, *4*, 301–327.

Klahr, D., & Wallace, J. G. *Cognitive development: An information processing view*. Hillsdale, N.J.: Lawrence Erlbaum Associates, 1976.

Mandler, G., & Shebo, B. J. Subitizing: An analysis of its component processes. *Journal of Experimental Psychology: General*, 1982, *III*, 1–22.

Newman D., Reil, M., & Martin, L. Cultural practices and Piagetian theory: The impact of a cross-cultural research program. In D. Kuhn & J. A. Meacham (Eds.), *On the development of developmental psychology*. Basel: Karger, 1982.

Piaget, J. How children form mathematical concepts. *Scientific American*, 1953, *189*, 74–79.

Piaget, J. *Success and understanding*. Cambridge, Mass.: Harvard University Press, 1978.

Piaget, J. *Experiments in contradiction*. Chicago: University of Chicago Press, 1974/1980.

Piaget, J., Grize, J. B., Szeminska, A., & Vinh-Bank. *Epistemology and psychology of functions*. Dordrecht: D. Reidel, 1977.

Piaget, J., Kaufmann, J., & Bourquin, J. La construction de communs multiples. In J. Piaget (Ed.) *Recherches dur l'abstraction reflechissante, l. L'abstraction des relations logico-arithmetiques*. Paris: Presses Universitaires de France, 1977.

Shatz, M. The relationship between cognitive processes and the development of communication skills. In C. B. Keasey (Ed.), *Nebraska symposium on motivation* (Vol. 26). Lincoln: University of Nebraska Press, 1978.

Siegler, R. S. Developmental sequences within and between concepts. *Monographs of the Society for Research in Child Development*, 1981, *46*, 1–84.

Siegler, R. S., & Robinson, M. The development of numerical understanding. In H. W. Reese & L. P. Lipsitt (Eds.), *Advances in child development and behavior* (Vol. 16). New York: Academic Press, 1982.

Starkey, P. Young children's performance in number conservation tasks: Evidence for a hierarchy of strategies. *Journal of Genetic Psychology*, 1981, *138*, 103–110.

Starkey, P. *Some precursors of early arithmetic competencies*. Paper presented at the Society for Research in Child Development meetings, Detroit, 1983.

Starkey, P., & Cooper, R. G. *The role of estimation skills in the development of number conservation*. Paper presented at the Jean Piaget Society meetings, Philadelphia, 1977.

Starkey, P., & Cooper, R. G. Perception of numbers by human infants. *Science*, 1980, *210*, 1033–1035.

Starkey, P., Spelke, E., & Gelman, R. *Detection of intermodal numerical correspondence by human infants*. Paper presented at the International Conference on Infant Studies meetings, Austin, Texas, 1982.

Strauss, M., & Curtis, L. Infant perception of numerosity. *Child Development*, 1981, *52*, 1146–1152.

Tollefsrud, L. *Preschoolers' use, understanding, and explanation of the number conservation principle*. Unpublished doctoral dissertation, University of Texas at Austin, 1981.

Tollefsrud, L., Campbell, R., Starkey, P., & Cooper, R. G. *Development of number conservation: The role of quantification and operator solutions*. In preparation.

Trabasso, T. R. Representation, memory and reasoning: How do we make transitive inferences? In A. D. Pick (Ed.), *Minnesota symposium on child psychology* (Vol. 9). Minneapolis: University of Minnesota Press, 1975.

8

Child as the Measurer of All Things: Measurement Procedures and the Development of Quantitative Concepts

Kevin Miller
The University of Texas at Austin

Procedures for measuring have been intimately connected to the development of mathematical procedures and mathematics itself (e.g., Kline, 1959, 1972). This relation ranges from the derivation of the word *geometry* from roots corresponding to "earth measurement" to Gauss' (unsuccessful) attempt to determine the applicability of non-Euclidean geometries by measuring the angles between three distant mountain peaks (Courant & Robbins, 1941). Despite the contribution that practical measurement problems in navigation, agriculture, and other fields have made to the development of mathematical thought, studies of the development of an understanding of numerical and physical concepts have largely neglected children's spontaneous measurement procedures.

An exception to this neglect of children's developing understanding of measurement is found in the work of Piaget (Piaget, Inhelder, & Szeminska, 1960). Piaget's findings suggest that young children's understanding of measurement is limited by their lack of a general understanding of quantity. As with other Piagetian tasks, Piaget found that young children tend to rely on unreliable perceptual strategies, to be misled by the appearance of stimuli, and to at times lose sight of the goals of their actions when measuring. For example, Piaget reported that preschoolers measuring the height of a tower in order to duplicate it either relied on perceptual estimates or attempted to measure it by maintaining their hands a distance apart. In the Piagetian view, it is only gradually and in conjunction with the realization that changes in position do not affect amount that children are able to make use of traditional procedures for measuring.

The idea that preschool children possess an understanding of quantitative invariance that is reflected in the measurement procedures they employ encounters an apparent paradox. Young children lack a general understanding of the

193

quantitative dimensions such as number, length, area, and volume to be measured, which would seem an insurmountable obstacle to successful measurement. The problem this presents to early measuring is expressed well in the rhetorical question, "How can children measure if they don't know what they're measuring?" Because measurement involves quantifying within a domain such as length or area, the ability to measure would seem to depend on a prior understanding of what constitutes that domain. The view that quantification is not possible without a general understanding of quantity has been emphasized by Inhelder, Sinclair, and Bovet (1974):

> The child's initial understanding of conservation is based on a general undifferentiated concept of invariance which provides the basis for subsequent, more specific quantifications and measurements (e.g., of height and length). This first notion of conservation of continuous (or physical) quantity is developed before any actual physical quantification of mass, volume, or weight is possible [p. 32].

Early measurement by children who do not possess such a general understanding of amount seems a contradiction in terms. Nonetheless, the research described here demonstrates that young children do possess a basic understanding of what measurement entails, and that much of what children understand about quantitative invariance relates to the nature and limits of their measurement procedures.

An example of the kind of early understanding about quantitative invariance that young children may possess is found in the results of Miller and Baillargeon (1982). This study replicated Piaget's (Piaget et al., 1960) finding that children under about 6 years of age believe two objects become closer together when some of the distance between them is occluded by a screen. In the same 15-minute session, however, a majority of 4-year-olds (and all older children) insisted that such occlusion would not affect which stick (from a set of sticks differing in length) would "just fit" between the two objects. Reasoning about the relation between length and distance in general seems to be more difficult than is reasoning about a specific implication of that relation.

This distinction between judgments of quantity in general and comprehension of specific implications of quantitative relations parallels a similar distinction made in J. J. Gibson's (1979) theory of affordances. Gibson argued that perception primarily concerns not interpreting sensations but rather determining functional relations such as "Can I carry this?" or "Will this stick fit across here?" Although information about weight and size are necessary to answer such questions, Gibson suggests that it is the affordances rather than the quantitative information on which they are based that are perceived.

This distinction between affordance and amount helps to explain the asymmetry found between judging the relation between length and distance versus judging an affordance based on that relation. Children may be expected to do better at solving problems that require them to use quantitative information to solve functional problems than they do at "directly" estimating or reasoning about amounts. Understanding that occluding part of a gap will not affect the length of stick needed to span it implies some understanding that occlusion does not affect distance. Being able to use information about quantity to solve this sort of problem does not, however, seem to imply any more general realization of the relation between length and distance.

The distinction between affordance and amount also suggests a solution to the paradox of children measuring without possessing a general understanding of what is being measured. Children may develop procedures for determining affordances without realizing the implications of such procedures for reasoning about amounts. Learning to relate affordances to amounts may represent a later elaboration of what children already know about the world, rationalizing previously existing system for determining functional relations.

Measurement procedures of the sort described here concern solving functional questions such as "Will this stick fit across this gap?" The set of procedures children may employ to answer such questions does not necessarily conform to Piaget's (Piaget et al., 1960) conceptualization of measurement. The spontaneous-measurement procedures of young children do fit more standard definitions of what measurement entails.

WHAT IS MEASUREMENT?

A description of children's measurement procedures relies on a working definition of what measurement is. Answers to this definitional question have important consequences for the apparent course of children's understanding of measurement. Piaget (Piaget et al., 1960) defined measurement as follows:

> To measure is to take out of a whole one element, taken as a unit, and to transpose this unit on the remainder of a whole: measurement is therefore a synthesis of subdivision and change of position [p. 3].

This flexible use of an arbitrary unit of measurement is a sophisticated accomplishment, and it is not surprising that Piaget found that such an understanding does not emerge for the case of volume measurement until adolescence. Defining measurement, as Piaget did, in relation to the flexibility and sophistication of adult behavior risks falling into the Procrustean trap of overlooking early competence that may reflect a real, but limited, understanding of quantitative invariance.

A more general definition of measurement is provided by S. S. Stevens (1946, 1975) who asserted that "measurement occurs whenever an element from one domain is matched, equated or conjoined to an element of another domain

[1975, p. 46]." Stevens' view distinguishes the basic question of whether measurement exists from description of the kind of measurement shown. The basic concept underlying measurement is that some quantitative rule must be applied systematically. Although the nature of such rules may change with development, children who understand the need to employ consistent procedures preserving some aspect of quantity in order to determine quantitative relations demonstrate this fundamental concept.

Stevens' definition of measurement includes counting as a possible measurement procedure. Counting involves pairing items from a physical set with a set of psychological markers (Beckwith & Restle, 1966; Gelman, 1972) such that one-to-one correspondence is preserved between items and markers. Counting is of interest because of evidence (Fuson, Secada, & Hall, 1983; Gelman, 1978; Gelman & Gallistel, 1978) that the counting procedures of preschoolers show a concern for numerical invariance that is often *not* evident when young children reason about numerical relations established in other ways.

What are the implications for the development of an understanding of measurement of young children's precocious understanding of number through counting? On the one hand, this early competence at one measurement procedure may imply little about understanding others. Counting and understanding number may be unique accomplishments: Counting is a procedure that children demonstrate early and practice spontaneously. Furthermore, there is recent evidence suggesting that infants demonstrate a sensitivity to small number that is general across transformations of size and shape (Antell & Keating, 1983; Cooper, this volume; Starkey & Cooper, 1980; Strauss & Curtis, 1981, this volume). Perhaps most remarkable are recent findings (Starkey, Spelke, & Gelman, 1980) that infants' sensitivity to number generalizes across visual and auditory modalities. Thus, number may be a special, limited area of early competence, with little meaning for cognitive development in general.

On the other hand, counting may be a model for the young child as a learner of procedures. The early development of counting may be only a particularly salient example of children's propensity for learning procedures for determining quantitative relations. As with counting, children may spontaneously learn and practice other procedures for determining amounts.

To anticipate my answer to the question of whether number and counting represent areas of exceptional competence, or a model for what children know about measurement procedures, some of both seem to apply. On the one hand, even 3-year-old children show systematic measurement procedures that reflect a concern for quantitative invariance. Although these procedures at times differ systematically from those of adults, children rarely make quantitative judgments on the basis of quantitative information, or confuse actions with their quantitative consequences. At the same time, number *is* different, and many of the difficulties confronting immature measurement procedures lie specifically in difficulties transcending numerical information when it gives a misleading picture of quantity.

I will describe the results of three studies from a project investigating the nature and development of spontaneous measurement procedures in children. The first study assessed whether young children demonstrate systematic procedures for determining quantitative relations, and described changes with age in the kinds of procedures they employ. The second study investigated whether measurement procedures play a role in children's reasoning about quantity beyond their role as procedures for determining amounts. The development of an understanding of transformations relevant to measurement procedures was compared with other transformations traditionally used to assess children's understanding of quantitative invariance. The third study shows how modifying a standard experimental paradigm to elicit children's measurement strategies and to involve affordance relations demonstrates the presence of precocious quantitative knowledge. In this study, a modification of procedures used to measure children's understanding of area revealed the presence in preschoolers of an understanding of the relation between dimensions in determining area.

THE DEVELOPMENT OF SPONTANEOUS
MEASUREMENT PROCEDURES

Where ought one look for early understanding of quantitative invariance? One obvious place to look is in contexts in which some familiar outcome of interest to children is a function of quantity. Dantzig (1967) suggested that mathematics itself had its origin in the development of procedures for keeping track of property. Informal observations suggest that equality of division is an affordance to which children in this culture are attuned from an early age. Thus, asking children to divide familiar materials evenly in an appropriate context might elicit maximal demonstration of early understanding of the importance of quantitative invariance.

Method

Subjects for this study (Miller, 1983b, 1983c, Study 1) were 64 children, equal numbers of boys and girls at each of ages 3 and 5 years, and grades 2 and 4. Children were presented with scenes like the one illustrated in Fig. 8.1, containing sets of two, three, or four turtles. Turtles were chosen because children had no difficulty accepting that turtles are stupid and would not be able to divide materials evenly. The turtles were shown prepared to enjoy a snack consisting of materials emphasizing number ("candies"), length (strips of clay "spaghetti"), area (clay squares of "fudge"), and volume (glasses of "kool-aid"). In each

FIG. 8.1. Materials used to investigate spontaneous measurement procedures.
Children were shown a snack consisting of materials emphasizing *number* (''candies''), *length* (strips of ''spaghetti''), *area* (squares of ''fudge''), and *volume*
(glasses of ''kool-aid''). They were asked to divide an extra snack among the
turtles present, and were provided with a knife, measuring cup, rulers, and a paper
strip to assist them in measurement.

scene an extra place was set with a snack for a missing turtle, with the explanation that another turtle had been invited to share the snack but was unable to show
up. Therefore the turtles were confronted with the task of dividing the snack
evenly. Children were told that, although the turtles did not know how to divide
the snacks fairly, they would still get upset if one of them ended up with more
than the others. Thus, the importance of dividing the material so that each turtle
had exactly the same amount as the others was stressed, and the child's help was
then enlisted in dividing the snacks evenly. Various measuring devices (rulers
and cups of different sizes) were presented, and the children were told that they
could use these implements if doing so would help in producing equivalent sets.

Results

Two kinds of data were collected from children's performances. The materials
divided by each child were retained and accuracy of division was evaluated by
determining the standard deviation of sets of items created to be equal. In

TABLE 8.1
Correlation Between Accuracy on Different
Operations (Partial Correlation, with Effect of
Age Removed)

Task:	Number	Volume	Length	Area
Number				
Volume	.297*			
Length	−.029	.032		
Area	−.095	.002	.646*	
		$p < .01$		

addition, the children's measurement behavior was videotaped for coding of strategies employed. Videotapes were coded in a two-pass procedure. An initial, low-level coding scheme was employed to transcribe the discrete "moves" of division (such as aligning two pieces of spaghetti, or folding a piece over to halve it). A second-level coding based on the resulting transcripts produced the strategy data discussed next.

Accuracy data are blind to strategies employed, but may indicate similarities in performance across tasks that suggest similarities in strategies used or the problems particular measurement tasks present to children. Intercorrelations of accuracy across tasks, with the overall effect of age partialed out, are presented in Table 8.1. Two pairs of tasks show significant intercorrelations. Accuracy of performance on the number task was significantly correlated with performance on the volume task, whereas relatively good performance on the length task was associated with good performance on dividing area. This pattern raises the question of what these pairs of task might have in common, such that good performance on one was associated with good performance on the other. Data on strategies are presented in the pairs number/volume and length/area suggested by the accuracy data.

Data on strategies used to divide number are presented in Fig. 8.2, which presents the number of children in an age group who used a particular strategy at any point during the session. Note first that use of a nonquantitative strategy, in which children simply dumped candies into the cups without apparent concern for the number involved, was limited to only one preschool child. A somewhat more sophisticated strategy has been described previously by Gelman and Gallistel (1978): dumping followed by counting to evaluate the outcome. This strategy was also found only among a small number of preschool subjects. The vast majority of children at all ages employed a strategy of distributive counting, in which pieces were distributed one at a time among the turtles, often accompanied by statements such as "one for you and one for you. . . ." Distributive counting incorporates one-to-one correspondence in a very general way, because it does not require children to determine the number present. This contrasts with the

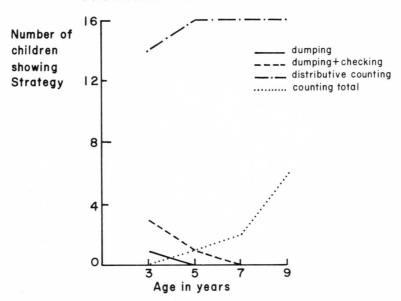

FIG. 8.2.   Frequency of various strategies for dividing number. Children were credited with using a strategy if they showed it at any point during the task.

earlier view of Gelman and Gallistel (1978), who suggested that young children's understanding of number is limited to specific, known numerosities. Gelman (1982) has since altered this view based on a training study in which children quickly learned that one-to-one correspondence is the basis for numerical equality. The present results support Gelman's recent position by suggesting that even without training young children possess a strategy that reflects a general understanding of one-to-one correspondence as the basis for equality of number.

Strategies involving determining the actual number of candies to be divided increased slowly with age. Despite the saving of time possible if one knew how many pieces were to be given to each turtle, counting the set to be divided was never shown by a majority of children in any age group. Thus, the basic strategies used to divide number showed little developmental change, with one strategy (distributive counting) being used by a majority of children at all ages.

The parallel between performance on the number and volume tasks seems to result not from use of common strategies across the two tasks, but from the fact that for each task a single basic strategy used by preschoolers was also retained by older subjects. Fig. 8.3 shows the distribution across age groups of strategies for measuring volume. As with division of number, the use of no apparent measuring procedure was limited to preschoolers. A quarter of the 3-year-olds showed no apparent evaluation of outcome in dividing volume at some point during the session. The vast majority of children at all ages visually compared levels of fluid to determine relative volume. More complicated strategies involving measuring the height of the column, or using a unit from a measuring cup developed slowly. Such strategies were employed by only a small percentage of even the older children.

For both number and volume measurement, the use of nonquantitative procedures failing to demonstrate a concern for number and volume was limited to a small number of preschoolers. A majority of subjects at all ages employed a common strategy within each task. Because most children were using the same strategy, variations in accuracy likely reflected factors such as the care with which children executed a particular strategy. Carefulness in assessing the outcome of a strategy might well be common across the two tasks and account for intercorrelations in accuracy of performance across the number and volume tasks.

Although even preschoolers demonstrated adequate strategies for measuring number and volume, there are obvious differences in the extent to which children at different ages are bound by these specific strategies. Tasks such as the conservation paradigm involve systematic violations of the assumptions underlying the measurement strategies employed by children. In the number-conservation task, children have to reason about number without the support of the distributive

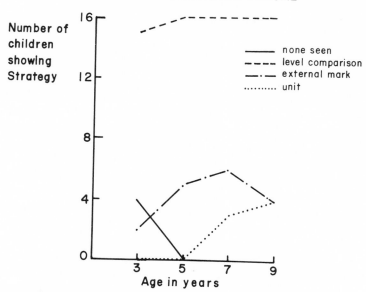

FIG. 8.3. Frequency of various strategies for dividing volume.

counting demonstrated here. Similarly, even though children at all ages made judgments based on comparing levels of liquid, conservation of volume tasks demonstrate that younger children have trouble abandoning that procedure when the use of containers of different areas makes it unsatisfactory. Although the majority of children at all ages demonstrate the same common strategies, older children resemble Hatano's (Hatano, 1982; Hatano & Inagaki, 1983) "adaptive experts," able to repair or abandon their procedures when circumstances change. Younger children, on the other hand, resemble Hatano's "routine experts" whose expertise does not extend to an ability to transcend the limitations of their preferred measurement procedures.

Number and volume measurement share another similarity that becomes more important in comparison to measurement of length and area. Neither task confronted children with problems concerning the need for units to be of consistent size. In dividing a set of pieces of equal size, the relevant units are given to children. In dividing volume into equivalent glasses, judgments based on height avoid any need to consider the size of volume units.

Measurement of length and area present children with a different set of problems, many of which relate to difficulties in creating equivalent units. It is in the division of length and area that Piaget found the strongest evidence for young children's indifference to quantitative invariance in measurement. For example, when Piaget (Piaget et al., 1960) required children to draw lines showing how to divide a paper "cookie" among various numbers of consumers, he found that young children seemed to get distracted by the act of drawing lines. Preschoolers would draw dozens of lines as if to divide the cookie into many pieces, without any relation to the number of pieces desired.

It is unfortunate that Piaget's task did not allow children to finish dividing the paper "cookie," because he might have drawn different conclusions from the way in which children divided the pieces thus created. Strategies for dividing length materials are shown in Fig. 8.4, and the predominance among preschoolers of cutting into pieces of arbitrary length replicates Piaget's report. This procedure of cutting into (typically many) arbitrary pieces was clearly the most common strategy among preschoolers. But a further aspect of young children's division of length casts a different light on this apparently nonquantitative behavior. Nearly all children who cut the materials into arbitrary pieces took care to count to ensure that the same *number* of pieces were distributed, although the pieces were often of different sizes.

Concern for equality of number at the expense of equality of size is best illustrated by a peculiar strategy shown by six preschoolers. These children ran out of pieces when distributing the pieces they had cut. To fix the inequality, they took a piece from the turtle who had not gotten enough, cut it in two, and returned it to the same turtle. It would be hard to find a better illustration of the predominance of numerical information in the quantitative reasoning of these children.

STRATEGIES FOR DIVIDING LENGTH

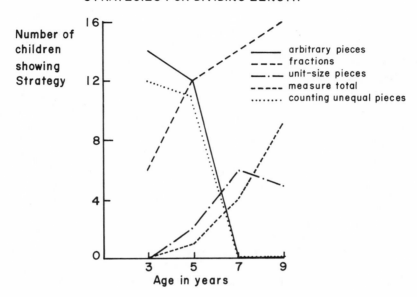

FIG. 8.4.   Frequency of various strategies for dividing length.

The peculiarity of this strategy also argues against the view that children are simply copying measurement procedures they have observed in the home. Presumably it is a rare as well as an unscrupulous parent who would attempt to fool a child into thinking he or she had more by cutting one piece into several. The strategy of producing equal numbers of pieces varying in size demonstrates the importance of number in children's reasoning about other quantitative dimensions, as well as their willingness to invent novel procedures for ensuring numerical equality.

Use of strategies in which children cut the material directly into fractions of approximately equal size increased with age. This involved either estimating the size and then cutting into fractions, or folding the piece in half or thirds. These procedures were used at some point during the study by a majority of children at all ages older than 3 years. Cutting into fractions indicates some concern for the length of pieces to be distributed, indicating that for these children equality of length involves considerations of the size as well as number of pieces. Such understanding need not imply, of course, the general understanding of the role and arbitrary nature of units used by Piaget to define measurement. Indeed, at times the use of this apparently straightforward fraction-cutting procedure showed confusion over how to produce the right number of fractions. As Piaget (Piaget et al., 1960) reported, many children had difficulty relating the number of cuts made to the number of pieces produced. This took two forms. In the first, children proceeded to make the same number of cuts as pieces desired, which resulted in an extra piece (which was then divided appropriately). The second confusion between the number of cuts and pieces is more interesting. Some children used a procedure of repeated halving, which was successful for dividing into halves or quarters. When attempting to divide into thirds, these children divided a piece in half, then halved the pieces again. After distributing three such pieces, they were left with a remaining piece to divide. One child (a 7-year-old) went through three iterations of halving the material twice, distributing three of the pieces, then repeating the halving of the remaining piece. All children who showed this pattern eventually cut a remaining piece approximately into thirds. The existence of these systematic "bugs" (Brown & Burton, 1978) suggests that even the apparently straightforward procedure of dividing material into roughly equal fractions is capable of undergoing elaboration with development.

Procedures involving the use of units of constant size increased in frequency with age, and were common among the school-aged children. An interesting strategy that peaked in the 7-year-old group involved cutting a series of unit-sized pieces. These were constructed in one of two ways. In the first, the child cut an initial arbitrary piece (as would be done as well by children who proceeded to cut a series of such arbitrary pieces). Children who showed this particular strategy, however, used the initial piece as a template for cutting later pieces. An alternative approach was to use a unit marker on a ruler (e.g., 1 cm or 1 inch) to cut a series of small pieces. In either case, the children ended up with many small pieces, with the important difference that children who used a first piece as a template produced pieces equal in length.

Finally, some children used the units provided by rulers in a more conventional manner, measuring the total amount and using the result to determine how long each fraction needed to be. This strategy, which corresponds most closely to "ordinary" length measurement by adults, was used by a majority of children only in the 9-year-old group. Along the way to such ordinary measurement children demonstrated a variety of strategies that reflect different understandings of what quantitative equivalence means and how one might go about creating equivalent sets.

Strategies employed in measuring area were similar to those used for length, as is shown in Fig. 8.5. Cutting into arbitrary pieces was again a frequent strategy among preschool children, whereas strategies involving the use of units of constant size were limited to older children. Some small differences between the tasks were observed. In particular, preschoolers were more likely on the area than the length task to cut pieces into fractions rather than into arbitrary pieces. Perhaps the increased difficulty of having to cut along two dimensions rather than one made it more difficult to implement a preferred strategy of cutting into many small pieces. Use of the same strategy across length and area tasks was the rule, with 77% of pairs of tasks (e.g., dividing length into thirds compared to dividing area into thirds) resulting in resort to the same strategy. Although the parallel in accuracy between number and volume tasks seems due to the role carefulness plays in determining accuracy, the parallel in accuracy between length and area tasks stems from a simpler source. The correlation in accuracy between length and area division is related to a strong tendency to use similar strategies in both cases, although there is substantial developmental variation in the nature of strategies employed.

The Nature and Limits of Early Measurement

What do these results imply concerning young children's understanding of measurement? It should be clear that a basic understanding of the importance of creating quantitative equality, and the use of systematic procedures to determine equality was demonstrated by most of even the youngest children studied on all tasks employed. Children 3 years of age and older demonstrate respect for this fundamental principle of measurement. Flavell's (1977) suggestion that preconserving children lack a ''general measurement attitude'' is contradicted by the systematic measuring preschoolers undertook in these tasks. Young children were measuring *an* invariance, although the invariance was often not the same as that adults would measure in similar circumstances. Much of the difficulty young children have in measuring length and area, including the apparently confused and nonquantitative procedures observed by Piaget, result from more specific difficulties in creating units of equal size.

The practical knowledge of preschool children includes a set of procedures for determining quantitative invariance. When these procedures are basically ade-

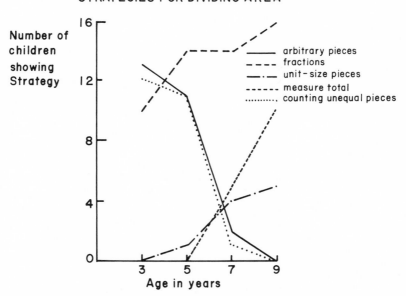

FIG. 8.5.   Frequency of various strategies for dividing area.

quate, as in ordinary number and volume division tasks, little developmental change occurs. In other domains the spontaneous measurement procedures of young children undergo a gradual elaboration and refinement as constraints such as the need for units to be equivalent are incorporated into children's measurement.

MEASUREMENT PROCEDURES AND REASONING ABOUT TRANSFORMATIONS

Although the results of this study suggest interesting early competencies as well as limitations to the measurement procedures of young children, the relation between such procedures and children's thinking about quantity is not clearly addressed by these findings. What connection is there between procedures for determining quantity and procedures for reasoning about quantities? Research on children's ability to conserve quantity across irrelevant transformations has not investigated the role that children's procedures for quantifying may play in their understanding of what affects quantity. If measurement procedures are central to the way in which children reason about amounts, then reasoning about transformations that are not reflected in a child's measurement procedures should be quite difficult. Put more simply, transformations that fool a measurement procedure should be transformations that fool children who use such procedures.

The first study is uninformative regarding the relation between measurement procedures and tasks traditionally used to assess understanding of quantity because children did not show strategies that might be expected from their performance on conservation tasks. Although children showed immature procedures such as contending that amount is increased by cutting a piece in two, no child attempted to increase number by spreading out a set of pieces or attempted to increase length by moving pieces. This nonfinding suggests that conservation-related transformations may be less important in children's reasoning about amounts than might be expected. It also raises questions concerning what relation there is between conservation transformations and transformations more directly related to measurement procedures. To evaluate the role of measurement procedures in children's quantitative reasoning, a second study was undertaken in which transformations related to measurement procedures were contrasted with transformations traditionally used to assess children's quantitative reasoning.

Method

A new group of 64 children at the ages used in the first study were shown a new task involving the same kinds of materials used in the measurement study (Miller, 1983c, Study 2). The children were presented with two turtles described as siblings who needed the child's help in determining when one of them had more than the other one, or when it just thought it did. In each case an initial, readily perceptible equivalence was demonstrated, as in the standard equivalence-conservation tasks. This was followed by a transformation, after which the turtle whose set had been changed claimed to have more because of the change. For example, after the number-conservation transformation of spreading out pieces, the turtle would say, "I have more than you because mine is longer than yours." Following a number transformation, in which one piece was cut in half, the turtle would assert that, "I have more than you because now I have 1 . . 2 . . 3 . . 4 . . 5 . . 6 . . 7 . . 8 . . 9 pieces while you only have 1 . . 2 . . 3 . . 4 . . 5 . . 6 . . 7 . . 8 pieces." Each child was then asked to determine whether the turtle actually did have more than the other, or just thought it did. Fig. 8.6 illustrates a transformation on the number task, in which larger pieces had been substituted for one turtle, who nonetheless claimed to have the same amount to eat because of the continued equality of number.

Except as noted, the transformations listed were shown for each domain of number, length, area, and volume:

1. *Color*: A change in color of stimulus was included in each domain to assess and, if possible, reduce any tendency of children to assert that any change in the stimulus would alter quantity. For example, the experimenter said, "One turtle decided she'd like to have red spaghetti instead, so she took a piece of red spaghetti." He then placed a piece of red clay the same size as the original in alignment with the other turtle's piece. As with the other transformations, one

FIG. 8.6.   Task used to study difficulty of quantitative transformations. After seeing initially identical arrays, one array was altered and the child had to evaluate the effect on quantity. In the example shown, one turtle was given the same number of pieces, but larger ones than the other had. The child had to evaluate one turtle's claim of having the same amount to eat as the other because of this continuing numerical equality.

turtle then claimed to have more because of the change, saying "I have more than you because now I have a red piece."

2. *Change in number:* One piece was cut into two, altering number without changing the amount present.

3. *Superimposition:* The material was folded (length, area), or two pieces were superimposed (number) to create an apparent decrease in quantity in the domain of interest, while not changing the amount present. Because volume is a three-dimensional construct, no such transformation in an unattended dimension was possible.

4. *Rolling out:* The material was rolled out, to increase the length (length) or area (area, number) of material while not altering the amount present. Once again, this transformation could not be done for volume.

5. *Change in size:* A substitution was made altering a possibly unattended dimension, substituting a wider piece of the same length (length), a thicker piece of same area (area), and larger pieces (number) for those originally present. This could not be done for volume.

6. *Conservation:* A conservation task was also administered in each domain with the same turtles and materials.

7. *Conservation + addition:* Conservation was also contrasted with addition to the set usually judged to have fewer. Following the report of Siegler (1981), it was expected that information about addition/subtraction of material would dominate the judgments of some children who otherwise believe that the conservation tasks result in changes in quantity.

When wider or thicker pieces were substituted, the larger pieces were constructed by doubling the width or area of the initial pieces. To ensure that differences in size were apparent, at the conclusion of the session children were presented pairs of stimuli as they appeared *after* the substition. When they had not seen the initial equivalence, children had no difficulty identifying which was larger.

Results

Because the main concern of this study was the relative difficulty of transformations within a domain, children's judgments were subjected to Guttman scaling using the Goodenough-Edwards technique (Edwards, 1948; Goodenough, 1944). The set of transformations within each domain produced a reasonably good Guttman scale, indicating that items could be arranged in a linear ordering with comparatively few off-diagonal entries. Although there are no universally accepted statistics for the goodness of fit of the Guttman model, each scale presented here conforms to commonly accepted values for the Goodenough–Edwards coefficient of reproducibility, and Green's (1956) minimal marginal reproducibility and index of consistency. I present the results for number, length, area, and volume

GUTTMAN SCALING OF NUMBER TRANSFORMATIONS.
Entries are number of children passing item.

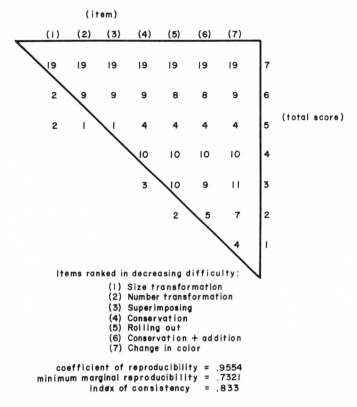

Items ranked in decreasing difficulty:
    (1) Size transformation
    (2) Number transformation
    (3) Superimposing
    (4) Conservation
    (5) Rolling out
    (6) Conservation + addition
    (7) Change in color

coefficient of reproducibility = .9554
minimum marginal reproducibility = .7321
Index of consistency   = .833

FIG. 8.7.   Guttman scaling of number transformations.

transformations separately before considering what the obtained pattern of difficulties of transformations across tasks indicates about the role of measurement
procedures in children's quantitative reasoning.

    Results for the set of transformations on number stimuli are presented in Fig.
8.7. The easiest transformation for children to understand was change in color;
all children understood that a change in the color of the pieces of candy had no
effect on the amount present. Only four children did not also understand that
addition to one row led to an increase in the amount present, even when the
addition followed the conservation transformation. Understanding that rolling
out a piece so that its area increased did not increase quantity was also easier than
the standard conservation task.

    Three transformations were more difficult for children to understand than the
conservation task. All involve fooling counting in some regard—changing num-

ber in a manner different from the way quantity is changed. Superimposing one piece on another (so that two pieces could be counted as one), cutting one piece into two, and replacing the standard pieces with the same number of larger pieces were all difficult for conserving children to understand. Although a majority of 5-year-olds passed the conservation task, it was not until the 7-year-old group that a majority understood that cutting a piece into two does not imply an increase in amount present.

Results from scalogram analysis of the length transformations also constituted a good Guttman scale. As Fig. 8.8 demonstrates, for length as well as for number, understanding the conservation transformation does not imply a complete understanding of which transformations affect length and which do not. Again, conservation was toward the easier part of the scale, and transformations that affect length in a manner different from their effect on quantity were more difficult for children to master. The most difficult transformation was rolling out

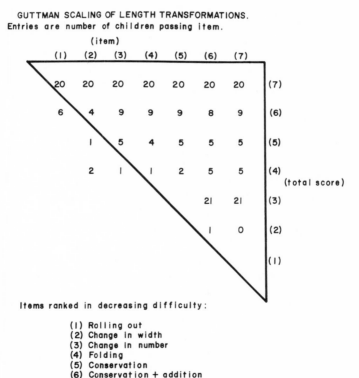

GUTTMAN SCALING OF LENGTH TRANSFORMATIONS.
Entries are number of children passing item.

(item)

	(1)	(2)	(3)	(4)	(5)	(6)	(7)	
	20	20	20	20	20	20	20	(7)
	6	4	9	9	9	8	9	(6)
		1	5	4	5	5	5	(5)
		2	1	1	2	5	5	(4) (total score)
						21	21	(3)
						1	0	(2)
								(1)

Items ranked in decreasing difficulty:

(1) Rolling out
(2) Change in width
(3) Change in number
(4) Folding
(5) Conservation
(6) Conservation + addition
(7) Change in color

coefficient of reproducibility = .9375
minimum marginal repreducibility = .6853
index of consistency = .8014

FIG. 8.8.   Guttman scaling of length transformations.

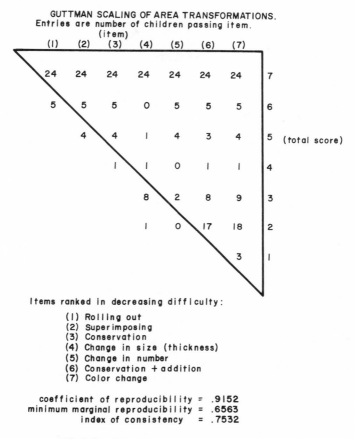

GUTTMAN SCALING OF AREA TRANSFORMATIONS.
Entries are number of children passing item.

Items ranked in decreasing difficulty:

(1) Rolling out
(2) Superimposing
(3) Conservation
(4) Change in size (thickness)
(5) Change in number
(6) Conservation + addition
(7) Color change

coefficient of reproducibility = .9152
minimum marginal reproducibility = .6563
index of consistency = .7532

FIG. 8.9. Guttman scaling of area transformations.

a piece, which increases length while not altering the amount of material present. Next most difficult was replacement of one piece with a wider piece of equal length. Folding a piece in half also created difficulty for children, with apparent length decreasing. It is interesting to note that change in number of pieces was also a relatively difficult transformation. Although difficult transformations generally involved conflicts between length and actual quantity, the difficulty of the number transformation is consistent with the first study in suggesting that numerical information extends beyond "number" tasks to affect judgments of other quantitative dimensions. Thus although children did not realize that a change in the width of a "length" piece implied a change in amount present, they thought that a change in the number of such pieces did indicate a change in quantity.

Results for judgments following area transformations are presented in Fig. 8.9, and show a generally similar pattern. Again the most difficult transformation was one specifically related to area; children had difficulty realizing that

GUTTMAN SCALING OF VOLUME DATA
Entries are number of children passing item.

(item)

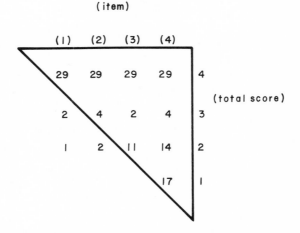

items ranked in order of decreasing difficulty:

(1) Change in number
(2) Conservation
(3) Conservation + addition
(4) Change in color

coefficient of reproducibility = .9609
minimum marginal reproducibility = .6758
index of consistency = .8795

FIG. 8.10.   Guttman scaling of volume transformations.

rolling out a piece does not imply an increase in quantity. The other transformation more difficult than the area-conservation task involved folding the piece in two, which reduced area without changing the amount present. On the other hand, understanding that changing the thickness of a piece increases the amount present was somewhat easier than the conservation transformation. This may be because substitution of a piece twice as thick as the one it is being compared to is particularly perceptually salient. Judging that changing number did not imply a change in amount present was also easier than conservation. This may relate to the difficulty of the area-conservation task more than it does to the ease of ignoring numerical information, because the number transformation was nonetheless a stumbling block for slightly more than a quarter of the children.

The volume task presented fewer options than the others concerning the range of possible transformations, but the scalogram presented in Fig. 8.10 is consistent with results for the other domains. Children had the most difficulty with understanding that dividing the contents of a glass into two glasses does not imply an increase in quantity. This was more difficult than the conservation task, which in turn was harder than tasks that contrasted conservation with addition to the glass judged as having less, or changing the color of the liquid. Although the three-dimensional nature of volume does not permit changing a dimension not relevant to volume, the interference of irrelevant numerical information in volume judgments provides another example of the importance of numerical information in a variety of quantitative judgments.

The relative difficulty of transformations across tasks is presented in Fig. 8.11 to facilitate comparing the difficulty of the same transformations over different domains. This Figure clearly shows the degree to which the relative difficulty of transformations interacts with the kind of material being judged. It is impossible to draw any general conclusion from these data concerning how difficult it is for children to realize that rolling material out, as in a conservation of quantity task (Piaget & Inhelder, 1974), does not affect the amount present. The difficulty of understanding the noneffects of this transformation is a function of the context in which it is presented. In a situation ostensibly involving number, this is a relatively easy conclusion for children to draw, even though it was the most difficult of the transformations presented for the length and area materials. Although some transformations were easy across all tasks (e.g., understanding the irrelevance of color or realizing that addition leads to increases in quantity), in general the difficulty of a transformation interacted to a large extent with the specific

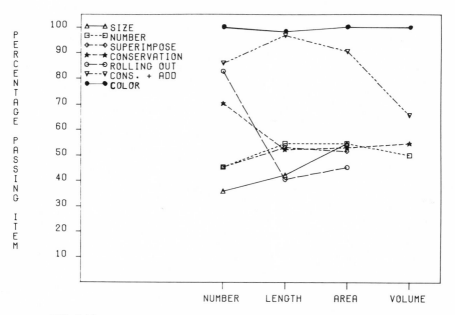

FIG. 8.11.   Relative difficulty of transformations across tasks. Percentage of children understanding the effect of a particular transformation is shown across the four tasks of number, length, area, and volume transformations.

context in which it was presented. Transformations that present children with problems are those that fool a relevant measurement procedure, such as increasing the length of a long piece by rolling it out. The effect of such transformations on a relevant quantitative dimension are different from their effect on quantity.

Even after children have learned that changes in irrelevant covarying dimensions do not affect quantity, as in the conservation tasks, they still have difficulty understanding that changes in relevant dimensions sometimes do not affect quantity. Learning what transformations affect "quantity" is more difficult than learning what transformations alter number, length, area, and volume. Measurement procedures exist for these separate quantitative domains, but learning how they interact may require yet another level of abstraction and organization. Procedures for measuring seem to leave their mark in the ways in which children conceive of and reason about the domains being measured.

Relations between Measurement and Reasoning about Transformations

Results of the two studies presented here support the view that the measurement strategies of children play a central role in their reasoning about quantity. Early measurement procedures provide evidence that children demonstrate a concern for the importance of quantitative invariance in determining whether equivalent amounts exist. If, as Stevens suggested, measurement involves the systematic use of some quantitative rule to determine relations between sets, even the youngest children studied demonstrate this fundamental concept of measurement. The development of measurement procedures consists of expanding the set of rules that determine quantitative relations, and learning the domain restrictions that determine when number, length, area, or volume are relevant in determining how much is present.

These measurement procedures play a more extensive role in children's reasoning about quantity than simply being methods of quantifying sets. The limitations of these measurement procedures appear to pose difficulties for children's understanding of quantity that include difficulties in understanding which transformations affect amount and which do not. In general, those transformations that are not incorporated into the measurement procedure for a particular domain are more difficult for children to understand than are the variations in dimensions studied in conservation tasks.

Results of the second study indicated that the limits of measurement procedures constitute real limits to children's ability to reason about quantitative transformations. Yet it would be a mistake to view such procedures as being merely limitations on children's understanding of quantity. If measurement procedures are indeed central to the way children reason about quantity, then understanding children's procedures should provide a way of improving performance. Eliciting a relevant measurement procedure should lead to increases in the sophistication with which children reason about quantitative invariants. Such was the logic of a third study (Miller, 1983a), part of which is discussed here, concerning children's understanding of the relation between height and width in determining area.

AFFORDANCE AND AMOUNT IN INFORMATION INTEGRATION

Representing and reasoning about stimuli that present more than a single salient dimension pose major difficulties for children. Piaget (Piaget et al., 1960) suggested that young children tend to center on a single salient dimension, unable to simultaneously consider two covarying dimensions. The Piagetian conservation tasks involve just this problem of learning that changes in a salient dimension (such as the height of a column of fluid) can be compensated by countervailing changes in a less obvious dimension (such as its width). Anderson and Cuneo (1978; Cuneo, 1980, 1982) have proposed an alternative to the view that young children center on a single dimension. They assert that children attend to more than one dimension, but use different rules than do adults in integrating dimensional information. Thus, whereas adults' judgments of the area of rectangles are a function of the *product* of length × width, children's judgments typically reflect the *sum* of these dimensions. Cuneo (1980) has suggested that children apply a "general purpose adding rule" to a variety of situations requiring the integration of dimensional information (such as judging numerosity of rows of items).

Yet use of such a "general purpose adding rule" may be an artifact of situations in which the appropriate measurement operations are not clear. One way to clarify for children the quantitative question they are being asked may be to ask about what area affords. Judging how large an area is may be more difficult than judging something that area affords. This difference in tasks may result in children's failing to utilize measurement procedures they possess that would be sufficient to solve the question being asked.

Perhaps the most basic affordance of area is the simple relation that one object will cover another as a function of their relative areas. "Will this cover that?" thus becomes the prototype for asking children to make judgments of what area affords. Children who resort to additive rules for making judgments of the size of areas may nonetheless know that the ability of one object to cover another is a function of their true areas.

Method

As part of a larger study, 16 3-year-olds were presented with two tasks requiring them to make estimates of the size of rectangles. The first was a replication of that used by Cuneo (1980); the second a modification designed to emphasize functional relations based on area and the procedures used to measure area.

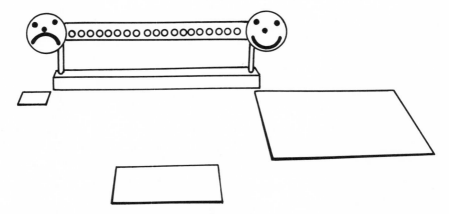

FIG. 8.12.   Modified graphic rating scale (Anderson & Cuneo, 1978) used to obtain area ratings of rectangles. Children rated the area of a target rectangle (shown in the center) in comparison to two end-anchors.

Area Ratings.   In the area-rating task based on (Anderson & Cuneo, 1978; Cuneo, 1980), children were presented with a "modified graphic rating scale," a scale with prominent "happy-face"/"sad-face" end anchors and 19 intermediate points. Fig. 8.12 illustrates the apparatus used. Children were told that the small circles between the happy and sad faces showed where tiny faces might go that are happier than the sad face but sadder than the happy one. Children were shown small (2 × 2 cm) and large (20 × 20 cm) cardboard squares as end anchors, which were identified as "cookies" that a hungry person might respectivley be quite sad and quite happy to eat. After this explanation, a practice task (reported in Cuneo, 1982) was administered until children could reach a monotonicity criterion in judging the degree of happiness associated with eating a set of seven circles of varying diameter. Three subjects (two girls and one boy) failed to meet this criterion and were replaced.

Following this practice task, children were administered two random replications of a set of nine rectangles representing the nine pairwise combinations of 8, 12, and 16 cm for height and width. As in the practice task, children were asked to point to the circle on the scale that showed how happy a child would be who was very hungry and had a cracker that size to eat.

Functional Judgments.   In the same session (with order counterbalanced), children also completed a functional-judgment task, using the same stimuli, illustrated in Fig. 8.13. This task was introduced as a game in which children had to help cover a floor with tiles. Children were shown the set of 4 × 4 cm tiles and were told that their job would be to figure out how many of the tiles would be needed to cover different floors. They were then administered a practice task in which they were asked to estimate the number of tiles needed to cover a series of three floors measuring 4×4, 4×68, and 4×32 cm. These sizes were chosen so that only one row of tiles would be required to cover a floor, avoiding the opportunity for any learning of how to integrate height and width information in judging area. Children were asked to count out the right number of tiles needed to just cover the floor and place them in a small cup. They were not allowed to solve the task by laying the tiles on the floor, but after the judgments were made in the practice task, the experimenter laid the tiles down to give feedback.

Following three practice judgments, children were told that they would be shown some more floors and asked to determine the number of tiles required to cover them. They were admonished to be careful in figuring out how many tiles were needed, because they would not be able to check to see whether they were correct. Children were then administered two random replications of the full set of nine rectangles, and asked to place into a small cup just enough tiles to cover each floor. Older children who counted to estimate the entire number of tiles needed before placing any in the cup were allowed, after several trials, to simply give a numerical response.

Results

Graphical Interpretation of Integration Rules.   In a graph of judgments by height and width, use of an additive-judgment rule implies that judgments will show additive, parallel effects. Therefore plots of judgment by width (with a curve factor of height) will consist of a series of parallel lines. Use of a multiplicative rule implies a "linear fan" (Anderson, 1974) with the lines corresponding to different widths diverging with increases in height. Fig. 8.14 illustrates a

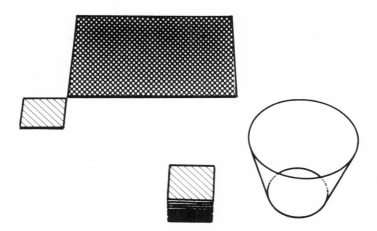

FIG. 8.13.   Materials used to obtain functional judgments of area. Children estimated the number of small square "tiles" required to cover a larger rectangular "floor" by placing enough tiles in a cup to cover the target rectangle.

pure additive model, Fig. 8.15 shows the linear-fan characteristic of a purely multiplicative model.

Statistical Analysis.   The additive and multiplicative models of Anderson (1974) have straightforward statistical interpretations within an analysis of variance framework. In a factorial design with height and width as factors, use of an additive model implies significant main effects for both factors, with minimal interaction between them. A multiplicative model implies a significant interaction between the two factors, which should be positive and concentrated in the linear × linear component.

Area-Rating Task.   Mean area ratings are presented in Fig. 8.16. The impression of a rough parallelism in the mean judgments is supported statistically, with a Sex × Height × Width ANOVA yielding significant main effects of Height ($F(2,28)112.98$, $p < .001$) and Width ($F(2,28) = 99.23$, $p < .001$). Neither the overall Height × Width interaction ($F(4,56) = .98$, *ns*), the Linear × Linear component ($F(1,14) = 3.45$, *ns*), nor the residual component ($F(3,42) = .37$, *ns*) were significant. Thus, this group of preschoolers conform to the constraints of the Height + Width adding rule of Anderson and Cuneo.

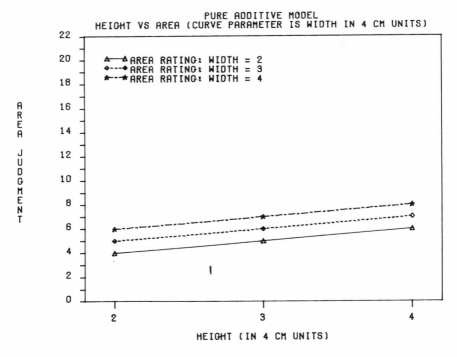

FIG. 8.14.   Graphical interpretation of a pure additive model of area judgments. Note the parallelism of slopes for different widths of rectangles.

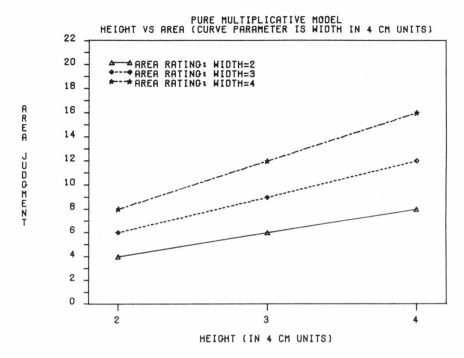

FIG. 8.15. Graphical interpretation of a pure multiplicative model of area judgments. Note the diverging "linear-fan effect" of slopes for different widths of rectangles.

The use of a general adding rule for rating area did not, however, extend to functional judgments. Fig. 8.17 depicts mean performance on this task. A Sex × Height × Width ANOVA indicates significant main effects of Height ($F(2,28) = 64.44, p < .001$), Width ($F(2,28) = 90.11, p < .001$), and a significant interaction between the two ($F(4,56) = 3.55, p < .05$ concentrated in the Linear × Linear component ($F(1,14) = 9.83, p < .01$). This discrepancy in performance across two parallel tasks indicates that under some circumstances young children can abandon a general purpose adding rule and replace it with a more sophisticated use of area information.

The pattern of judgments found in this study can be described simply. Preschool children make judgments of what area affords that correspond to the normative relation between dimensions. Young children do demonstrate the general adding strategy described by Anderson and Cuneo, but this strategy appears to be a response to questions requiring judgments of size rather than judgments of what size affords.

Judging an affordance rather than directly estimating size may be easier for children because doing so clarifies an ambiguity present in tasks that require children to make judgments of amount. As shown in the second study, "amount"

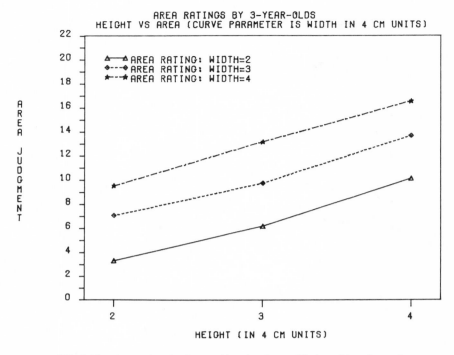

FIG. 8.16.   Area ratings by 3-year-olds using the modified graphic rating scale show a rough parallelism consistent with an additive model.

can at times involve number, length, area, and volume, or combinations of these quantitative dimensions. Which is relevant may not be clear when children are asked to judge size, and lacking understanding of what is required, they may revert to some primitive general purpose amount rule. Judging whether one can lay an object on another one requires a judgment of its size relative to the other object, and this task would seem more difficult than simply reporting perception of its size. Yet as E. J. Gibson has stressed (E. J. Gibson & Rader, 1979), perception is in large part determined by the performances that perception supports. Presenting children with tasks in which the requisite performance is unclear can often mask competence. Presenting tasks that tap into familiar procedures and problems can lead to discovery of areas of early competence.

Measurement and Understanding

The indication that children's procedures for measuring play a significant role in their understanding of the domain being measured turns the Piagetian view of measurement on its head. Practical measurement procedures appear *not* to be late-developing concomitants of a more general understanding of quantity. In-

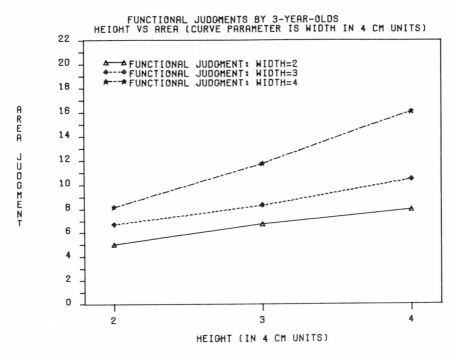

FIG. 8.17.   Functional judgments by 3-year-olds (using the tile materials) show a divergence consistent with some form of multiplicative rule.

stead, the measurement procedures of children embody their most sophisticated understanding of the domain in question. The limitations of these procedures constitute significant limits on children's understanding of quantity, while the domain of practical knowledge contained in measurement procedures may presage the more general understanding of quantitative invariance that characterizes older children and adults.

TWO VIEWS OF MEASUREMENT: IMPLICATIONS FOR COGNITIVE DEVELOPMENT

The Piagetian view that quantitative development proceeds from a general (qualitative) understanding of quantity to specific quantifications is challenged by the demonstration that children possess an early, if limited, understanding of quantitative invariance contained in measurement procedures. The difference between these views involves more than an argument over the age at which children acquire skills. If early and limited understanding of quantitative invariance based on measurement exists, this knowledge cannot be overlooked as the basis for developing a more general understanding of quantity. The presence in preschoolers of such precursors of concepts acquired later also provides the basis for a modified view of the nature of early skills and the role of induction in cognitive development.

The contrast between the view that successful measurement requires a more general understanding of quantity and the belief that previously-learned measurement procedures are the basis for more general understanding may be clarified by comparison with a parallel controversy in a different field. Wittgenstein (1974a;b; Diamond, 1976) contended that research on the logical foundations of mathematics such as that of Whitehead and Russell (1910) and their successors did not really provide the *basis* for mathematics, but rather represented a systematization of existing procedures. As Wittgenstein (1974a) characterized the distinction:

> A system's being based on first principles is not the same as its being developed from them. It makes a difference whether it is like a house resting on its lowest walls or like a celestial body floating free in space which we have begun to build beneath although we might have built anywhere else [p. 297].

Wittgenstein argued that mathematics stands in the latter relation to its putative foundations. People judge the adequacy of logical foundations for mathematics relative to the previously-known characteristics of mathematics, rather than actually using the ''foundations'' of mathematics as the basis for developing mathematics. Furthermore, he emphasized the priority of mathematical procedures over their logical foundations by suggesting that no one would abandon arithmetic because of any conceivable paradox that might be shown in some model of arithmetic.

In contrast to Wittgenstein's assertions that logical foundations for mathematics are misnamed, the Piagetian view (Beth & Piaget, 1961/1966; Piaget, 1970/1972, 1975/1977) takes logical foundations for quantity literally. In this view, it is only the possession of basic principles such as compensation and reversibility that render children's quantification meaningful to themselves and others. Because of this emphasis on general understanding, Piagetians have tended to disregard evidence of early but limited competence, believing that acquisition of general logical principles is required to turn children's limited *physical* abstraction into a *reflective* abstraction that implies real understanding. Whatever quantitative procedures and algorithms children may master before developing the logical basis are disparaged as being merely verbal learning.

Recent evidence including that described here indicating that young children structure their interactions with the quantitative world through the measurement procedures available to them suggests that such procedures need to be taken more seriously. Measurement procedures do indeed seem to be connected to children's reasoning about the quantitative domains being measured. The development of a more general understanding of why measurement works, as in learning that a principle of one-to-one correspondence underlies counting, does resemble the development of logical foundations for mathematics in that both provide explanations for why previously existing procedures work.

The belief that procedures can be based on or follow principles without having been developed from more general understanding resembles the recent view that much of development involves attaining more general access to knowledge previously limited to specific situations. The obvious (to adults) parallel between knowledge that children possess in one context but lack in another has led to the characterization (Brown, 1981; Gelman, 1982; Gelman & Gallistel, 1978; Pylyshyn, 1978; Rozin, 1976) of young children as lacking an ability to access information or processes from one procedure when required for another. With development two kinds of cross-task access develop (Pylyshyn, 1978). Children show an increased ability to use information acquired in one context when it is required in another. At the same time they become more conscious of the information, able to refer to and reflect upon it. Over time, children can become conscious of principles such as one-to-one correspondence that they previously followed in measuring, while gradually learning the relations between measuring in different domains.

WHAT ARE CHILDREN MEASURING?

This idea that children can access invariant information about quantity without possessing any more general awareness or understanding of invariance fits in well with J. J. Gibson's (1974, 1979) explanation of perception. As discussed previously, perception in Gibson's view primarily involves the determination of functional relations that are based on invariant features but need not imply any concepts or consciousness of these features. Instead of being inferences from more basic quantitative information, answers to questions such as "Will this fit in here?" or "Are any of my candies missing?" are seen as the basic information that perception produces. The measurement procedures discussed here share with Gibson's model of perception a concern for determining information about affordances. The distinction between an affordance (such as whether this stick will be long enough to reach a desired object) and the invariant information on which it is based is helpful in considering the situations in which children are sensitive to quantitative invariance. Judging affordances, such as judging a "winner" from a set that has more items after learning that the "winner" will be the more numerous set (Gelman, 1972), is easier than is the task of judging number without this context (e.g., Cuneo, 1982). The "reflective access" reflected in a general and conscious understanding of one-to-one correspondence, or the relations between length, width, and area involves the development of a conscious understanding of the invariant information on which previously understood affordances were based.

How might such an understanding develop? The transition from an understanding of quantity limited to measurement procedures and yielding information about affordances to a more general understanding of quantity may be a consequence of learning about the effects of measurement procedures. Exploration of the results of applying procedures under different circumstances, and induction of the constancies that emerge from such experimentation, provides one plausible explanation for the development of conscious and general understanding of concepts that were previously tacit and local. Given Piaget's belief that general understanding of quantity is a prerequisite for the development of measurement procedures, it is interesting that he gives an example of how measurement procedures might lead to an understanding of quantity that is no longer tied to specific procedures. Consider the following account (Piaget, 1974):

> I should like to give an example . . . in which knowledge is abstracted from actions, from the coordination of actions, and not from objects. This example, one we have studied quite thoroughly with many children, was first suggested to me by a mathematician friend who quoted it as the point of departure of his interest in mathematics. When he was a small child, he was counting pebbles one day; he lined them up in a row, counted them from left to right, and got ten. Then, just for fun, he counted them from right to left to see what number he would get, and was astonished that he got ten again. He put the pebbles in a circle and counted them, and once again there were ten. He went around the circle in the other way and got ten again. And no matter how he put the pebbles down, when he counted them, the number came to ten. He discovered here what is known in mathematics as the principle of commutativity, that is, the sum is independent of order. But how did he discover this? Is this commutativity a property of the pebbles? It is true that the pebbles, as it were, let him arrange them in various ways; he could not have done the same thing with drops of water. But the order was not in the pebbles; it was he, the subject, who put the pebbles in a line and then in a circle. Moreover, the sum was not in the pebbles themselves; it was he who united them. The knowledge that this future mathematician discovered that day was drawn, then, not from the physical properties of the pebbles, but from the actions that he carried out on the pebbles. This knowledge is what I call logical mathematical knowledge and not physical knowledge [pp. 16–17].

Piaget terms this an example of logico-mathematical learning for two reasons. The first is his belief that number is not a perceptible attribute of objects in the way that weight is. The evidence for early perceptual sensitivity to number presented elsewhere in this volume indicates that this distinction between perceptible and constructed attributes is a tenuous one. A second reason for terming this learning locico-mathematical rather than physical is that the child was not counting to determine how many pebbles there were, but was rather investigating the non-effects of spatial arrangement on numerosity.

In order for such an experiment to be convincing, however, the child needs confidence that counting will show how many pebbles are present. Measurement procedures provide a source of information about the physical world that can lead to the development of a general understanding of quantity that is less closely tied to specific measurement procedures. Research such as that of Bearison (1969) showing the effectiveness of training in measurement strategies in producing conservation suggests that such training can be quite successful. Training in measurement can be successful in inducing a more general understanding of quantitative invariance because even young children are familiar with the basic requirement of measurement: the need to employ systematic procedures to determine quantitative equivalence.

The inductive role of measurement procedures hypothesized here has more than a superficial resemblance to a developmental model proposed for the acquisition of number concepts by Klahr and Wallace (1976). They proposed that infants possess an early perceptual sensitivity to number (subitizing) that provides the foundation for early learning about counting, a system for ascertaining number that can be extended beyond the limits of such subitizing. In the Klahr and Wallace model, early subitizing plays a propaedeutic role in the development of counting. This perceptually-based sensitivity to number paves the way for later acquisition of counting by providing children with means of evaluating their counting while also ensuring early sensitivity to number. Measurement procedures may occupy a similarly propaedeutic position to the generalized reasoning about quantities that adults can demonstrate, pointing beyond themselves to an understanding of quantitative constancies that at times make measurement unnecessary.

Lorenz (1971a,b, 1977) has suggested that species such as humans that are "specialists in nonspecialization" come prepared with innate teaching mechanisms. These mechanisms produce sensitivity to certain kinds of information and involve (Lorenz, 1977) "structures that direct learning into profitable channels and produce the teaching mechanisms which ensure that the gaps in the various programmes are filled in relevant ways [p. 89]. Even though Lorenz is talking about biologically innate structures, the kinds of measurement procedures described in this chapter may play a similar role in determining later development. Measurement procedures may channel induction in the direction of certain kinds of (measurable) regularities and away from others, ensuring that children will develop the kinds of general knowledge that will permit them to dispense with measurement in some kinds of tasks.

The measurement procedures described in this chapter provide children with methods of solving important practical problems. If they did no more, their significance for cognitive development would be limited. In fact they may do much more, laying an experiential basis from which one might induce, as Piaget's mathematician did, the nature of quantitative invariance by experimenting with the effects of transformations on measurement procedures. Along with providing means of solving mundane problems, measurement procedures provide children with tools for exploring their environment and determining its regularities. In this may lie their most important contribution to cognitive development. In the same way that practical problems of navigation contributed to the discovery of geometrical and physical constancies, the measurement procedures young children develop to solve mundane tasks may in time form the basis for reasoning about the regularities and transformations that define the quantitative world.

ACKNOWLEDGMENTS

The first two studies described here were part of a dissertation submitted to the University of Minnesota in partial fulfillment of the requirements for the Ph.D. I would like to acknowledge the contributions of my advisor, Herbert L. Pick, Jr., and the other members of my committee: Marion Perlmutter, Anne Pick, Albert Yonas, Ruth Pitt, and Richard Weinberg. Rochel Gelman also contributed significantly to the development of the work reported here. Thanks are also due Craig Barclay, Robert Flodin, and James Stigler for comments on earlier versions of this chapter. The research reported here was supported by fellowships and a dissertation grant from the Danforth Foundation and the Graduate School of the University of Minnesota.

REFERENCES

Anderson, N. H. Algebraic models in perception. In E. C. Carterette & M. P. Friedman (Eds.), *Handbook of Perception* (Vol. 2). New York: Academic Press, 1974.

Anderson, N. H., & Cuneo, D. O. The height + width rule in children's judgments of quantity. *Journal of Experimental Psychology: General*, 1978, *107*, 335–378.

Antell, S. E., & Keating, D. P. Perception of numerical invariance in neonates. *Child Development*, 1983, *54*, 695–701.

Bearison, D. J. The role of measurement operations in the acquisition of conservation. *Developmental Psychology*, 1969, *1*, 653–60.

Beckwith, M., & Restle, F. The process of enumeration. *Psychological Review*, 1966, *73*, 437–444.

Beth, E. W., & Piaget, J. *Mathematical epistemology and psychology.* New York: Gordon & Beach, 1966. (Originally published, 1961.)

Brown, A. L. Learning and development: The problems of compatibility, access and induction. *Human Development*, 1981, *25*, 89–115.

Brown, J. S., & Burton, R. R. Diagnostic models for procedural bugs in basic mathematical skills. *Cognitive Science*, 1978, *4*, 379–426.

Courant, R., & Robbins, H. *What is mathematics?* New York: Oxford University Press, 1941.

Cuneo, D. H. A general strategy for quantity judgments: The height + width rule. *Child Development*, 1980, *51*, 299–301.

Cuneo, D. H. Children's judgments of numerical quantity: A new view of early quantification. *Cognitive Psychology*, 1982, *14*, 13–44.

Dantzig, T. *Number: The language of science.* New York: Free Press, 1967.

Diamond, C. *Wittgenstein's lectures on the foundations of mathematics: Cambridge, 1939*. Ithaca, N.Y.: Cornell University Press, 1976.

Edwards, A. On Guttman's scale analysis. *Educational and Psychological Measurement*, 1948, *8*, 313–318.

Flavell, J. *Cognitive development*. Englewood Cliffs, N.J.: Prentice-Hall, 1977.

Fuson, K. C., Secada, W. G., & Hall, J. W. Matching, counting and conservation of numerical equivalence. *Child Development*, 1983, *54*, 91–97.

Gelman, R. The nature and development of early number concepts. In H. Reese (Ed.), *Advances in child development and behavior* (Vol. 7). New York: Academic Press, 1972.

Gelman, R. Counting in the preschooler: What does and does not develop. In R. S. Siegler (Ed.), *Children's thinking: What develops?* Hillsdale, N.J.: Lawrence Erlbaum Associates, 1978.

Gelman, R. Accessing one-to-one correspondence: Still another paper about conservation. *British Journal of Psychology*, 1982, *73*, 209–220.

Gelman, R., & Gallistel, C. R. *The child's understanding of number*. Cambridge, Mass.: Harvard University Press, 1978.

Gibson, E. J., & Rader, N. The perceiver as performer. In G. Hale & M. Lewis (Eds.), *Attention and cognitive development*. New York: Plenum Press, 1979.

Gibson, J. J. A note on ecological optics. In E. C. Cartarette & M. P. Friedman (Eds.), *Handbook of perception* (Vol. 1). New York: Academic Press, 1974.

Gibson, J. J. *The ecological approach to visual perception*. Boston: Houghton-Mifflin, 1979.

Goodenough, W. H. A technique for scale analysis. *Educational and Psychological Measurement*, 1944, *4*, 179–180.

Green, B. F. A method of scalogram analysis using summary statistics. *Psychometrika*, 1956, *21*, 79–88.

Hatano, G. Cognitive consequences of practice in culture specific procedural skills. *Quarterly Newsletter of Laboratory of Comparative Human Cognition*, 1982, *4*, 15–18.

Hatano, G., & Inagaki, K. *Two courses of expertise*. Paper presented at the Conference on Child Development in Japan and the United States, Stanford, California, April 1983.

Inhelder, B., Sinclair, H., & Bovet, M. *Learning and the development of cognition*. Cambridge, Mass.: Harvard University Press, 1974.

Klahr, D., & Wallace, J. G. *Cognitive development: An information-processing view*. Hillsdale, N.J.: Lawrence Erlbaum Associates, 1976.

Kline, M. *Mathematics and the physical world*. New York: Thomas Y. Crowell, 1959.

Kline, M. *Mathematical thought from ancient to modern times*. New York: Oxford University Press, 1972.

Lorenz, K. Part and parcel in animals and human societies: A methodological discussion. In K. Lorenz, *Studies in animal and human behaviour* (Vol. 2). Cambridge, Mass.: Harvard University Press, 1971. (Originally published, 1950.) (a)

Lorenz, K. Psychology and phylogeny. In K. Lorenz, *Studies in animal and human behaviour* (Vol. 2). Cambridge, Mass.: Harvard University Press, 1971. (Originally published, 1954.) (b)

Lorenz, K. *Behind the mirror*. New York: Harcourt Brace Jovanovich, 1977. (Originally published, 1973.)

Miller, K. *Affordance and amount in information integration*. Paper presented at the biennial meeting of the Society for Research in Child Development, Detroit, April 1983. (a)

Miller, K. *Early measurement revisited: The nature of immature strategies*. Paper presented at the biennial meeting of the Society for Research in Child Development, Detroit, April 1983. (b)

Miller, K. *The nature and role of spontaneous measurement procedures*. Unpublished manuscript, Michigan State University, 1983. (c)

Miller, K., & Baillargeon, R. *Length versus distance: Bridging gaps in preschoolers' knowledge*. Paper presented at the annual convention of the American Psychological Association, Washington, D.C., September 1982.

Piaget, J. *Genetic epistemology*. New York: Columbia University Press, 1970.

Piaget, J. *Psychology and epistemology*. London: Penguin Press, 1972.

Piaget, J. *The development of thought: Equilibration of cognitive structures*. New York: Viking Press, 1977. (Originally published, 1975.)

Piaget, J., & Inhelder, I. *The child's construction of quantities: Conservation and atomism*. London: Routledge and Kegan Paul, 1974.

Piaget, J., Inhelder, I., & Szeminska, A. *The child's conception of geometry*. London: Routledge and Kegan Paul, 1960.

Pylyshyn, Z. W. When is attribution of beliefs justified? *The Behavioral and Brain Sciences*, 1978 *4*, 592–593.

Rozin, P. The evolution of intelligence and access to the cognitive unconscious. In J. M. Sprague & A. D. Epstein (Eds.), *Progress in psychobiology and physiological psychology* (Vol. 6). New York: Academic Press, 1976.

Siegler, R. S. Developmental sequences within and between concepts. *Monographs of the Society for Research in Child Development*, 1981, *46*(2 Serial No. 189).

Starkey, P., & Cooper, R. G. Numerosity perception in human infants. *Science*, 1980, *210*, 1033–1035.

Starkey, P., Spelke, E., & Gelman, R. *Number competence in infants: Sensitivity to numeric invariance and numeric change*. Paper presented at the meeting of the International Conference on Infant Studies, New Haven, Connecticut, April 1980.

Stevens, S. S. On the theory of scales of measurement. *Science*, 1946, *103*, 677–680.

Stevens, S. S. *Psychophysics*. New York: Wiley, 1975.

Strauss, M. S., & Curtis, L. E. Infant perception of numerosity. *Child Development*, 1981, *52*, 1146–1152.

Whitehead, A., & Russell, B. *Principia mathematica* (Vols. 1–3). Cambridge, Eng.: Cambridge University Press, 1910.

Wittgenstein, L. *Philosophical grammar*. Oxford: Basil Blackwell, 1974. (a)

Wittgenstein, L. *Remarks on the foundations of arithmetic*. Cambridge, Mass.: MIT Press, 1974. (b)

9

Strategy Choices in Addition and Subtraction: How Do Children Know What to Do?

Robert S. Siegler
Jeffrey Shrager
Carnegie-Mellon University

Out of all of the problem-solving strategies that people could use, how do they decide which ones to use? Even a task as mundane as spelling reveals the variety of strategies that people can employ. Suppose that someone was trying to spell the word "accommodation." One approach would be to retrieve the spelling. An alternative would be to try to form an image of what the word looks like. Another possibility would be to write out several alternative spellings and to try to recognize the correct one. Yet another strategy would be to look up the word in a dictionary. These variations in strategies are not only "between-subjects" phenomena. Individuals often use each of the approaches at different times, even on a single word.

Good reasons exist for people to know and to use multiple strategies for achieving a goal. Strategies differ in their accuracy, in the amounts of time they require, in their memory demands, and in the range of problems to which they apply. Strategy choices involve tradeoffs among these properties so that people can cope with cognitive and situational constraints. These cognitive and situational constraints can vary from moment to moment, even within what ordinarily is viewed as a single problem. The broader the range of strategies that people know, the more precisely they can shape their approaches to meet these changing circumstances. As becomes evident in the course of this chapter, even young children can choose strategies in adaptive ways. Our goals are to specify how they make such strategy choices, how the ability to make them develops, and what functions the strategy-choice process serves.

The particular strategy choices that we examine are those that preschoolers make in solving simple arithmetic problems. Previous reports indicate that children use a variety of strategies to add and subtract. They count from 1, count on

229

from the first or the higher number, put up their fingers and count them, tap their feet rhythmically, and decompose complex problems into simpler ones (e.g., 3 + 4 = (3 + 3) = 1). The reports of these visible and audible strategies have been largely anecdotal, but they have been sufficiently persistent to leave little doubt of their existence. Left undescribed, however, have been the mechanisms by which children arrive at a strategy on a particular problem and whether their use of overt strategies results in more effective problem solving. These issues are the focus of the present research.

We begin the chapter by discussing current views on how people select strategies and on how they solve simple addition problems. Then we examine several recent experiments indicating that a single child may use as many as four distinct strategies in solving such problems. The particular strategy that children use on each problem turns out to be closely related to the problem's difficulty. Next we present a distribution of associations model that accounts for this close relation between strategy use and problem difficulty as well as for the existence of the four strategies and for their temporal characteristics. Following this, we present evidence that the model applies to performance on a broader range of addition problems and also to performance on subtraction problems. Then we present a second distribution of associations model that subsumes the first model's assumptions about performance but that also accounts for how strategy choices on simple addition and subtraction problems develop. This second model is expressed as a running computer simulation that initially generates poor performance but that learns from its experience in such a way that it eventually produces patterns of strategy use, solution times, and correct answers and errors much like those of 4- and 5-year-olds. Finally, we speculate about how the revised model might apply to other domains, such as spelling and beginning reading, and discuss its general implications for how people arrive at strategies.

A BRIEF REVIEW OF THE LITERATURES ON STRATEGY CHOICE AND ELEMENTARY ADDITION

The Issue of Strategy Choice

Cognitive psychologists who study adults have devoted considerable effort to determining *the* strategy people use to perform particular tasks. Out of these efforts have come models of sentence verification (Clark & Chase, 1972; Just & Carpenter, 1975; Trabasso, Rollins, & Shaughnessy, 1971), spatial information processing (Cooper & Shepard, 1973; Shepard & Metzler, 1971), transitive inference (H. H. Clark, 1969; Huttenlocher & Higgins, 1971; Sternberg, 1977), and many other tasks. Recently, however, a number of investigators have noted that people's strategies vary. They have suggested that cognitive theories should explain how people choose among alternative approaches. Consider three recent comments:

> Discussion of the appropriate models for psycholinguistic tasks is usually couched in general terms (i.e., "What models apply to people?"). Our results can be seen as a reminder that this approach is too simplistic. The same ostensibly linguistic task can be approached in radically different ways by different people (MacLeod, Hunt, & Mathews, 1978, p. 506).

> Too often psychologists set out to study *the* way that a task is performed, and miss one of the most interesting and general aspects of human cognitive performance: that there is more than one way to skin a cat. Once we accept this flexibility as a significant characteristic of the way that humans think and learn, rather than a troublesome source of variation in our data, it becomes important to understand the factors that control the adoption of one strategy over others (Farah & Kosslyn, 1982, p. 164).

> Information processing psychologists have little to say on "how it is that the child knows what to do" and "what" inside the child's head makes the decisions [Gardner, 1982, p. 421].

These opinions and recommendations have been accompanied by a growing amount of research demonstrating that people do use diverse strategies on tasks for which cognitive psychologists previously had proposed a single model. Hunt and his colleagues demonstrated that different people use different approaches to verify sentences (MacLeod et al., 1978; Mathews, Hunt, & MacLeod, 1980). Cooper and her colleagues described alternative strategies that people use to perform a spatial comparison task (Cooper & Regan, 1982; Glushko & Cooper, 1978). Egan and Grimes-Farrow (1982) and Sternberg and Weil (1980) identified several strategies that people use to draw transitive inferences.

All of these studies of strategy differences followed the comparative approach. That is, they defined groups on some preexisting status variable and demonstrated that group membership predicted behavioral differences. Hunt's, Egan's, Cooper's, and Sternberg's studies all used spatial and verbal abilities as the covariate. People relatively high in spatial ability used one strategy; people relatively high in verbal ability used another. Cross-cultural investigators (e.g., Wagner, 1978) and those interested in aging (e.g., Reder, 1982) have also contrasted the strategies used by members of different groups.

Developmental psychologists have a longer tradition of attending to strategy differences than do psychologists who study adults. One of the central phenomena of developmental psychology is that people of different ages often vary in their approaches. Five-year-olds rarely rehearse when asked to remember arbitrary lists of words; 8-year-olds usually do rehearse; 11-year-olds rehearse in a more comprehensive, less repetitive, way than 8-year-olds (Flavell, Beach, & Chinsky, 1966; Naus, Ornstein, & Aivano, 1977). Five-year-olds judge which side of a balance scale will go down solely on the basis of weight; 9-year-olds usually consider both weight and distance from the fulcrum but do not know the proportionality rule for combining them; at least some 18-year-olds compute relative torques on the two sides of the balance (Inhelder & Piaget, 1958; Siegler, 1976). Similar strategy differences among different-aged children have been found on analogical reasoning, probability learning, visual scanning, and many other tasks (Sternberg & Rifkin, 1979; Vurpillot, 1968; Weir, 1964).

Investigations showing that people of a particular age, ability profile, or culture tend to use a particular strategy are useful in at least three ways. They document the range of strategies that people can use to solve the problem. They illustrate that different people spontaneously choose different strategies. They show that these choices frequently correlate with group membership. However, they may also divert attention from an issue of even greater interest: *how* strategy choices are made. A person high in spatial ability need not always use a spatially oriented strategy, nor one high in verbal ability a verbally oriented one. Egan and Grimes-Farrow (1982), Mathews et al. (1980), and Sternberg and Ketron (1982) have all demonstrated that people who ordinarily use one strategy will use a different one if instructed to do so. Cooper and Regan (1982) showed that aspects of the particular stimulus configuration also influence which strategy people adopt. Even if people were not so flexible, they would still need strategy-choice procedures. Before entering the experimental situation, most people do not have extensive experience with the tasks that they encounter (e.g., solving three-term syllogism problems). How does a person high in spatial aptitude know to use a spatially rather than a verbally oriented strategy?

One set of efforts to explain strategy choices is included under the heading of metacognition. Underlying much metacognitive research is the plausible belief that people use explicit knowledge of their cognitive capacities, available strategies, and task demands to determine which strategy to use. When confronted with a problem, they might reason, "This is a difficult problem, too difficult to solve without a powerful strategy such as *x*, I'd better use *x*."

Several difficulties have arisen in metacognitive research that make this mode of explanation less promising than it once appeared. On an empirical level, research has revealed only modest correlations between metacognitive knowledge and performance measures (see reviews by Flavell & Wellman, 1977, and by Cavanaugh & Perlmutter, 1982). On a theoretical level, there is considerable lack of clarity about how metacognitive knowledge would lead to strategy choices. Do people make explicit judgments about their intellectual capacities, about available strategies, and about task demands every time they face a task that they could perform in two or more ways? If not, how do they decide on which tasks to do so? Do they consider every strategy that they conceivably could use on the task or only some subset of them? If only a subset, how do they decide which ones? How do people know what their cognitive capacity will be or what strategies they could apply when they are presented a novel task? Determining how metacognitive knowledge leads to strategy choices is much more complex than initially might be supposed.

There also appears to be a mismatch between the seemingly useful strategies that very young children at times adopt and their apparent lack of metacognitive knowledge. DeLoache (this volume) reported that when $1\frac{1}{2}$ year olds in a laboratory situation saw an experimenter hide objects that they later needed to find, they engaged in more labeling and other types of discussion of the objects than when the experimenter hid them in the children's own homes. The children did not discuss the objects at all when they remained visible throughout the waiting period. DeLoache concluded that the children used the labeling and discussion strategy when they needed it to keep alive a memory trace that otherwise might fade. This conclusion seemed consistent with the data. But how did the $1\frac{1}{2}$-year-olds make this decision? Did they possess sufficient knowledge of their memory capacities and of task demands to anticipate that their memory traces might fade if they did not talk about the hidden objects?

In sum, a decade of research on people's explicit metacognitive knowledge has not explained how they arrive at their strategies. This lack of success raises an intriguing possibility. Perhaps people can arrive at adaptive strategies without explicitly considering capacity limitations, available strategies, and task demands. This possibility will be the focus of the present chapter.

The development of addition skills.   Research on how addition skills develop, like research on strategy choice, has followed the comparative approach of equating the performance of one group with one strategy and the performance of another group with another. The two best-known models are those of Groen and Parkman (1972) and Ashcraft (1982). Groen and Parkman proposed the *min* model. This model indicates that when people are given a problem with two addends, they add by selecting the larger addend and counting up from it the number of times indicated by the smaller. Groen and Parkman hypothesized that the time needed to identify the larger number was a constant for all problems. Therefore, solution times depended only on the number of increments indicated by the smaller number (hence the name min model). The only exception to this formula involved ties, problems with equal augend and addend. Groen and Parkman suggested that answers to these problems were retrieved directly, at a uniformly rapid rate, so that solution times for all tie problems would be faster than solution times for any other problem (excepting those with zero as an addend, which would be retrieved as quickly as ties, due to their not requiring any increments of the larger number).

Several types of evidence supported this model. Groen and Parkman found that the solution times of both first graders and adults increased by constant amounts with each increase in the minimum number. Svenson (1975) and Svenson and Broquist (1975) found that the model fit the performance of third graders, and, with a small modification, slow-learning older children. Ginsburg (1977) found that children's verbalizations about their ongoing solution processes often alluded to counting on from the larger number.

Even though Groen and Parkman's adult data fit the min model, they were reluctant to conclude that adults used the approach. One reason was implausibility; it seemed unlikely that adults had failed to memorize the addition facts after years of using them. A second reason was the shallow slope (20 msec/increment) of the regression equation that fit the adults' performances. For the min model to apply, the incrementing process would need to be faster than any known elementary information process. Therefore, Groen and Parkman postulated a different model of adult performance. On 95% of trials, adults would retrieve the answer. On the remaining 5%, they would fail to retrieve and instead use the min process. By assuming equally rapid retrieval on all retrieval trials and incrementing times similar to those of children on min process trials, Groen and Parkman were able to fit this model to adults' performances.

Ashcraft (1982) formulated a different account, which he labeled the fact-retrieval model. Ashcraft's alternative was motivated by his observation that the magnitude of the squared sum was a better predictor of adults' solution times than was the magnitude of the minimum number. (Groen and his colleagues do not appear to have examined this predictor variable). To account for the predictive value of sum squared, Ashcraft hypothesized that adults represent addition facts in a form much like a standard addition table, with augends (first numbers) heading each column and addends (second numbers) heading each row. In this mental table, distances between columns and between rows would increase exponentially with increases in the absolute magnitude of the augend and addend. For example, the distance between the third and fourth rows would be greater than that between the second and third rows. Adults would locate the answer to each problem by traveling from the origin to the appropriate augend, traveling down to the appropriate addend, then reading out the sum. Solution times would be directly proportional to distance traveled. The exponential spacing of the rows and columns would lead to a more than linear increase of solution time with increases in the sum. Ashcraft (1982) reported that this model did not fit first graders' performance as well as did the min model, that the two models fit the performance of third graders equally well, and that the fact-retrieval model fit better the performance of fourth through sixth graders and adults. He therefore concluded that young children use the min approach and that older children and adults use the fact-retrieval model.

Like the previously cited comparative research, these studies of how people solve simple addition problems highlight the fact that people with different demographic characteristics often use different strategies. Also like the previous research, however, they do not indicate how people arrive at which strategy to use. Further, both models have a somewhat ad hoc flavor. Why should children treat all ties in one way and all nonties in another? Why are columns and rows in the fact-retrieval matrix spaced exponentially? How would children make the transition from the min process to the exponentially spaced matrix?

The models may also underestimate the diversity of children's addition strategies. As noted previously, observational studies have revealed that children sometimes put up their fingers and count them; other times they tap their feet rhythmically; yet other times they count aloud with no obvious referent (Hebbeler, 1976; Ilg & Ames, 1951; Yoshimura, 1974). What is the purpose of using these strategies? What is their relation to the min and fact-retrieval models? How do children decide when to use each approach?

Some Methodological Issues

It is not coincidental that researchers working with chronometric data have tended to postulate a single strategy for all subjects within a given age or ability group, whereas researchers relying on direct observation have postulated multiple strategies. Solution-time data are sufficiently noisy and sufficiently remote from the processes that produce the behavior that strategies can be inferred from them only by aggregating over a large number of trials. Even given a large number of trials, it is extraordinarily difficult to infer from a person's solution times that he or she used multiple strategies. In contrast, simply observing a child can reveal multiple strategies if visible or audible behavior accompanies the strategies. Such observations, however, do not yield sufficiently precise data to allow use of powerful methods for inferring the processes by which children execute each particular strategy.

Videotaping young children's performance seemed to combine the advantages of the two approaches. It would chronicle the behavior occurring between presentation of the problem and statement of the answer, thus allowing assessment of the range of strategies that children used. It would also allow precise measurement of solution times and identification of particular errors. These objective indices would help in inferring how each strategy was executed and how children chose among strategies. Together, the visual record of the strategies and the solution time and error data promised to make the strategy-choice issue tractable.

The possibility that even a single person performing a single task may use a variety of strategies at different times raises several issues. What strategies are used? What are their accuracy and temporal characteristics? How does a person arrive at the strategy to use on a given occasion? Does use of diverse strategies aid the efficiency or accuracy of solutions? If so, how? In the next section, we describe a recent empirical study that addressed these issues.

AN EMPIRICAL STUDY OF CHILDREN'S ADDITION

Method

Siegler and Robinson (1982) examined 4- and 5-year-olds' addition strategies. The 30 children who participated, 17 boys and 13 girls, were students at a university-run preschool.

Children were videotaped as they solved 25 addition problems. The problems were the possible combinations of augends from one to five and addends from one to five. The instructions were the following:

> I want you to imagine that you have a pile of oranges. I'll give you more oranges to add to your pile; then you need to tell me how many oranges you have altogether. Okay? You have m oranges, and I'm going to give you n to add to your pile. How many do you have altogether?

After four or five questions, many children indicated that they preferred to hear the problem in the form "How much is $m + n$?" We complied with their request.

Each child was presented each problem on two occasions; thus, children were eventually presented 50 trials. These 50 trials were divided among six sessions, with eight or nine problems in each session. Children performed the problems while sitting at a desk with a bare top; no external objects were present for them to manipulate while they solved the problems. The experimenter praised the children and gave each child a star following each correct answer. Sessions lasted approximately 5 minutes apiece.

Results

The videotapes revealed four strategies. Three were overt (visible or audible) approaches. Sometimes children raised fingers corresponding to each addend and counted them (the *counting-fingers strategy*). Other times they lifted fingers corresponding to each addend but answered without counting them (the *fingers strategy*). Yet other times they counted aloud (or moved their lips in a visible, silent-counting sequence), but their counting did not have any obvious external referent (the *counting strategy*). The fourth approach involved no visible or audible behavior. For reasons that become apparent in the course of the chapter, we labeled this the *retrieval strategy*.

As shown in Table 9.1, the four strategies differed in their frequency of use and in their temporal and accuracy characteristics. Of particular interest within the analysis that follows were relative solution times. For each pair of strategies, we compared mean solution times on each of the 25 problems for those trials on which children used one strategy to the mean solution times on trials on that problem on which they used the other. (Only the solution times of children who

TABLE 9.1
Characteristics of Arithmetic Strategies (Siegler & Robinson, 1982)

Strategy	Trials on Which Strategy Used (%)	Mean Solution Time (Sec)	Correct Answers (%)
Counting fingers	15	14.0	87
Fingers	13	6.6	89
Counting	8	9.0	54
Retrieval	64	4.0	66

used both strategies being compared at least twice were included in this analysis). Retrieval was significantly faster than the fingers strategy, $t(24) = 3.10$, which in turn was faster than the counting-fingers strategy, $t(23) = 3.96$. Retrieval was also significantly faster than counting, $t(23) = 8.87$ which in turn was faster than counting fingers, $t(23) = 3.91$ (all p's $< .01$).[1]

The most intriguing finding of the experiment was unexpected. The preschoolers proved to be surprisingly adept at matching their use of strategies with the difficulty of the problems. There was a very close association ($r = .91$) between percentage of errors on the 25 problems and percentage of use of the three overt strategies on them (Fig. 9.1). Children most frequently used overt strategies on exactly those problems that were the most difficult to answer correctly. Percentage of overt strategy use on each problem was a better predictor of percentage of errors on that problem than were any of the other variables that we included in the regression analysis: the sum, the larger number, the smaller number, the first number, the second number, the square of the sum, or the min model. (For details of this and subsequent regression analyses, see Appendix A.)

The relation between overt strategy use and errors was not a simple causal one in which use of overt strategies caused children to err. Viewing each problem individually, on 24 of the 25 problems children erred on a *lower* percentage of trials on which they used overt strategies than on trials on which they did not, $t(24) = 6.87$, $p < .01$. For example, on the problem $3 + 4$, children erred on 31% of trials on which they used overt strategies versus 80% of trials on which they did not.

Children's use of overt strategies was also closely related to a second measure of problem difficulty, mean solution times. The longer the mean solution time on a problem, the higher the percentage of overt strategy use on that problem ($r = .90$). The relation could not be explained solely as the overt strategies' taking longer to execute (although they did). Even when we excluded from our calculation of mean solution times those trials on which children used overt strategies, the relation remained substantial. Specifically, the correlation between mean

---

[1]No children used the counting or the counting-fingers strategy on the problem $1 + 1$, thus leading to 23 rather than 24 degrees of freedom on comparisons involving those strategies.

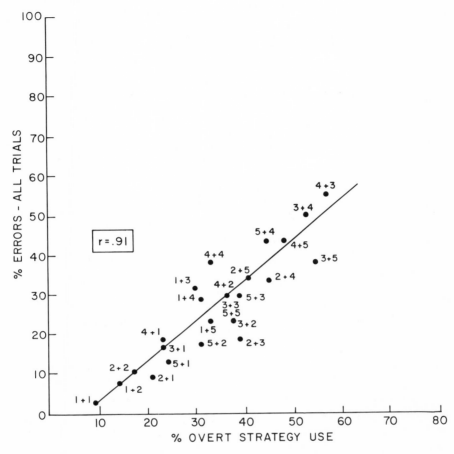

FIG. 9.1.   Relation between overt strategy use and errors. Data from Siegler and Robinson (1982). Addends ≤ 5, sum ≤ 10.

solution times on retrieval trials on each problem and percentage of overt strategy use on that problem was $r = .76$.[2]

To summarize, children used four strategies: fingers, counting fingers, counting, and retrieval. Retrieval was the fastest strategy, fingers the next fastest, and counting and counting fingers the slowest. Use of the overt strategies helped

---

[2]In computing the mean solution times on all trials, the two longest and two shortest times were ignored. These four times were also excluded in the computation of the mean solution time for each strategy (i.e., if two of the four longest trials were retrieval trials, these two would be excluded from the computation of the mean solution time on retrieval trials). The reason for doing this was that the attention of the 4- and 5-year-olds sometimes drifted, leading to long pauses or to extremely rapid answers that seemed intended "to get it over with."

children solve problems. On 24 of the 25 problems, children added more accurately on trials on which they used overt strategies than on trials on which they did not. Finally, strong relations among the percentage of errors, the mean solution time, and the percentage of overt strategy use on each problem indicated that children had some systematic way of choosing when to use overt strategies. We next consider how children might have arrived at their strategies.

A DISTRIBUTION OF ASSOCIATIONS MODEL OF STRATEGY CHOICE

Fig. 9.2 outlines a model of how children generated their addition performance. We have labeled it the *distribution of associations model,* because within it errors, solution times, and overt strategy use are all functions of a single variable: the distribution of associations between problems and potential answers.

The model includes a representation and a process. The representation consists of associations of varying strengths between each problem and possible answers to the problem. The numerical values in the Fig. 9.2A matrix are the estimated strengths of these associations.[3] For example, an associative strength of .05 links the problem 1 + 1 and the answer "1," and an associative strength of .86 links 1 + 1 and "2."

The process that operates on this representation can be divided into three phases: retrieval, elaboration of the representation, and counting. As shown in Fig. 9.2B, the child (who we here imagine as a boy) first retrieves an answer. If he is sufficiently confident of it, he states it. Otherwise, he next generates a more elaborate representation of the problem, perhaps by putting up fingers, and tries again to retrieve an answer. As before, if he is sufficiently confident of the answer he states it. Otherwise, he counts the objects in the representation and states the last number as the answer.

Now we can examine the process in greater detail. The first phase (Steps 1 to 8) involves an effort at retrieval. The child sets two parameters: a confidence criterion and a search length. The confidence criterion defines a value that must be exceeded by the associative strength of a retrieved answer for the child to state that answer. The search length indicates the maximum number of retrieval efforts the child will make before moving on to the second phase of the process. Once

---

[3]These estimated strengths were derived from performance in a separate "overt-strategies-prohibited" experiment. In this experiment, 4-year-olds were presented the Siegler and Robinson procedure except that they were explicitly asked to "just say what you think the right answer is without putting up your fingers or counting." The purpose of these instructions was to obtain the purest possible estimate of the strengths of associations between problems and answers. Each associative strength in the Fig. 9.2A matrix corresponds to the proportion of trials on which children advanced the particular answer to the particular problem in the overt-strategies-prohibited experiment.

these parameters are set, the child retrieves an answer. The probability of any given answer's being retrieved on a particular retrieval effort is proportional to the associative strength of that answer for that problem. Thus, the probability of retrieving "2" as the answer to "1 + 1" would be .86 (Fig. 9.2A). If the associative strength of the retrieved answer exceeds the confidence criterion, the child states that answer. Otherwise, the child examines whether the number of

A. Representation (Associative Strengths)

PROBLEM	0	1	2	3	4	5	6	7	8	9	10	11	OTHER
1 + 1	.05	.86			.02		.02					.02	.04
1 + 2		.09	.70	.02			.04			.07	.02	.02	.05
1 + 3	.02			.11	.71	.05	.02	.02					.07
1 + 4					.11	.61	.09	.07				.02	.11
1 + 5					.13	.16	.50	.11		.02	.02		.05
2 + 1	.07	.05	.79	.05									.04
2 + 2	.02		.04	.05	.80	.04		.05					
2 + 3			.04	.07	.38	.34	.09	.02	.02	.02			.04
2 + 4	.02			.07	.02	.43	.29	.07	.07				.04
2 + 5	.02			.05	.02	.16	.43	.13			.02		.18
3 + 1	.02			.09	.79	.04		.04					.04
3 + 2			.09	.11	.11	.55	.07						.07
3 + 3	.04			.05	.21	.09	.48		.02	.02	.02		.07
3 + 4				.05	.11	.23	.14	.29	.02				.16
3 + 5				.07		.13	.23	.14	.18		.05		.20
4 + 1			.04	.02	.09	.68	.02	.02	.07				.07
4 + 2			.07	.09		.20	.36	.13	.07		.02		.07
4 + 3				.05	.18	.09	.09	.38	.09		.02		.11
4 + 4	.04			.02	.02	.29	.07	.07	.34		.04		.13
4 + 5					.04	.09	.16	.09	.11	.18	.11	.04	.20
5 + 1			.04		.04	.07	.71	.04	.04		.04		.04
5 + 2			.05	.20	.02	.18	.27	.25	.02		.02		
5 + 3			.02	.11	.09	.18	.05	.16	.23		.05		.11
5 + 4					.11	.21	.16	.05	.11	.16	.04		.16
5 + 5	.04					.07	.25	.11	.02	.04	.34	.04	.11

FIG. 9.2.   The strategy choice model. In Fig. 9.2B, "answer$_a$" refers to whichever answer is retrieved on the particular retrieval effort. Also in Fig. 9.2B "problem-answer$_a$ associative strength" refers to the association between the elaborated representation and the retrieved answer.

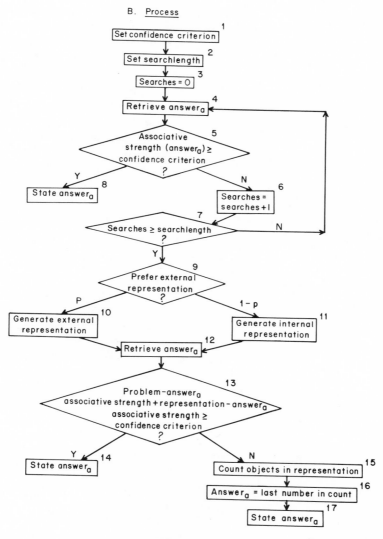

FIG. 9.2. (*cont.*)

searches that have been conducted is within the permissible search length. If so, the child again retrieves an answer, compares it to the confidence criterion, and advances it as the solution if its associative strength exceeds the criterion. Retrieval efforts continue as long as the associative strength of each retrieved answer is below the confidence criterion and the number of searches does not exceed the search length. If the point is reached at which the number of searches does exceed the search length, the child proceeds to the second phase.

In the second phase, the child creates an elaborated representation of the problem. This can be either an elaborated external representation, for example one in which the child puts up his fingers, or an elaborated internal representation, for example one in which the child forms a mental image of objects corresponding to augend and addend. Putting up fingers or forming an image adds visual associations between the elaborated representation and various answers to the already-existing association between the problem and various answers. If the elaborated representation involves the child's fingers, it adds kinesthetic associations as well. We refer to these visual and kinesthetic associations as *elaborated representation-answer associations* as opposed to the *problem-answer associations* discussed previously. Having formed the elaborated representation, the child again retrieves an answer.[4] If that answer's associative strength exceeds the confidence criterion, the child responds. If it does not, the child proceeds to the third phase, an algorithmic process in which he or she counts the objects in the elaborated representation and advances the number assigned to the last object as the sum.

It may be useful to examine how a child using the model would solve a particular problem. Suppose a girl was presented the problem "3 + 4." Initially, she chooses a confidence criterion and a search length. For purpose of illustration, we assume that she selects the confidence criterion .50 and the search length two. Next, she retrieves an answer. As shown in Fig. 9.2A, the probability of retrieving 3 is .05, the probability of retrieving 4 is .11, the probability of retrieving 5 is .21, and so on. Suppose that the child retrieves 5. This answer's associative strength, .21, does not exceed the current confidence criterion, .50. Therefore, the girl does not state it as the answer. She next checks whether the number of searches has reached the search length. Because it has not, she again retrieves an answer. This time she might retrieve 7. The associative strength of 7, .29, does not exceed the confidence criterion, .50. Because the number of searches, two, has reached the allowed search length, the child proceeds to the second phase of the process.

In this second phase, the girl initially represents the problem either by forming a mental image or by putting up fingers. We assume that she puts up three fingers on one hand and four on the other. Next, she again retrieves an answer. As indicated in Footnote 4, combining the problem-answer and the representation-answer associative strengths increases the child's probability of retrieving 7

---

[4]The probability of a given answer's being retrieved at this point is determined by adding the problem–answer and the elaborated representation–answer associative strengths and dividing by one plus the elaborated representation–answer associative strength. In our computer simulation (described later), we arbitrarily decided that each external representation added a constant .05 to the answer corresponding to the number of objects in the representation. Thus, if the problem 1 + 4 was represented with five fingers, and the initial associative strength of 1 + 4 = 5 was .61, the new associative strength would be .66/1.05 = .63.

from .29 to .32. Suppose that she retrieves 7. Its associative strength still does not exceed the .50 confidence criterion. Therefore, the child does not state it. She instead proceeds to the third phase of the process. Here, she counts her fingers and states the last number as the answer to the problem. If she counts correctly, she will say "7."

This model accounts for the strategies that children use, for the temporal characteristics of the strategies, and for the close relations among the percentage of overt strategy use, the percentage of errors, and the mean solution times on each problem. First consider how it accounts for the existence of the four strategies. The retrieval strategy appears if children retrieve an answer whose problem-answer associative strength exceeds their confidence criterion (Steps 1 to 5, sometimes Steps 6 and 7, Step 8). The fingers strategy emerges when children fail to retrieve an answer whose problem-answer associative strength exceeds their confidence criterion, put up their fingers, and then retrieve an answer in which the sum of the problem-answer and the elaborated representation-answer associative strengths exceeds their confidence criterion (Steps 1 to 7, 9 to 10, 12 to 14). The counting-fingers strategy appears if children fail to retrieve an answer whose problem-answer associative strength exceeds their confidence criterion, put up their fingers, fail to retrieve an answer in which the sum of the elaborated representation-answer and problem-answer associative strengths exceeds the confidence criterion, and finally count their fingers (Steps 1 to 7, 9 to 10, 12 to 13, 15 to 17). The counting strategy is observed if children fail to retrieve an answer whose problem-answer associative strength exceeds their confidence criterion, form an elaborated internal representation, fail to retrieve an answer in which the sum of the elaborated representation-answer and problem-answer associative strengths exceeds the confidence criterion, and finally count the objects in the internal representation (Steps 1 to 7, 9, 11 to 13, 15 to 17).[5]

The relative solution times of the strategies arise because the faster strategies are component parts of the slower ones. To use the fingers strategy, children must execute all of the steps in the retrieval strategy and four additional ones. To execute the counting-fingers strategy, children must proceed through all of the steps in the fingers strategy and two additional ones. To execute the counting strategy, children must execute all of the steps in the retrieval strategy plus six others. If we can equate the time needed to form elaborated internal and elaborated external representations, children using the counting strategy must execute all of the steps in the fingers strategy plus two others. Thus, the retrieval strategy should be faster than any of the other strategies, the fingers strategy should be

---

[5]Any trials on which children generated an internal representation and then stated the answer that they retrieved (Steps 1 to 7 and 10 to 13) would also be classified as retrieval trials. This path was expected to be rare, however. Kinesthetic cues would not be available to mediate the elaborated representation-answer association, and visual cues would be weaker than if the objects in the elaborated representation were visible.

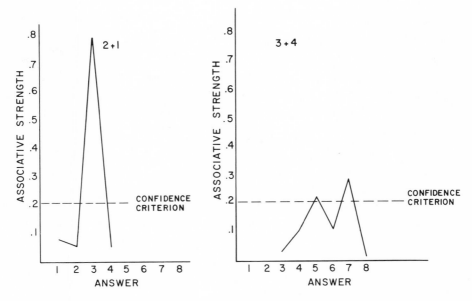

FIG. 9.3.   Distribution of associative strengths for a peaked and a flat distribution. Data from overt-strategies-prohibited experiment.

faster than the counting-fingers strategy, and, if the time needed to form an external representation does not exceed the time needed to form an internal one, the fingers strategy also should be faster than the counting strategy.[6]

Perhaps the most important feature of the model is that it generates close associations among percentage of errors, mean solution time, and percentage of overt strategy use on each problem. The associations arise because all three dependent variables are functions of the same independent variable: the distribution of associations linking problems and answers. The way in which this dependency operates becomes apparent when we compare the outcomes of a peaked distribution of associations, such as that for 2 + 1 in Fig. 9.3, with those of a flat distribution, such as that for 3 + 4. A low percentage of use of overt strategies, a low percentage of errors, and a short mean solution time all accompany the peaked distribution. Relative to the flat distribution, the peaked distribution results in: (1) less frequent use of overt strategies (because the answer that is retrieved is more likely to have high associative strength, which allows it to exceed more confidence criteria, thus leading to use of retrieval rather than overt strategies); (2) fewer errors (because of the higher probability of retrieving and

---

[6]The relative accuracy of the four strategies can also be explained within the framework of the model, though the explanation involves several considerations external to the model. See Siegler and Robinson (1982, pp. 298–299) for this explanation.

stating the answer that forms the peak of the distribution, which is generally the correct answer); and (3) shorter solution times (because the probability of retrieving on an early search an answer whose associative strength exceeds any given confidence criterion is greater the more peaked the distribution of associations).

At least two nonintuitive predictions follow from this model. One is that the correlation between percentage of errors on each problem and percentage of overt strategy use on that problem is primarily a correlation between the *percentage of errors on retrieval trials on each problem* and the percentage of overt strategy use on the problem. That is, the correlation does not depend on the percentage of errors on counting, counting-fingers, and fingers strategy trials. The reasoning underlying this prediction is that percentage of overt strategy use on a problem and percentage of errors on retrieval trials on that problem both depend entirely on the distribution of associations, but percentage of errors on nonretrieval trials on the problem depends on other factors.

This logic may become clearer when we examine the model's account of the way in which errors are produced by each of the four strategies. On retrieval trials, the percentage of errors on each problem depends only on the distribution of associations. Errors are made when an incorrect answer retrieved from the distribution exceeds the confidence criterion. The flatter the distribution, the greater the proportion of retrieval trials on which this will happen. The distribution's flatness increases both the likelihood of an incorrect answer's being retrieved and the likelihood of its having sufficient associative strength to be stated. Thus percentage of errors on retrieval trials, like percentage of overt strategy use, depends entirely on the distribution of associations.

In contrast, the percentage of errors on counting and counting-fingers trials is unaffected by the distribution of associations. The counting and counting-fingers strategies arise when children fail to retrieve a statable answer from the distribution of associations. Instead, they base answers on their counts of the objects in their elaborated representations. Errors are made when they misrepresent the number of objects in the problem or when they miscount them. The greater the sum, the more objects that can be misrepresented or miscounted, and therefore the greater the likelihood of errors. Thus, colinearity with the sum should account for whatever correlation emerges between the percentage of errors on counting and counting-fingers trials on each problem and the percentage of overt strategy use on the problem.

Correlations involving the percentage of errors on fingers-strategy trials should occupy a middle ground. Recall that the fingers strategy is produced when children first fail to retrieve an answer whose associative strength exceeds their confidence criterion, then elaborate the representation by putting up their fingers, and then retrieve an answer in which the sum of the problem-answer and the elaborated representation-answer associative strengths exceeds the confidence criterion. Under such circumstances, the percentage of errors is a function of both the distribution of associations between problems and answers and the distribution of associations between elaborated representations and answers. A relatively peaked distribution of associations increases the probability that the problem-answer and elaborated representation-answer associations together will lead to retrieval of an answer whose associative strength exceeds the confidence criterion. However, the sum also may influence this likelihood. Presumably, children more often correctly represent the addends on problems with small sums, which leads to the elaborated representation-answer association's more often being added to the correct rather than to an incorrect answer on these problems. Thus, the percentage of errors on fingers-strategy trials on each problem should correlate somewhat with percentage of overt strategy use on that problem, but not as highly as percentage of errors on retrieval trials on the problem.

The logic of these predictions can be summarized as follows:

A. If percentage of overt strategy use on each problem is a function of only the distribution of associations; and
B. If percentage of errors on retrieval trials on each problem is also a function of only the distribution of associations; and
C. If percentage of errors on fingers trials is in part a function of the distribution of associations; and
D. If percentage of errors on counting and counting-fingers trials is not at all a function of the distribution of associations, instead being a function of the sum;

Then

1. Percentage of errors on retrieval trials should correlate highly with percentage of overt strategy use.
2. Percentage of errors on counting and counting-fingers trials should correlate less highly with percentage of overt strategy use, especially when the contribution of the sum is partialed out.
3. Percentage of errors on fingers trials should show an intermediate degree of correlation with percentage of overt strategy use.

The data were entirely consistent with these predictions. As shown in Fig. 9.4, percentage of errors on retrieval trials on each problem correlated $r = .92$ with percentage of overt strategy use on the problem. This correlation was actually slightly higher than the correlation reported earlier between the percentage of errors on all trials and the percentage of overt strategy use. The correlation between percentage of errors on counting and counting-fingers trials on each problem and the percentage of overt strategy use on that problem ($r = .38$) was significantly lower, $t(22) = 6.47, p < .01$. Yet more striking was the difference between the partial correlations. When the contribution of the sum was partialed out, percentage of overt strategy use correlated $r = .87$ with percentage of errors on retrieval trials. The corresponding partial correlation between percentage of

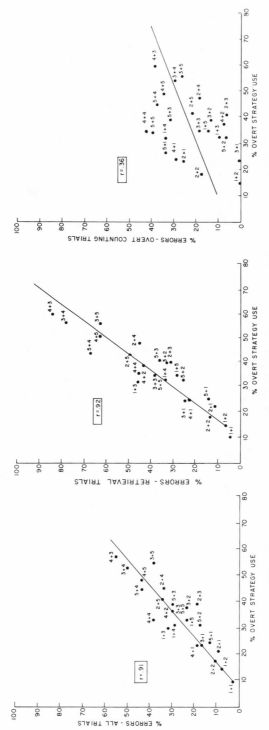

FIG. 9.4. Correlations between percentage of overt strategy use on each problem and percentage of errors on all trials, retrieval trials, and counting and counting-fingers trials. Data from Siegler and Robinson (1982).

247

overt strategy use and percentage of errors on counting and counting-fingers trials was $r = -.23$. The difference between the two partial correlations was highly significant $t(22) = 7.45, p < .01$.

Also as predicted, the correlation between percentage of errors on fingers trials and percentage of overt strategy use on each problem was in between ($r = .68$). It did not differ significantly from either of the other correlations. When the contribution of the sum was partialed out, the correlation became $r = .66$. This correlation was significantly lower than the one involving errors on retrieval trials $t(22) = 2.10, p < .05$ and significantly higher than the one involving errors on counting and counting-fingers trials $t(22) = 5.08$.[7] The findings supported the view that the original correlation between errors and overt strategy use was due primarily to overt strategy use and errors on retrieval trials being functions of the same variable, the distribution of associations, and of errors on overt strategy trials depending on other variables.

Similar logic can be applied to analyzing the correlation between solution times and overt strategy use. Solution times on retrieval trials should derive exclusively from the distribution of associations. The more peaked this distribution, the more quickly children should retrieve an answer whose associative strength exceeds their confidence criterion. On counting and counting-fingers trials, the amount of time needed to generate an elaborated representation and to count the objects in it would influence the times. These would depend on the number of objects that need to be represented and counted—in short, on the sum. The model made no direct prediction concerning solution times on fingers trials on each problem. Thus, the prediction of the model was that the correlation between percentage of overt strategy use and mean solution times on retrieval trials on each problem would be higher than the correlation between percentage of overt strategy use and mean solution times on counting and counting-fingers trials. The pattern would be most evident with the contribution of the sum partialed out from both correlations.

A multiple regression analysis indicated that, as predicted by the model, percentage of overt strategy use was the most powerful predictor of mean solution times on retrieval trials on the 25 problems ($r = .76$) (Appendix A). Contrary to expectation, however, the best predictor of solution times on counting and counting-fingers trials on each problem was also percentage of overt strategy use ($r = .83$). The partial correlations showed the same pattern. With the contribution of the sum partialed out, the correlation between percentage of overt strategy use on each problem and mean solution times on retrieval trials on the

---

[7]This finding argued against the possibility that the difference in the magnitudes of the correlations involving errors on retrieval trials and those involving errors on counting and counting-fingers trials was due to the latter's being based on fewer trials per problem. If trials per problem were the key variable, we would not expect percentage of overt strategy use to correlate more highly with the percentage of errors on fingers trials than with the percentage of errors on counting and counting-fingers trials. There were fewer fingers trials than counting and counting-fingers trials.

problem was $r = .68$. The corresponding partial correlation between overt strategy use and solution times on counting and counting-fingers trials was $r = .71$.[8]

In summary, all but one of the model's predictions were consistent with the data. The model accounted for the four strategies that children used, the relative solution times of the strategies, the correlations among percentage of errors, mean solution times, and percentage of overt strategy use on each problem, and the source of at least the correlation between errors and strategy use's being percentage of errors on retrieval trials. The model also possessed several other properties that seemed desirable. It allowed children to strike a balance between speed and accuracy demands. When possible, they would use the relatively rapid retrieval approach. When retrieval yielded no answer that was sufficiently strongly associated with the problem, they would fall back on successively more time-consuming overt approaches. The model also had the advantage of treating all problems in the same way. It did not assume that ties have a special status or that the mental distance between sums increases exponentially with their sizes. Finally, as is discussed in more detail later in the chapter, the model suggests how development might occur. As children's distributions of associations become increasingly peaked, they rely increasingly on retrieval, advance the correct answer more often, and answer more quickly. In short, their performance becomes increasingly adultlike.

A MATHEMATICAL EXPRESSION OF THE MODEL

We wanted to provide a rigorous test of the sufficiency of the model to produce strong relations among overt strategy use, frequency of errors on retrieval trials, and length of mean solution times on each problem. Therefore, we translated the model's predictions into algebraic equations, inserted a large range of parameter values into the model, and compared the model's behavior to that that children had displayed.

The following equations were used to describe, for each problem, the probability of retrieving an answer that exceeded the confidence criterion, the probability of overt strategy use, the probability of an error on a retrieval trial, and the expected solution time on a retrieval trial.

Probability of Retrieving Answer on a Problem that Exceeds Confidence Criterion =

$$R = \sum_{a=1}^{A} (AS_a)(p(AS_a > CC))/(\sum_{a=1}^{A} AS_a)$$

---

[8]As becomes evident later, patterns of solution times in all subsequent experiments conformed to the predictions of the model. Therefore, no effort was made to explain why the solution times in this experiment did not.

Probability of Overt Strategy Use on a Problem $= (1 - R)^N$

Probability of Error on Retrieval Trials on Each Problem $=$

$$1 - ((p(AS_{ca} > CC))(AS_{ca})/\sum_{a=1}^{A} (AS_a(p(AS_a > CC)))$$

Expected Solution Time on Retrieval Trials on Each Problem $=$

$$\sum_{n=1}^{N} nR((1 - R)^{n-1}) + N(1 - (\sum_{n=1}^{N} R((1 - R)^{n-1})))$$

where R refers to the probability that the answer retrieved on any given search will exceed the confidence criterion, AS_a refers to the associative strength of answer a, CC refers to the confidence criterion, N refers to the search length, and $ASca$ refers to the associative strength of the correct answer.

The correspondence between each equation and the process it models is quite straightforward. The probability on each problem of retrieving an answer that exceeds the confidence criterion is the sum of the associative strengths of answers to that problem that exceed the criterion divided by the sum of the associative strengths of all answers to the problem. The probability of overt strategy use on a problem is the probability that on none of the searches will an answer be retrieved that exceeds the confidence criterion. The probability of an error on a retrieval trial is the probability of retrieving an incorrect answer whose associative strength exceeds the confidence criterion divided by the probability of retrieving a correct or incorrect answer whose associative strength exceeds the confidence criterion. The expected solution time on retrieval trials is proportional to the expected value of the number of searches on each problem before an answer is stated.

We examined the operation of this mathematical model under the 72 possible combinations of confidence criteria (.05, .10, .15, .20, .30, .40, .50, .60, .70, .80,.90, 1.00) and search lengths (one to six). For each confidence-criterion–search-length pair, we applied the four equations to each of the 25 problems that children had been presented. Then we combined the results to obtain expected percentages of errors on retrieval trials, mean solution times on retrieval trials, and percentages of overt strategy use.

The model was tested in two ways, corresponding to measures of internal and external validity. First we wanted to establish the sufficiency of the equations to generate the high correlations among the three variables that we had observed. To do this, we entered into the equations associative strengths (operationally defined here as the relative frequencies of answers given on retrieval trials in Siegler and Robinson) and used the output of the equations to estimate percentages of errors, mean solution times, and percentages of overt strategy use on each problem. If the equations operated as anticipated, this procedure would produce high intercorrelations among the expected values for the three variables. The equations passed this test. The intercorrelations among the output of the equations for errors, solution times, and overt strategy use ranged from $r = .92$ to $r = .99$.

As another measure of internal validity, we tested whether the model's predictions for each measure would correlate highly with the children's mean solution times, percentage of overt strategy use, and percentage of errors in the Siegler and Robinson experiment. The correlation between modeled and observed percentage of errors on retrieval trials was $r = .94$, between modeled and observed frequency of overt strategy use $r = .89$, and between modeled and observed mean solution times on retrieval trials $r = .92$.

We next tested the mathematical model's ability to predict across data sets. We used the associative strengths displayed in Fig. 9.2A to predict performance in the Siegler and Robinson experiment. As indicated in Footnote 2, these associative strengths were estimated from the performance of different children under somewhat different experimental conditions (no overt strategies allowed) than the data being predicted. The correlation between the predicted and observed percentage of overt strategy use on each problem was $r = .87$. The correlation between the predicted and observed percentages of errors on each problem was $r = .77$. The correlation between the predicted and observed mean solution times on each problem was $r = .83$. These results demonstrated that estimates of associative strengths obtained in one experiment could be used to predict experimental data in another.

A REPLICATION AND EXTENSION EXPERIMENT

Many results from the initial experiment were unanticipated. Also, it seemed possible that the generality of the findings would be limited to problems in which the fingers and counting-fingers strategies were easy to use—that is, problems with addends no greater than 5 and/or sums no greater than 10. We therefore performed a second experiment replicating the initial condition and adding problem sets on which overt strategies would be more difficult to execute.

A further purpose of the experiment was to test an alternative to the Fig. 9.2 model of strategy choice. In this alternative, the close connection between errors, solution times, and overt strategy use arises because children explicitly judge each problem's difficulty and use an overt strategy when they judge the difficulty to be high. Thus:

problem difficulty→ judgments of problem difficulty→ overt strategy use

This depiction suggests that judgments of problem difficulty should correlate highly with both actual problem difficulty (as measured by percentage of errors on each problem) and overt strategy use. Otherwise the observed high correlation between percentage of errors and overt strategies would be difficult to explain.

In a preliminary test of this alternative, Siegler and Robinson (1982) asked a group of 5 year olds, students at a nursery school similar to the one at which the original experiment had been run, to label each of the 25 problems as hard, easy, or in between. "Hard" ratings were quantified as 2, "easy" ratings as 0, and "in-between" ratings as 1. It was found that the mean difficulty ratings on each of the 25 problems correlated $r = .47$ with the percentage of errors on the problem and $r = .51$ with the percentage of overt strategy use on the problems. These correlations were substantially lower than the previously noted $r = .91$ correlation between percentage of overt strategy use on each problem and percentage of errors on the problem. Because the judgment data were collected from different children than the addition performance data, however, the experiment provided only a preliminary index. The replication and extension experiment, in which both types of data were obtained from the same children, would provide a more definitive test.

Method

The 42 children who participated, 23 boys and 19 girls, attended either a university preschool or a nursery school in a middle-class area of Pittsburgh. In each of the three conditions, there were eight 4 year olds and six 5-year-olds.

Children in Group 1 of this experiment (the replication condition) were presented the same 25 problems as the children studied by Siegler and Robinson. These were all of the problems on which both addends were less than or equal to 5 and on which the sum was less than or equal to 10. Children in Group 2 were presented 25 problems on which the sum again was less than or equal to 10 but on which either addend could be as great as 9. Children in Group 3 were presented a third set of 25 problems; in this set, the sum could be as high as 12 and the addends as large as 11. To maintain the interest of children who were not especially skillful at adding, Groups 2 and 3 included two subsets of problems. In each group, 13 of the problems were selected from the relatively easy items presented in Group 1 in which addends never exceeded 5 and sums never exceeded 10. The remaining 12 problems in Group 2 all had one addend between 6 and 9 and a sum that did not exceed 10. The remaining 12 problems in Group 3 all had one addend between 6 and 11 and sums of 11 or 12.

The instructions began in the same way as those used by Siegler and Robinson. However, to ensure that all children knew that they could use overt strategies, we added the following instructions at the end: "You can do anything you want to help you get the right answer. If you want to use your fingers or count aloud, that's fine." It seemed possible that these instructions would increase overall use of the overt strategies, but unlikely that they would influence the correlation between use of overt strategies and problem difficulty.

Within a week of their last counting session, children in all three groups were presented the metacognitive judgment task that peers in the Siegler and Robinson study had performed. They were told, ''Remember the problems I asked you about? Well, some of those problems were easy, some were hard, and some were in between easy and hard. I'm going to ask you about each problem and you tell me whether you think that it is easy, hard, or in between.''

Results

Existence of Strategies.   The model suggested that children would use four strategies: counting fingers, fingers, counting, and retrieval. As shown in Table 9.2, children in all groups used each of these approaches. We had anticipated that the new instructions' explicit statement that children could use overt strategies might result in more frequent use of such strategies. The data showed little tendency in this direction, however. In the Siegler and Robinson study, children used overt strategies on 36% of trials; in the replication and extension experiment, they used them on 43%. These percentages did not differ significantly, $t <$ 1.[9]

Children in Group 3 encountered items on which the sum exceeded their number of fingers. This situation appeared to lead them to adopt new procedures, because on 8% of trials they used strategies that did not fall neatly into the four categories. The two most common variants, each accounting for 3% of total trials, were counting/counting fingers on and counting fingers/fail. In the first of these, children would count up to one addend without putting up their fingers, then put up their fingers to represent the other addend, and then count their fingers starting with the number one greater than the result of their initial counting procedure. As long as the addend that children represented on their fingers was no greater than 10, this procedure circumvented the difficulty of the sum's exceeding their number of fingers. The second relatively common procedure involved representing as many numbers as the child had fingers, counting all of them, and then arbitrarily naming a larger number if both addends had not been totally represented. Several other procedures were used very occasionally, none of them exceeding 1% of total trials. Like the procedures just described, these

---

[9]A variant of the counting strategy that was not observed by Siegler and Robinson appeared in this experiment. On some trials, children put up fingers synchronously with counting the sum. That is, they put up a first finger while saying ''1,'' a second finger while saying ''2,'' and so on. These trials could not be classified as counting-fingers trials, because there was no evidence that the fingers were being used to represent the addends. Unlike the trials that were labeled counting fingers, children did not represent the addends separately from counting out the sum, did not pause between addends, and did not represent addends on separate hands. Accuracy rates on these trials were also more similar to those observed on counting than on counting-fingers trials. Therefore, these approaches were viewed as a form of counting in which fingers were incidental accompaniments, much as tapping one's feet might be.

TABLE 9.2
Characteristics of Arithmetic Strategies:
Replication and Extension Experiment

	Strategy	Trials on Which Strategy Used (%)[a]	Mean Solution Time (Sec)	Correct Answers (%)
Group 1	Counting fingers	9	9.1	97
	Fingers	10	3.9	99
	Counting	29	8.2	69
	Retrieval	50	3.6	70
Group 2	Counting fingers	10	11.1	70
	Fingers	11	4.9	86
	Counting	10	13.2	60
	Retrieval	68	4.3	61
Group 3	Counting fingers	11	13.2	74
	Fingers	12	4.2	93
	Counting	16	14.1	56
	Retrieval	53	5.1	62

[a]Children in Group 3 used strategies other than the usual 4 on 8% of trials.

involved combining the usual strategies in innovative ways, and appeared aimed at overcoming the difficulty associated with sums greater than 10.

Relative Accuracy of Strategies.   The relative accuracy of the four strategies was identical to that found in the earlier study. In all three groups, the fingers strategy was the most accurate, the counting-fingers strategy the next most accurate, and the retrieval and counting strategies the least accurate. Also as previously, children performed more accurately on those trials on each problem on which they used overt strategies than on those trials on which they did not (for Group 1, $t(24) = 5.14$; for Group 2, $t(24) = 2.89$; for Group 3, $t(24) = 3.61$; all p's $< .01$). Thus, using the overt strategies seemed to help children solve the problems.

Relative Solution Times of Strategies.   The model predicted that retrieval would be the fastest strategy, that fingers would be the next fastest, and that counting and countng fingers would be the slowest. The data were in accord with these predictions. As shown in Table 9.2, the retrieval and fingers strategies were substantially faster than the counting and counting-fingers strategies in each of the three groups. Including those children from all three groups who used both of the pairs of strategies at least twice, retrieval was significantly faster than the fingers strategy, $t(18) = 2.34$, $p < .05$, which in turn was significantly faster than the counting strategy, $t(14) = 2.42$, $p < .05$, or the counting-fingers strategy, $t(13) = 3.53$, $p < .01$.[10]

Relations among Errors, Solution Times, and Overt Strategy Use. The model predicted that the percentage of errors, mean solution times, and percentage of overt strategy use on each problem would vary together. The expected pattern emerged in all three groups. In Group 1, percentage of overt strategy use on each problem correlated $r = .79$ with percentage of errors on that problem. In Group 2, the two variables correlated $r = .79$. In Group 3, they correlated $r = .81$. The relation is illustrated in Fig. 9.5 and in Appendix A.

A similar relation was present between overt strategy use and solution times. In Group 1, mean solution times correlated $r = .91$ with percentage of overt strategy use; in Group 2, the two variables correlated $r = .81$; and in Group 3, the two variables correlated $r = .92$. As in Siegler and Robinson, the relations were present even when only solution times on retrieval trials were considered: $r = .80$, $r = .75$, and $r = .90$ for Groups 1, 2, and 3, respectively (Appendix A).

The Source of the Relations among Strategy Use, Errors, and Solution Times. The model predicted that the correlations among these three variables derived primarily from percentage of errors and mean solution times on retrieval trials. This prediction again proved accurate. First consider analyses involving errors on retrieval trials. In each of the three groups, the best predictor of the percentage of errors on retrieval trials on each problem was the percentage of overt strategy use on that problem (Appendix A). The correlations ranged from $r = .80$ to $r = .88$ (Table 9.3). In all three cases, as in the Siegler and Robinson data, these correlations were greater than the correlations involving the overall percentage of errors. When the contribution of the sum was partialed out, the correlation between errors on retrieval trials and overt strategy use remained quite high, ranging from $r = .56$ to $r = .70$. The correlations involving percentage of errors on counting and counting-fingers trials showed a different pattern. In none of the three groups was overt strategy use the best predictor of percentage of errors on these trials. The raw correlations ranged from $r = .37$ to $r = .51$. With the contribution of the sum partialed out, the correlations ranged from $r = .23$ to $r = .42$.

For each of the three groups, the raw correlation between percentage of errors on retrieval trials and percentage of overt strategy use was significantly greater than the corresponding correlation between percentage of errors on counting and counting-fingers trials and percentage of overt strategy use. The difference be-

---

[10]The reason for comparing the solution times of children in all three groups in a single analysis, rather than comparing the times in each group separately, was to obtain enough children who used each pair of strategies to make a statistical comparison reasonably powerful. In many cases, only five or six children in each group used a particular pair of strategies.

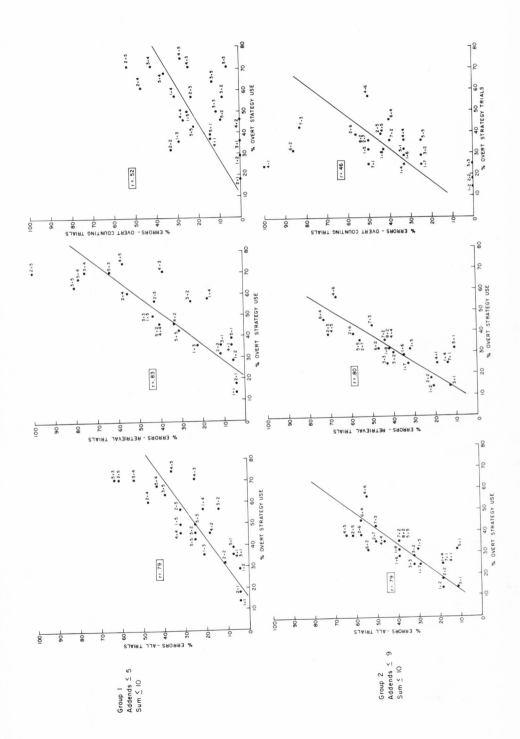

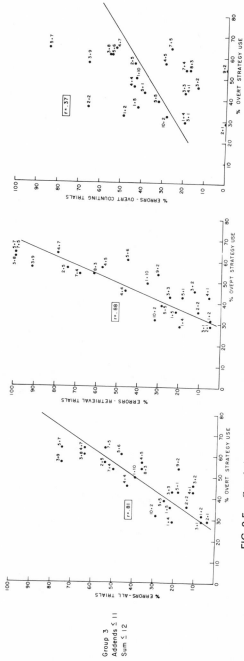

FIG. 9.5. Correlations between percentage of overt strategy use on each problem and percentage of errors on all trials, retrieval trials, and counting and counting- fingers trials. Data from replication and extension experiment.

TABLE 9.3
Source of Correlations of Overt Strategy Use with Errors and
Solution Times: Replication and Extension Experiment[a]

A. *Raw Correlations*

	Errors			Solution Times	
	Retrieval Trials	*Fingers Trials[b]*	*Counting and Counting-Fingers Trials*	*Retrieval Trials*	*Counting and Counting-Fingers Trials*
Group 1	.83		.51	.79	.42
Group 2	.80	.68	.47	.75	.54
Group 3	.88		.37	.84	.79

B. *Partial Correlations (Correlations with the Sum Partialed Out)*

	Errors			Solution Times	
	Retrieval Trials	*Fingers Trials[c]*	*Counting and Counting-Fingers Trials*	*Retrieval Trials*	*Counting and Counting-Fingers Trials*
Group 1	.67		.42	.75	.10
Group 2	.56	.66	.23	.50	.00
Group 3	.70		.26	.74	.38

[a]Numbers in the Table indicate correlations of percentage of overt strategy use on each problem with the variable specified in the Table. For example, the top left value of .83 indicates a raw correlation of $r = .83$ between percentage of errors on retrieval trials on each problem and percentage of overt strategy use on that problem for Group 1.

[b]Summing across the performance of children in all three groups, the correlation was $r = .68$.

[c]Summing across the performance of children in all three groups, the correlation was $r = .66$.

tween the correlations for Group 1 was $t(22) = 2.82$; for Group 2, $t(22) = 2.26$; and for Group 3, $t(22) = 5.03$ (all p's $< .05$). For the partial correlations, the difference between the correlations' magnitudes was significant for Group 3, $t(22) = 2.81, p < .01$. It did not reach significance for Group 1, $t(22) = 1.64$, or for Group 2, $t(22) = 1.32$, despite the rather large differences between the correlations ($r = .67$ versus $r = .42$ for Group 1 and $r = .56$ versus $r = .23$ for Group 2).

The model predicted that the correlation between the percentage of errors on fingers-strategy trials and percentage of overt strategy use would be intermediate between the correlations of overt strategy use with errors on retrieval trials and with errors on counting and counting-fingers trials. Children made too few errors on fingers trials on each problem for us to analyze their performance separately in each of the three groups. Children in Group 1, for example, erred only twice on fingers trials. Combining across the three groups, however, the correlation between percentage of errors on fingers-strategy trials on each problem and percentage of overt strategy use on that problem was $r = .68$, which was, as predicted, intermediate between the other two correlations. With the contribution of the sum partialed out, the correlation was $r = .66$.

The source of the correlation between solution times and overt strategy use was also in accord with the prediction of the model. In all three groups, the best predictor of mean solution times on retrieval trials on each problem was percentage of overt strategy use on that problem (Appendix A). In contrast, in all three groups the sum was a better predictor of mean solution times on counting and counting-fingers trials on each problem than was the percentage of overt strategy use on that problem. The differences in the magnitudes of the raw correlations was significant for Group 1, $t(22) = 2.60$, $p < .05$, though not for the other two groups, t's$(22) = 1.45$ and .84. The comparisons of the partial correlations yielded more striking results. As shown in Table 9.3, large differences separated the magnitudes of the partial correlations involving solution times on retrieval and on counting and counting-fingers trials. The differences were significant for all three groups (t's$(22) = 3.38$, 2.24, and 5.07 for Groups 1, 2, and 3, respectively, all p's $< .05$).

Explicit Judgment Data.   Explicit judgments of problem difficulty collected from the same subjects who provided the addition performance data showed a similar pattern to that previously reported with between-subjects data. The correlations between mean rating of problem difficulty for each problem and percentages of errors on that problem were $r = .64$, $r = .34$, and $r = .70$ for Groups 1, 2, and 3, respectively. The correlations between mean rating of difficulty for each problem and percentage of overt strategy use on that problem were $r = .73$, $r = .50$, and $r = .53$, respectively. All six of these correlations were lower than any of the three correlations between percentages of overt strategy use and errors. Four of the six were also lower than the corresponding correlations between the metacognitive judgments and the size of the larger addend, suggesting that it was not unreliability of measurement of the metacognitive judgments that led to the lower correlations. The slippage that would be entailed in going from problem difficulty to judgments of problem difficulty and then from judgments of problem difficulty to use of overt strategies added to the unlikelihood that the accuracy of the metacognitive judgments of difficulty could account for the correlations between overt strategy use and errors.

Summary of Replication and Extension Experiment Findings.   The results of the replication and extension experiment indicated that the earlier results were not due to any peculiarity of the problem set. The data from each of the three groups closely paralleled the Siegler and Robinson findings concerning the existence of the four strategies, their relative accuracy, their relative solution times, the correlations among percentage of overt strategy use, mean solution time, and percentage of errors on each problem, and the source of these correlations being errors and solution times on retrieval trials. On the new problems, as on the original ones, young children demonstrated the ability to make adaptive strategy choices even without the ability to make highly accurate judgments about problem difficulty.

AN EXPERIMENT ON SUBTRACTION

Although the model was developed to account for strategy choices on addition problems, it seemed to provide a plausible model of strategy choices on simple subtraction problems as well. To use the counting-fingers strategy, children could raise fingers to represent the larger number, lower fingers corresponding to the smaller number, and count the remaining fingers. To use the fingers strategy, they could put up fingers representing the larger number, put down fingers representing the smaller number, and answer without counting the remainder. To use the counting strategy, they could count backward from the larger number, or count up to it from one and then count backward, without putting up fingers. To use the retrieval strategy, they could retrieve an answer and state it without any intervening visible or audible behavior. The expectations for the relative solution times of the strategies, the relations among percentage of overt strategy use, mean solution times, and percentage of errors on each problem, and the source of these relations' being errors and solution times on retrieval trials would be the same as in addition. The subtraction experiment was performed to test whether subtraction did resemble addition in these ways.

Method

Participants were 34 children, half 5-year-olds and half 6-year-olds, half of each age group boys and half girls. The 5-year-olds attended a university preschool. The 6-year-olds attended the first grade of an upper-middle-class suburban school.

The problems were the inverses of the 25 addition problems presented by Siegler and Robinson. For every problem of the form $a + b = c$ in the Siegler and Robinson study, here there was a problem of the form $c - b = a$. The instructions were:

> I want you to imagine that you have a pile of oranges. Then imagine that I take some oranges away from your pile. Tell me how many you have left. You can do anything you want to help you get the right answer. If you want to use your fingers or count aloud, that's fine. Okay? Suppose you have m oranges, how many would you have if I took away n of them?

TABLE 9.4
Characteristics of Arithmetic Strategies: Subtraction Experiment

Strategy	Trials on Which Strategy Used (%)	Mean Solution Time (Sec)	Correct Answers (%)
Counting fingers	21	9.8	83
Fingers	14	4.4	94
Counting	7	9.1	25
Retrieval	58	4.4	68

Results

Existence of Strategies. The videotapes revealed that children used the same four strategies as they had in the addition experiments. As indicated in Table 9.4, children used overt strategies on subtraction problems at least as often as peers previously had used them in adding. Also as previously, retrieval was the most frequently used strategy, being employed on 58% of trials, a figure comparable to the 64% and 57% in the previous studies. The relative accuracy of the four strategies was also identical to those obtained in the addition studies. Fingers was the most accurate strategy, counting fingers the next most accurate, and retrieval and counting the least accurate.

Relative Solution Times of Strategies. The relative solution times again followed the pattern predicted by the model. The retrieval strategy was significantly faster than the fingers strategy $t(17) = 2.70$, which was significantly faster than either the counting strategy $t(7) = 3.43$ or the counting-fingers strategy $t(17) = 7.15$ (all p's $< .05$).

Relations among Errors, Solution Times, and Overt Strategy Use. As shown in Fig. 9.6, a strong relation again emerged between the percentage of errors on each problem and the percentage of overt strategy use on that problem. The correlation ($r = .83$) was of the same magnitude that had appeared in the addition studies. As previously, percentage of overt strategy use on each problem correlated more highly with the error rate on the problem than did any of the other variables that were tested (remainder, remainder squared, larger number, smaller number, the Woods, Resnick, and Groen (1975) subtraction model,[11] or

---

[11]In this subtraction model, children chose whichever of two strategies was easier to execute. They could either count down from the larger number the number of times indicated by the smaller, or they could count up from the smaller number the number of times needed to reach the larger, whichever took fewer counts. On $7 - 3$, they would count down from 7 because it required three rather than four counts; on $7 - 4$, they would count up from 4 for the same reason.

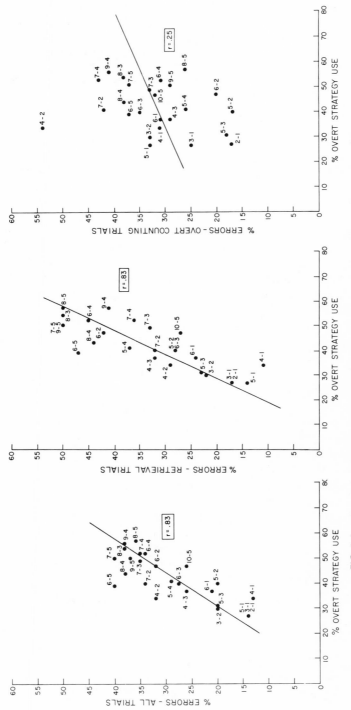

FIG. 9.6. Correlations between percentage of overt strategy use on each problem and percentage of errors on all trials, retrieval trials, and counting and counting-fingers trials. Data from subtraction experiment. Larger number $\leq$ 10, remainder $\leq$ 5.

the sum) (Appendix A). The correlation between mean solution times on each problem and percentage of overt strategy use on that problem ($r = .88$) was also similar in magnitude to those obtained in the earlier experiments.

The Source of the Relations among Strategy Use, Errors, and Solution Times. The model predicted that the correlations among these three variables derived primarily from errors and solution times on retrieval trials. Errors and solution times on these trials, like overt strategy use, would derive from the distribution of associations. By contrast, errors and solution times on counting and counting-fingers trials would derive from the size of the numbers being counted. In the operation of addition the size of the numbers being counted corresponds to the sum. In subtraction, it corresponds most naturally to the size of the larger number. Illustratively, a child who is counting fingers first needs to represent the larger number, then to put down the number of fingers corresponding to the second number, and then to count the remainder. Adding the larger number, the smaller number, and the remainder yields a sum that is twice the larger number. Therefore, the percentage of overt strategy use seemed likely to be an accurate predictor of errors and solution times on retrieval trials in subtraction, but not of errors and solution times on counting and counting-fingers trials, especially when the contribution of the larger number was partialed out.

These predictions proved accurate. First consider the data on retrieval-trial errors. Percentage of errors on retrieval trials on each problem correlated $r = .83$ with percentage of overt strategy use on the problem. When the contribution of the size of the larger number was partialed out, the correlation between percentage of errors on retrieval trials and percentage of overt strategy use remained high: $r = .72$. In contrast, percentage of errors on counting and counting-fingers trials correlated only $r = .25$ with percentage of overt strategy use (Fig. 9.6). With the contribution of the larger number partialed out, the correlation between errors on counting and counting-fingers trials and overt strategy use became $r = .00$. On both the raw and the partial correlations, percentage of errors on retrieval trials was significantly more closely related to percentage of overt strategy use than was percentage of errors on counting and counting-fingers trials. For the raw correlations, the difference in the correlations was $t(22) = 4.09$. For the partial correlations, the difference between the two correlations was $t(22) = 3.51$ (both p's $< .01$).

The model predicted that the correlation between percentage of errors on fingers-strategy trials and percentage of overt strategy use would be lower than the correlation of overt strategy use with errors on retrieval trials and higher than the correlation of overt strategy use with errors on counting and counting-fingers trials (for the same reason as on addition problems). The raw correlation between percentage of errors on fingers-strategy trials on each problem and percentage of overt strategy use on that problem was $r = .39$, which was between the other two raw correlations. This correlation was significantly lower than the raw correlation with errors on retrieval trials, $t(22) = 3.51, p < .01$, but not significantly different than the raw correlation with errors on counting and counting-fingers trials $t < 1$. With the contribution of the larger number partialed out, the correlation was $r = .11$. This partial correlation again was in between the other two. It was significantly lower than the partial correlation involving errors on retrieval trials, $t(22) = 3.36, p < .01$, and did not differ significantly from the partial correlation involving errors on counting and counting-fingers trials, $t < 1$.

A similar pattern emerged for solution times. Overt strategy use correlated highly with mean solution times on retrieval trials ($r = .83$). The magnitude of the correlation was reduced somewhat but remained substantial when the magnitude of the larger number was partialed out ($r = .62$). Solution times on counting and counting-fingers trials also correlated highly with overt strategy use ($r = .73$). This correlation, however, was based largely on covariation with the larger number. When the contribution of the larger number's size was partialed out, the correlation between percentage of overt strategy use and mean solution times on counting and counting-fingers trials fell to $r = .25$. The difference between the raw correlations did not reach significance, $t(22) = 1.20, p > .10$, but the difference between the partial correlations was significant, $t(22) = 2.45$, $p < .05$.

These results indicate that in subtraction, as in addition, the types of strategies that children use, the relative solution times of the strategies, the correlations among percentage of errors, mean solution times, and percentage of overt strategy use on each problem, and the source of the correlations' residing in errors and solution times on retrieval trials all matched the pattern predicted by the distribution of associations model. Next we consider how young children might develop such an adaptive strategy-choice procedure.

THE DEVELOPMENT OF STRATEGY CHOICES

How might children acquire their distributions of associations, and how might they acquire a process for operating on them? First consider the distributions of associations themselves. A satisfactory acquisition theory would need to explain learning of both correct answers and errors, because children's distributions of associations include incorrect as well as correct responses. Our basic assumption about how children acquire these distributions is that each time they answer a problem, the associative strength linking that answer to the problem increases. This idea has frequently been used to account for the learning of correct answers but has rarely been used to explain the learning of particular errors. A recent finding by Jacoby (personal communication), however, suggests that the mechanism may apply there as well. Jacoby found that showing college students words spelled incorrectly slowed their later recognition of correct spellings. He interpreted the result to mean that the college students retained the incorrect spellings and that the incorrect spellings interfered with efforts to retrieve the correct one. Given the assumption that people retain whatever answer they advance to a problem, the issue becomes to determine what answers they will advance. Three factors that we hypothesize influence the answers that preschoolers advance on addition problems are preexisting associations from the counting string, the sum of the numbers being added, and the frequency of exposure to the problems.

Counting-String Associations

Even before learning to add, most children know the counting string, at least as high as 10 (Pollio & Reinhardt, 1970; Pollio & Whitacre, 1970). Examination of the particular addition errors that children made in our experiments suggested that this prior knowledge of the counting string influences the formation of distributions of associations for adding. As shown in Fig. 9.7A, on all ties (problems on which the first and second number are the same, such as 3 + 3), and ascending-series problems (items on which the second number is larger than the first one, such as 2 + 4), the most frequent error in Siegler and Robinson's data and in the data of the replication and extension experiment was for children to state the number one greater than the second number. That is, they would say that 3 + 3 = 4 and that 3 + 5 = 6. Fig. 9.7B shows an identical pattern in the overt-strategies-prohibited experiment. Here too, the answer one greater than the second number was the most frequent error on all 10 ties and ascending-series problems. Our interpretation was that such problems triggered associations with children's knowledge of the counting string and that the children simply advanced the next number in the series (e.g., 2 + 4 = 5). The phenomenon is reminiscent of Winkelman and Schmidt's (1974) finding that college students are slow to reject propositions such as 5 + 3 = 15—that is, problems on which a different numerical operation provides an interfering association. It is also consistent with Miller and Gelman's (in press) finding that counting string relations are the main determinant of 5-year-olds' judgments of similarity among numbers.

The specific reason that counting-string associations influenced responses on ascending-series and tie problems but not on descending-series problems was open to speculation. The simplest account—that the more similar the problem to the counting string, the greater the likelihood of the association's being triggered—fit the data only crudely. Problems with discrepant addends, such as 2 + 5, and tie problems, such as 3 + 3, elicited counting-string errors as often as problems that more closely paralleled the counting string, such as 3 + 4 and 4 + 5.

A somewhat less straightforward explanation was in considerably better accord with the data. The last addend in an addition problem may always activate its immediate successor as a potential answer. However, other knowledge that preschoolers have, namely that answers to addition problems should be at least as great as the larger addend, may prevent them from stating counting-string associates as answers on descending-series problems. On 4 + 1, for example, children would not say 2 as an answer because it did not exceed 4. This explanation was

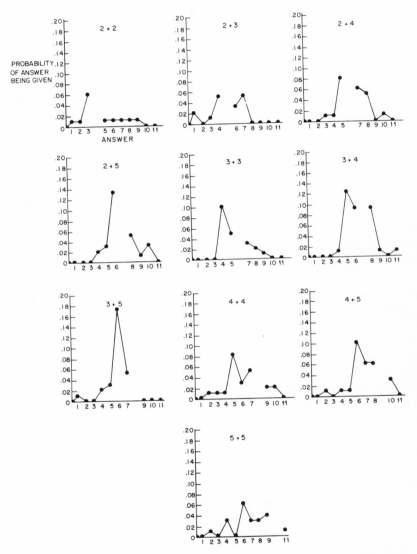

FIG. 9.7. Frequency of each incorrect answer on ties and ascending-series problems.

B. Overt - Strategies - Prohibited Experiment Data

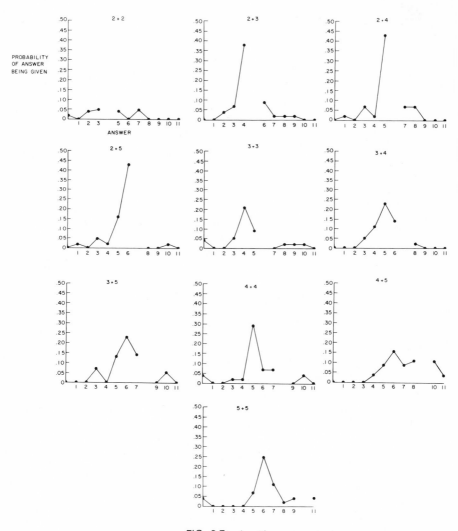

FIG. 9.7. (cont.)

consistent with the pattern of problems in which the counting-string associations did and did not influence answers, and also with three other pieces of evidence. First, in the addition experiments reported in this chapter, children rarely advanced answers smaller than the larger addend. They did so on only 5% of trials. Second, when we presented eight 4- and 5-year-olds a single digit (4, 5, or 6) and asked them to name the first number they thought of, all eight responded with the immediate successor of the number—that is, with the counting-string associate. Here, as on the addition problems, the absence of a larger prior number allowed the counting-string association to manifest itself. Third, Brush (1978) and Cooper, Starkey, Blevins, Goth, and Leitner (1978) found that 3- to 5-year-olds know that adding objects to a collection increases its number. How children acquire such knowledge, and how it combines with their other knowledge to influence addition performance, are unknown, but it seems at least plausible that counting-string associations always operate, but are manifested in children's answers only if the answers produced are greater than either addend.

The Sum of the Numbers

A second potential influence on the distribution of associations was the answers yielded by children's efforts to count their fingers or the objects in their mental images. Presumably, the greater the number of objects people need to count, the greater the probability that they will err somewhere in the counting process. Gelman and Gallistel (1978) provided evidence that 3-, 4-, and 5-year-olds do err more frequently in counting large than small sets. In the addition context, learning of responses advanced after incorrect counting of the objects in the representation would lead to problems with higher sums' having flatter distributions of associative strengths than problems with smaller sums.

Frequency of Exposure to Problems

A third factor that could influence the formation of the distribution of associations is frequency of exposure to each problem. Parents, preschool teachers, and older children might present preschoolers with some problems more often than others. Greater opportunity to learn particular problems, rather than any inherent characteristics of the learners or the problems, might account for those problems having relatively peaked distributions of associations.

To test this view, Sue Hamman and I asked 30 adults, all parents of 2- to 4-year-olds who attended a local preschool, to teach their children about addition as they might at home. The parents were instructed:

> We know that parents sometimes teach their children arithmetic problems even before the children enter elementary school. We are interested in learning how parents do this, since they often seem to be quite successful. Please give your child some addition problems as you might at home, so that we can learn how parents go about teaching.

The experimenter ended the session once the parent had presented 10 problems or once 5 minutes had passed, whichever came first.

The frequency with which parents presented various problems is shown in Table 9.5. The most frequently posed problems were ones that children answered quite accurately in the previous studies. The frequency with which parents pre-

TABLE 9.5
Distribution of Parental Input[a]

		Addend				
	1	*2*	*3*	*4*	*5*
1	15	6	1	1	0
2	14	12	1	0	0
Augend *3*	14	3	0	0	0
4	9	5	0	1	1
5	4	0	1	0	3

[a]The data indicate the number of parents (out of 30) who presented the given problem at least once.

sented the 25 problems generated by the combinations of augend (1 to 5) + addend (1 to 5) correlated $r = .69$ with percentage of errors in the Siegler and Robinson data, $F(24) = 21.37$, $p < .01$.

The parental input data also suggested why certain problems were easier than might have been expected on other grounds. Illustratively, in Siegler and Robinson and in the replication and extension experiment, children were more often correct on each "+1" problem (e.g., 4 + 1) than on the inverse "1+" problem (e.g., 1 + 4). Groen and Parkman (1972) and Svenson (1975) have reported similar findings on solution-time measures with first through third graders. Yet both the min model and the sum-squared model predict that the two types of problems should be of identical difficulty, and 1 + 4, unlike 4 + 1, has helpful counting-string associations working for it. Parental input may be a crucial factor in explaining this apparent anomaly. As shown in Table 9.5, parents presented "+1" problems five times as often as they presented "1+" items. Ties, which similarly have been found to be easier than the sizes of their minimum numbers or squared sums would suggest, were also presented relatively often. Thus, the frequency with which children encounter a problem, as well as the sizes of sums and associations from counting, seemed likely to be among the factors influencing the development of the distribution of associations.[12]

---

[12]Another interpretation of the parental input data is that the parents had accurate intuitions about which problems were easy to learn, and that these intuitions, rather than differential exposure, were responsible for the correlation between problem presentation rates and children's performance. We are currently testing this interpretation. If "+1" problems are indeed easier to learn than "1+" problems, then children who have not yet learned either of them should more quickly master the "+1" items. With roughly one-fourth of the data from the experiment collected, this does not seem to be the case; the two types of problems seem equally difficult to learn. If the pattern continues, it would render unlikely the view that accurate parental intuitions about learnability created the correlation between parental input and problem difficulty.

To test the adequacy of this account of development, we quantified each of the hypothesized predictor variables and examined how well they together accounted for the Fig. 9.2A distribution of associations. The acquisition model was expressed as a regression equation with three indpendent variables. One predictor was associations from the counting string. All ties and ascending-series problems on which counting-string associations yielded a correct answer (e.g., 1 + 3) were assigned a value of two, all ties and ascending-series problems on which such associations yielded an incorrect answer (e.g., 2 + 3) were assigned a value of zero, and all descending-series problems (e.g., 3 + 2) were assigned a neutral value of one. A second predictor was the likelihood that children would err in counting the objects in their elaborated representations. This variable was defined operationally as the sum of the numbers in the problem, because the more objects children had to represent, and the more objects they had to count, the more likely they would be to err. The third predictor was the frequency of exposure to each problem. The Table 9.5 data on frequency of parental presentation of each problem was the operational measure of exposure to that problem.

The regression analysis supported the preceding analysis of development in several ways. The three predictor variables accounted for 85% of the variance in the percentage of errors on the 25 problems in Fig. 9.2A. Each of the predictors added significant amounts of variance to that explained by the other two. The sum variable was the first to enter the equation, accounting for 68% of the variance, the counting-associations variable was the next to enter, adding 10%, and the parental-input variable also added significant variance, 7%. These results were consistent with the view that preexisting associations from the counting string, likelihood of mistakes in counting objects in elaborated representations, and frequency of exposure to different problems contribute to the development of associations between problems and answers.

How might the process develop? Here, our account is largely speculative. The first issue is how children acquire each of the four strategies. Retrieval is as basic and as generally applicable a strategy as any that people possess. It almost certainly is present well before the preschool period. Retrieval seems inherently to entail standards akin to confidence criteria and search lengths. Illustratively, Mervis and Canada (1982) observed reliable "refusal responses" by 1-year-olds. That is, when infants were asked by their mothers to identify a given object from an array of objects in front of them, they consistently refused to choose any of them when none fit into the appropriate category. The refusal response did not arise when the named object was available. For the 1-year-olds to defy the social demand implicit in being asked for an object by their parents, they would need to know that each available object did not exceed their confidence criterion for belonging to the category. The fact that children at times said "there aren't any" indicated that they also possessed a "stop rule" akin to a search length for governing the number of retrieval efforts they would make.

The way in which the other three strategies develop is at least as much a matter of speculation. The counting-fingers strategy is probably acquired through imitation of, and direct instruction by, other children and adults. Informal observation and discussion with parents indicates that such instruction is quite common. Whether the fingers and counting strategies develop independently of the counting-fingers approach, or whether they develop as attempts to execute or modify it, is unknown at present.

Another issue about the development of the process concerns how its three phases are assembled into an overall problem-solving procedure. Retrieval is so rapid, so generally applicable, and, ordinarily, so nearly effortless, that attempting it first may be the "default option" for a wide range of cognitive activity. Until children form an elaborated representation, they have nothing to count; thus, problem elaboration naturally precedes counting. In sum, assembling the process in the order retrieval first, problem elaboration second, and counting third does not seem to require great insight.

Might the process exist in a more rudimentary form before assuming the shape depicted in Fig. 9.2B? It seems plausible that at an early point in development, children might use only the retrieval strategy. This point would need to be quite early, however; Starkey and Gelman (1982) observed that 3-year-olds sometimes solved addition problems by putting up fingers (or putting out other objects) and counting them. Again, the existence of such a simple process at an early point in development is only speculation at present. Studying children younger than those we have examined to date may allow more solidly grounded statements about how the process develops.

A COMPUTER SIMULATION OF THE DEVELOPMENT OF THE DISTRIBUTION OF ASSOCIATIONS

A number of critics of information-processing approaches, among them Neisser (1976) and Beilin (1981), have argued that computer simulations have not, and probably cannot, account for development. They noted that most existing simulations of development generate performance but do not undergo transitions from one state to the next. Transition mechanisms are postulated at a verbal level, but not incorporated into the simulations themselves. In this section, we discuss a computer simulation of addition that incorporates learning and performance mechanisms into a single model and that proceeds from producing relatively poor performance to producing the sophisticated performance typical of 4- and 5-year-olds.

An Outline of the Simulation

The simulation can be described in terms of the beginning state of its representation and its process and in terms of six features of its operation. At the outset, the representation includes only two types of knowledge. One is the understanding that numbers as a general class are appropriate answers to addition problems. We depicted this information as a set of minimal associations (associative strength = .01) between each problem under consideration and each possible answer (each whole number between 1 and 12). Second, when an ascending or tie problem is presented, the association between that problem and the answer one higher than the second number is momentarily strengthened, much as in semantic priming. For ease of description, and because this momentary association is identical to an enduring association in its effects on the probabilities of retrieving an answer and stating it, we have grouped together the two types of associations throughout the remainder of this discussion.

Now consider the initial state of the process. Biology has given it the ability to retrieve information from memory. Direct instruction and modeling have taught it to put up fingers (or their equivalent) and count them. Thus, the process at the beginning of the simulation resembles that shown in Fig. 9.2B.

This initial representation and process are insufficient to produce the performance of 4- and 5-year-olds. For example, when we presented to the simulation in its initial state a set of 10,000 problems, 400 each of the 25 problems in Siegler and Robinson, it stated a retrieved answer on only 7% of the trials. Percentage of errors and percentage of overt strategy use on each problem correlated $r = .01$. However, the initial representation and process do provide a base from which learning can occur. Six aspects of the acquisition process seem critical:

1. The simulation is presented the 25 problems in accord with their relative frequency in the parental input study described earlier.[13]
2. Before each problem, the simulation generates a confidence criterion and a search length. Both are selected by a random process, with the confidence criterion varying from .05 to .99 and the search length from 1 to 3.
3. The probability of retrieving an answer is proportional to its associative strength. A retrieved answer is stated if its associative strength exceeds the current confidence criterion. Retrieval attempts continue until either the associative strength of a retrieved answer exceeds the confidence criterion or the number of searches matches the allowed search length.
4. If the number of retrieval efforts reaches the allowed search length, and no answer has been stated, the program generates an elaborated representation of the number of objects in the augend and addend. In the program's present implementation, this elaboration always corresponds to the fingers approach, in which the presentation, once generated, does not fade. Once

---

[13]In the relatively small sample of parental input data that we had available at the time that this chapter was written, parents had never presented some problems (Table 9.5). This seemed unlikely to reflect the real-world input. Therefore, we added a constant to each percentage in the input data. This ensured that all problems would be encountered on at least 2% of trials, while also ensuring that the simulation most frequently encountered the most frequently presented problems.

the representation is generated, the model temporarily (for the duration of the trial) adds .05 to the associative strength of the answer corresponding to the number of objects represented. It then retrieves an answer, and states it if its associative strength exceeds the confidence criterion.

5. If this last retrieval effort is unsuccessful, the model counts the objects in the elaborated representation. On each count, there is a fixed probability of skipping over the object being counted and a fixed probability of counting it twice.

6. Every time the system advances an answer, the association between that answer and the problem increases. The increment is twice as great for correct answers, which presumably are reinforced, as for incorrect answers, which presumably are not.

The Simulation's Behavior

The simulation runs in two phases: a learning phase and a test phase. The learning phase is designed to resemble children's experience with addition prior to the time at which they enter the experiment. The test phase is intended to resemble behavior in the experimental setting, given children's prior experience.

The learning phase includes 2000 trials, an average of 80 for each of the 25 problems (range = 60 to 158 trials per problem). During this phase, children develop more or less peaked distributions of associations on each problem. In accord with the previously discussed regression equations, three variables shape the learning process: associations from the counting string, frequency of presentation of each problem, and the sum of the numbers. To highlight the contribution of each of these variables, we compare pairs of problems that differ on that variable but whose status is the same on the other two variables.

First consider $1 + 4$ and $2 + 3$, problems that have identical sums and frequencies of presentation, but one with a helpful and one with an interfering association from counting. As shown in Fig. 9.8A, the item that has the helpful association, $1 + 4$, rapidly builds a peak at the answer 5. The association between the item with the interfering association, $2 + 3$, and the answer 5 starts from a lower point and grows more slowly. At the end of the learning phase, after 2000 trials, the answer 5 has 77% of the total associative strength for $1 + 4$ versus 46% for $2 + 3$. The peak for $1 + 4$ is also higher in absolute terms: .67 versus .37. The greater percentage of total associative strength at 5 for $1 + 4$ means that the simulation will retrieve 5 more often on this problem. The higher absolute peak for $1 + 4$ means that when the simulation retrieves 5, it will state it more often.

Fig. 9.8B illustrates the developmental course for two problems that have identical sums and that lack specific counting-string associations, but that differ in frequency of presentation. The problem $4 + 1$ is presented on 5.4% of trials, whereas the problem $3 + 2$ is presented on 3.7%. The presentation rate has a

A. Problems Differing in Type of Counting Association

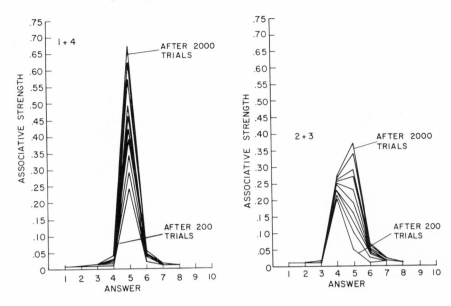

B. Problems Differing in Frequency of Presentation

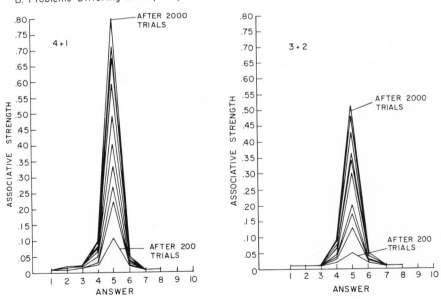

FIG. 9.8. Computer simulation's learning of associations: effects of counting-string associations, frequency of presentation, and sum. Curves represent associative strengths after each 200 trials; the lowest curve represents strengths after 200 trials, the next lowest after 400 trials, and so on.

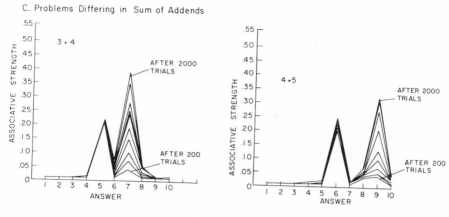

C. Problems Differing in Sum of Addends

FIG. 9.8. *(cont.)*

marked effect on how high the peak rises as well as some effect on how peaked the distribution is. After 2000 trials, the absolute associative strength of the peak for 4 + 1 was .80, whereas for 3 + 2 the associative strength was .51. The percentages of associative strength that were located in the peak were 76% and 69%, respectively. These differences indicate that 4 + 1 would be retrieved somewhat more often than 3 + 2, and would be stated on a considerably higher percentage of those trials on which it was retrieved.

Finally, as shown in Fig. 9.8C, the sum exerted an effect even when the frequency of presentation and the type of counting-string association was constant. The problems 3 + 4 and 4 + 5 are identical in frequency of presentation and in having an interfering counting association. However, they differ in their sums. The peak of the item with the lower sum rises somewhat more rapidly and at the end of 2000 learning trials is higher (.39 versus .32) than that for the item with the higher sum. The distribution is also somewhat more peaked, with the peak of 3 + 4 having 50% of the total associative strength and the peak of 4 + 5 having 43%. Thus, all three variables influence the percentage of trials on which the correct answer is retrieved and the likelihood that it will be stated once it is retrieved.

After the simulation completes the learning phase, it proceeds to the test phase. Whereas the learning phase was intended to model children's experience prior to the experiment, the test phase was intended to parallel their experience in the experiment. The test phase differed from the learning phase in two respects. First, to parallel the empirical experiments that we conducted, all problems were presented equally often in the test phase. Second, because each child who participated in the empirical experiments received only two exposures to each problem, thereby providing very little opportunity to learn, we turned off the learning mechanism that added associative strength to each answer that was stated. The

TABLE 9.6

Computer Simulation's Performance Before and After Learning Phase

Intramodel Correlations	Correlations Between Children's[a] and Model's Behavior
A. Before Learning Phase	
$r_{\%}$ errors and % overt strategy use = .01	$r_{\%}$ errors produced by model and children = .78[b]
$r_{\%}$ errors and $\bar{x}$ solution times = .11	$r_{\%}$ overt strategy use produced by model and children = −.03
$r_{\%}$ overt strategy use and $\bar{x}$ solution times = .82[b]	$r_{\bar{x}}$ solution times produced by model and children = .00
B. After Learning Phase	
$r_{\%}$ errors and % overt strategy use = .94	$r_{\%}$ errors produced by model and children = .87
$r_{\%}$ errors and $\bar{x}$ solution times = .94	$r_{\%}$ overt strategy use produced by model and children = .87
$r_{\%}$ overt strategy use and $\bar{x}$ solution times = .99	$r_{\bar{x}}$ solution times produced by model and children = .80

[a]Children's data are combined results of Siegler and Robinson and replication condition of replication and extension experiment.

[b]The strength of these correlations is due to the influence of the counting-string associations that exist prior to the learning phase. The model's percentage of overt strategy use and mean solution times correlate highly even before the learning phase because both are relatively low for the 15 problems with counting-string associations (due to these problems' having distributions of associations with a peak at the number one higher than the second addend) and relatively high for the 10 without them (where no such peaks exist). The correlation between the children's and the model's errors is due to the counting associations' producing correct answers on the five "1+" problems, which are relatively easy for children, and incorrect answers on the other 10 ties and ascending-series problems, which the children find relatively difficult.

276

goal was to model a large number of children, each having a brief experimental session, rather than a single child having a very long session.

The computer program's behavior in the test phase resembled that of children much more closely than had its behavior prior to the learning phase. It generated three of the four strategies: retrieval, fingers, and counting fingers (recall that the counting strategy has not yet been implemented in the simulation). The relative accuracies and the relative solution times of the three modeled strategies were identical to those of the children. The simulation's error patterns also were like the children's; the simulation's most frequent error on all 10 ascending and tie problems was the answer one greater than the second addend.

The simulation's performance also resembled that of the children in which problems elicited the greatest percentage of errors, which took the longest to answer, and which elicited the highest percentage of overt strategies. As shown in Table 9.6, all of the correlations of greatest interest between the simulation's behavior and that of the children exceeded $r = .80$. Moreover, the intrasimulation correlations among percentage of errors, percentage of overt strategy use, and mean solution times on each problem all exceeded $r = .90$.[14]

The results of the simulation also suggested two hypotheses about the developmental sequence of addition skills. First, in examining the correlations between the model's and the children's percentages of overt strategies and errors, we noticed that the correlations between the two sets of errors started higher and grew more rapidly than did the correlations between the percentages of overt strategy use (Table 9.6). The reason lay in the dominating effect of the counting-string associations at the outset of the learning phase. These counting-string associations produce relative numbers of correct answers on the 25 problems much like those that will be present after the learning phase. The five problems with helpful associations remain relatively easy, and the 10 with interfering associations remain difficult. The effect on overt strategy use is different, however. The five problems with helpful associations continue to elicit relatively frequent use of the retrieval strategy. However, the 10 problems with interfering associations, which early elicit relatively frequent use of retrieval, are later among the problems that least often elicit use of retrieval. The reason is that before the learning phase, they are among the 15 problems whose distribution of associations have any peak, but after the learning phase, they are the only problems whose associative strength is divided among two peaks, one at the counting-string association and one at the correct answer. Thus, one testable hypothesis that emerges from the simulation is that the first age at which children's errors correlate significantly with the errors of 4- and 5-year-olds will be

---

[14]The model's solution times were operationally defined as the number of searches that it made before finding an answer on each problem.

earlier than the first age at which their pattern of overt strategy use correlates with that of the older children. We plan to test this hypothesis by presenting the problems to 3½-year-olds and seeing which correlation emerges earlier.

A second, related prediction that follows from the computer model is that early in development, counting-string associations should be an especially powerful predictor of performance. At the outset of the computer simulation's learning phase, neither errors made in counting nor frequency of problem presentation has much effect on the distribution of associations. Their effects depend on children's having experience with the problems. Counting associations, however, exercise a strong effect from the outset. Thus, the percentage of responses in accord with counting-string associations should be greater early in development than later. Again, experiments with very young children can test these predictions.

In sum, a computer simulation that takes into account relative frequency of problem presentation, associations from the counting string, and the likelihood of errors in executing overt strategies can produce performance much like that of children. The simulation both learns and performs. At the outset, its performance is not very accurate, and is unlike that of 4- and 5-year-olds in many ways. After having an opportunity to learn, its performance is much more childlike. The simulation demonstrates that children could acquire their distributions of addition associations through the three hypothesized mechanisms, and that if they did, their performance would be much like what we observed.

DEVELOPMENT BEYOND THE PRESCHOOL PERIOD

Although we have not yet simulated development of addition skills beyond the level displayed by 4- and 5-year-olds, the simulation suggests ways in which the knowledge of older children and adults might develop. Ashcraft (1982), Groen and Parkman (1972), and Svenson (1975) have all noted two characteristics of 7- to 9-year-olds' performance on simple addition problems. The children make few errors, and their solution times are proportional to the size of the minimum addend. The present research complements these findings on the min strategy in at least four ways. It indicates the chronological period during which children learn the strategy, the range of problems on which they might apply it, the mechanisms by which they might decide when to use it, and how it could be integrated with the process that younger children use.

Our research provided almost no evidence of preschoolers' using the min strategy. In particular, on trials in which they counted aloud, preschoolers started counting from 1 rather than from the larger addend on more than 99% of trials. Thus, most children must acquire the min strategy at age 6 or 7—that is, in first or second grade.

Our finding that even 4-year-olds accurately retrieve answers to many problems makes it unlikely that children use the min strategy on every problem once they do acquire it. Why would children use a reconstructive process when they could accurately retrieve the answer? Instead, children who use the min strategy probably use it only on relatively difficult problems—that is, on problems for which they possess relatively flat distributions of associations.

Older children could arrive at the min strategy through the same mechanisms by which 4- and 5-year-olds arrive at other overt strategies. They would use it when they could not in the allotted search length retrieve an answer whose associative strength exceeded the confidence criterion. As their distribution of associations for a problem grow more peaked, they would use the min strategy less and less frequently. This hypothesis is consistent with Ashcraft's (1982) finding that the minimum number ceases to be the best predictor of children's solution times after age 9.

Only two modifications would be needed to integrate the min strategy with the Fig. 9.2B process. First, the elaborated representation would include the number of objects indicated by the smaller addend, rather than the number indicated by the sum (Step 11). Second, counting would proceed from the number one greater than the larger addend rather than from "1" (Step 15). Otherwise, the process could be the same as that used by 4- and 5-year-olds. Such a process, like its predecessor, would have the desirable properties of yielding answers to all problems, of leading to use of the relatively effortless retrieval process on those problems in which it could yield consistently correct performance, and of eventually yielding a state in which retrieval would always be used on these simple addition problems. It would have the added advantage of reducing the number of objects that needed to be represented, thus reducing both the time needed to solve problems and the likelihood of counting errors.

AN OVERVIEW OF THE MODEL

The present model of strategy choice in addition and subtraction is sufficiently complex that there may be a danger of losing the forest for the trees. Figure 9.9 provides an overview of the model that strips away much of the complexity. The distribution of associations, the key to the operation of the model, is at the center. Performance is produced by a three-phase process operating on this distribution. The three phases are retrieval, elaboration of the representation, and counting. Development of the distribution of associations is influenced by three factors: preexisting associations from the counting string, frequency of exposure to the problems, and the sum of the two addends. These three factors determine the peakedness of the distribution of associations, which in turn determines the percentage of overt strategy use, the percentage of errors on retrieval trials, and the mean solution times on retrieval trials.

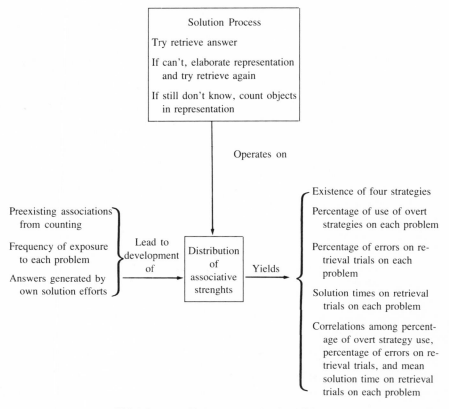

FIG 9.9.   Model of strategy choice in addition.

EXTENSIONS OF THE MODEL TO OTHER DOMAINS

The distribution of associations model provides a framework for considering strategy choices in domains as diverse as reading, spelling, and multiplication. The particular associations will vary among domains, but the organization of the process may be quite similar. In each case, the process could include three sequential phases. The first phase would be retrieval of an answer from a distribution of associations. The second phase, contingent on the failure of the first to yield a statable answer, would involve elaboration of the problem representation. The particulars of this elaborative process would vary with the task domain. The third phase, again contingent on the answer's not yet having been stated, would involve an algorithmic process certain to yield an answer but slower than the other strategies. As in the second phase, the particular algorithmic process varies with the domain of application. In all domains, the distribution of associations on particular problems would determine when each strategy was most likely to be used, when errors would most frequently occur, and when problems would be answered most rapidly.

Table 9.7 indicates how the model might be applied to the reading of words, spelling, and multiplication. Children use at least three strategies to decode words. Sometimes they retrieve a word's pronunciation and state it with no intervening overt behavior. Other times they proceed phoneme by phoneme in an attempt to "sound out" the word. Yet other times, they ask a parent, teacher, or older child to identify the word. The prediction of the model is that words that elicit frequent errors and long solution times should also elicit frequent use of "sounding out" and seeking help from other people.

Spelling is another domain in which people may base strategy choices on their distribution of associations. As discussed at the outset of this chapter, people can use at least four strategies to spell. They can retrieve the letters in a word, they can form a mental image of how the word might look, they can write out several possible spellings, or they can look in a dictionary. These strategies closely parallel the ones used in addition and subtraction. Familiar words, short words, words with unambiguous sound–letter correspondences, and words that conform to typical orthographic patterns would be expected to have peaked distributions of associations. They, therefore, also would be associated with short solution times, frequent correct answers, and frequent use of retrieval.

Multidigit multiplication presents another domain in which people might use a similar strategy-choice procedure. For some problems, such as 20×20, many people can retrieve the correct answer. For others, people might elaborate the problem representations in ways that take advantage of specific aspects of the numbers. For example, if asked to multiply 54×11, they might decompose 11 into 10 and 1, multiply each by 54, and finally add 540 and 54 to obtain the product. On yet other problems, people typically follow the long multiplication algorithm. This algorithm is applicable to all problems but, like looking up words in the dictionary or counting one's fingers, is cumbersome and time

TABLE 9.7
Strategy-Choice Model Applied to Three Other Tasks

		Phase of Model	
Task	Retrieval	Elaboration of Representation	Solution Algorithm
Multiplication	Retrieve product	Try to use "shortcut"	Use long multiplication algorithm
Oral reading	Retrieve word's pronunciation	Sound out pronunciation	Ask the teacher
Spelling	Retrieve word's spelling	Write out alternative spellings and try to recognize correct one	Look up spelling in dictionary

consuming to use. Again, we would expect to find strong correlations among percentage of errors on a problem, mean solution times, and percentage of overt strategy use, at least if percentage of errors and mean solution times were measured by a procedure in which overt strategies were not allowed.

SOME FINAL COMMENTS ABOUT STRATEGY CHOICE

In this concluding section, we discuss three issues raised by the present research: the role of explicit metacognitive decisions in strategy choices, the relation of the distribution of associations model to previous rule-oriented models that we have formulated, and the way in which the distribution of association model may help reconcile our intuitions of commonalities in reasoning across domains with the persistent empirical data to the contrary.

The Role of Metacognitive Decisions in Strategy Choices

The distribution of associations model illustrates a way in which people could choose strategies without extensive knowledge about their cognitive capacities and the demands of particular tasks. This type of model has several advantages. An obvious one is that the model provides a basis for the empirical finding that metacognitive knowledge often correlates weakly with strategy choices. Because it is possible to arrive at useful strategies without any metacognitive knowledge, the two do not need to be highly correlated.

Closely related, the model renders understandable the finding that despite 1- to 3-year-olds' minimal metacognitive knowledge, they make sensible strategy choices in certain situations. Specifically, in domains in which they have extensive experience, such as memory for object locations and production and comprehension of language, young children often use reasonable strategies (Clark, 1983; DeLoache, this volume; Perlmutter, 1980). In these domains, even young children have extensive associative networks to guide their performance. These associations may render explicit metacognitive knowledge unnecessary.

This view should not be confused with the frequently expressed hypothesis that young children are associative animals whereas older ones are conceptual (e.g., Kendler & Kendler, 1962; Lange, 1978; White, 1965). In our model, the process that operates on the associations is both powerful and general; it certainly seems to qualify for the title "conceptual." Adults and older children may sometimes use more abstract processes for choosing strategies that would not depend on associations within particular domains (as may young children). However, the problem isomorph literature (e.g., Kotovsky, 1983) suggests caution in postulating such processes and especially in hypothesizing their widespread use. Even adults frequently do not transfer strategies that they have learned in the context of a particular problem to other problems with identical structural characteristics. Specific associations between problems and means for answering them may often dominate adults' as well as young children's strategy choices.

It is impossible to demonstrate that a particular process does not occur in a problem-solving procedure. It can be demonstrated, however, that such a process would be redundant. In the present context, children could explicitly judge a problem's difficulty and their own problem-solving capacity, but it is difficult to see what purpose such judgments would serve. The model in its present form arrives at adaptive strategies without the judgments. Even if we postulated that children explicitly judged problem difficulty, we would still need to account for how they made their judgments and why the correlations among overt strategy use, errors, and solution times would be greatest for percentages of errors and mean solution times on retrieval trials. We would also need to explain how the four strategies were generated and to account for their relative solution times. In short, it is unclear what utility explicit metacognitive judgments would have within this model, either for children or for the researcher trying to model their thought processes.

It might be argued that the model already incorporates a metacognitive judgment in a slightly disguised form. This is the judgment that the associative strength of a retrieved answer does or does not exceed the confidence criterion. Due to the diversity of uses of the term *metacognitive*, we are unsure whether this judgment is best viewed as fitting within the metacognitive category. Regardless of its placement, the ability to make such decisions seems to us one of the most basic cognitive qualities. Without it, how would the 1-year-olds in the Mervis and Canada (1982) experiment have known not to answer their mothers' request when none of the available responses was appropriate? More generally, how would children know when to ask questions? Whether we label such judgments "metacognitive" is immaterial to our claim that on simple arithmetic problems, children choose strategies by a procedure like that shown in Fig. 9.2, rather than on the basis of their knowledge of their cognitive capacities, available strategies, and task demands.

The Relation of the Distribution of Associations Model to Rule Models

In previous research, one of us has characterized children's knowledge in terms of rules. Associations between problems and specific answers played no explicit role. Why might rule-based models be appropriate in some contexts and associative models in others?

A major difference between the tasks for which we have postulated rule-based models and the tasks for which we have postulated associative models concerns people's prior knowledge. Before the experimental session, people would have had little, if any, experience with balance scale, liquid-quantity conservation, or fullness problems. They would certainly be unlikely to have formed strong associations between particular answers—such as that the left side of the balance scale will go down—and particular items, such as three weights on the third peg on the left side versus four weights on the second peg on the right. In contrast, children have extensive experience with specific addition, subtraction, spelling, and reading items. Associations between problems and particular answers would directly influence performance on many items.

Even in domains usually thought of as rule governed, associations involving particular items seem to play a crucial role when people have extensive experience with the domain. Support for this position comes from research on language development. Children's overgeneralizations of the English past-tense and pluralization rules have often been cited as evidence for the rule-governed nature of language use (e.g., Brown, 1973; Cazden, 1968). Yet language rules never attain the consistency of those observed on the balance scale, liquid-quantity conservation, and other unfamiliar tasks. At all times, children continue to produce some correct irregular past-tense and plural forms (MacWhinney, 1978; Moratsos, 1983). These correct irregular uses tend to occur on the most common verbs, those for which children would have the greatest opportunity to form distributions of associations with strong peaks at the correct irregular form. Thus, models that focus exclusively on rules may be useful primarily in situation in which people have little experience with specific items. Associations involving particular items must also be considered in domains in which people have had experience.

Domain Specificity and Domain Generality

In the past decade, many cognitive developmentalists have been torn between their intuitions that commonalities in reasoning across domains do exist and the evidence that children reason in different ways on different tasks. Articles by Flavell (1982), Fischer (1980), Case (1978), and many others attest to this conflict. Each investigator has proposed means for reconciling the discrepancy. For example, Flavell suggested that commonalities may exist for some individuals, in some task domains, and at some points in the developmental process. The present research suggests an additional possibility. A common process, such as that depicted in Fig. 9.2B, may be utilized across numerous domains. Because the distributions of associations are distinct for each domain, indeed for each problem within each domain, this common process will not yield parallel behavior on different tasks. A child might form very peaked distributions for arithmetic problems, leading to good performance, and relatively flat ones on spelling items, leading to poor performance. The child's behavior would not be parallel, but the process used to produce the behavior would be. Behavior comes about through processes' operating on specific content knowledge. Only by considering the latter as well as the former are we likely to detect many of the unities in children's thinking.

ACKNOWLEDGMENTS

This research was supported by Grant #HD 16578 from the National Institute of Child Health and Human Development and by a grant from the Spencer Foundation. Useful comments and suggestions of William Chase, David Klahr, Brian MacWhinney, and Catherine Sophian on earlier versions of the manuscript are gratefully acknowledged.

REFERENCES

Ashcraft, M. H. The development of mental arithmetic: A chronometric approach. *Developmental Review*, 1982, *2*, 213–236.

Beilin, H. *Piaget and the new functionalism. Eleventh Symposium of the Jean Piaget Society*, Philadelphia, 1981.

Brown, R. *A first language. The early stages.* Cambridge, Mass.: Harvard University Press. 1973.

Brush, L. R. Preschool children's knowledge of addition and subtraction. *Journal of Research in Mathematics Education*, 1978, *1*, 44–54.

Case, R. Intellectual development from birth to adulthood: A neo-Piagetian approach. In R. S. Siegler (Ed.), *Children's thinking: What develops?* Hillsdale, N.J.: Lawrence Erlbaum Associates, 1978.

Cavanaugh, J. C., & Perlmutter, M. Metamemory: A critical examination. *Child Development*, 1982, *53*, 11–28.

Cazden, C. B. The acquisition of noun and verb inflections. *Child Development*, 1968, *39*, 433–448.

Clark, E. V. Meanings and concepts. In W. Kessen (Ed.), *History, theory, and methods* (Vol. in P. Mussen, Ed., *Handbook of child psychology*). New York: Wiley, 1983.

Clark, H. H. Linguistic processes in deductive reasoning. *Psychological Review*, 1969, *76*, 387–404.

Clark, H. H., & Chase, W. G. On the process of comparing sentences against pictures. *Cognitive Psychology*, 1972, *3*, 472–517.

Cooper, L. A., & Regan, D. Attention, perception, and intelligence. In R. Sternberg (Ed.), *Handbook of human intelligence*. New York: Cambridge University Press, 1982.

Cooper, L. A., & Shepard, R. N. Chronometric studies of the rotation of mental images. In W. G. Chase (Ed.), *Visual information processing*. New York: Academic Press, 1973.

Cooper, R. G., Starkey, P., Blevins, B., Gath, P., & Leitner, E. *Number development: Addition and subtraction.* Paper presented at the meeting of the Jean Piaget Society, Philadelphia, May, 1978.

Egan, D. E., & Grimes-Farrow, D. D. Differences in mental representations spontaneously adopted for reasoning. *Memory and Cognition*, 1982, *10*, 297–307.

Farah, M. J., & Kosslyn, S. M. Concept development. In H. W. Reese & L. P. Lipsitt (Eds.), *Advances in child development and behavior* (Vol. 16). New York: Academic Press, 1982.

Fischer, K. W. A theory of cognitive development: The control and construction of hierarchies of skills. *Psychological Review*, 1980, *87*, 477–531.

Flavell, J. H. On cognitive development. *Child Development*, 1982, *53*, 1–10.

Flavell, J. H., Beach, D. R., & Chinsky, J. M. Spontaneous verbal rehearsal in a memory task as a function of age. *Child Development*, 1966, *37*, 283–299.

Flavell, J. H., & Wellman H. M. Metamemory. In R. V. Kail, Jr. & J. W. Hagen (Eds.), *Perspectives on the development of memory and cognition*. Hillsdale, N.J.: Lawrence Erlbaum Associates, 1977.

Gardner, H. *Development psychology: An introduction*. Boston: Little, Brown, 1982.

Gelman, R., & Gallistel, C. R. *The child's understanding of number*. Cambridge, Mass.: Harvard University Press, 1978.

Ginsburg, H. *Children's arithmetic: The learning process*. New York: D. Van Nostrand, 1977.

Glushko, R. J., & Cooper, L. A. Spatial comprehension and comparison processes in verification tasks. *Cognitive Psychology*, 1978, *10*, 391–421.

Groen, G. J., & Parkman, J. M. A chronometric analysis of simple addition. *Psychological Review*, 1972, *79*, 329–343.

Groen, G. J., & Poll, M. Subtraction and the solution of open sentence problems. *Journal of Experimental Child Psychology*, 1973, *16*, 292–302.

Hebbeler, K. *The development of children's problem-solving skills in addition*. Unpublished doctoral dissertation, Cornell University, 1976.

Huttenlocher, J. J., & Higgins, E. T. Adjectives, comparatives and syllogisms. *Psychological Review*, 1971, *78*, 487–504.

Ilg, F., & Ames, L. B. Developmental trends in arithmetic. *Journal of Genetic Psychology*, 1951, *79*, 3–28.

Inhelder, B., & Piaget, J. *The growth of logical thinking from childhood to adolescence*. New York: Basic Books, 1958.

Jacaby, L. Effects of recent prior experience on spelling. Paper presented at the Psychonomic Society Conference, San Diego, CAL., November, 1983.

Just, M. A., & Carpenter, P. A. Sentence comprehension: A psycholingusitic processing model of verification. *Psychological Review*, 1975, *82*, 26–44.

Kendler, H. H., & Kendler, T. S. Vertical and horizontal processes in problem solving. *Psychological Review*, 1962, *69*, 1–16.

Kotovsky, K. *Tower of Hanoi problem isomorphs and solution processes*. Unpublished doctoral dissertation, Carnegie-Mellon University, 1983.

Lange, G. Organization-related processes in children's recall. In P. A. Ornstein (Ed.), *Memory development in children*. Hillsdale, N.J.: Lawrence Erlbaum Associates, 1978.

MacLeod, C. M., Hunt, E. B., & Mathews, N. N. Individual differences in the verification of sentence–picture relationships. *Journal of Verbal Learning and Verbal Behavior*, 1978, *17*, 493–507.

MacWhinney, B. The acquisition of morphophonology. *Monographs of the Society for Research in Child Development*, 1978, *43*(Serial No. 174).

Maratsos, M. Some current issues in the study of grammar. In P. Mussen (Ed.) *Handbook of child psychology Vol. 3, Cognitive Development*, (J. H. Flavell and E. Meekum Volume editors). New York: Wiley, 1983.

Mathews, N. N., Hunt, E. B., & MacLeod, C. M. Strategy choice and strategy training in sentence–picture verification. *Journal of Verbal Learning and Verbal Behavior*, 1980, *19*, 531–548.

Mervis, C. B., & Canada, K. Notes and discussion on the existence of competence errors in early comprehension: A reply to Fremgen & Fay and Chapman & Thomson. *Journal of Child Language*, 1982, *10*, 1–10.

Miller, K., & Gelman, R. The child's representation of number: A multidimensional scaling analysis. *Child Development*, in press.

Naus, M. J., Ornstein, P. A., & Aivano, S. Developmental changes in memory: The effects of processing time and rehearsal instructions. *Journal of Experimental Child Psychology*, 1977, *23*, 237–251.

Neisser, U. General, academic, and artificial intelligence. In L. B. Resnick (Ed.), *The nature of intelligence.* Hillsdale, N.J.: Lawrence Erlbaum Associates, 1976.

Permutter, M. (Ed.). *New directions for child development.* San Francisco: Jossey-Bass, 1980.

Pollio, H. R., & Reinhardt, D. Rules and counting behavior. *Cognitive Psychology,* 1970, *1,* 388–402.

Pollio, H. R., & Whitacre, J. Some observations on the use of natural numbers by preschool children. *Perceptual and Motor Skills,* 1970, *30,* 167–174.

Reder, L. M. Plausibility judgments versus fact retrieval: Alternative strategies for sentence verification. *Psychological Review,* 1982, *89,* 250–280.

Shepard, R. N., & Metzler, J. Mental rotation of three-dimensional objects. *Science,* 1971, *171,* 701–703.

Siegler, R. S. Three aspects of cognitive development. *Cognitive Psychology,* 1976, *8,* 481–520.

Siegler, R. S., & Robinson, M. The development of numerical understandings. In H. Reese & L. P. Lipsitt (Eds.), *Advances in child development and behavior.* New York: Academic Press, 1982.

Starkey, P., & Gelman, R. The development of addition and subtraction abilities. In T. P. Carpenter, J. M. Moser, & T. A. Romberg (Ed.), *Addition and subtraction: A cognitive perspective.* Hillsdale, N.J.: Lawrence Erlbaum Associates, 1982.

Sternberg, R. J. *Intelligence, information processing, and analogical reasoning.* Hillsdale, N.J.: Lawrence Erlbaum Associates, 1977.

Sternberg, R. J., & Ketron, J. L. Selection and implementation of strategies in reasoning by analogy. *Journal of Educational Psychology,* 1982, *74,* 399–413.

Sternberg, R. J., & Rifkin, B. The development of analogical reasoning processes. *Journal of Experimental Child Psychology,* 1979, 27, 195–232.

Sternberg, R. J., & Weil, E. M. An aptitude × strategy interaction in linear syllogistic reasoning. *Journal of Educational Psychology,* 1980, *72,* 226–239.

Svenson, O. Analysis of time required by children for simple additions. *Acta Psychologica,* 1975, *39,* 289–302.

Svenson, O., & Broquist, S. Strategies for solving simple addition problems. *Scandinavian Journal of Psychology,* 1975, *16,* 143–151.

Trabasso, T., Rollins, H., & Shaughnessy, E. Storage and verification stages in processing concepts. *Cognitive Psychology,* 1971, *2,* 239–289.

Vurpillot, E. The development of scanning strategies and their relation to visual differentiation. *Journal of Experimental Child Psychology,* 1968, *6,* 632–650.

Wagner, D. A. Memories of Morocco: The influence of age, schooling and environment on memory. *Cognitive Psychology,* 1978, *10,* 1–28.

Weir, M. W. Developmental changes in problem-solving strategies. *Psychological Review,* 1964, *71,* 473–490.

White, S. H. Evidence for a hierarchical arrangement of learning processes. In L. P. Lipsitt & C. C. Spiker (Ed.), *Advances in child development and behavior* (Vol. 2). New York: Academic Press, 1965.

Winkelman, H. J., & Schmidt, J. Associative confusions in mental arithmetic. *Journal of Experimental Psychology,* 1974, *102,* 734–736.

Yoshimura, T. *Strategies for addition among young children.* Paper presented at the 16th annual convention of the Japanese Association of Educational Psychology, 1974.

APPENDIX A: ZERO-ORDER CORRELATIONS FOR ALL PREDICTORS USED IN REGRESSION ANALYSES OF PERCENTAGE OF ERRORS AND MEAN SOLUTION TIME ON EACH PROBLEM

Siegler and Robinson Experiment

Dependent Variable	Predictor Variables	Correlation	F-To-Enter[a]
% Errors All Trials	% Overt Strategy Use	.91	109.41
	Min Model	.59	
	Sum	.72	
	Larger number	.58	
	Smaller number	.66	
	First number	.34	
	Second number	.68	
	Sum squared	.66	
% Errors Retrieval Trials	% Overt Strategy Use	.92	126.90
	Min Model	.62	
	Sum	.67	
	Larger number	.53	
	Smaller number	.62	
	First number	.31	
	Second number	.64	
	Sum squared	.62	
% Errors Counting and Counting-Fingers Trials	% Overt Strategy Use	.36	
	Min Model	.14	
	Sum	.68	18.46
	Larger number	.50	
	Smaller number	.64	
	First number	.48	
	Second number	.43	
	Sum squared	.69	
Mean Solution Time All Trials	% Overt Strategy Use	.90	93.05
	Min Model	.74	
	Sum	.67	
	Larger number	.62	
	Smaller number	.52	
	First number	.28	
	Second number	.66	
	Sum squared	.61	
Mean Solution Time Retrieval Trials	% Overt Strategy Use	.76	31.67
	Min Model	.74	
	Sum	.51	
	Larger number	.56	
	Smaller number	.31	
	First number	.21	
	Second number	.51	
	Sum squared	.46	

Siegler and Robinson Experiment (*Continued*)

Dependent Variable	Predictor Variables	Correlation	F-To-Enter[a]
Mean Solution Time Counting and Counting-Fingers Trials	% Overt Strategy Use	.83	47.41
	Min Model	.66	
	Sum	.61	
	Larger number	.41	
	Smaller number	.61	
	First number	.31	
	Second number	.52	
	Sum squared	.59	

[a]All F statistics have 24 degrees of freedom.

Replication and Extension Experiment—Group 1

Dependent Variable	Predictor Variables	Correlation	F-To-Enter[a]
% Errors All Trials	% Overt Strategy Use	.79	
	Min Model	.44	
	Sum	.64	
	Larger number	.58	
	Smaller number	.51	
	First number	.08	
	Second number	.82	48.16
	Sum squared	.58	
% Errors Retrieval Trials	% Overt Strategy Use	.83	51.21
	Min Model	.53	
	Sum	.70	
	Larger number	.63	
	Smaller number	.56	
	First number	.22	
	Second number	.75	
	Sum squared	.64	
% Errors Counting and Counting-Fingers Trials	% Overt Strategy Use	.52	
	Min Model	.19	
	Sum	.32	
	Larger number	.29	
	Smaller number	.26	
	First number	−.20	
	Second number	.64	15.02
	Sum squared	.25	
Mean Solution Time All Trials	% Overt Strategy Use	.91	115.76
	Min Model	.65	
	Sum	.75	
	Larger number	.76	
	Smaller number	.53	
	First number	.26	

(*continued*)

Replication and Extension Experiment—Group 1 (*Continued*)

Dependent Variable	Predictor Variables	Correlation	F-To-Enter[a]
	Second number	.80	
	Sum squared	.68	
Mean Solution Time	% Overt Strategy Use	.80	41.33
Retrieval Trials	Min Model	.42	
	Sum	.49	
	Larger number	.56	
	Smaller number	.30	
	First number	.02	
	Second number	.64	
	Sum squared	.43	
Mean Solution Time	% Overt Strategy Use	.40	
Counting and Counting-	Min Model	.42	
Fingers Trials	Sum	.65	
	Larger number	.58	
	Smaller number	.53	
	First number	.16	
	Second number	.72	23.27
	Sum squared	.64	

[a]All *F* statistics have 24 degrees of freedom.

Replication and Extension Experiment—Group 2

Dependent Variable	Predictor Variables	Correlation	F-To-Enter[a]
% Errors All Trials	% Overt Strategy Use	.79	38.85
	Min Model	.65	
	Sum	.71	
	Larger number	.44	
	Smaller number	.62	
	First number	.17	
	Second number	.54	
	Sum squared	.69	
% Errors Retrieval	% Overt Strategy Use	.80	41.20
Trials	Min Model	.64	
	Sum	.70	
	Larger number	.35	
	Smaller number	.72	
	First number	.16	
	Second number	.53	
	Sum squared	.67	
% Errors Counting and	% Overt Strategy Use	.46	
Counting-Fingers Trials	Min Model	.37	
	Sum	.42	
	Larger number	.52	8.62

Replication and Extension Experiment—Group 2 (*Continued*)

Dependent Variable	Predictor Variables	Correlation	F-To-Enter[a]
	Smaller number	−.02	
	First number	.34	
	Second number	.06	
	Sum squared	.36	
Mean Solution Time All	% Overt Strategy Use	.81	44.16
Trials	Min Model	.68	
	Sum	.73	
	Larger number	.52	
	Smaller number	.52	
	First number	.15	
	Second number	.58	
	Sum squared	.64	
Mean Solution Time	% Overt Strategy Use	.75	30.11
Retrieval Trials	Min Model	.60	
	Sum	.65	
	Larger number	.45	
	Smaller number	.50	
	First number	.18	
	Second number	.47	
	Sum squared	.65	
Mean Solution Time	% Overt Strategy Use	.54	
Counting and Counting-	Min Model	.35	
Fingers Trials	Sum	.67	
	Larger number	.67	19.10
	Smaller number	.20	
	First number	.42	
	Second number	.23	
	Sum squared	.56	

[a]All *F* statistics have 24 degrees of freedom.

Replication and Extension Experiment—Group 3

Dependent Variable	Predictor Variables	Correlation	F-To-Enter[a]
% Errors All Trials	% Overt Strategy Use	.81	
	Min Model	.68	
	Sum	.77	
	Larger number	.62	
	Smaller number	.64	
	First number	.15	
	Second number	.82	47.05
	Sum squared	.76	

(*continued*)

Replication and Extension Experiment—Group 3 (*Continued*)

Dependent Variable	Predictor Variables	Correlation	F-To-Enter[a]
% Errors Retrieval Trials	% Overt Strategy Use	.88	79.80
	Min Model	.80	
	Sum	.79	
	Larger number	.60	
	Smaller number	.72	
	First number	.28	
	Second number	.72	
	Sum squared	.79	
% Errors Counting and Counting-Fingers Trials	% Overt Strategy Use	.37	
	Min Model	.26	
	Sum	.27	
	Larger number	.16	
	Smaller number	.33	
	First number	−.27	
	Second number	.60	12.81
	Sum squared	.28	
Mean Solution Time All Trials	% Overt Strategy Use	.92	125.16
	Min Model	.79	
	Sum	.84	
	Larger number	.70	
	Smaller number	.65	
	First number	.26	
	Second number	.79	
	Sum squared	.82	
Mean Solution Time Retrieval Trials	% Overt Strategy Use	.90	103.58
	Min Model	.81	
	Sum	.79	
	Larger number	.63	
	Smaller number	.66	
	First number	.31	
	Second number	.69	
	Sum squared	.79	
Mean Solution Time Counting and Counting-Fingers Trials	% Overt Strategy Use	.78	
	Min Model	.63	
	Sum	.79	38.59
	Larger number	.77	
	Smaller number	.44	
	First number	.24	
	Second number	.76	
	Sum squared	.78	

[a]All F statistics have 24 degrees of freedom.

Subtraction Experiment

Dependent Variable	Predictor Variables	Correlation	F-To-Enter[a]
% Errors All Trials	% Overt Strategy Use	.83	50.67
	Groen and Poll Model	.55	
	Sum	.80	
	Difference	.24	
	First number	.71	
	Second number	.77	
	Sum squared	.73	
	Difference squared	.24	
% Errors Retrieval Trials	% Overt Strategy Use	.83	52.32
	Groen and Poll Model	.45	
	Sum	.76	
	Difference	.14	
	First number	.65	
	Second number	.78	
	Sum squared	.70	
	Difference squared	.14	
% Errors Counting and Counting-Fingers Trials	% Overt Strategy Use	.25	
	Groen and Poll Model	.26	
	Sum	.28	
	Difference	.24	
	First number	.31	2.43
	Second number	.20	
	Sum squared	.25	
	Difference squared	.25	
Mean Solution Time All Trials	% Overt Strategy Use	.88	80.88
	Groen and Poll Model	.65	
	Sum	.80	
	Difference	.45	
	First number	.79	
	Second number	.67	
	Sum squared	.74	
	Difference squared	.36	
Mean Solution Time Retrieval Trials	% Overt Strategy Use	.83	52.33
	Groen and Poll Model	.55	
	Sum	.76	
	Difference	.34	
	First number	.72	
	Second number	.68	
	Sum squared	.69	
	Difference squared	.24	
Mean Solution Time Counting and Counting-Fingers Trials	% Overt Strategy Use	.73	
	Groen and Poll Model	.59	
	Sum	.74	
	Difference	.54	
	First number	.78	35.29
	Second number	.56	
	Sum squared	.67	
	Difference squared	.50	

[a]All F statistics have 24 degrees of freedom.

10 Commentary: An Embarrassment of Number

David Klahr
Carnegie-Mellon University

WHO IS A NUMBER EXPERT?

When Catherine Sophian first asked me to comment on these chapters, I began wondering about what essential quality of mine she was seeking to exploit. So I took a look at the list of discussants from the previous 17 Carnegie Cognition Symposia in order to determine what common attributes they all shared. I discovered that past discussants have usually, but not always, combined such features as charm, grace, good looks, cultivated tastes, entertaining style, and an air of casual hilarity. Included in the collection of several dozen discussants were aging gurus, old friends, stand-up comedians, incisive critics, departmental loiterers, and even retired ballplayers.

However, the defining criterion for previous discussants—and the one that I hope Catherine used—is *expertise*. It seems pretty clear that one chooses a discussant by looking for someone who is an expert in the area.

Having concluded that expertise was the key factor here, the next step was to determine whether or not number development is one of my areas of expertise. How can I be sure of that? How do you decide what you *think* you are an expert in? Although there is a lot of research (much of it done here in Pittsburgh) about how experts think, there is not much known about self-defined expertise.

Lacking any rigorous approach, I decided to use my favorite definition of expertise. It comes from a friend of mine with a world-wide reputation in a discipline unrelated to psychology. He once told me that when attempting to draw the boundaries of his own areas of expertise he used the following criterion:

> If you hear a fact about area X, and if you are embarrassed that you do not already know that fact, then you consider yourself an expert in area X.

This definition, together with the chapters in this section, confirm my hunch that number development *is* one of my areas of expertise. Strauss, Curtis, Cooper, Miller, Shrager, and Siegler presented us with new ideas in theory, in methodology, and in empirical results, and I blush not to have known them all in the first place. Hence the title of this commentary: *An Embarrassment of Number*.

Perhaps I can extricate myself from total mortification by providing a structure within which we might evaluate the various contributions. Rather than list fatal flaws and brilliant breakthroughs for each chapter, I outline a research agenda on the development of number skills. In doing so, I will try to get those of you outside the area of number development to see the world through the lens of those committed to solving some of its problems, and to appreciate the difficulties we face. My questions about these chapters are organized around three related topics: (1) the number concept; (2) developmental processes; and (3) information-processing models.

WHAT'S SO SPECIAL ABOUT "NUMBER"?

Why do we study the number concept? What makes number different from, say, shape, or color, or heaviness? We do study the perceptual basis for color, but not the color concept *as such*. "Conservation of color" is just not an issue in developmental psychology. Why is that? After all, we do have a clear set of well-established color constancies. We generally do not expect color to change abruptly, and when it does, we infer a color-changing transformation. What then, is so special about number?

I will try to answer the question indirectly, by focusing on a few key issues about number. Some of what I have to say is speculative, but speculation is absolutely necessary if we are to construct theories of quantitative development. It does my heart good to see such careful experimentalists as the authors of these chapters—some of them the best in the business—beginning to postulate developmental mechanisms. Nevertheless, I am aware that proximity to speculation elicits bizarre behavior from many psychologists, ranging from apology to apoplexy, so instead of *speculation*, I call these comments *design criteria* for a model of quantitative development.

DESIGNING A NUMBER CONCEIVER

One way to appreciate the issues here is to ask the following question: If you were to build a system that "had" the number concept, with what properties would you endow it? Contrastively, how would it differ from a system that *lacked* the number concept?

Formulating issues in terms of the design of an information-processing system is not just a rhetorical device. It forces the conceptual clarification of issues that otherwise remain ambiguous and it suggests appropriate experimental investigations. For example, the most fundamental decision in the design of a system that "has" quantitative knowledge is how to represent quantity. As I try to illustrate in the next section, even this basic issue is not yet resolved.

What is a Quantitative Symbol?

There are two senses in which we may talk about quantitative symbols. In the first, *quantitative symbol* refers to the internal representation produced by encoding processes operating on any quantitative features of the environment. Early versions of quantitative symbols may be inaccurate, or they may have only partial information about all the quantitative aspects of the external situation they purportedly represent. In this first sense, then, a quantitative symbol is whatever gets produced by processes that attempt to encode quantity. Cooper's "subitized states" are an example of this use of the concept of a quantitative symbol.

The second sense of quantitative symbol applies to internal symbols that have all the essential properties of quantity. Most importantly, in the case of number, quantitative symbols in the second sense have both cardinal and ordinal properties. That is, given two such quantitative symbols, the system can determine their relative magnitudes. Otherwise, the system can only determine their sameness or differentness. Thus, it can determine that three is less than four, but only that red is not the same as blue or long or three.

What is it about the internal representation for the things we call quantities in general, and numbers in particular, that makes them special, that endows them with properties unlike other symbols? And how does such a representation develop? More specifically, how does *quantitative symbol* in the first sense develop into *quantitative symbol* in the second? Ten years ago, Wallace and I addressed these questions (Klahr & Wallace, 1973), but our proposed answers seem to have sunk like stones. However, I have not since seen any other serious proposals, so let me resurrect some of our ideas here.

I propose a specific form for representing discrete quantity, and then, in this section and subsequent ones, I describe some possible developmental consequences of this assumption. Consider the early representation for a pair of identical objects, shown in A of Fig. 10.1. The total collection X is represented by two identical symbol structures, each comprised of some elementary symbols that completely characterize the objects. If the objects being represented here were, say, fingers, we could think of this early representation for two fingers as "a finger and a finger."

This is a redundant and inefficient representation, and at some later stage, the system adopts an alternative representation for a set of identical objects. B in Fig. 10.1 shows one possibility. The complete object is represented only once, and its

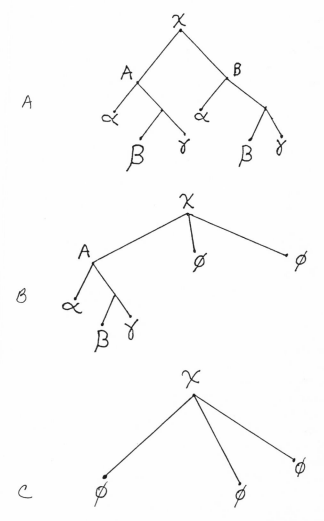

FIG. 10.1.   Hypothetical forms for representing discrete quantity. a) Rudimentary and redundant representation for a pair of specific objects; b) More efficient
and abstract representation for 3 specific items; c) Most abstract representation for
any three items.

other occurrences are represented by a kind of internal ''ditto'' mark. In the
representation for three things shown here, we have something like: a finger and
another and another. For quite some time, the infant may maintain many different object-specific representations for small sets of identical objects, particularly
the ones he or she frequently encounters. This idea is elaborated by Strauss and
Curtis' notion of item specificity and number specificity. Even as adults, we

have several ways of expressing two things, depending on what those things are: pair, couple, set, team, twin, brace, and so on.

Eventually, the system exploits the structural similarity between the representations for the same amount of different things, and develops a representation for cardinal number that is independent of the thing being quantified. Such a representation for "threeness" might be just the simple list of null markers shown in C of Fig. 10.1. This representation differs from the previous one in the same way that "three" differs from "three dolls."

All that I have described so far is a representation for cardinality, not ordinality. As Cooper notes, these early representations for number, or "subitized states" as he calls them, are initially unordered. However, as we will see, ordinality is inherent in the symbols, and their particular form plays a crucial role in quantitative relations.

Extracting Ordinality from Cardinality

Strauss and Curtis have a very interesting idea on this. First, they endow the baby with an innate ability to detect magnitude differences. Then they suggest that the covariation of discrete and continuous quantities enables the infant to order the numerical symbols according to the ordering of the corresponding continuous, nonnumerical representations of physical dimensions.

I think that there are two problems with this idea. First, it seems unlikely that the required cooccurrences are really there. In general, covariation of continuous ordinal and discrete cardinal quantities are quite rare. In the standard conservation situation, length, density, and number do not cooperate. In the infant's world, two hands remain two hands no matter how far apart or close they are, fingers spread and close and yet remain the same in number, two blocks and three blocks can be fit into the same space, and so on.

Strauss and Curtis, seated in their armchairs opposite mine, disagree: "In the natural environment, differences in discrete quantities naturally covary with differences in continuous quantities." This difference of opinion illustrates the importance to any developmental theory of a good account of the environmental inputs to the developing system. I return to this point later. It also underscores the need for detailed naturalistic studies of infants' transactions with their quantitative environments (c.f. Langer, 1980).

The second problem with the Strauss and Curtis idea is that it finesses the issue of what it means to make ordinal judgments about continuous quantity, because we can ask of continuous quantity the same question that Strauss and Curtis ask of number: How do we know that infants are responding to order and not just to difference in magnitude? What does it mean to know that one sound is louder than another rather than just different from another? Even if we are sure that an ordinal judgment is being made, how can we represent that internally? Of course, we can build in ordinality with respect to continuous quantity and then just transfer it to discrete quantity, but that seems to take a lot of the fun out of the endeavor.

Cooper has a different proposal, one that is in some respects quite similar to my own view, but different in important ways. His proposal is similar in the extent to which it emphasizes the importance of the infant's ability to encode quantity before and after transformations, and to detect regularities under different classes of transformations. (Although Miller's subjects were older than those being discussed here, his careful analysis of children's understanding of the relevance of different transformations is quite important and might be adapted for assessing younger children's transformational knowledge.) However, Cooper does not go quite far enough in explaining how he would account for ordinality solely on the basis of transformational correspondences. If it were that simple, then why do other, nonnumerical domains not acquire an inherent ordering of their own? For example, the baby might notice that pouring milk into water makes the water turn white. Why do the symbols for white and clear not get ordered via the milk-pouring transformation?

Cooper alludes to an answer, one that I would like to take a bit further. I think that the *form* of the quantitative symbols, such as the ones shown earlier, enables the system to generate ordinal information. There are two unique properties of quantitative symbols that produce an implicit ordinality in representations for cardinality. The first property derives from the form of the symbols. When the innate symbol-processing routines compare two such symbols for sameness or differentness, they get a little more information than they need. If the symbols are different, that difference is represented by the actual structure of the residual symbol. This residual is itself a quantitative symbol, capable of being matched to another, and this provides the rudiments of internally generated ordinal knowledge. Once this knowledge is available, then the system can use the results of transformations in the manner suggested by Cooper.

The second source of ordinality derives from another unique property of the encoding of small, discrete quantities: multiple representation. When three objects are encoded, so are subsets of two and one. This multiple activation of "detectors" or subitizers occurs asymmetrically, however. When three items are encoded, symbols are generated for two and one as well as for three, but, of course, when two items are present, there is no encoding of three. This inherent asymmetry of cardinality encoders provides the data base for the ultimate representation of ordinality via internal analysis of correspondences. (See Wallace, Klahr, & Bluff, in press, for a full explication of the process.)

The Role of Counting in Childhood and Infancy

What is the role of counting in the development of number concepts in general and in arithmetic computation in particular?

First, let us consider young children, and then we will look at infants. As Siegler and Shrager's work indicates, children appreciate the tremendous utility of finger counting. In fact, children's use of finger counting shows an interesting correspondence with the cognitive skills of primitive cultures. Although anthropological analogies are considered bad form in psychology, I cannot resist quoting from Dantzig's (1954) book, first published nearly 50 years ago, on the history of number:

> wherever a counting technique, worthy of the name, exists at all, *finger counting* has been found to either precede it or accompany it. And in his fingers man possesses a device which permits him to pass imperceptibly from cardinal to ordinal number. Should he want to indicate that a certain collection contains four objects he will raise or turn down four fingers *simultaneously;* should he want to count the same collection, he will raise or turn down these fingers *in succession.* In the first case he is using his fingers as a cardinal model, in the second as an ordinal system. Only a few hundred years ago, finger counting was such a widespread custom in western Europe that no manual of arithmetic was complete unless it gave full instructions in the method [p. 11].

Before you get too smug at the idea of adults counting on their fingers, try the following exercise: Sit on your hands and then figure out what month it will be 7 months from today.

It is clear from the work of Siegler and Shrager that preschoolers are quite sophisticated in the deployment of their counting technology. What about infants? The important issue here is the role of counting in the *development* of the number concept. Is counting the *basis* of true quantitative thinking, or is it a *reflection* of it, an acquired technology to extend already-developed quantitative processes and representations into higher numbers, with increased speed and accuracy?

In their excellent summary of the empirical work on infant quantification, Strauss and Curtis make a convincing critique of Gelman's view of the primacy of counting. As they note, it seems implausible that infants have the capacity to systematically scan visual arrays, to coordinate an internal tagging process with that scan, to partition the array into tagged and untagged items, and to use the "cardinality principle" to label the set with the last of the ordered tags. Cooper's brief-exposure studies further discredit the notion that infants count.

On One-to-One Correspondence

The role of one-to-one correspondence in quantitative development is still controversial. My own view is that it is a relatively late acquisition (c.f. Klahr & Wallace, 1976, pp. 76–80), but I do not have space to elaborate that view here.[1]

---

[1]Viewing one-to-one correspondence as a late acquisition is not inconsistent with the assumption of innate processes that underlie the account of internal symbol comparison described earlier. One-to-one correspondence is a high-level strategy for producing or comparing external collections with specific ordinalities. It requires noticing, marking, tagging, and so on. The comparison of internal symbols is a low level, automatic, innate process.

Rather, I want to argue for an alternative interpretation of Miller's results. His clever procedure for getting kids to generate "fair" distributions may or may not actually index their understanding of one-to-one correspondences, for they may simply be executing a distributional procedure that has been socially transmitted without any real appreciation of its quantitative basis. That is, for the youngest children, the one-for-you, one-for-me procedure may simply be a ritual associated with the eliciting conditions of "fairness." Miller argues against the ritualistic copying view by noting that parents rarely attempt to fool children by confusing number of pieces with total amount, but one could equally argue that there are many occasions in which children must accept that equal number is equivalent to equal amount (as in pieces of pie, fruit, etc., with obvious variation in size).[2] As Miller notes, it is clear that children are treating the thing that is equitably distributed as number of pieces, rather than total amount, but do they really believe that each turtle has the same amount to eat? If children could choose which snack to consume, would they be indifferent to the "fair" distributions they have created?

Nevertheless, although I quibble over some of his interpretations, I think that Miller's idea of assessing children's abilities to *produce* specific quantitative outcomes, rather than just assess them, has begun to add important information to our understanding of quantitative development, and it is worthy of extension. In particular, his procedure for assessing children's ability to judge area—in which children count out a specific number of tiles to "cover" an area—provides a challenging alternative to N. H. Anderson's (1974) information-integration model.

ON DEVELOPMENTAL PROCESSES

A complete account of the development of some skill should take a position on three issues:

1. What is the innate kernel of processes and structures with which the system is endowed?
2. What are the developmental mechanisms—that is, the self-modification processes?
3. What are the environmental experiences that, in combination with the innate kernel, provide grist for the developmental mill?

If I could control the format of all the chapters in this volume (or, while I am fantasizing, *all* publications about cognitive development) I would require au-

---

[2]My disagreeement with Miller is another example of arguments based on assumptions about the naturally occurring quantitative experiences of the child (c.f. my earlier comments on Strauss and Curtis). The only way to resolve such differences of opinion is to observe what really happens, as in Siegler's study of parental input of addition problems.

thors to indicate clearly what they have to say about each of these issues. My own summary of how the four chapters address the three questions is as follows:

Strauss and Curtis make a clear statement of their position on what is not necessarily innate. They systematically rule out some of the knowledge structures that might, at first blush, seem to underlie children's numerical performances. Such properties are thus eliminated from contention as necessary members of the innate kernel. They then suggest that "very possibly" there are innate cardinality detectors, but that these have, at first, no ordinal properties. However, ordinality is inherent in innate magnitude-discrimination processes that operate on continuous perceptual dimensions such as size, brightness, length, and so on.

With respect to developmental mechanisms, Strauss and Curtis simply mention that infants' "ability to make [ordinal] judgments with continuous quantity may serve as the foundation for both their eventual knowledge of discrete ordinal concepts and their knowledge of how discrete cardinal and ordinal properties are related." Implied but not specified in their account are processes that can actually build on this foundation. The crucial environmental experience for this (implicit) process to operate is the covariation of differences in continuous and discrete quantity mentioned earlier.

Miller alludes to a notion that humans may be endowed with self-teaching mechanisms that are sensitive to specific information. One such innate mechanism might be sensitive to the results of experimentation with measurement procedures. Miller also seems to view rudimentary forms of counting as "spontaneous." Rudimentary counting provides the requisite stability for the detection of quantitative constancies.

This, in turn, provides the basis for Miller's model of the developmental process, which consists of the "gradual elaboration and refinement" of measurement procedures. Finally, according to Miller, the major environmental experience that drives all of this is the child's practical need to construct and evaluate quantitative equivalences.

Like Strauss and Curtis, Cooper also posits an innate mechanism, a "numerosity detector," that provides cardinal information. He proposes that this base of unorganized "subitized states" undergoes an extensive and subtle bootstrapping process that is sensitive to quantitative transformations and their effects on numerosity. His series of decision trees represents a modest step toward a process model of how this bootstrapping might take place. The requisite environmental experiences, in Cooper's account, are repeated occurrences of transformations involving small (in both set size and increment) discrete quantities. I have to give Cooper high marks for the way in which he has clearly stated his position on the three key issues. In particular, his entire research program is commendably motivated by relatively well-specified working hypotheses about developmental mechanisms.

The Siegler and Shrager chapter is harder to evaluate. On the one hand, their model for performance on the addition task itself, and for the learning of the interitem associations, is more precise, better articulated, and better supported empirically than anything else we have in this set of chapters. They also propose an important environmental regularity—parental input—to account for initial (but not innate!) interitem associations. On the other hand, with respect to both the innate kernel and the general developmental mechanisms that affect the strategy-choice process, they have less to say. Nevertheless, given the unambiguous way in which they have cast their performance model, they are in a good position to address the other issues with equal precision.

ON INFORMATION-PROCESSING PSYCHOLOGY

This final section of my commentary has to do with the potentially rich interplay between the central issues in cognitive development, and the concepts and methods of what is generally known as *information-processing (IP) psychology.* I illustrate a few ways in which recurring issues in cognitive development might be resolved by constructing systems that exhibit the phenomena of interest, and I suggest that current IP models require substantial extension before they can fully capture some of these phenomena.

On Tacit Knowledge

Developmentalists, including many of those writing in this volume, seem compelled to talk of children's tacit knowledge. How is tacit knowledge expressed in information-processing models?

1. Does a calculator have tacit knowledge of the principles of arithmetic?
2. Does a system that knows the "addition facts" have tacit knowledge of the "multiplication facts"?
3. Does an adult have tacit knowledge that each letter appears only once in the alphabet?

In order to construct an information-processing model that has tacit knowledge of some domain, we have to decide which of several possible definitions of "tacit" is intended.

1. TACIT1: Derivable by examination of internal structures, but not explicit before such examination. (The alphabet example.)
2. TACIT2: Computable indirectly from current processes and data structures, or directly if there is memory for results of past processing. (The multiplication example.)
3. TACIT3: Consistent with that knowledge, but nowhere derivable without external intelligence. (Calculator example.)

Here are some examples from number development; I leave the mapping of these examples onto the set of definitions as an exercise for the reader.

1. I proposed earlier that ordinal knowledge was tacit in the representation for cardinality.

2. In Siegler and Shrager's model the associative strengths reveal some surprising tacit knowledge in children's own assessments of their confidence. Recall that the associative strength is used in two very different ways. Its primary use is to determine the likelihood of producing a tentative answer. But it also is compared with the criterion. In this second use, it is as if the child, having produced an answer with some likelihood, is now asking, "Is this answer sufficiently likely for me to say it with confidence?" It seems that with adults, one could test this multiple use directly by getting confidence ratings of some of their retrievals. Note that this form of tacit knowledge is often studied by developmentalists under the rubric of "metacognition." Siegler and Shrager's concluding comments about metacognition and strategy choice shed some welcome light on this often murky area.

3. Miller also deals with tacit knowledge. He concludes from children's performances on his equivalence-creation task that they have tacit knowledge about measurement in general and one-to-one correspondence in particular. He argues that "children can access invariant information about quantity without possessing any more general awareness or understanding of invariance."

Strategy Choice

How do we know what to do? This sort of question is so fundamental that most psychologists would rather not raise it, but it is the core of Siegler and Shrager's work on strategy choice. They have made a series of fascinating discoveries about children's arithmetic skills, and such discoveries are clearly relevant to the full development of number concepts.[3] Siegler and Shrager hope to extend their basic ideas into domains unrelated to arithmetic in particular or to number in general. Thus, I comment only on the *general* implications that their work might have for information-processing models of cognitive functioning.

The basic question is how you decide what to do. As I noted earlier, it is unusual for psychologists to confront this question so directly. Siegler and

---

[3]Those of you who are familiar with Siegler's previous work may be surprised to find him working in the general area of number development, but, in fact, he has been interested in number for quite some time. This long-term interest is best revealed by looking at the titles of a few of his papers published over the past several years: "*Three* Aspects of Cognitive Development" (Siegler, 1976); "*Seven* Generalizations about Cognitive Development" (Siegler, 1981); "*Five* Generalizations about Cognitive Development" (Siegler, 1983); The Development of *Two* Concepts (Siegler & Richards, 1983). The efficiency of Siegler's research program is evidenced by the fact that he has focused, thus far, exclusively on prime numbers.

Shrager have not only confronted it, they have provided a remarkably complete and empirically supported model of how children make a specific decision. The completeness of their answer derives in part from their considerable ingenuity, and in part from the limited scope that they have placed on the general question. Rather than address the general issue of "what to do," they have focused on a simpler one: How do you decide whether to retrieve or recompute something? However, they have great aspirations for this model.

I suspect that as Siegler and Shrager generalize their model to work in other domains, it will start to approach the form that people in artificial intelligence use to characterize the same general question. In artificial intelligence these issues go under the rubric of *method selection*. Given the full set of weak and strong methods than one might use to solve a problem, how does one design a system to make the choice intelligently? Recent work by Laird and Newell on "Universal Subgoaling" and "A Universal Weak Method" may be relevant here (Laird & Newell, 1983a, Laird & Newell, 1983b).

A key idea in artificial intelligence is that intelligent behavior consists of search through a problem space from an initial state to a goal state. The general search problem (search in the artificial intelligence sense, not in the more specific use of Siegler and Shrager) is to find operators and apply them, evaluating progress toward the goal. In the addition case, Siegler and Shrager propose a few operators: direct retrieval, external representation, and internal representation. What Siegler and Shrager call search is just one particular type of application of the retrieval operator. At some point, elegantly and fully specified by Siegler and Shrager, the retrieval operator is abandoned and the other operators get their shot at producing a solution.

Siegler and Shrager focus on stable facts, acquired over a protracted period, such as the "addition combinations." They give other examples of similar decisions about compute versus recall, such as spelling a word. They might have focused on a wide variety of similar situations, such as those in Table 10.1. Each example shows a situation in which you would be likely to use retrieval, and one

TABLE 10.1
Operator Selection for Memory
Tasks

Retrieval	Other
2 + 2	4 + 5
	[Count fingers]
What comes after A?	What comes before H?
	[Start at A, search forward]
Pittsburgh population	Wilmerding population
	[Use almanac]
Lunch Today	Lunch last Sunday
	[Directed Associations]

in which you would be likely to use some other operator (as indicated in brackets) to compute the answer.

Note that the last example does not refer to stable knowledge, but rather to a temporary value of a state variable. Nevertheless, it seems that people make the same kind of recall versus compute decision for this sort of transitory knowledge as they do for stable facts like the addition combinations.

The Role of Development in Information-Processing Psychology

In closing, I would like to make a few comments on the appropriateness of having these papers about developmental issues form the core of the Carnegie Symposium on *Cognition*.

This volume is based on the 18th Symposium in the series. It is the third one devoted to cognitive development (Farnham-Diggory, 1972; Siegler, 1978). If you compare the volume from the 1972 symposium with the chapters in this volume, it is clear that the intervening decade has produced substantial advances in the quality of research in cognitive development: in the sophistication of the questions being addressed, in the analytic power of the methodology being used, and in the conceptualization of the theories being proposed.

One common attribution for the source of this rapid advance in research in cognitive development is the "information-processing revolution" in adult psychology. Most cognitive psychologists who study adult behavior are of the opinion that (quoting one of my colleagues) "the theoretical issues in developmental psychology are usually defined by the theories of adult performance." If this is the case, then it is only a matter of time until developmental psychologists adapt the adult theories and paradigms for use with children.

I think that such a viewpoint is incorrect. One cannot fully understand the adult system without understanding *first* its developmental history. This is perhaps the one common theme in the diverse contributions of such profoundly influential psychologists as Freud, Piaget, and Skinner. A strong case for the primacy of a good developmental theory has been well stated by Don Norman (1980):

> . . . in the study of adult cognition there seems to be the implicit assumption that once we come to understand adults, children will simply be seen to be at various stages along the pathway toward the adult. Perhaps. But perhaps also that the complexity and experience of the adult will forever mask some properties. Automatic behavior masks the underlying structure, pushing things beneath the conscious surface to the inaccessibility of subconscious processes. Well established belief and knowledge systems mask their content [p. 18].

The primacy of developmental issues is nowhere more evident than in the challenge that development presents to theories of self-modification. I have long been an advocate of the relevance to developmental theory of self-modifying information-processing models (c.f. Anderson, Kline, & Beasley, 1980; Langley, in press, Lewis, 1978; Waterman, 1975). Nevertheless, it is still the case that the models currently available are inadequate to explain many fundamental developmental phenomena. Although they can often account for taking a system from state N to $N + 1$, they fail the crucial induction step: They have not (yet) addressed the question of the innate kernel of information processes. That is, many of the currently available models have little developmental tractibility, although they may provide a reasonable account of the learning mechanisms in an already well-developed system.

There is no reason to believe that this is an inherent limitation of the approach, but there are still some difficult problems to solve. The construction of truly developmental models requires advances in two areas.

1. First, we need theoretical advances in the area of information-processing models, especially in the area of system architectures. Right now it is very difficult to figure out how to start a system with very little—with an innate kernel—and have it evolve into an intelligent system. Even if we solved the conceptual issues, we are currently limited by the tools at our disposal. A serious information-processing model of development—that is, one that actually went through an important developmental process—requires more speed and storage capacity than is currently available on any of the machines around. However, within a few years, we may see specialized production-system machines that run 1000 times faster and that can support systems of 100,000 productions. With such tools at our disposal, we are likely to see some exciting advances in information-processing models of development.

2. Second, we need a more robust empirical foundation. The work described in these chapters exemplifies just the sort of necessary theory-driven methodology. The results from such studies help to constrain and evaluate the proposed models.

It should be clear that the creation of information-processing theories of cognitive development will have a profound effect on theories of adult cognition. As the chapters in this part and in the rest of this volume attest, developmentalists do their best work not when they attempt to harvest the riches of work in adult cognition, but rather when they plow their own rows, and sow their own intellectual seeds.

I look forward to some very embarrassing moments in the years to come.

ACKNOWLEDGMENTS

Preparation of these comments was supported, in part, by grants from the Spencer Foundation and the National Science Foundation (BSN 81–12743). Useful comments on earlier drafts were provided by Robert Siegler and Catherine Sophian.

REFERENCES

Anderson, J. R., Kline, P. J., & Beasley, C. M., Jr. Complex learning processes. In R. E. Snow, P. A. Federico, & W. E. Montague (Eds.), *Aptitude, learning and instruction: Cognitive processes analyses*. Hillsdale, N.J.: Lawrence Erlbaum Associates, 1980.

Anderson, N. H. Algebraic models in perception. In E. C. Carterette & M. P. Friedman (Eds.), *Handbook of perception* (Vol. 2). New York: Academic Press, 1974.

Dantzig, T. *Number, the language of science* (4th ed.). New York: Macmillan, 1954.

Farnham-Diggory, S. (Ed.). *Information processing in children*. New York: Academic Press, 1972.

Klahr, D., & Wallace, J. G. The role of quantification operators in the development of conservation of quantity. *Cognitive Psychology*, 1973, *4*, 301–327.

Klahr, D., & Wallace, J. G. Cognitive development: An information-processing view. Hillsdale, N.J.: Lawrence Erlbaum Associates, 1976.

Laird, J. E., & Newell, A. Universal subgoaling: An initial investigation. Computer Science Department, Carnegie-Mellon University, 1983. (a)

Laird, J. E., & Newell, A. A universal weak method. Computer Science Department, Carnegie-Mellon University, 1983. (b)

Langer, J. *The origins of logic: Six to twelve months*. New York: Academic Press, 1980.

Langley, P. A general theory of discrimination learning. In D. Klahr, P. Langley, & R. Neches (Eds.), *Production system models of learning and development*. Cambridge, Mass.: Bradford Books/The MIT Press, in press.

Lewis, C. H. *Production system models of practice effects*. Doctoral dissertation, University of Michigan, 1978.

Norman, D. A. Twelve issues for cognitive science. *Cognitive Science*, 1980, *4*, 1–32.

Siegler, R. S. Three aspects of cognitive development. *Cognitive Psychology*, 1976, *8*, 481–520.

Siegler, R. S. The origins of scientific reasoning. In R. S. Siegler (Ed.), *Children's thinking: What develops?* Hillsdale, N.J.: Lawrence Erlbaum Associates, 1978.

Siegler, R. S. Seven generalizations about cognitive development. *Psychology*, 1981, *June*, 60–67 (in the Japanese journal *Psychology*.).

Siegler, R. S. Five generalizations about cognitive development. *American Psychologist*, 1983, *38*, 263–277.

Siegler, R. S., & Richards, D. D. The development of two concepts. In C. Brainerd (Ed.), *Recent advances in cognitive development theory*. New York: Springer-Verlag, 1983.

Wallace, J. G., Klahr, D., & Bluff, K. A self-modifying production system for conservation acquisition. In D. Klahr, P. Langley, & R. Neches (Eds.), *Production system models of learning and development*. Cambridge, Mass.: Bradford Books/The MIT Press, in press.

Waterman, D. Adaptive production systems. In *The Proceedings of the Fourth International Joint Conference on Artificial Intelligence*. Cambridge, Mass.: Artificial Intelligence Laboratory, MIT, 1975.

ORIGINS OF CATEGORIES

11 A Descriptive Taxonomy of Psychological Categories Used By Infants

Marc H. Bornstein
New York University

This chapter describes four types of psychological categories and the earliest development of categorizing by human infants. In the first section, I review briefly practical and theoretical characteristics and functions of categorization in mental life. In the second section, I offer a fourfold typology of category processes and review relevant data on infants' capacities to categorize. In the third section, I indicate biological and experiential substrates of the different category types in infants. In the fourth and final section of this chapter, I assess merit for the developmental nature of the typology.

The chief aim of this chapter is to bring rudimentary order to a variety of categorization processes now well documented in the first year of life. It is important to indicate at the outset, therefore, that my use of the term *category* is broader than is traditional, for I include (and justify) as categories a variety of phenomena presently known by other names, including, for example, perceptual constancies and cross-modal transfer. Moreover, this treatment is heuristic and selective and is not intended to constitute a comprehensive review of infant cognition. Finally, the literature I present suggests that some types of categorization of which infants are capable early in life are based on perceived similarity among entities and might be innate, whereas other categorization processes are clearly cognitive and must be based on experience. I do not, however, take as my purpose here the final adjudication of the origins of diverse categorization abilities.

CATEGORIZATION

Categorization is essential and pervasive in adult mental life: to perceiving, thinking, remembering, and speaking. *Categorization is the treatment of discriminable entities—properties, objects, or events—as similar by an equivalence*

313

rule. Entities in a category may be coclassified because they share a common attribute, element, or relationship, because their membership status is affirmed relative to an extant or idealized prototype of the category, or simply because they constitute the logical or have been defined to constitute the conventional set included in the category. Categorization therefore automatically entails a decision rule whereby the membership status of new properties, objects, or events in the category can be judged.[1] Categorization functionally advances perception, memory, thought, and language in many ways, and as a consequence categorization is linked to basic mechanisms of mental adaptation and advancement. Several comprehensive treatments of categorization already exist (e.g., Bornstein, 1981a, 1981b; Bruner, Goodnow, & Austin, 1956; Rosch & Lloyd, 1978; Smith & Medin, 1981). To set the main task of this chapter in focus, however, it will be helpful initially to classify and, however briefly, to enumerate selected functions of categorization.

Categorization reflects mental activity in three distinct modes that I distinguish here as perception, cognition, and information processing. First, categories structure and clarify *perception.* People experience the world out of a constant biological flux, and the environment into which they are born and in which they develop is physically unstable. Both these major sources of variation must to some extent be reduced if perception is to proceed with any degree of organization, order, or coherence. Categorization promotes structured perception by surmounting natural variation. Categorization offers further perceptual advantage in that categorizing enhances clarity between different properties or objects or events—that is, mutually exclusive categorizations help to distinguish among entities.

Second, categories serve *cognition* and *memory* in ways that outstrip inchoate perceptual filtering. Categories help us recognize familiar information. Moreover, categories facilitate the assimilation of new information. As categories imply generalization over variation, they serve further to enhance memory capacity: initially, by providing "receptacles" into which incoming information can be encoded; further, by reducing variety so that fewer items need to be retained individually after encoding; and, finally, by supplying a principle of organization whereby more information can be stored more efficiently in memory.

Third, even elementary kinds of categorization anticipate modes of advanced *information processing.* The principle of equivalent treatment of discriminable entities is formally identical to concept formation. Further, in categorization the knowledge of some attribute or property often implies knowledge of other attributes or properties; thus categorization also entails a rudimentary kind of inference.

---

[1]Any such decision rule—usually involving *similarity*—presents a vexing philosophical issue: viz., any two things are similar or dissimilar in one or many respects; categorical similarity, therefore, demands qualification.

In brief, categorization is a many-to-one reduction process that functions adaptively in diverse spheres of mental life. For these several reasons it would be difficult to overstate the significance of categorization in cognition and its development. Putting the obverse case is telling: Could we think without categorizing? The difficulties would be formidable. Experiences would not be organized or structured. Biological variation and environmental diversity would overwhelm us. Distinctions among some properties, objects, and events would fade. Information or stimulation would need to be encoded on a piecemeal basis, thereby retarding cognitive processes and necessitating significantly greater storage. Recognition would need to proceed on a stimulus-by-stimulus basis. Higher conceptual abilities would have to develop de novo without prior, simpler formats on which to build. Finally, if every entity required a different name, language would be more complex than it is already, and communication considerably more difficult.

Clearly, categorization implies a basic, economical, and sophisticated cognitive approach to the world: Categorization simultaneously embraces unity *and* diversity, constancy *and* variation, and it is central to a host of significant mental functions.[2] Yet, infants and very young children categorize. Of what kinds of categorization are they capable? How does categorization develop so quickly? Are the sophisticated decisions inherent in categorization innate, or do infants meet the complex requirements for categorization through some exponential experiential development? What mechanisms ensure the ubiquitous accomplishment and rapid growth to categorization in early infancy?

In the second section of this chapter, I propose a fourfold classification of category types. The scheme is based on the small set of different possible relationships that unite physical stimuli, their possible different appearances, and our eventual psychological categorization of them. Simultaneously, I adduce developmental evidence for the existence and function of each category type in infants. In the third and final sections of this chapter, I explore substrates of category function in infants and then show that the accomplishment of diverse categorization is tied (at least loosely) to developmental level.

CATEGORIZATION PROCESSES: TYPOLOGY AND DEVELOPMENT

Information that eventuates in a psychological category originates in physical stimulation and, somewhere in the sensory–perceptual–cognitive chain, assumes one or more different appearances. Four types of categories that encompass increasingly greater and more comprehensive variation among stimuli and ap-

---

[2]The ledger ought to be balanced: Categories do have liabilities. To wit: Categorization entails a loss of detail and information, memories based on categorizations are inexact, and inference from categorization is bound sometimes to be improper.

pearances can be distinguished. These categories are: identity categories, referent equivalence categories, perceptual equivalence categories, and conceptual equivalence categories.

Identity Categorization

Identity categorization denotes the *perception of a single physical stimulus whose appearance is basically unitary.* This is the simplest format in perception, and in a sense it begins the typology with a weak connotation of "category" because an identity category only involves generalization over variation through time. It is clearly a rudimentary category type. For example, a line element of constant length, width, orientation, and chromatic character is recognized as such over time, and it is treated as discriminable from line elements of other length, width, orientation, and chromatic character, as well as from all other patterns.

Identity involves simply perceiving and recognizing a stimulus and has been demonstrated at or near birth (e.g., Friedman, 1975; Kessen, 1967). When the task is made more difficult, however, differences emerge in infants' abilities to recognize stimuli. So, for example, newborns will not usually show clear recognition of a stimulus to which they have previously been merely exposed (Fantz, Fagan, & Miranda, 1975), but procedures for familiarization that entail individual learning to a criterion, as, for example, via habituation, provoke successful stimulus recognition (Bornstein, 1984; Friedman, 1975; Siqueland, 1981).

Referent Equivalence Categorization

Referent equivalence denotes the *categorization of a single physical stimulus across variations in its phenomenal appearance.* In referent equivalence, a single physical stimulus may assume many appearances but all still converge into a single psychological category. Thus, referent equivalence surpasses identity categorization in generality, or breadth of application, because phenomenal manifestations of the original physical stimulus source may vary though they are still treated as equivalent. Three kinds of referent equivalence categories can be distinguished. The first is a perceptual constancy that is confined to a single sensory modality. For example, a single cube of fixed dimensions is rotated in space so as to provoke successively different perceptions, yet these perceptions are categorized as having a single referent—the "cube." The second kind of referent equivalence category involves recognition of a stimulus as the same across various dimensional translations of the stimulus. For example, a cube is seen three dimensionally in real life, and later a two-dimensional static photograph or dynamic picture or a holograph is recognized to have the same referent—the "cube." The third kind of referent equivalence category involves recognition of the same stimulus across two (or more) modalities. For example, a cube is palpated tactually in the absence of visual or other stimulation and is later recognized visually as the same in the absence of tactual information—the "cube." In each case, the original source or referent stimulus is a single property, object, or event that provokes discriminably distinct phenomenal appearances that in turn eventuate in a unitary psychological category more or less faithful to the original referent stimulus. The following brief reviews provide evidence for each type of referent category in infancy.

Perceptual Constancy.   A constancy is the perceived stability of an object despite variation in projective properties of the object, such as shape, size, or color. In a recent review, Day and McKenzie (1977) concluded that infants only 2 months of age display constancies of size and of shape. Though exact age claims may be disputed, results of pertinent studies consistently support the main conclusion that infants early in the first year of life show perceptual constancies of several kinds.

Definitive studies of shape constancy, for example, have been conducted by Caron, Caron, and their associates (Caron, Caron, & Carlson, 1978, 1979; Caron, Caron, Carlson, & Cobb, 1979). In this programmatic line of research that used the habituation paradigm, the Carons have demonstrated that 3-month-old infants treat as familiar a shape to which they have been habituated even though it may vary in slant or other projective properties. Using habituation designs as well, Schwartz and Day (1979), Bornstein, Gross, and Wolf (1978), and Gibson, Owsley, Walker, and Megaw-Nyce (1979) have provided converging data on constancy of simple shapes in babies in the 2 to 4-month age range and Cohen and Strauss (1979) on constancy of complex shapes in 7.5-month-old babies. Bower (1966a), Ruff (1978), and Fagan (1979) have provided further converging evidence for shape constancy based on conditioning and familiarization-test paradigms in babies between 2 and 7 months of age.

Infants show other perceptual constancies as well. McKenzie, Tootell, and Day (1980) used an habituation-test procedure to investigate the development of size constancy in the first year of life. They found that some 4-month-olds and virtually all 6 to 8–month-olds conserved the size of an object over relatively near ranges when the distance of the object changed but its size remained constant; infants in control conditions discriminated a change in size with distance constant and a change in size and distance with visual angle constant. Bower (1966b) and McKenzie and Day (1972) had previously provided suggestive evidence for size constancy in 1.5 to 2- and in 4-month-olds, respectively. Burnham and Day (1979) have also found that 2 to 5-month-old infants show color constancy, as, for example, between stationary and moving objects, and that babies maintain this discrimination over velocity changes in a target object.

Conclusions about *how early* in life perceptual constancies emerge may depend on methodologies employed to chart their development (see McKenzie et al., 1980; Ruff, 1978, 1980). However, conclusions about *whether* such constancies exist in early infancy are not now disputed. Perceptual constancies therefore constitute one kind of referent equivalence category infants possess.

Dimensional Translation.   Young infants also display referent equivalence categorization when information about an object is carried across dimensional transformations of the object. Dirks and Gibson (1977), for example, habituated 5-month-old babies to a live face and found that the babies would later reliably generalize habituation to a chromatic photograph of the same face but dishabituate to a photograph of a novel face. Likewise, Rose (1977) and DeLoache, Strauss, and Maynard (1979) found that 5 to 6-month-olds will treat two-dimensional representations of familiar three-dimensional geometric stimuli as similar—even when photographs of the stimuli are degraded from chromatic to black and white.

These results do not imply that babies cannot tell the difference between two- and three-dimensional versions of the same target object. Several types of experiments show that they can. For example, newborns reach and visually orient toward real objects more frequently than toward photos of the same objects (Bower, 1972; DiFranco, Muir, & Dodwell, 1978); 1 to 2- and 5-month-olds prefer three-dimensional to two-dimensional representations of the same stimuli (DeLoache et al., 1979; Pipp & Haith, 1977); and, 3 to 5-month-olds habituate more efficiently to three-dimensional than to two-dimensional representations of the same stimuli (Day & McKenzie, 1973; Ruff, Kohler, & Haupt, 1976). Further, these experiments include many additional appropriate controls. In some, investigators familiarize or habituate babies with the two-dimensional version of the stimulus and test with the three-dimensional one, and they then familiarize or habituate with the three-dimensional version and test with the two-dimensional one; happily, the results of such balanced assessments usually show stable discriminations. Other ancillary control conditions show that babies can treat a two-dimensional or a three-dimensional representation of a novel stimulus as different from the "familiar" stimulus. These several experimental controls confirm that infants are able to detect differences between different dimensional representations of the same target stimuli. Yet the main body of research shows clearly that in certain contexts infants also categorize different dimensional representations of a stimulus together.

Cross-Modal Transfer.   A third kind of referent equivalence is exemplified in cross-modal transfer. Cross-modal transfer reflects an ability to convey information about an object that is acquired in one modality to another modality. Cross-modal transfer is therefore recognition of some common property, object, or event across qualitatively heterogeneous inputs to the sensory systems, and thus conforms to the definition of referent equivalence categorization. This kind of intermodal matching has been investigated between different sensory systems (e.g., touch and vision) and has been demonstrated (at least in a rudimentary form) in babies within the first 6 months of life.

In a demonstration of the earliest emergence of this capacity to date, Meltzoff and Borton (1979) showed that babies as young as 1 month of age were influenced in which of two shapes they looked at if one of the two matched a shape the babies had previously explored orally. Other systematic studies have demonstrated infants' capacities for this and similar simple cross-modal transfer between 6 and 12 months (e.g., Bryant, Jones, Claxton, & Perkins, 1972; Bushnell, 1981; Gottfried, Rose, & Bridger, 1977, 1978; Rose, Gottfried, & Bridger, 1978, 1979, 1981a, 1981b; Ruff & Kohler, 1978). In the typical paradigm, Rose and her colleagues permit a 6-month-old to palpate a simple geometric stimulus for 60 seconds without being able to see the stimulus; afterward, they show the baby the "familiar" object and a "novel" (equally attractive) object, without permitting the baby the opportunity to touch either test stimulus. Babies at this age and older look more and reach more for the novel object, thereby demonstrating *visual* familiarity with an object with which they have had only *tactual* experience. These studies also contain controls in which infants demonstrate that they possess requisite intramodal recognition capacities.

In summary, referent equivalence categories are illustrated in three kinds of infant capacities: in perceptual constancies, in the equivalent treatment of dimensional translations, and in cross-modal transfer. Further, there is good evidence that these different capacities function reasonably efficiently by the end of the first half-year of postnatal life.

Before concluding a consideration of referent equivalence categories in infants, I wish to draw two inferences about this competence. The problem of referent equivalence is a basic one in perception; indeed, in the view of many theorists, constancies constitute "one of the major problems of classical perceptual research" (e.g., Hochberg, 1978). In many quarters it is believed that the distal physical stimulus, or real object in the world, is best known through proximal patterns of stimulation it projects on the sensory apparatus; yet, appearances of real-world stimuli constantly vary. It is therefore the task of the perceptual system to unmask diverse guises of proximal stimulation to identify permanent features of the real object. Referent equivalence achieves this transcendence. Insofar as referent equivalence overcomes the vagaries of environmental flux and sensory input, it contributes to perceived stability of the perceptual world. In doing so, moreover, referent equivalence in early infancy may anticipate a major accomplishment of middle infancy: constancy of the object. Thus, the hypothesis might be advanced that, initially, attributes of objects stabilize perceptually, only after which the object's existence stabilizes independent of sensory feedback.

The second inference about referent equivalence I wish to draw concerns its power. Synthesis across qualitatively distinct appearances of an entity—cross-modal transfer—means (at least) that seeing an object informs about its feel (or vice versa). That is, cross-modal transfer implies prediction and inference. By itself, then, referent equivalence constitutes a very impressive and effective perceptual mechanism.

Perceptual Equivalence Categorization

Perceptual equivalence denotes the *categorization of different physical stimuli (from one dimension) across variations in appearance.* The perceptual equivalence category advances in comprehensiveness over the referent equivalence category in that here original physical stimuli vary, as do their phenomenal appearances. Still all converge onto the same psychological category. For example, different lights of short wavelength give rise to a discriminable series of colors, all of which are blue in hue. Different physical stimuli giving rise to different perceptions eventuate in a common category. Perceptual categories are, however, limited in this typology in the number of dimensions over which stimulation may vary, and they are limited to concrete (as opposed to abstract) relations.

Perceptual equivalence categories in at least two modalities have been isolated and studied in infancy. The first shows infants' equivalent treatments of physically and phenomenally discriminable stimuli in vision and the second in audition. In one example experiment, Bornstein, Kessen, and Weiskopf (1976) demonstrated infants' competence at wavelength-to-hue perceptual categorization. Hue is the psychological correlate of the physical dimension of wavelength. Adults discriminate many more wavelengths than they see hues (Graham, 1965)—that is, adults coclassify select discriminable wavelengths under the same hue (Bornstein & Korda, 1984). Bornstein et al. (1976) found similar perceptual equivalence categorization of hue in 3 to 4-month-old infants. Babies were habituated to one wavelength from a given adult hue category (e.g., blue), and they were then tested with the habituation wavelength, with another wavelength from the same adult hue category (e.g., blue), and with a third wavelength from a different adult hue category (e.g., green). Both of the two new test wavelengths were selected so as to be equally distant from the habituation wavelength in physical terms (nanometers); thus, amount of physical change was eliminated as an explanation of differential psychological responsivity. As a rule, babies generalized habituation to the new wavelength from the familiar category, but dishabituated to the new wavelength from the different category. In a control study, Bornstein (1981a) showed that babies can discriminate among (at least some of) the wavelengths they group into a hue category. In this study, babies habituated faster to the re-presentation of a single wavelength from a hue category and habituated slower to a series of six wavelengths selected from the same category; if wavelengths within a category were *in*discriminable for infants, they ought to have habituated to physical variety and to physical identity equally quickly. These complementary studies confirm that hues exemplify perceptual equivalence categories: Different physical stimuli from the same dimension give rise to discriminable perceptions, which in turn converge on a single psychological class.

A wholly different example of infants' perceptual equivalence categorization can be found in audition. A demonstration is Eimas, Siqueland, Jusczyk, and Vigorito's (1971) classic study of infants' categorization of different voice-onset times into "phonemes" that adults perceive as discrete stop consonants. Other auditory perceptual equivalence categories include, in the speech domain, place of articulation and liquids and, in the nonspeech domain, rise time and temporal onset (for reviews, see Bornstein, 1979b; Eimas, Miller, & Jusczyk, 1984; Jusczyk, 1984).

In summary, infants give evidence that, while still in the first months of life, they categorize by perceptual equivalence in at least two modalities; they may do so in others—for example, gustation (for a discussion, see Bornstein, 1981b). This is a very substantial mental accomplishment of early life because it implies the abilities to abstract what is common among physically different, perceptually discriminable entities and to generalize on the basis of that abstraction.

Conceptual Equivalence Categorization

Conceptual equivalence denotes the *categorization of different physical or mental stimuli (from the same or different dimensions) across variations in appearance*. Conceptual equivalence categories advance in comprehensiveness beyond perceptual equivalence categories: Not only can they refer to physical or to phenomenal variation that shares common attributes or properties within a single dimension, but they can refer to relations whose common attribute or property transcends two or more dimensions and is abstract. For example, a variety of objects resembling one another only a little physically or phenomenally (e.g., an infant's high chair, a "Breuer," a rocking chair, a "Barcelona," a living-room recliner, etc.) converge on a single psychological category—"chair."

"Conceptual" must be thought of as a generic term because it is possible to distinguish among three different kinds of conceptual categories: One is sensory, one is conceptual, and one is linguistic. In the case of referent equivalence, we found three different *spheres* of examples; in the case of conceptual equivalence, we find that there are three different *levels* of examples. The sensory kind of conceptual category applies to classes of stimuli whose membership is connected on some natural stimulus basis. By contrast, conceptual and linguistic kinds of categories apply to classes whose membership is rooted in experience or in convention. The latter two fit our general understanding of a "concept." But distinctions can be made between these two. Conceptual categories are non-nameable, nameable only by exhaustive description of their common features, or nameable only by ad hoc terms (e.g., "threeness"). Linguistic variants of conceptual categories are readily nameable conceptual categories (e.g., "chairs" or "truths"). Again, the term *conceptual equivalence* is used here in the generic sense to encompass sensory, conceptual, and linguistic categories.

A variety of studies shows that young infants will habituate to discriminable discrete entities in a stimulus series and appropriately generalize habituation to novel instances of the same series when the series itself connects into a simple, natural stimulus class. For example, Bornstein (1979a) found that 4-month-old babies would habituate to a variety of wavelengths of different hues and subsequently generalize habituation to a novel wavelength of a novel hue but dishabituate to an achromatic form, indicating that the babies perceived chromaticity as common to the habituation stimulus series. Schwartz and Day (1979), Milewski (1979), and Caron and Caron (1981) have found that 2-, 3-, and 4.5-month-old babies would habituate to simple spatial relations shared by a group of patterns (an angle, an arrangement, an above–below configuration) and subsequently generalize habituation to novel patterns in that same spatial relation, but that they dishabituate to a new spatial relation, indicating that they abstracted a common spatial relation among the original forms. Similarly, Gibson, Owsley, and Johnston (1978) have found that 5-month-old babies would habituate to three types of rigid motion and subsequently generalize habituation to a fourth type of rigid motion, but that they dishabituate to a deformation, indicating that they perceived rigidity as an invariant property of objects. Another stimulus sphere in which like sensory–conceptual categorization has been demonstrated by infants is in the classification of faces. Shown a series of faces of different individuals, 6-month-olds give evidence that they can abstract and generalize upon the common gender of the models (Cornell, 1974; Fagan, 1979), and shown a series of faces of different individuals, 7-month-olds give evidence that they can abstract and generalize upon a common facial expression of the models (Nelson, Morse, & Leavitt, 1979).

All of these experiments employed proper control procedures to show discrimination within as well as between categories. Together these studies therefore show "conceptual" attainments of chromaticity, spatial relations, object properties, and facial qualities in infants before or around their 6-month birthdays. These achievements, however, represent a sensory kind of conceptual categorization. They are sensory in that the stimuli and dimensions abstracted over are immediately perceivable, and they differ from perceptual equivalence because the connection among entities may be abstract. Thus, although the size, shape, and color of a configuration may vary its spatial relations will still be immediately apparent. Nevertheless, the distinction between perceptual equivalence categorization and the sensory format of conceptual equivalence categorization is not always transparent. In color, for example, perceptual equivalence means that different physical stimuli from a localized region of the spectrum give rise to different (but related) phenomenal appearances that are grouped naturally into a single hue (e.g., blue), whereas sensory conceptual equivalence means that different physical stimuli from widely different regions of the spectrum give rise to different phenomenal appearances that are grouped into a single class (i.e., color). There is clearly something about the degree of variation and the natural domain of that variation that distinguishes sensory–conceptual equivalence.

In contrast to a conceptual stimulus series related by some immediately perceivable—sensory—characteristic, other conceptual categories seem to be related ad hoc or by cultural convention. Among these, as well, infants habituate and generalize habituation in ways that give evidence that they categorize conceptually. An experiment by Ross (1980) exemplifies conceptual equivalence of conventional categories in babies. Ross first familiarized 12 to 24-month-olds with multiple examples of food in one condition or of furniture in another. Afterward, she presented children with a choice between a novel instance of the familiar category and an instance of the unfamiliar category. In the test, children reached out more and looked more at novel-category stimuli. These preverbal infants clearly abstracted and acted upon a conceptual linkage among conventionally related items of food and furniture.

A converging and successful technique used to assess conceptual classification among preverbal infants involves infants' sequential touching and sorting of objects (Vygotsky, 1962). Sequential touching of conceptually similar objects has been observed as early as 12 months and spatial grouping by similarity somewhat later (Nelson, 1973; Ricciuti, 1965; Starkey, 1981; Sugarman, 1981, 1982). Ricciuti (1965), for example, presented an unorganized array of dolls and cubes to 18-month-olds and instructed the babies to "fix them all up." Babies promptly touched the dolls in turn, selectively passing over the cubes. Many investigators argue that perceptual similarity (sensory categorization) motivates children's earliest sorts, conceptual grouping their later sorts. As Vygotsky (1962) observed, younger children sort objects into "precategorical" arrangements based on perceived similarities between contiguous objects, whereas older children employ superordinate (i.e., functional and clearly conceptual) principles.

Before concluding this section, a word needs to be said about how sensory, conceptual, and linguistic kinds of conceptual equivalence categories relate to one another. As defined, the three are formally identical in that in each different physical stimuli (from the same or from different dimensions) that provoke discriminable phenomenal appearances are in turn enveloped by a single category. The three differ, however, in that conceptual categories of the sensory kind are constituted of stimulus series that appeal naturally and directly to the sensory apparatus and are immediately perceivable, whereas conceptual and linguistic kinds of conceptual categories are based on experience or on convention.

In addition, age seems to play a significant role in differentiating sensory from conceptual–linguistic categories. In general, infants seem to be capable of sensory kinds of grouping earlier in life than conceptual, and conceptual earlier than linguistic. For example, Strauss and Curtis (this volume) habituated 10 to 12-month-olds to a series of pictures in which item type (dog, house, etc.), item size, and item position varied while the number of items (2, 3, or 4) remained constant; they then tested infants with new pictures that either contained the same number of items or contained one item more or less. The attempt in this study was to isolate "numerosity" as a concept. Infants generalized among two- and among three-item arrays, but they also discriminated between two- and three-item arrays, suggesting that they successfully abstracted "concepts" of "two-ness" and "threeness." Importantly, however, infants younger than 1 year of age failed at such numerosity judgments with numbers greater than four. The rationale that has been offered to explain this difference is that quantities less than four may be perceived directly, whereas larger quantities need to be counted in a traditional and conceptual sense. This ability is not possessed until child-hood.

Few studies have actually compared infants' grouping of sensory versus conceptually related objects. In her 1980 study, Ross presented 12 to 24-month-olds with multiple instances of Ms or Os as well as food or furniture for successive trials of fixed duration. She reasoned, as I have here, that these two sets of stimuli might differ in level of "conceptual" interrelatedness, the first set in our terms sensory and the second conceptual (or conventional). Children in Ross' study habituated to variation in Ms and Os, but they did not actually habituate to variation in food and furniture. This relative ease of encoding attests to the greater similarity of variation of sensory as opposed to conventionally related stimuli. In the posthabituation choice test, children preferred stimuli from a novel category to stimuli from a familiar one across all habituation categories. The test results support the conclusion that infants 1 year or older can abstract conceptual linkages among familiar stimuli (i.e., what is conventional) as well as they can abstract sensory similarity, whereas the habituation data suggest that sensory similarity is a more felicitous basis of categorization.

With regard to the conceptual–linguistic décalage, infants certainly can conceive of a class of related items before they have acquired a label that unites members of the class, as in the case of Ross' (1980) furniture. For our purposes, conceptual and linguistic are identical types of categories, except that in one labels are readily available and applied. In this respect, the argument I have adopted here is consonant with that proposed by developmental psycholinguists, like Lenneberg (1967): "concept-formation [is] the primary cognitive process, and naming (as well as acquiring a name) the secondary cognitive process [pp. 332–333]." A critical point of future research will be to disentangle further purely linguistic influences on conceptual equivalence that are not at first conceptual, à la Whorf (1964). This could be done with direct comparisons that bound the child's first birthday—that is, before and after the onset of formal language.

In summary, conceptual categories are in evidence when babies treat different physical or mental stimuli (from the same or from different dimensions) that provoke discriminably different perceptions as in some sense psychologically equivalent. Conceptual categories may be distinguished as having three levels—sensory, conceptual, and linguistic; the three are formally or definitionally similar, except that the first is tied to sensory function and seems to occur earlier in life, whereas the last overlays "names" on concepts. Linguistic structure may also determine category structure.

Summary and Comparison

Four types of psychological categories have been identified, defined, and illustrated with reference to infancy: identity categories, referent equivalence categories, perceptual equivalence categories, and conceptual equivalence categories. By mapping many entities into a single concept, categorization reduces variation that is the natural concomitant of biological and environmental flux. The four kinds of categories encompass increasing complexity and variation—from identification of a single physical stimulus having a single phenomenal appearance to coclassification of multiple physical stimuli having different appearances or coexisting in an abstract relation. Each category type, however, eventually converges on a unitary psychological representation.

Beyond this summary, several words of comparison about the four category types are warranted. First, identity and referent classes each refer to (more or less) singular, original physical sources of stimulation, whereas perceptual and conceptual equivalence classes each refer to discrete, multiple, original physical sources of stimulation. Second, identity categories may assume only a single phenomenal appearance, whereas the latter three category types integrate over more than one appearance of stimulus or stimuli. Third, the number, variety, and abstractness of dimensions along which source stimuli vary differ among category types: Identity, referent, and perceptual equivalence categories refer to single and concrete dimensions of stimulation, even though they may assume one or many appearances; conceptual equivalence categories refer to multiple, original sources of information that may be concrete or abstract. As a consequence of these several considerations, movement from identity to referent equivalence to perceptual equivalence and, finally, to conceptual equivalence constitutes movement away from simple psychophysical correspondence toward reducing more and more complicated and abstract physical and psychological variation in the organism and in the environment.

Two related characteristics of the category typology are also notable. First, identity, referent equivalence, and perceptual equivalence categories refer in many instances to identifiable biological substrates (see the next section) and seem either to be innate or quickly learned; though the etiological status of sensory concepts is undetermined, clearly conceptual and linguistic equivalence categories emerge later in infancy and depend more on experience accrued in development. The obvious developmental prediction is that younger infants would be capable of the first three types of categorization, whereas only older infants or young children will demonstrate the ability to conceptualize.

Second, the category structures described in this typology assume different levels of complication; however, the achievements of perceptual and conceptual categorization are formally identical. Both function by reducing variation at the physical *and* phenomenal levels. However, conceptual equivalence exceeds the accomplishment of perceptual equivalence in important qualitative respects. For example, variety in source stimulation and phenomenal appearance may be great in perceptual equivalence, but it is still limited to a physical dimension, whereas conceptual equivalence includes abstract relations. If perceptual equivalence precedes conceptual equivalence, accomplishments of the perceptual kind may contribute to attaining the higher conceptual form of mental activity. On this account, perceptual equivalences, which have been shown to be present in the earliest months after birth, would constitute veritable *Anlagen,* or more primitive forms, of conceptual equivalence. Alternatively, it may be that perceptual equivalence serves one of two other roles in the achievement of conception. More conservatively, perceptual equivalence may be related to conceptual equivalence only superficially, simply because the two share the same formal structure and same mode of function in reducing physical and phenomenal variation. Or, more liberally, it may be that conceptual equivalence is made possible because identity, referent, and perceptual equivalence together attenuate blooming, buzzing confusion in the infant's world.

SUBSTRATES OF CATEGORIZATION

Infants in the first 6 months of life have been shown to possess and make use of identity, referent equivalence, and perceptual equivalence rules, a set to which they seem around their 6-month birthdays to add higher-order forms of conceptual equivalence. What are the bases in biology and in experience for these four main category types?

The fact that infants engage in some types of categorization near birth (that is, prior to extensive experience) strongly suggests that some categorical equivalences have biogenetic bases. By contrast, conceptual equivalence appears to be based on experience. It is not possible here to document substrates of categorization exhaustively; select illustrations suffice to show the biogenetic basis of referent and perceptual equivalence categorization in contrast to the experiential nature of conceptual categorization.

One perceptual domain used to exemplify referent equivalence is shape constancy—that is, stimulus equivalence across retinal translation. Do neural mechanisms exist to accomplish this constancy? The inferior convexity of the temporal lobe in primates is well known to be essential in visual discrimination, recognition, and associative memory, and neurons in this region of the brain are sensitive to several stimulus parameters, such as contrast, wavelength, orientation, and direction of movement. Based on experiments with rhesus monkeys, Gross and Mishkin (1977) identified two further characteristics of groups of neurons in the inferior temporal cortex: Some of these cells have unusually large receptive fields—fields that even extend across the visual midline into both visual half-fields—and they respond similarly to a given stimulus anywhere within their receptive fields. (Indeed, most can be activated through either eye.) As a consequence, single neurons located in the inferotemporal cortex help to mediate object recognition no matter what part of the retina is stimulated; these neural mechanisms may subserve shape constancy.

A second mode of referent equivalence is similarity across dimensional translation. Although no physiological data exist that directly show a biological substrate for this ability, two indirect sources converge to support this conclusion. Hochberg and Brooks (1962) have cogently argued on the basis of deprivation studies, which reveal that a Western child sheltered from pictures for the first 19 months of his life could still readily identify pictures and line drawings of objects, and Jahoda, Deregowski, Ampene, and Williams (1977) have argued on the basis of analogous cross-cultural studies, which reveal that non-Western children reared in pictureless environments can still identify pictured objects, that the ability to "read" two-dimensional representations need not be learned.

A third type of referent equivalence is cross-modal transfer. Wilson (1965) has indicated two classes of relevant neural mechanisms that may subserve transfer. First, it is known that some neurons are polysensory; they respond to specific inputs from more than a single sense modality. Second, it is known that information from modality-specific cortical projection regions is integrated at specific cerebral association areas; cortical damage in these areas results in specific deficits of cross-modal functioning. In short, some types of referent equivalence have identifiable central nervous system substrates, whereas others may be inferred to have them.

There is well-founded speculation that perceptual categories directly reflect psychophysiological function as well. Neural mechanisms subserving wavelength discrimination, for example, have been identified in primates at the level of the lateral geniculate nucleus (DeValois & DeValois, 1975). The envelope of maximal sensitivity of their individual discriminability functions is nonmonotonic, characterizing the native functioning of the sensory apparatus, and it is congruent with the animal's behavioral capacity for wavelength discrimination (DeValois & DeValois, 1975; A. A. Wright, 1972; W. D. Wright, 1947). By the "inverse law" (Lashley & Wade, 1946), organisms generalize along a physical dimension where their discrimination is poor, and that generalization naturally contributes to categorization.

Although nervous-system correlates of referent equivalence and perceptual equivalence categories have been identified (or deduced), similar substrates have not yet been observed or identified for conceptual equivalence categories. This is not to say that conceptual categorization does not imply some change in the central nervous system—mental representation, or memory of any kind, must; it is likely, however, that conceptual categories assume an imaginal, symbolic, or propositional status that reflects integrative rather than localized cerebral activity (Uttal, 1984).

The fact that some category types have at least some identifiable neurological substrates does not, of course, necessarily imply that the mechanisms involved in their action are innate or congenital or without experiential foundation. However, the more obvious and accessible biogenetic bases of identity, referent, and perceptual categories distinguish them from conceptual categories. That is, the existence of identifiable neurological bases for referent and perceptual equivalence categories suggests, though it certainly does not confirm, a developmental priority of these category types. The origin and action of conceptual categories are, by contrast, manifestly dependent on experience.

DOES THE CATEGORY TYPOLOGY FORM A DEVELOPMENTAL PROGRESSION?

Infants give evidence that they categorize in at least four major ways. However, the empirical research in infant categorization reviewed earlier suggests a tentative age grading among category types; moreover, the fact that identity, referent, and perceptual equivalences have at least some identifiable biological substrates whereas conceptual equivalences are almost certainly experiential in origin further suggests that identity, referent, and perceptual equivalence categories may in fact precede conceptual equivalence categories in ontogeny. The question of whether these category types as a series constitute a true ontogenetic progression must be left open, however, in the absence of developmental data that show that infants at an early point in ontogeny are capable of categorizing only by means of identity equivalence, at a later point by means of referent and perceptual equivalence as well,[3] and still later by conceptual equivalence. Further, it may be that within conceptual equivalence categorization sensory, conceptual, and linguistic formats generate their own developmental progression.

In order to demonstrate a developmental progression among category types, experimental conditions (i.e., stimuli, parameters, etc.) would have to be equated across tasks. The shortcoming of most extant related studies of infancy is that, drawn as they are from different laboratories that have used different stimuli and procedures, they do not assert proper stimulus control to test the proposed developmental schemes. Quite clearly, until such experimental control is brought to bear in a complete developmental design, a latent developmental progression could emerge or fail to be found on account of nondevelopmental factors. For

---

[3]If both referent and perceptual equivalence are founded in the biology of the organism, they may of course come "on line" simultaneously.

example, if younger infants were given a referent equivalence problem and passed it, and they were then given a conceptual equivalence problem and failed it, an investigator might conclude in favor of the progression even though the referent problem was "easy" in some sense and the conceptual problem "difficult." If, however, older infants had been given an "easy" conceptual equivalence problem and passed it, but they had also been given a "difficult" referent equivalence problem and failed it, the same investigator might just as readily have concluded against a developmental progression.

Three data sets can be marshaled to assess validity of developmental progressions between and within category types. The first derives from empirical age-graded research with normal infants. The second compares categorization in normal versus developmentally delayed infants. The third assesses the décalage between sensory and conceptual–linguistic formats of conceptual equivalence categories.

Age-Graded Studies of Normal Infants

Among the few empirical studies of normal infants that can be used to assess development among category types is a study by Cohen and Strauss (1979). These investigators adopted the multiple-habituation generalization-test design to document the acquisition of different categories of faces. Three groups of infants at each of three ages—4.5, 6, and 7.5 months—participated: One group at each age habituated to a single female face in a single "orientation" (position and expression), one group habituated to a single female face shown in any of 12 different orientations, and one group habituated to different female faces shown in any of 12 different orientations. Following habituation in each condition, babies were shown two test stimuli, including a female face they had seen but in a novel orientation and a totally novel female face in a novel orientation. The first experimental group assessed identity discrimination, the second referent equivalence, and the third conceptual equivalence in the terms developed here. Although a complex pattern of results ensued, the relevant findings may be summarized easily: Whereas babies at all ages treated both test stimuli as "different" in the discrimination condition, 4.5-month-olds showed *neither* referent *nor* conceptual equivalence, 6-month-olds showed referent *but not* conceptual equivalence, and 7.5-month-olds showed *both* referent *and* conceptual equivalence. That is, older and older babies abstract more inclusively across tasks and habituation stimulus sets. This rather fortuitously designed study demonstrates that, if the stimuli and situation are properly controlled, identity may be developmentally differentiated from referent equivalence, and referent equivalence may be developmentally differentiated from conceptual equivalence. Moreover, the three form a developmental progression.

Other recent studies support parts of the same progression, indicating that, ceteris paribus, younger babies do not abstract common relations among stimuli whereas older babies do. Caron and Caron (1981), for example, habituated 4, 6, and 8-month-olds to four pairs of patterns all in a relation that had a small version of the pattern above and a large version below, and they then tested babies with a familiar pattern pair, with a novel pattern pair in the same relation, and with a novel pattern pair in a novel relation. Comparison of the first and second conditions assessed identity versus conceptual equivalence. The younger age groups dishabituated in each of the change conditions; only the oldest babies generalized habituation to the novel pattern pair in the familiar relation, thereby giving evidence of the later *development* of conceptual equivalence.

Normal Infants Versus Infants Who Are Developmentally Delayed

If the categorization typology adheres to a developmental progression, then infants who are developmentally delayed (whatever the reason) ought to lag behind normal infants in categorization but follow the same ontogenetic course. A plethora of comparative studies of normal versus delayed neonates, infants, and young children supports this proposition.

Consider, for example, preterm–term differences in the development from identity to referent equivalence classification. Rose et al. (1978) found that term and preterm 12-month-olds could both visually recognize a stimulus that they had previously seen, but that only the term babies could visually recognize a stimulus that they had previously touched or sucked. In short, matched term and preterm babies show identity (intramodal recognition), but only term babies show referent equivalence (i.e., cross-modal transfer). A follow-up, systematic comparison study by the same research group demonstrates exactly the predicted developmental ordering and lags between term and preterm babies for referent equivalence: Preterm 6-month-olds fail both intramodal and cross-modal tasks, preterm 12-month-olds and term 6-month-olds pass intramodal tasks but fail cross-modal tasks, and only term 12-month-olds pass both intramodal and cross-modal tasks (Rose et al., 1979).

Caron and Caron (1981) compared acquisition of a relational concept by 4.5-month-old term and preterm babies. Babies habituated to different pairs of identical forms (e.g., stars, bulls-eyes, etc.), a large version always below a small one in a pair. After they were shown four different examples of this above–below relation, babies were tested with novel forms in the same relation (above–below) and with novel forms in a novel relation (below–above). Term babies generalized habituation to novel pairs of forms in the original invariant relation and dishabituated to novel forms in a novel configuration, giving evidence that they had abstracted the relational invariance shared among habituation stimuli. By contrast, matched preterm babies failed to abstract this invariance successfully, even though they discriminated novel pattern information.

In summary, categorization processes are developmentally delayed in preterm babies relative to term babies even as both groups develop through the same progression in category competence.

Sensory Versus Conceptual Categorization and the Development of First-Word Meaning

Children begin to speak at about 1 year of age, and the words they use usually refer to categories of objects rather than to particular objects in the world—for example, *doggie* for all four-legged animals, and so on (Anglin, 1977; Brown, 1973; Rosch, Mervis, Gray, Johnson, & Boyes-Braem, 1976). Moreover, children give us an idea about the pervasiveness of this strategy because, when just beginning to speak, they commonly describe objects with which they are unfamiliar by names they know. Such "overextensions" confirm that children have larger classes of word meaning in mind. Thus, children bring diverse cognitive competences to language comprehension and production (Kessen & Nelson, 1978); one such noteworthy competence is equivalence categorization (Brown, 1973; Macnamara, 1972; Nelson, 1974a; Slobin, 1974).

Initial categorizations in children could be driven by directly perceptible features of entities, or they could be conditioned by conceptual—conventional or functional—associations, or both could operate simultaneously. Which stimulus features determine initial equivalence classifications and guide first-word development in children? If a developmental progression holds within conceptual equivalence categorization, then sensory classifications ought to lead conceptual–linguistic classifications.

Children categorize in domains linked by sensory equivalence earlier and more efficiently than they categorize in domains linked by conceptual equivalence. Nelson (1974b), for example, studied the composition of nine natural-language categories in children at two ages, 5 and 8 years; the categories included animals, clothes, colors, flowers, fruit, furniture, insects, tools, and vegetables. Nelson employed a production paradigm in which children were asked simply to name as many instances as they could of each category; afterward, Nelson analyzed, among other things, production diversity among the children, the number of responses children gave in each category, and adult-judged appropriateness of the children's productions. Less diverse but more numerous responses within a category in which the instances possess a high level of adult-judged appropriateness are indicative of more mature categorization. Among the nine categories, *colors* is the only perceptually natural (sensory) equivalence category, and among the nine categories, color was responded to in the most mature fashion. Production of colors was the least diverse among children, colors was second in terms of the number of responses children gave, and children's color examples were the most appropriate for any category as judged by adults. As Nelson (1974b) observed, "Of these categories, colors is unquestionably the best defined category of the entire group [p. 581]." Whereas clothes, flowers, fruit, furniture, insects, tools, and vegetables are *conceptual–linguistic*—that is, conventional and culturally learned—categories, color is a *sensory* category. It is not surprising, therefore, that categorization of colors reaches a stable, mature level earliest in development, at least among these nine.

Several language theorists posit that perceptual attributes also constitute the primary basis of the child's earliest lexicon. For Clark (1973), first-word meaning is determined by *perceptual features* of entities (size, texture, etc.), and overextensions are principally analyzable in terms of the misperception or misapplication of such features. The child-language observations of Bowerman (1976), Anglin (1977), and Gentner (1978) support such a perception-based hypothesis. An alternative conceptual view has been proposed by Nelson (1973, 1974a), for whom the semantic bases of referential words are not perceptual features but *functional relations* that are meaningful for the child (things go together that can be rolled, eaten, etc.). Can these theoretical positions be evaluated empirically?

Tomikawa and Dodd (1980) pit these perceptual and conceptual views against one another in a series of five systematic studies of the development of initial referential meaning. Their subjects were 2 to 4-year-old children, and their studies used both a sorting task and a word-learning task; these investigators were also careful to employ stimulus objects that were novel for the children (so that no prior learned categorization or familiarity would intrude), objects that contrasted salience of perceptual versus conceptual relations, and objects that could be varied independently in appearance and in function. Thus, both the materials and the experimental design were specifically organized to avoid bias toward the perceptual or toward the conceptual hypothesis. Tomikawa and Dodd's first two experiments showed that young children initially categorize on the basis of perceptual similarity rather than functional relations: Regardless of the high or low salience of perceptual cues, children categorized objects on the basis of their perceptual features approximately 75% of the time and on the basis of functional relations approximately 15% of the time. Daehler, Lonardo, and Bukatko (1979) had previously demonstrated that 2 to 3-year-olds match objects on the basis of identity best, basic-level categorization next, superordinate categorization third, and conceptually complementary relationships least well, thereby confirming the role of perceptual over conceptual cues governing children's natural equivalence judgments. The third and fourth of Tomikawa and Dodd's experiments were directed at assessing bases for categorization and word acquisition. They showed that children actually learn referential words that label perceptually similar objects more easily and quickly than children learn the *same* referential words when used to label functionally related objects. Again, regardless of the salience of perceptual versus functional cues, children in experimental conditions that had perceptual cues met a learning criterion and made few errors in doing so, whereas children in experimental conditions that had functional cues failed to reach the same learning criterion and made many more errors.

In summary, young children tend predominantly to abstract perceptual properties of objects to inform their earliest conceptual groupings and word use. Nonperceptual dimensions play a secondary role to perceptual ones in children's first categorizations and in the earliest development of word meaning. It would appear that categorizing different entities as a psychological unit on the basis of their perceptual (as opposed to conventional or functional) similarity has priority in language development.

Summary

There exist in the developmental literature diverse studies whose results suggest that when stimuli and situation are controlled, but categorization task is varied with age, category types can be differentiated developmentally. It remains possible that infants (or young children) would be capable of conceptual equivalence categorization (say, in an "easy" task) when they might not be capable of referent equivalent categorization (say, in a "difficult" task). Other things being equal, however, appropriate data from age-graded studies of normal infants, from comparisons between normal and developmentally delayed infants, and from the foundations of early-language development indicate that, in the ontogeny of categorization, identity may precede referent and perceptual equivalence and that referent and perceptual equivalence may precede conceptual equivalence. Moreover, among formats of conceptual equivalence, sensory may precede conceptual, and conceptual precede linguistic.

CONCLUSIONS

The first chapter of *Genesis* tells us that immediately following the creation of the heavens, the earth, and light, God "*separated* the light from the darkness" and "*called* the light Day and the darkness . . . Night," God *separated* the waters above and below the firmament and "*called* the firmament Heaven," and God *separated* "the waters under the heavens" from the "dry land" and "*called* the dry land Earth, and the waters that were gathered together he *called* Seas." Categorization followed by naming. Ontogenesis follows the same pattern, first creating order out of chaos and then naming ordered categories of experience.

The awe-inspiring accomplishment of the first year of postnatal life is the transition from sensorimotor behavior to linguistic intelligence. Though this process is well recognized to be ordered and universal, the leap is still vast, and the achievement impressive. We can now see, however tentatively, that when meaning begins, the categorization processes children invoke may be built directly on prior category abilities and are even formally identical to at least one category process they have newly mastered. Even little babies give evidence that they naturally perceive equivalences—that is, constancy and invariance—out of a flux of biology and ambient energy. Presumably this accomplishment helps pave the way for seemingly more difficult tasks involving cognition and language. From this perspective, linguistic acts are another step in a progression that, viewed as a connected series rather than a special event, can be perceived to continue a program in the child of reducing stimulation, collapsing variation, and facilitating cognition and creativity. The category typology I have introduced here connects biology, perception, cognition, and language. Very young children can categorize; and, as I have endeavored to show, categorization *is* essential and pervasive in the child's mental life, as it is in the adult's: to perceiving, remembering, thinking, and speaking.

ACKNOWLEDGMENTS

This chapter was prepared while the author was a J. S. Guggenheim Memorial Foundation Fellow and was supported in part by a research grant and by a Research Career Development Award from the National Institute of Child Health and Human Development (R01 HD17423 and K04 HD00521). I thank R. Adamo, H. Bornstein, S. Krinsky, C. Miner, C. Sophian, C. Tamis, and M. Tress for comments and assistance.

REFERENCES

Anglin, J. M. *Word, object, and conceptual development.* New York: Norton, 1977.

Bornstein, M. H. Effects of habituation experience on posthabituation behavior in young infants: Discrimination and generalization among colors. *Developmental Psychology,* 1979, *15,* 348–349. (a)

Bornstein, M. H. Perceptual development: Stability and change in feature perception. In M. H. Bornstein & W. Kessen (Eds.), *Psychological development from infancy: Image to intention.* Hillsdale, N.J.: Lawrence Erlbaum Associates, 1979. (b)

Bornstein, M. H. Psychological studies of color perception in human infants: Habituation, discrimination and categorization, recognition, and conceptualization. In L. P. Lipsitt (Ed.), *Advances in infancy research* (Vol. 1). Norwood, N.J.: Ablex, 1981. (a)

Bornstein, M. H. Two kinds of perceptual organization near the beginning of life. In W. A. Collins (Ed.), *Minnesota symposia on child psychology* (Vol. 14). Hillsdale, N.J.: Lawrence Erlbaum Associates, 1981. (b)

Bornstein, M. H. Habituation of attention as a measure of visual information processing in human infants: Summary, systematization, and synthesis. In G. Gottlieb & N. A. Krasnegor (Eds.), *Measurement of audition and vision in the first year of postnatal life: A methodological overview.* Norwood, N.J.: Ablex, 1984.

Bornstein, M. H., Gross, J., & Wolf, J. Perceptual similarity of mirror images in infancy. *Cognition,* 1978, *6,* 89–116.

Bornstein, M. H., Kessen, W., & Weiskopf, S. Color vision and hue categorization in young human infants. *Journal of Experimental Psychology: Human Perception and Performance,* 1976, *2,* 115–129.

Bornstein, M. H., & Korda, N. O. Some psychological parallels between categorization processes in vision and in audition. In S. Harnad (Ed.), *Categorical perception.* New York: Cambridge University Press, 1984.

Bower, T. G. R. Heterogeneous summation in human infants. *Animal Behaviour,* 1966, *14,* 395–398. (a)

Bower, T. G. R. Slant perception and shape constancy in infants. *Science,* 1966, *151,* 832–834. (b)

Bower, T. G. R. Object perception in infants. *Perception,* 1972, *1,* 15–30.

Bowerman, M. Semantic factors in the acquisition of rules for word use and sentence construction. In D. M. Morehead & A. E. Morehead (Eds.), *Normal and deficient child language*. Baltimore: University Park Press, 1976.

Brown, R. *A first language: The early stages*. London: George Allen, 1973.

Bruner, J. S., Goodnow, J. J., & Austin, G. A. *A study of thinking*. New York: Wiley, 1956.

Bryant, P. E., Jones, P., Claxton, V. C., & Perkins, G. M. Recognition of shapes across modalities by infants. *Nature*, 1972, *240*, 444–448.

Burnham, D. K., & Day, R. H. Detection of color in rotating objects by infants and its generalization over changes in velocity. *Journal of Experimental Child Psychology*, 1979, *28*, 191–204.

Bushnell, E. W. The ontogeny of intermodal relations: Vision and touch in infancy. In R. D. Walk & H. L. Pick, Jr. (Eds.), *Intersensory perception and sensory integration*. New York: Plenum Press, 1981.

Caron, A. J., & Caron, R. F. Processing of relational information as an index of infant risk. In S. L. Friedman & M. Sigman (Eds.), *Preterm birth and psychological development*. New York: Academic Press, 1981.

Caron, A. J., Caron, R. F., & Carlson, V. R. Do infants see objects or retinal images? Shape constancy revisited. *Infant Behavior and Development*, 1978, *1*, 229–243.

Caron, A. J., Caron, R. F., & Carlson, V. R. Infant perception of the invariant shape of objects varying in slant. *Child Development*, 1979, *50*, 716–721.

Caron, R. F., Caron, A. J., Carlson, V. R., & Cobb, L. S. Perception of shape-at-a-slant in the young infant. *Bulletin of the Psychonomic Society*, 1979, *1*, 229–243.

Clark, E. V. What's in a word? On the child's acquisition of semantics in his first language. In T. E. Moore (Ed.), *Cognitive development and the acquisition of language*. New York: Academic Press, 1973.

Cohen, L. B., & Strauss, M. S. Concept acquisition in the human infant. *Child Development*, 1979, *50*, 419–424.

Cornell, E. H. Infants' discrimination of photographs of faces following redundant presentations. *Journal of Experimental Child Psychology*, 1974, *18*, 98–106.

Daehler, M. V., Lonardo, R., & Bukatko, D. Matching and equivalence judgments in very young children. *Child Development*, 1979, *50*, 170–179.

Day, R. H., & McKenzie, B. E. Perceptual shape constancy in early infancy. *Perception*, 1973, *2*, 315–320.

Day, R. H., & McKenzie, B. E. Constancies in the perceptual world of the infant. In W. Epstein (Ed.), *Stability and constancy in visual perception: Mechanisms and processes*. New York: Wiley, 1977.

DeLoache, J. S., Strauss, M. S., & Maynard, J. Picture perception in infancy. *Infant Behavior and Development*, 1979, *2*, 77–89.

DeValois, R. L., & DeValois, K. K. Neural coding of color. In E. C. Carterette & M. P. Friedman (Eds.), *Handbook of perception* (Vol. 5). New York: Academic Press, 1975.

DiFranco, D., Muir, D. W., & Dodwell, P. C. Reaching in very young infants. *Perception*, 1978, *7*, 385–392.

Dirks, J., & Gibson, E. J. Infants' perception of similarity between live people and their photographs. *Child Development*, 1977, *48*, 124–130.

Eimas, P. D., Miller, J. L., & Jusczyk, P. W. On infant speech perception and the acquisition of language. In S. Harnad (Ed.), *Categorical perception*. New York: Cambridge University Press, 1984.

Eimas, P. D., Siqueland, E. R., Jusczyk, P., & Vigorito, J. Speech perception in infants. *Science*, 1971, *171*, 303–306.

Fagan, J. F. The origins of facial pattern recognition. In M. H. Bornstein & W. Kessen (Eds.), *Psychological development from infancy: Image to intention*. Hillsdale, N.J.: Lawrence Erlbaum Associates, 1979.

Fantz, R. L., Fagan, J. F., & Miranda, S. B. Early visual selection. In L. B. Cohen & P. Salapatek (Eds.), *Infant perception: From sensation to cognition* (Vol. 1). New York: Academic Press, 1975.

Friedman, S. Infant habituation: Processes, problems and possibilities. In N. R. Ellis (Ed.), *Aberrant development in infancy: Human and animal studies*. New York: Halstead, 1975.

Gentner, D. What looks like a jiggy but acts like a zimbo? A study of early word meaning using artificial objects. *Paper and Reports on Child Language Development*, 1978, *15*, 1–6.

Gibson, E. J., Owsley, C. J., & Johnston, J. Perception of invariants by five-month-olds: Differentiation of two types of motion. *Developmental Psychology*, 1978, *14*, 407–415.

Gibson, E. J., Owsley, C. J., Walker, A., & Megaw-Nyce, J. Development of the perception of invariants: Substance and shape. *Perception*, 1979, *8*, 609–619.

Gottfried, A. W., Rose, S. A., & Bridger, W. A. Cross-modal transfer in human infants. *Child Development*, 1977, *48*, 118–123.

Gottfried, A. W., Rose, S. A., & Bridger, W. A. Effects of visual, haptic, and manipulatory experiences on infants' visual recognition memory of objects. *Developmental Psychology*, 1978, *14*, 305–312.

Graham, C. H. Discriminations that depend on wavelength. In C. H. Graham (Ed.), *Vision and visual perception*. New York: Wiley, 1965.

Gross, C. G., & Mishkin, M. The neural basis of stimulus equivalence across retinal translation. In S. Harnad (Ed.), *Lateralization in the nervous system*. New York: Academic Press, 1977.

Hochberg, J. *Perception*. Englewood Cliffs, N.J.: Prentice-Hall, 1978.

Hochberg, J., & Brooks, V. Pictorial recognition as an unlearned ability: A study of one child's performance. *American Journal of Psychology*, 1962, *75*, 624–628.

Jahoda, C., Deregowski, J., Ampene, E., & Williams, N. Pictorial recognition as an unlearned ability. In G. Butterworth (Ed.), *The child's representation of the world*. New York: Plenum Press, 1977.

Jusczyk, P. W. The high amplitude sucking technique as a methodological tool in speech perception research. In G. Gottlieb & N. A. Krasnegor (Eds.), *Measurement of audition and vision in the first year of postnatal life: A methodological overview*. Norwood, N.J.: Ablex, 1984.

Kessen, W. Sucking and looking: Two organized congenital patterns of behavior in the human newborn. In H. W. Stevenson, E. H. Hess, & H. L. Rheingold (Eds.), *Early behavior: Comparative and developmental approaches*. New York: Wiley, 1967.

Kessen, W., & Nelson, K. What the child brings to language. In B. Z. Presseisen, D. Goldstein, & M. H. Appel (Eds.), *Topics in cognitive development* (Vol. 2). New York: Plenum Press, 1978.

Lashley, K. S., & Wade, M. The Pavlovian theory of generalization. *Psychological Review*, 1946, *53*, 72–87.

Lenneberg, E. *The biological foundations of language*. New York: Wiley, 1967.

Macnamara, J. Cognitive basis of language learning in infants. *Psychological Review*, 1972, *79*, 1–13.

McKenzie, B. E., & Day, R. H. Distance as a determinant of visual fixation in early infancy. *Science*, 1972, *178*, 1108–1110.

McKenzie, B. E., Tootell, H. E., & Day, R. H. Development of visual size constancy during the 1st year of human infancy. *Developmental Psychology*, 1980, *16*, 163–174.

Meltzoff, A. N., & Borton, R. W. Intermodal matching by human neonates. *Nature*, 1979, *282*, 403–404.

Milewski, A. E. Visual discrimination and detection of configurational invariance in 3-month infants. *Developmental Psychology*, 1979, *15*, 357–363.

Nelson, C. A., Morse, P. A., & Leavitt, L. A. Recognition of facial expressions by seven-month-old infants. *Child Development*, 1979, *50*, 1239–1242.

Nelson, K. Some evidence for the cognitive primacy of categorization and its functional basis. *Merrill-Palmer Quarterly*, 1973, *19*, 21–39.

Nelson, K. Concept, word, and sentence: Interrelations in acquisition and development. *Psychological Review*, 1974, *81*, 269–285. (a)

Nelson, K. Variations in children's concepts by age and category. *Child Development*, 1974, *45*, 577–584. (b)

Pipp, S., & Haith, M. M. Infant visual scanning of two and three-dimensional forms. *Child Development*, 1977, *48*, 1640–1644.

Ricciuti, H. Object grouping and selective ordering behavior in infants 12–24 months old. *Merrill-Palmer Quarterly*, 1965, *11*, 129–148.

Rosch, E., & Lloyd, B. B. (Eds.). *Cognition and categorization*. Hillsdale, N.J.: Lawrence Erlbaum Associates, 1978.

Rosch, E., Mervis, C. B., Gray, W. D., Johnson, D. M., & Boyes-Braem, P. Basic objects in natural categories. *Cognitive Psychology*, 1976, *8*, 382–439.

Rose, S. A. Infants' transfer of response between two-dimensional and three-dimensional stimuli. *Child Development*, 1977, *48*, 1086–1091.

Rose, S. A., Gottfried, A. W., & Bridger, W. H. Cross-modal transfer in infants: Relationship to prematurity and socioeconomic background. *Developmental Psychology*, 1978, *14*, 643–652.

Rose, S. A., Gottfried, A. W., & Bridger, W. H. Effects of haptic cues on visual recognition memory in fullterm and preterm infants. *Infant Behavior and Development*, 1979, *2*, 55–67.

Rose, S. A., Gottfried, A. W., & Bridger, W. H. Cross-modal transfer and information processing by the sense of touch in infancy. *Developmental Psychology*, 1981, *17*, 90–98. (a)

Rose, S. A., Gottfried, A. W., & Bridger, W. H. Cross-modal transfer in six-month-old infants. *Developmental Psychology*, 1981, *17*, 661–669. (b)

Ross, G. S. Categorization in 1- to 2-year-olds. *Developmental Psychology*, 1980, *16*, 391–396.

Ruff, H. A. Infant recognition of the invariant form of objects. *Child Development*, 1978, *49*, 293–306.

Ruff, H. A. The development of perception and recognition of objects. *Child Development*, 1980, *51*, 981–992.

Ruff, H. A., & Kohler, C. J. Tactual–visual transfer in six-month-old infants. *Infant Behavior and Development*, 1978, *1*, 259–264.

Ruff, H. A., Kohler, C. J., & Haupt, D. L. Infant recognition of two- and three-dimensional stimuli. *Developmental Psychology*, 1976, *12*, 455–459.

Schwartz, M., & Day, R. H. Visual shape perception in early infancy. *Monographs of the Society for Research in Child Development*, 1979, *44* (7, Serial No. 182).

Siqueland, E. R. Studies of visual recognition memory in preterm infants: Differences in development as a function of perinatal morbidity factors. In S. L. Friedman & M. Sigman (Eds.), *Preterm birth and psychological development*. New York: Academic Press, 1981.

Slobin, D. *Psycholinguistics*. Glenview, Ill.: Scott Foresman, 1974.

Smith, E. E., & Medin, D. I. *Categories and concepts*. Cambridge, Mass.: Harvard University Press, 1981.

Starkey, D. The origins of concept formation: Object sorting and object preference in early infancy. *Child Development*, 1981, *52*, 489–497.

Sugarman, S. The cognitive basis of classification in very young children: An analysis of object ordering trends. *Child Development*, 1981, *52*, 1172–1178.

Sugarman, S. Developmental change in early representational intelligence: Evidence from spatial classification strategies and related verbal expressions. *Cognitive Psychology*, 1982, *14*, 410–449.

Tomikawa, S. A., & Dodd, D. H. Early word meanings: Perceptually or functionally based? *Child Development*, 1980, *51*, 1103–1109.

Uttal, W. R. Psychology and biology. In M. H. Bornstein (Ed.), *Psychology and its allied disciplines (Vol. III): Psychology and the natural sciences*. Hillsdale, N.J.: Lawrence Erlbaum Associates, 1984.

Vygotsky, L. S. [*Thought and language*] (E. Hanfmann & G. Vakar, trans.). Cambridge, Mass.: MIT Press, 1962.

Whorf, B. L. *Language, thought and reality.* Cambridge, Mass.: MIT Press, 1964.

Wilson, W. A. Intersensory transfer in normal and brain-operated monkeys. *Neuropsychologia,* 1965, *3,* 363–370.

Wright, A. A. Psychometric and psychophysical hue discrimination functions for the pigeon. *Vision Research,* 1972, *12,* 1447–1464.

Wright, W. D. *Researches on normal and defective colour vision.* St. Louis: C. V. Mosby, 1947.

12 Early Lexical Development: The Contributions of Mother and Child

Carolyn B. Mervis
University of Massachusetts, Amherst

A complete theory of lexical development must be concerned with at least three questions. First, what is the nature of the child's initial concepts? Second, what do parents or other caregivers know about, and how do they respond to, these initial concepts? Third, how does an initial concept evolve to correspond to a mature concept? The formation of such a theory of lexical development, as with all other psychological theories, must involve three parts: obtaining a data base relevant to the phenomenon, providing a description of these data, and providing an explanation for the description.

Until now, theories of lexical development have focused on the child's role in this process. It is not surprising, then, that the available data base does not include data on caregiver behavior. More surprising, in view of the proliferation of theories, is the minimal amount of data concerning the child. Theories generally have been based on minimally detailed observations, as exemplified by the word lists contained in many of the diary studies from the early 1900s. Thus, the data base has been inadequate for an accurate description of the acquisition and evolution of children's initial concepts. Without accurate description, adequate explanation is impossible.

The preliminary theory of early lexical development that I describe is concerned with all three of the questions I raised previously, for the domain of categories of concrete objects. This theory is founded on a new and substantial data base, including both normal children and Down syndrome (DS) children and their mothers. The inclusion of DS children serves two major purposes. First, because young normal children and young DS children differ considerably in their cognitive and social competence, the effects of perceived child competence on maternal accommodation to the child's concepts during the period of early lexical development can be determined. Second, if the two sets of mothers tend to name objects differently for their children, a comparison of initial concepts and conceptual evolution for normal children and DS children may be particularly useful in delineating the roles of mother and child in the process of early lexical development.

I began this research because of the contrast between what I had read about the semantic aspects of maternal speech to young children and some statements I heard my neighbor make to her 14-month-old daughter. According to the literature, mothers are concerned about the semantic correctness of their children's utterances, and consistently correct their children's semantic errors (e.g., Slobin, 1972; for a recent reiteration, see Miller, 1982). However, my neighbor produced a number of utterances that were at variance with the literature. For example, consider the following situation. Sarah, her mother, and I were in their front yard. Her mother picked up a walnut from the grass and said, "Sarah, look at the ball." Apparently, this mother was not as concerned about correct semantics as one might have expected. I suspected that what she was actually concerned about was making the semantics correct from her daughter's perspective. This hypothesis raised the set of questions listed previously. First, what is the relationship between the child's initial concepts and the corresponding adult concepts? Second, if differences between child concepts and adult concepts occur, how does the mother come to realize that they do? How does the mother respond to any differences? Third, what is the course of evolution from any initially different child concepts to ones that correspond to adult concepts? What role does the mother play in this evolution?

A theory was developed to address these questions. The theory's two major starting points are consistent with current views of categorization and of social interaction. First, I assume, based on the work of Rosch and Mervis (Mervis & Rosch, 1981; Rosch, Mervis, Gray, Johnson, & Boyes-Braem, 1976), that there exists one taxonomic level of categorization, the basic level, that is more fundamental than the remaining levels. The principles governing the determination of which categories are basic are universal, but the actual categories that serve as basic-level categories vary, depending on a person's knowledge of the relevant domain (Dougherty, 1978; Rosch et al., 1976). Applied to early lexical development, this suggests that young children initially form basic-level categories, and that these categories are governed by the same principles as adults' basic categories, but that child-basic categories may differ substantially from adult-basic categories. Children do not share adults' knowledge of culturally appropriate functions and their correlated form attributes, and attributes that are unimportant to an adult for a given object may be important to a child. Second, I assume, based on the work of Bell (Bell, 1964; Bell & Harper, 1977) and of Jones (1977, 1979, 1980), that mothers of young, normally developing children tend to follow their children's initiatives when interacting with their children, whereas mothers of young handicapped children are less likely to follow their children's initiatives under the same circumstances. More generally, maternal accommodation to the child is a function of maternal perception of the child's competence. Therefore, I propose that mothers of normally developing children who are at the earliest stages of lexical development are likely to encourage their children's categories, even when they differ from adult categories. Mothers of young handicapped children at the same stage are likely to discourage any aberrant child categories and instead encourage adult categories. If these hypotheses are correct, then a comparison of the initial concepts of normal children and DS children may provide the basis for determination of whether initial concepts are based on the child's cognitive structures or on maternal input. The rest of this theory is derived more specifically from the results of a cross-sectional study of maternal behavior (Mervis & Mervis, 1982) and a longitudinal study of both maternal and child behavior during the period of early lexical development (Mervis, 1981; Mervis & Canada, 1983). The theory has been tested and refined on the basis of an additional cross-sectional study (see Cardoso-Martins & Mervis, 1981) and a considerably longer longitudinal study involving both normal children and Down syndrome children and their mothers. In the remainder of this chapter, I first outline the theory of early lexical development. I then present the relevant data from the second longitudinal study in support of this view. Finally, I make suggestions for further research and extension of the theory.

PRELIMINARY THEORY OF EARLY LEXICAL DEVELOPMENT

Children's Initial Categories

Children's initial categories are basic-level categories. This seems reasonable, because as Rosch and I have argued previously (Rosch et al., 1976), categories at the basic level are more fundamental psychologically than categories at other hierarchical levels. For example, *chair* is more fundamental than either *kitchen chair* or *furniture*. The basic level is the level at which within-category similarity is maximal relative to between-category similarity. Thus, categories at the basic level "stand out" as categories. In our world, these basic-level categories are the most general categories whose members share similar overall shapes and similar functions or characteristic actions. (Tversky & Hemenway, in press, have provided data suggesting that these latter characteristics of basic-level categories are due to the fact that basic-level categories [but not categories at other hierarchical levels] differ from one another on the basis of object parts.) Recent research has indicated that 2-year-olds can easily form basic-level categories, while formation of superordinate and subordinate categories is considerably more difficult (Daehler, Lonardo, & Bukatko, 1979; Mervis & Crisafi, 1982).

But children's initial basic-level categories often will not correspond to the adult basic-level category labeled by the same word. Such differences are to be expected, because both Dougherty (1978) and Rosch and Mervis (Rosch et al., 1976) have argued that only the principles governing the determination of basic-level categories should be universal. The actual categories formed on the basis of these principles will vary both between cultures and for subgroups within a culture (for example, experts versus nonexperts in a particular domain). This variation occurs because different groups notice or emphasize different attributes of the same object as a function of different experiences or different degrees of expertise. Because very young children have limited experience and limited knowledge of the culturally appropriate functions of objects and the form attributes correlated with these functions, these children are likely to emphasize different attributes from adults, for the same object. Therefore, very young children's basic-level categories will sometimes differ from the corresponding adult-basic-level categories.

When these deviations occur, several relationships between the two types of basic-level categories could result. First, the child-basic category could be broader than the corresponding adult-basic category. In this case, the child's category will sometimes correspond to a more general level in the same taxonomy (see also Brown, 1958, 1978). For example, the child-basic *kitty* category might correspond to the adult *feline* category. Alternatively, the child's broad category will contain exemplars from several adult taxonomies. For example, the child-basic *ball* category might include round candles, round banks, and multisided beads, as well as objects adults would consider balls. Second, the child's category may be narrower than the corresponding adult category. For example, the child-basic *chair* category might not include bean-bag chairs. Third, the child's category may overlap the adult's category—that is, the child's category may include objects that are excluded from the adult category while at the same time excluding objects that are included in the adult category. For example, the child-basic *car* category might include trucks, but exclude dune buggies.

Previous theories of lexical development have frequently accounted for the differences between child and adult categories on the basis that children and adults attend to different numbers of attributes. Thus, Clark (1973) has claimed that children attend to fewer attributes than adults, whereas Nelson (1974) has argued that children attend to more attributes than adults. Development consists of either adding attributes (Clark, 1973) or subtracting attributes (Nelson, 1974) until the appropriate adult concept is acquired. In contrast, I believe (see Mervis, 1982; Mervis & Canada, 1983) that although some differences between child and adult categories may be due to variations in the number of attributes attended to, this is not the major source of difference. Instead, one of the most important causes of the differences between child and adult categories is that children are attending to or emphasizing different attributes from adults.

For child-basic categories that are broader than the corresponding adult-basic category, there are three reasons why a child might attend to a different set of attributes or assign a different weight to an attribute. First, the child may not know about certain culturally significant attributes. For example, the child may not realize that a bank is for storing money. Therefore, the slot and the keyhole of a round bank may be ignored, in favor of known attributes such as round, rolls, can be thrown. The round bank will accordingly be assigned to the child's *ball* category. In contrast, when an adult considers a round bank, he or she ignores the attributes to which the child attends, and instead concentrates on culturally significant attributes such as slot, keyhole, for storing money. The round bank is accordingly assigned to the adult's *bank* category. Second, the child may be aware of the attributes that are important to the adult category assignment, but the salience of these attributes may sometimes be less for him or her than the salience of a different set of attributes. For example, a child may realize that a bank is for storing money and may therefore notice the slot and keyhole. The object may accordingly be assigned to the child's *bank* category. But sometimes the attributes that contribute to the round bank's ballness may be more salient to the child. At these times, the round bank will be assigned to his or her *ball* category. Thus, the child may consider the round bank to be both a bank and a ball. Third, the child may include false attributes in his or her decision process. For example, the knowledge that a leopard says ''meow'' (as the child's mother is likely to tell him or her; Mervis & Mervis, 1982) may contribute to the child's decision to categorize it as a *kitty*. However, leopards do not really say ''meow''; instead, they say ''grr.''

For child-basic categories that are narrower than the corresponding adult-basic category, the child often defines the acceptable range of values for a given attribute more narrowly, for attributes that both children and adults include in their decision processes. For example, both children and adults expect *bunnies* to have fur. However, children may require this fur to be plush, whereas adults are willing to accept a wider range of fur types. Thus, a toy rabbit made out of a flowerprint cotton fabric may be excluded from a child's *bunny* category but included in an adult's *bunny* category. In those cases for which the child-basic category overlaps the corresponding adult-basic category, the factors that contribute to overly broad and overly narrow categories operate simultaneously.

As with adult-basic-level categories, child-basic categories are characterized by gradients of goodness-of-example. That is, some members of the category are more representative of the category than other members. The principles of family resemblance and contrast set (see Rosch & Mervis, 1975) govern the goodness-of-example of child-basic categories, just as for adult-basic categories. Thus, the most representative exemplars are those that share large numbers of attributes with many other exemplars of the category, while at the same time sharing few attributes with exemplars of related categories. However, the goodness-of-example structure of the child-basic category is not determined simply on the basis of the goodness-of-example structure of the corresponding adult-basic category. The two structures will sometimes differ, because children may attend to or emphasize different attributes from adults. For example, for an adult, a football is an example of *ball,* whereas a round candle is not. For a young child, a round candle may be a better exemplar of *ball* than a football is; for some children, the football may not even be a *ball.*

In summary, very young children form basic-level categories that sometimes differ from adult-basic-level categories in both content and structure. These differences occur because the child's limited knowledge of culturally appropriate functions of objects and the form attributes correlated with these functions leads him or her to emphasize different attributes than adults do, for the same object. However, child-basic categories and adult-basic categories are both formed and structured according to the same principles.

Maternal Response to Children's Initial Concepts

In order for a mother to interact with her child according to her child's categories, she must first realize that the child's categories sometimes differ from her own. This realization may be prompted either by her child's nonverbal demonstration of his or her categories, or by his or her verbal demonstrations, or by knowledge the mother has gained from observing other children.

A child cannot demonstrate his or her categories nonverbally until he or she enters the fifth stage of the sensorimotor period. Prior to this stage, according to Piaget (e.g., 1954), children tend to interact with all objects in the same manner—for example, by looking, mouthing, shaking, or banging. The child is interested in his or her own actions, rather than in the properties of the object with which he or she is interacting. Thus, the child provides no clues to the mother concerning his or her categories. The main change that occurs during the fifth stage is the development of an interest in objects for their own sake. During this stage, children actively explore objects, and in so doing discover many of the characteristic functions of specific types of objects, and the form attributes that predict these functions. The child therefore begins to treat different types of objects differentially (Piaget, 1954; Uzgiris & Hunt, 1975). At this point, the child provides the mother with information concerning his or her categorization scheme. For example, unless angry or frustrated, the child is likely to throw only ball-like objects. These include both objects the mother considers balls and objects that are similar to balls but are not really balls, such as round candles and round bells. Once the mother notices these behaviors, she is likely to realize that her child's categorization scheme sometimes differs from her own. Thus, child function appears to be extremely important initially in leading mothers to notice differences between child and adult categorization schemes.

If the mother does not notice these differences on the basis of the child's nonverbal cues, or if she chooses to ignore these differences, the child has another chance to impress these differences upon her. Once the child starts to talk, he or she will label objects to correspond to his or her own categories, rather than to his or her mother's categories. Thus, the child provides the mother with verbal evidence of his or her categorization scheme. The child also continues to provide nonverbal evidence in the form of his or her mode of interaction with objects.

In some cases, the mother may realize that some of her child's categories differ from her own, without receiving specific input from her child concerning a particular category. First, the mother might anticipate specific differences between child and adult categorization schemes on the basis of previous experience with her older children or with other very young children. Such anticipations could occur even before her child entered sensorimotor stage five. Second, the mother might generalize the idea that her child's categories sometimes differ from her own, on the basis of differences she has observed between other of her child's categories and the corresponding adult categories. For example, once a mother realizes that her child thinks tigers and leopards are kitties, she may anticipate that the child will think zebras and giraffes are horsies.

Once the mother realizes that there are differences between her categorization scheme and her child's categorization scheme, how does she respond? Mothers of normal children tend to respect their children's initiatives (Bell, 1964; Bell & Harper, 1977; Jones, 1977, 1979, 1980). Therefore, the mother should accommodate her own naming behavior and play behavior to match her child's scheme. Thus, the mother will often name objects according to their child-basic category membership, and she will often interact with objects in a manner appropriate to their child-basic category assignment. This accommodation should occur even before the child begins to talk.

In contrast, because maternal accommodation is a function of perceived child competence, mothers of handicapped children are much less likely to respect their children's initiatives. The handicapped child is expected to follow the mother's initiative (Bell, 1964; Bell & Harper, 1977; Jones, 1977, 1979, 1980). Even though the mother realizes that some of her child's categories differ from her own, she will usually label objects with their adult names, and she is much less likely than the mother of a normal child to interact with objects in a manner appropriate to their child-basic category assignment.

What happens once the child begins to talk? The mother of a normal child will continue to label objects and interact with objects according to their child-basic category assignment. The incidence of these behaviors may increase, especially for categories that are more difficult to infer based on child nonverbal behavior alone. In addition, the mother of a normal child will accept and encourage her child's use of child-basic labels to name members of the child-basic category. However, she will correct her child's use of a label to name an object that she does not consider to be a member of the child-basic category. For example, the mother might accept the label ''car'' for a truck, but not for an airplane.

What about the mother of a handicapped child? The onset of language production (either verbal or manual sign) is important to all mothers, whether the child is normal or handicapped. However, language onset is particularly important to mothers of handicapped children, because it is perceived as indicating a major increase in the child's competence. This perception is especially true for mothers of DS children, because these mothers often fear that their children will never learn to talk (Jones, 1980). According to Bell and Harper's (1977) lower-limit control theory, maternal perception of dramatically increased child competence should result in a decrease in maternal intrusiveness and demands. This should lead to a corresponding increase in respect for the child's perspective. Therefore, the mother of a handicapped child should be more likely to use child-basic labels herself and to interact with objects according to their child-basic functions once her child begins to talk. In addition, she should often accept her child's use of child-basic labels to name members of the child-basic category that are not also members of the corresponding adult-basic category. However, she should correct her child's use of a label to name an object that she does not consider to be a member of the child-basic category.

In summary, mothers come to realize that their children's categories sometimes differ from adult categories by noticing differences in the way in which very young children and adults interact with certain objects. Additional clues are provided by the child's naming behavior once he or she begins to talk. Maternal accommodation to her child is a function of perceived child competence. Mothers of normal children tend to follow their children's initiatives; therefore, they are likely to treat objects as members of the appropriate child-basic category as soon as they realize that the children's category assignment differs from their own. Mothers of handicapped children tend to expect their children to follow their initiatives, and therefore seldom treat objects as members of the child-basic category until the children begin to talk. At that point, they perceive their children as considerably more competent, and therefore are more willing to accept the children's perspectives. Mothers of both types of children correct labeling errors that extend beyond the boundaries of the child-basic category.

Category Evolution

Some initial child-basic categories will be identical to the corresponding adult-basic categories. However, many initial child-basic categories will not be. These categories must change, in order to become isomorphic to the corresponding adult-basic categories. Child-basic categories can evolve in either of two directions (or in the case of overlapped categories, in both directions) in becoming more similar to adult categories: The child-basic category can become narrower, or it can become broader. This evolution can be initiated by either the child or the mother.

Evolution of Initially Broad Categories.   In cases in which the child-basic category becomes narrower, the general process involves the breakdown of a single child-basic category into two or more new child-basic categories. In order for the breakdown to be initiated, the child must realize that one or more members of the single category have important form and/or function characteristics that are not present in other category members. These characteristics may be ones that the child had not previously noticed or known about, or they may be ones that he or she had noticed but had not considered important. The child may note these attributes on his or her own, based on his or her interactions with the object, or by watching someone else interact with the object, or by observing something the object does on its own. The child might then call these attributes to the mother's attention. The mother would be likely to respond by labeling the object with its adult-basic name (assuming the attributes pointed out are salient characteristics of members of the adult-basic category). For example, the child might point out a candle's wick to the mother, in which case she would probably respond by labeling the object "candle." This labeling accomplishes two purposes. First, it provides the child with a name for the new child-basic category. Second, it serves as acknowledgment that the mother also thinks the difference the child has noticed is important.

If the child has not noticed these important attributes on his or her own (or if he or she has noticed them, but the mother does not realize he or she has), the mother may choose to point them out. This may be accomplished in two ways. First, the mother can show the child a critical form attribute(s) and/or demonstrate a critical function attribute(s) of an object, which serves to differentiate the object from other members of the child-basic category. Coincident with this highlighting of a critical attribute, she may label the object with its adult-basic name. These illustrations are often accompanied by verbal descriptions. For example, the mother might run her finger along the slot of a bank, drop a coin in, and tell her child that this is a slot into which you put money. She would then label the object "bank". Alternatively, the mother might provide a verbal description, without a concrete demonstration. For example, she might tell her child that an object was a candle because you can burn it, without either showing the child the wick or lighting the candle. Both these strategies could be used either spontaneously or in response to the child's use of a child-basic name to label the object in question.

Finally, the mother may label the object with its adult-basic name without either an implied request from the child (the first circumstance described) or some form of explanation (the second and third circumstances). The use of an adult-basic label alone constitutes an implicit statement of the existence of attributes that separate the labeled object from other objects included in the same child-basic category; if such attributes did not exist, then there would be no reason for the mother to use a different label. This strategy may also be used spontaneously or as a correction of the child's use of a child-basic name to label the object in question.

The first evidence that the child's conceptual system is beginning to evolve (that is, that the child has realized the importance of one or more distinguishing attributes) occurs when the child comprehends a more appropriate name for an object that has previously been included in a different child-basic category. For example, the child might comprehend "truck" in relation to a dump truck, which until then had been included only in the *car* category. The four circumstances under which the mother labels an object with its adult-basic name should be differentially associated with success at leading the child to comprehend the new adult-basic label. In addition, the success of some of these methods should be associated with the child's vocabulary size. Success should be most likely to occur if either the child points out a relevant attribute (the first circumstance) or the mother provides a concrete illustration of a relevant attribute (the second circumstance). Success when the mother provides a verbal explanation alone is less likely, but should increase as the child's vocabulary size increases (making it more likely that the child will understand the explanation). Success when the mother uses an adult-basic label without either a request from the child or an explanation is extremely unlikely for very young children. The metacognition required to realize that an object already assigned to one category should be assigned to a different one simply because a different label is used is considerably more complex than that required to accept the other types of label introduction.

The child is most likely to notice/acknowledge important form and/or function differences for those objects that are least similar to the best example of the child-basic category. (In general, these objects will also be the ones least similar to the best examples of the adult-basic category labeled by the same word as the child-basic category.) Therefore, when the child begins to break down an initial child-basic category, the first new category(ies) to emerge should be the one(s) represented by the most atypical member(s) of the original child-basic category. For example, when breaking down an initial child-basic *kitty* category, the child should form a *tiger* category before forming a *panther* category, because tigers are less similar to domesticated cats than panthers are. Similarly, if all the members of a new child-basic category are not assigned to that category simultaneously, the objects (of those ultimately to be assigned to the new category) least similar to the other members of the initial child-basic category should be assigned to the new category first. (In general, these objects will be the better examples of the new category.) For example, if a child does not simultaneously assign all trucks to the new *truck* category, he or she should assign dump trucks before pickup trucks, because dump trucks are less similar to other members of the initial child-basic *car* category than pickup trucks are. (Dump trucks are also more representative of *truck* than pickup trucks are.)

Comprehension of the adult-basic name (or a name more appropriate than the previous child-basic one) for an object previously included in an initial child-basic category is the first step in the evolution of that child-basic category to conform to the adult-basic category labeled by the same word. It has often been argued (e.g., Barrett, 1978, 1982; Clark, 1973, 1983) that upon learning a more appropriate name for an object, the child immediately discards the former name. That is, the old and the new categories immediately become disjunctive. This claim has been based on data from either diary studies (which actually include a few contradictions; see Lewis, 1936) or observations of play rather than on systematic testing. In contrast, I would like to argue that the complete separation of the two categories is gradual. The child, in considering the object(s) that is(are) changing category membership, at first finds two sets of attributes salient: the set that makes the object a member of the initial category and the set that makes the object a member of the new category. Consequently, the child includes the object in both categories. That is, the very young child does not have a principle that precludes the simultaneous assignment of objects to two basic-level categories. (Older children and adults generally do operate according to such a principle; see Tversky & Hemenway, in press.) In order for a child to decide that an object should be excluded from its initial category, he or she must decide that only the set of attributes that makes the object a member of the new category is important, or in the case of previously included false attributes, that the two sets of attributes are contradictory (e.g., that a single animal cannot say both "meow" and "grr"). At this point, the separation of the two categories will be complete. It is not clear what causes the child to finally make this decision. Three possible influences include: (1) the child's advancing knowledge of culturally appropriate ways to interact with particular objects, and the form attributes that correlate with these interaction patterns; (2) the increasing use of adult-basic, rather than child-basic, labels by the mother; and (3) the (potentially increasing) incidence of maternal corrections when her child either interacts with an object according to its child-basic assignment or labels the object with its child-basic name. If such an increase does occur, there are three likely times for it to begin: when the child initially comprehends a particular adult-basic label; when the child initially produces that adult-basic label; or when the child comprehends or produces a large number of adult-basic labels. In the first two cases, corrections should be made only when the already-comprehended or produced word should have been used or the relevant object was interacted with inappropriately; in the third case, corrections should consistently be made.

Evolution of Initially Narrow Categories.   A category can be initially narrow for either of two reasons. First, some members of the adult category may be included only in a different child category. For example, a bean-bag chair may be included only in the child's *pillow* category. Second, some members of the category from an adult perspective may not be included in any of the child's categories. For example, a child may have no idea to what category a sachet rabbit should be assigned. Only the second reason is considered here, because most instances of underextension seem to occur this way.

In order for the category in question to become broader, the child must realize that the acceptable range of values for one or more important form and/or function attributes is larger than he or she had previously thought. The child may realize this on his or her own. For example, the child may compare the object to known members of various categories, and the comparison may indicate that the object is much more similar to members of one of these categories than to members of any of the others. Alternatively, the child may decide that he or she does not know what a given object is, and then point out this object to his or her mother by asking, "What's that?" In this case, the mother would label the object for her child.

If the child has not realized that his or her acceptable range of values is too narrow, the mother may point this out to him or her. She may make her point implicitly, simply by using a child-basic label to name an object that the child has not previously considered a member of that child-basic category. Alternatively, the mother may make her point explicitly, by using the child-basic label to name the object and simultaneously providing an explanation of why the new object really does belong to the particular category. (To the extent that this explanation is linguistic, rather than demonstrated concretely, the effectiveness of the explanation will depend on the linguistic sophistication of the child.) If the child agrees that his or her acceptable range of values was narrow, then he or she will accept the mother's label (as indicated by comprehension) and accordingly expand the range of values he or she considers acceptable.

Summary.   Child-basic categories that are not initially identical to adult-basic categories must evolve in order to become identical. In cases in which the child-basic category becomes narrower, the general process involves breaking down an initial child-basic category into two or more new child-basic categories. In order for the breakdown to be initiated, the child must realize that one or more category members have important form and/or function attributes that are not present in other category members. The first evidence that the breakdown has begun occurs when the child comprehends the adult-basic name of an object that was previously included in only its child-basic category. This comprehension is most likely to occur when either the child has realized the importance of the relevant attributes on his or her own and has pointed them out to the mother, who responded by providing the object's adult-basic name; or when the mother provides a concrete illustation of these attributes, accompanied by the object's adult-basic name. Once the breakdown begins, the separation of the new category(ies) from the initial child-basic category is gradual. This separation is completed only when the child realizes that the attributes that led him or her to include the object in the initial child-basic category are either irrelevant for that object or not true of that object. In cases in which the child-basic category becomes broader, the child must realize that the acceptable range of values for one or more important form and/or function attributes is larger than he or she had previously thought.

SUPPORTING DATA

The preliminary theory just described was based on the results of a cross-sectional study (Mervis & Mervis, 1982) and a longitudinal study (Mervis, 1981; Mervis & Canada, 1983), both involving only normal children. More recently, another cross-sectional study (Cardoso-Martins & Mervis, 1981) and another longitudinal study, both involving normal children and DS children, have been conducted in order to test certain aspects of the theory. In the present chapter, I concentrate on the results of the second longitudinal study. As discussed in the introduction, a comparison of normal children and DS children permits the determination of the effects of perceived child competence on maternal accommodation to the child's concepts during the period of early lexical development. Additionally, if the mothers of the two types of children label objects differently, then a comparison of the children's initial concepts and conceptual evolution may be useful in delineating the roles of mother and child in the process of early lexical development. In particular, to the extent that the two types of children form the same categories despite differences in maternal input, the importance of the child in determining his or her initial categories would be evidenced.

Method

Subjects.   Six DS children (three girls and three boys) and their mothers and six normal children and their mothers participated in the second longitudinal study. The DS children constituted the entire known surviving population of DS children born in two small midwestern cities during the months of July, August, and September, 1979. The normal children were matched to the DS children for sex and birth-order position. All children had hearing and vision within the normal range. All the families were middle class, and in all cases the mother was the primary caregiver. (The mothers of one DS child and one normal child worked part time outside the home.) At the start of the study, the DS children were between 17- and 19-months-old. The normal children were 9-months-old. None of the children was able to comprehend or produce language referentially. The children were visited at home every 6 weeks for between 14 and 21 months.

Procedure.   Each visit began with a 30-minute play period during which mother and child played together with a specially chosen set of toys. The play period was audiotaped. In addition, one observer recorded all the nouns and pronouns used by either mother or child, along with their referents. A second observer audiotaped a running commentary describing the nonverbal interaction (including, for the DS children and their mothers, any manual signs produced and the context in which they were used). After the play period, the child was asked to name the toys, if there was any possibility that he or she could produce the names. Such a possibility was considered to exist if the child had produced any of the object names, either spontaneously or in imitation of the mother, during the play period, or if the mother thought her child could produce any of the object names. Next, the child's comprehension was tested. Four objects were placed in front of the child, and he or she was asked, "Is there an [X]?" The distractor objects were selected according to predetermined rules, to ensure that the objects most similar to members of the target category were used. For example, if (as determined by previous testing) a child did not consider trucks to be *cars,* then a typical *car* trial would include a sedan, a van, a dump truck, and a boat. If the child did consider trucks to be *cars* (and if his or her mother considered this categorization acceptable), then a typical *car* trial would include a sedan, a boat, an airplane, and a randomly chosen (nonvehicle) fourth object. A second *car* trial would include the van as the target object, and a third trial would include the dump truck as the target object. Only words that the mother or child had used during that play period, or that the child had comprehended during a previous play period, were tested. These words were tested for all possible referents. The words tested were deliberately limited in this manner, in order to avoid biasing the mother's use of object labels in subsequent play periods. Similarly, in order to try to avoid biasing the range of referents the mother considered acceptable for a particular word, each comprehension trial included one exemplar that the mother considered appropriate for the word. For example, if the mother consistently labeled the round candle "candle," then the comprehension trial used to determine if the child considered the round candle a ball would include both the round candle and a "true" ball. (It was impossible to preclude the possibility that the mother's labeling would be influenced by her child's responses on the comprehension test.) If the child appeared tired or fussy, comprehension testing was discontinued, and then completed within a few days.

Stimuli. The categories studied had to meet three criteria. First, the child-basic categories had to be expected to differ from the adult-basic categories. Second, the labels for these categories had to be among children's earliest words. (See Nelson, 1973, for early word lists for normal children and Gillham, 1979, for such lists for both normal and DS children.) Third, a variety of exemplars expected to be included in the child-basic category but not the adult-basic category had to be available. Several categories met the first two criteria, but only three of these met the third: *kitty, car,* and *ball.* All three were included in the study. The toys used included true members of each category (by adult standards), related objects that I predicted to be members of the child-basic categories, and unrelated objects from the same superordinate categories, that were predicted not to be included in either the adult-basic or the child-basic categories. In order to predict which items should be included in a child-basic category, I used the principle that basic-level categories are the most general categories whose members share similar overall shapes and similar functions or characteristic actions. I began by observing the functions for normal 13-month-olds of the prototypical exemplar (in toy form) of the adult-basic category labeled by each

TABLE 12.1
Toys Used in the Play Sessions[a]

	Category		
Predicted Membership	Ball	Car	Kitty
Adult-basic and child-basic	rubber ball[b]	sedan car[b]	house cat[b]
	whiffle ball[b]	sports car[b]	sachet cat[c]
	soccer ball	wooden car[c]	bean-bag cat[b,c]
	football[b,c]	jeep[c]	potholder cat[c]
Child-basic only	round candle[b]	van	tiger[b]
	multisided beads[b]	moving truck	leopard
	Christmas ornament[b]	dump truck[b]	cheetah
	owl bank[b]	cement truck	lion[b]
	round bell	fire engine	cougar
		bus[b]	panther
Neither	wooden blocks[b]	airplane	dog[b]
	frisbee	helicopter	frog
	plastic keys	boat[b]	parrot
			zebra
			squirrel
			rabbit
			walrus
			turtle
			elephant
			duck
			giraffe
			lobster
			camel
			dinosaur

[a]Note: A subset of these toys was used in each of the play sessions. At the start of the study, five objects from each category were included; one predicted adult-basic and child-basic, three predicted child-basic only, and one predicted neither. By the end of the study, nine objects from each category were included: two predicted adult-basic and child-basic, five predicted child-basic only, and two predicted neither.

[b]Several different exemplars have been used.

[c]Potential undergeneralization object.

target word. I then predicted that any object that could fulfill these functions (whether or not these functions were appropriate from an adult perspective) and that had a shape similar to the prototypical exemplar would be a member of the child-basic category. For example, I predicted that anything that could be thrown, could roll, and was approximately spherical would be included in the child-basic category *ball*. Starting with the fifth visit, I included objects that were predicted to be members of the adult-basic categories, but that might be excluded from the child-basic categories. The specific toys used were varied occasionally, in order to keep the mothers and children from becoming bored. The toys used are listed in Table 12.1.

Results

The results of this study are presented in four parts. I first present evidence concerning the initial extension of children's categories. Second, I discuss the mother's response to her child's initial categories. Third, I consider how the process of category evolution is initiated. Finally, I discuss the course of this evolution.

Children's Initial Categories.   In order to determine the initial extension of the children's *ball, car,* and *kitty* categories, the data from the first comprehension test on which each word was comprehended by a given child were considered. These data were compared to the predictions I made earlier based on basic-level theory. A summary of these comparisons is given in Table 12.2. Seventeen out of 18 of the normal children's initial categories corresponded exactly to the predicted child-basic categories. One category was slightly overextended. Fourteen out of 16 of the DS children's initial categories corresponded exactly to those predicted. The remaining two categories were slightly undergeneralized. (One DS child never comprehended either "car" or "kitty.") Thus, virtually all of the initial categories, for both the normal children and the DS children, corresponded exactly to the predicted child-basic categories.

In order to consider the question of whether the internal structure of children's categories is determined separately from the internal structure of the corresponding adult categories, the data from the later comprehension tests were considered for all three categories. Beginning with the fifth visit, one poor exemplar of each of the adult-basic categories (e.g., football, solid wooden car, sachet cat) was included among the play-session toys. Adult ratings confirmed that these objects

TABLE 12.2
Correspondence of the Initial Child-Basic Category to the Predicted
Initial Category[a]

| | | Relationship | |
Category Label	Predicted Child-Basic	Overgeneralized	Undergeneralized
Normal children			
ball	6		
car	5	1	
kitty	6		
Down syndrome children			
ball	4		2[c]
car	5[b]		
kitty	5[b]		

[a]The data reported are from the first session in which the relevant word was comprehended.
[b]One child never comprehended either "car" or "kitty".
[c]In both instances, only the football was excluded.

were the poorest exemplars of each category, of those available during the play sessions, but that these objects were definitely category members. The ratings also confirmed that the predicted child-basic-only items were definitely not members of the category by adult standards. Because it is not possible to obtain goodness-of-example ratings from children as young as those in the study, the basic measure of goodness-of-example available was undergeneralization. The percentage of adult subjects who indicate that an object is not a category member is highly negatively correlated with the goodness-of-example rating that an object is assigned by those persons who consider the object to be included in the category. That is, the more subjects who indicate that an object is not a category member, the poorer the goodness-of-example rating assigned to that object by people who do consider it a category member. Thus, objects that are excluded by some children should be considered poorer examples of the category than objects included by all children.

I did not expect all of the children to undergeneralize, because, as Kogan (1971) has pointed out, individual differences in conceptual breadth are common. In addition, the poor exemplars were not included at the beginning of the study. Thus, most of the children had already begun to comprehend the category names before the poor exemplars were introduced. If undergeneralization is most likely when children first begin to form a category, then potential instances of undergeneralization may have been missed, due to the late introduction of the poor exemplars.

The number of children who ever evidenced undergeneralization for any of the categories is indicated in Table 12.3. Two normal children undergeneralized; in both cases, the poorest exemplar of the adult-basic category was excluded, whereas all objects predicted to be in only the child-basic category were included. Eight instances of undergeneralization occurred for the DS children. (Five of the six DS children evidenced some undergeneralization.) All eight fit the same pattern as described for the normal children. Thus, the goodness-of-example structure of the child-basic category is not composed simply of the goodness-of-example structure of the adult-basic category, with the child-basic-

TABLE 12.3
Number of Children Who Evidenced Undergeneralization[a]

	Category		
Children	Ball	Car	Kitty
Normal	0	2 (wooden car)	0
Down syndrome[b]	2 (football)	4 (wooden car)	2 (sachet cat)

[a]In all cases of undergeneralization, the object excluded was a poor exemplar of the adult-basic category, rather than one of the child-basic-only items.

[b]One Down syndrome child never comprehended either "car" or "kitty".

only items tacked on as the poorest exemplars. For the category exemplars included in the present study, the same objects served as poor exemplars for both children and adults. However, the nonexemplars from the adults' perspective (the predicted child-basic-only objects) were actually good or moderate exemplars from the children's perspective.

Maternal Response.   Within two or three sessions after the start of the study, all of the children had demonstrated functional use of the toys provided, from a child's perspective. The children were throwing or rolling only round things, pushing four-wheeled vehicles along the floor, and so on. Thus, the children were providing nonverbal evidence of the differences between their categories and their mothers' categories. As predicted, mothers of normal children tended to use child-basic labels to refer to objects. In contrast, mothers of DS children tended to use adult-basic labels. In order to confirm this difference statistically, a comparison between the mothers of the two types of children was made. The dependent variable was whether or not the mother labeled at least one of the child-basic-only objects with its child-basic name during the play period on the day the child first demonstrated comprehension of a particular target word ("ball," "car," "kitty"). (Because the play period preceded the comprehension test, the mothers were not yet aware that their children had demonstrated comprehension on our test.) The mothers of the normal children used the target word in 12 of the 18 test cases (six "ball," two "car," four "kitty"). In contrast, the mothers of the DS children used the target word in only five of the 16 test cases (three "ball," zero "car," two "kitty"). (One of the DS children never comprehended two of the target words.) This difference is significant by a sign test ($p = .03$). The difference is reflected in the following examples taken from the transcript of the play period on the day the child first comprehended the target word. The first three examples are from mother–normal-child dyads.

Jennifer
    Child: (picks up bank, then looks at its bottom)
    Mother: What is that?
    Child: (lets go of bank, and it rolls across the floor)
    Mother: Does it roll like a ball?
    Mother: (laughs)
    Mother: Yes.
    Mother: Look at its eyes.
    Child: (vocalizes five times, during which she picks up the bank)
    Mother: Can you throw it here?
    Child: (drops bank and it rolls)
    Mother: Uh-oh.
    Mother: Go get it.
    Child: (walks toward bank)
    Mother: Get the ball.

Nikki

Mother: (lines up car, van, bus, and moving truck in front of child)
Mother: Let's play with the cars.
Mother: There we go.
Mother: See the cars?
Mother: These are all cars.
Mother: Hm?
Mother: Make the cars go.

Zachary

Mother: (holds leopard in front of child)
Mother: What is that?
Mother: Is that a kitty-cat huh?
Mother: That's a big kitty-cat.
Mother: Meow.
Mother: Meow.
Mother: Meow. (as she moves leopard toward child)

Consider the contrast between these examples and the following three examples from mother–DS-child dyads (the names of the DS children are pseudonyms).

Suzanne

Mother: What else is in there?
Child: (reaches into small box and takes out candle)
Mother: That's a candle.
Child: (vocalizes as she throws candle)
Mother: Yeah, a candle.

Francis

Mother: Truck. (as she points to the moving truck)
Mother: See the truck?
a few minutes later . . .
Mother: (holds bus in front of child)
Mother: Bus.

Kenneth

Mother: Where's the kitty-cat? (Mother wants child to get house cat.)
Child: (reaches for lion, indicating that he thinks the lion is a kitty-cat)
Mother: There's a lion.
Mother: Yeah.

We now have available the data to answer the question: Are the child's initial categories determined by maternal input—that is, by the labels the mother uses? Or are these categories determined by the child, on the basis of his or her cognitive structures? Mothers of normal children tend to label objects with their child-basic names, whereas mothers of DS children tend to label objects with their adult-basic names. Thus, if the normal children initially formed child-basic categories, whereas the DS children initially formed adult-basic categories, then the maternal-input hypothesis might be supported. On the other hand, if both types of children initially formed child-basic categories, then, as predicted on the basis of the present theory, the child-cognitive-structure hypothesis would be supported. The results reported earlier indicate convincingly that both normal children and DS children initially formed the predicted child-basic categories.

What happens to the labeling patterns of mothers of DS children, once the children start to talk? According to the proposed theory, these mothers should now use child-basic labels, because demonstration of greatly increased competence (in this case, starting to talk) should lead to a reduction in maternal intrusiveness and an increase in respect for the child's perspective. In order to test this hypothesis, the data concerning maternal labeling patterns on the day her child first spontaneously produced the name of any of the play-period toys were considered. In 13 of the 18 test cases (five "ball," three "car," five "kitty"), the mothers of the DS children labeled at least one of the predicted child-basic-only objects with its child-basic name. A comparison, for the mothers of the DS children, of maternal labeling patterns during the play period in which her child first demonstrated comprehension of a particular target word with maternal labeling patterns during the play session in which her child first demonstrated referential production indicates a consistent difference in labeling patterns (sign test, $p = .06$). Four of the six mothers increased the number of categories for which child-basic labels were used, whereas two mothers used child-basic labels for the same number of categories as before. Thus, mothers of DS children tend to change their labeling patterns to more closely conform to their children's categories, once the children begin to talk.

One mother of a DS child never used child-basic labels, even after her child began to sign. However, this mother did accommodate in a different way, after the onset of language production. Before Suzanne began to sign, her mother never provided illustrations of the critical form or function attributes of the child-basic-only objects (except for occasionally shaking the bell). That is, she never provided any explanation for her use of adult-basic labels. The following exchange was typical:

Suzanne
    Child: (holds bank)
    Mother: What is that?
    Child: (Vocalizes)
    Mother: (Imitates child's vocalization)
    Mother: Say, a bank.
    Mother: Bank. (as she holds bank in front of child)
    Child: (Vocalizes)

Mother: A bank. (as child takes bank from mother)
Child: (throws bank into toy box)
Mother: A yellow bank.

However, once Suzanne began to sign, her mother almost always provided illustrations when using adult-appropriate lables for the child-basic-only objects whose names Suzanne had not yet comprehended. Thus, the following type of exchange became typical:

Suzanne

Mother: (holds bank in front of child)
Mother: It's a bank.
Mother: See the hole? (as she runs her finger along the bank's slot)
Child: _____. (sign only)
Mother: What's that?
Mother: (taps on bank)
Mother: Bank. (as child takes bank from her)

This form of accommodation was also shown by some of the mothers of the other DS children.

Once the child begins to talk, he or she provides the mother with direct evidence concerning his or her categorization scheme. The mother can indicate acceptance or rejection of the child's scheme by her acceptance or rejection of the child's labels. The child-naming data have not yet been formally analyzed. Informal examination of the data, however, indicates that as expected, mothers usually accepted the use of child-basic labels when a child first began to produce a word. However, use of a word to label an object not predicted to be included in the child-basic category was always rejected.

Initiation of Category Evolution. Despite the initial differences that have been shown between some child-basic categories and the corresponding adult-basic categories, the child's categories will eventually conform to the adult categories. The first evidence that a child's system is beginning to evolve occurs when the child comprehends a name more appropriate than the previous one (from an adult perspective) for an object that has previously been included in a child-basic category labeled by a different name—for example, when the child comprehends "tiger" in reference to a stuffed tiger, which has previously been included only in the child's *kitty* category.

In order for the child to comprehend this more appropriate name, he or she must first hear the name used. In the discussion of theory presented earlier, I indicated that there were four circumstances under which mothers used adult-basic names in speech to their children. These circumstances were predicted to be differentially associated with success (as measured by correct comprehension). In order to best evaluate the predictions, controlled experiments are necessary. In these experiments, the method of introduction of an adult-basic name could be systematically varied, and children of different ages and vocabulary levels could be studied. Such experiments are currently being planned. To provide a preliminary assessment in the meantime, I have examined the transcripts from the longitudinal study play periods for mother–child interactions with members of the child-basic (but not adult-basic) category *ball*. These objects are listed in Table 12.1. Of the six DS children, all learned to comprehend "bell," three learned "candle," three learned "bank," one learned "bead," and one learned "ornament." In every case, the mother provided a concrete illustration of crucial form and/or function attributes (the second circumstance) during the play period immediately preceding the comprehension test on which the child first demonstrated that he or she had learned the word in question. In one of these cases, the mother's initial use of the adult-basic label was also immediately preceded by the child's demonstration of a crucial form attribute of the object (the first circumstance). Informal examination of the data indicates that in the preceding sessions, the mothers hardly ever provided concrete demonstrations, although the adult-basic labels were frequently used.

Of the six normal children, all learned to comprehend "bell," all learned "candle," four learned "bank," two learned "bead," and two learned "ornament." In 16 of the 20 cases, the mother provided a concrete illustration of crucial form and/or function attributes just before the name was comprehended. In two of these cases, the mother's initial use of the adult-basic label was also immediately preceded by the child's demonstration of a crucial function attribute of the object. Of the four cases that did not involve concrete illustrations by the mother, three involved maternal provision of only a verbal description of crucial form and/or function attributes of the object (the third circumstance). The fourth involved maternal use of the adult-basic label without an explanation or a request from the child (the fourth circumstance; strictly speaking, this case does not fit the fourth circumstance because the child had received a set of beads during the interval between two play sessions, had apparently learned the word during that interval, and labeled the object correctly before his mother labeled it at all). Informal examination of the data indicates that in the preceding sessions, the mothers hardly ever provided concrete demonstrations, although adult-basic labels were occasionally used. Instances of correct comprehension after a concrete illustration occurred at age $10\frac{1}{2}$ months for one child and by 15 months for several others. The first instance of correct comprehension after only a verbal demonstration occurred at 19 months, although informal examination of the transcripts indicates that verbal demonstrations were used occasionally when the children were younger. Strictly speaking, no instance of correct comprehension following maternal use of the adult-basic label in isolation has occurred, although use of adult-basic labels under this circumstance did occur. (Correct comprehension under this circumstance would be more likely to occur with children older than the ones included in this study.) Thus, the data from the longitudinal study provide preliminary support for the hypothesis that for very young children, comprehension of an adult-basic name for an object previously included only in its child-basic category (and thus, the beginning of the evolution of that child-basic category) is most likely to occur when a concrete demonstration of crucial form and/or function attributes of the object is provided. If such a demonstration is not provided, then correct comprehension is more likely to occur when a verbal explanation of crucial form and/or function attributes of the object is provided than when the adult-basic name of the object is used without any form of explanation.

The results of this analysis indicate that the mother plays an important role in initiating the evolution of her child's categories. The manner in which the adult-appropriate label is presented is a major factor in determining if the child will comprehend this label. The child, too, plays a major role; the potential success of the presentation depends on convincing him or her that an attribute previously considered an irrelevant aspect of an object is in fact an important aspect.

Course of Category Evolution. The evolution of one child's initial child-basic "ball" category is presented in Table 12.4. This child's category is used to illustrate the general course of category evolution; data from all 12 children, for all three categories, are summarized in Tables 12.5, 12.6, and 12.7. By the end of the study, Zachary's initial *ball* category had not yet completely evolved to correspond to the adult-categorization scheme. This incomplete evolution was characteristic; complete evolution occurred for only four of the 34 initial child-basic categories.

Zachary first comprehended *ball* when he was 12 months old. His initial *ball* category corresponded exactly to the predicted child-basic *ball* category. The category began to evolve when Zachary was $16\frac{1}{2}$ months old. In order to consider the hypothesis that the first new categories acquired were the ones whose exemplars are least similar to the best example of the old category, the following procedure was used: First, 18 adults were asked to rate each of the predicted child-basic-only objects on a 1 to 7 scale, according to how much the object was "like an [X]," where X was either ball, car, or kitty. The modal ratings were then used to generate a predicted order of acquisition. For categories emerging from the child-basic category *ball,* this order was: (1) bell; (2) bank; (3) candle, ornament, bead. Zachary demonstrated acquisition of *bell* first, then *bank* and *candle,* and finally *ornament.* This order fits well with the predicted order.

For categories emerging from the child-basic category *car,* the predicted order was: (1) truck; (2) bus. For categories emerging from the child-basic category *kitty,* the predicted order was: (1) lion; (2) tiger, leopard; (3) panther. The correspondence between the predicted orders of acquisition and the obtained orders is indicated in Table 12.5, for all 12 children for all three categories. These data indicate that the obtained orders of acquisition correspond quite well to the predicted orders.

TABLE 12.4
Evolution of Zachary's Initial *Ball* Category[a]

| Session | Category | | | | | |
	Ball	Football	Bell	Bank	Candle	Ornament
1–2	—					
3 (age 12 months)–5	ball bell bank ornament bead[b]					
6–8	ball football[c] bell bank candle[d] ornament bead		bell			
9–10	ball football bell bank candle ornament bead	football	bell	bank	candle	
11	ball football bank candle ornament bead	football	bell	bank	candle	
12	ball football ornament bead	football	bell	bank	candle	ornament
13 (age 25 months)	ball football bead	football	bell	bank	candle	ornament

[a]Based on data from the comprehension tests.
[b]The beads were added to the play-period toy box beginning with the fifth visit.
[c]The football was added to the play-period toy box beginning with the seventh visit.
[d]The candle was added to the play-period toy box beginning with the sixth visit.

TABLE 12.5
Correspondence between Predicted and Obtained Orders of
Acquisition of Categories Emerging from Initial Child-Basic
Categories

Initial Category	First Term[a]		Second Term[b]		Third Term[c]	
	P	NP	P	NP	P	NP
Normal children						
ball	5	1	4	2	4	0
car	6[d]	0	6	0	—	—
kitty	4	1	5	0	0	1
Down syndrome children						
ball	6	0	3	1	2	0
car	4	0	4	0	—	—
kitty	3	1	4	0	1	0

[a]When a child comprehended one term, it was the predicted term (P) or an unpredicted term (NP).

[b]When a child comprehended two terms, they included the predicted first and second terms (P) or they did not (NP).

[c]When a child comprehended three terms, they included the predicted first, second, and third terms (P) or they did not (NP).

[d]Includes two cases in which initial comprehension of "truck" and "bus" was demonstrated in the same session.

Once the category breakdown begins, do the new categories separate immediately from the initial child-basic category, or is there a period during which certain objects are included in both the new and the old categories? That is, do children initially perceive the old and new categories as overlapping, or is membership in them mutually exclusive? For categories emerging from Zachary's initial *ball* category, the old and new categories did not separate immediately. Thus, the bell was included in both *bell* and *ball* for five sessions, and the bank was included in both *bank* and *ball* for three sessions. The candle was included in both *candle* and *ball* for three sessions, and the ornament was included in both *ornament* and *ball* for one session.

In order to test the prediction that the old and the new categories initially overlap, each child's responses on the comprehension test for the day on which he or she first comprehended a new label for an object previously included in one of the initial child-basic categories were considered. These data are presented in Table 12.6. Only categories that are mutually exclusive by adult standards were included in the analysis. The results clearly indicate that these categories are not mutually exclusive from the children's perspectives. For categories emerging from *ball*, membership was initially simultaneous in 95% of the test cases for normal children and in 93% of the test cases for DS children. For categories

TABLE 12.6
Incidence of Simultaneous versus Exclusive Membership in Two
Categories That Are Mutually Exclusive by Adult Standards[a]

Child	Ball		Car		Kitty	
	S[b]	E[c]	S	E	S	E
Normal						
Eric	4	0	6	0		
Zachary	4	0	6	0	2	0
Mark	3	1	5	0	2	0
Dori	4	0	6	0	5	0
Jennifer	2	0	6	0	2	2
Nikki	2	0	6	0	3	0
Down syndrome						
Daniel	3	1	6	0	3	0
Francis	2	0	5	0	3	0
Kenneth	1	0				
Suzanne	4	0	5	0	1	2
Myra	2	0	5	0	2	0
Andrea	1	0				
Mean						
Normal	95%	5%	100%	0%	88%	12%
Down syndrome	93%	7%	100%	0%	82%	18%

[a]The data reported are for the first session in which a new label was comprehended with respect to a given object.

[b]Simultaneous.

[c]Exclusive.

emerging from *car*, membership was initially simultaneous in every case, for both types of children. For categories emerging from *kitty*, membership was initially simultaneous in 88% of the test cases for the normal children and in 82% of the test cases for the DS children. Overall, membership was initially simultaneous in 96% of the test cases for the normal children and in 93% of the test cases for the DS children.

The theoretical predictions concerning the order of complete separation of the new categories from the initial child-basic category are identical to those made for the order of acquisition of the new categories. For Zachary's initial *ball* category, the order of complete separation was the same as the order of initial acquisition. Thus, the obtained order corresponded well to the predicted order.

The correspondence between the predicted and obtained orders of complete separation for all 12 children for the three categories is summarized in Table 12.7. As the relatively small numbers contained in the Table indicate, complete separation of many of the new categories from the old categories did not occur

TABLE 12.7
Correspondence between Predicted and Obtained Orders of
Separation of Categories from Initial Child-Basic Categories[a]

Initial Category	First Term[b]		Second Term[c]		Third Term[d]	
	P	NP	P	NP	P	NP
Normal						
ball	4	1	3	1	3	0
car	3	2	2	0	—	—
kitty	5	0	4	0	1	1
Down syndrome						
ball	4	0	3	0	1	0
car	3	0	1	0	—	—
kitty	3	0	2	0	0	0

[a]Separation is defined as the exclusion of at least one exemplar of the new category from the initial child-basic category.

[b]When separation occurred for one category, it was the predicted category (P) or an unpredicted category (NP).

[c]When separation occurred for two categories, they included the predicted first and second categories (P) or they did not (NP).

[d]When separation occurred for three categories, they included the predicted first, second, and third categories (P) or they did not (NP).

during the period studied. However, in those cases in which complete separation did occur, the obtained orders corresponded well to the predicted ones.

SUMMARY AND CONCLUSION

In this chapter, I have presented a preliminary version of a theory of early lexical development. The starting points of the theory are derived from Rosch and Mervis's research on basic-level categories and on the internal structure of categories, and from Bell's and Jones's research on mother–child interaction patterns. The remainder of the theory has emerged from the results of a cross-sectional and a longitudinal study of mother–child interaction and early lexical development. Many of the hypotheses have been tested in the second longitudinal study just described, and as indicated previously, the data provided support for each of these hypotheses. The hypotheses are summarized here:

1. Children's initial categories are child-basic-level categories, formed according to the same principles as adult-basic-level categories, but whose membership will sometimes differ substantially. These differences are due to the children's limited experiences and limited knowledge concerning the culturally appropriate functions of objects and the form attributes correlated with these

functions, which sometimes lead the children to emphasize different attributes from adults for the same object. The internal structure of these child-basic categories is based on the same principles as for adult categories, but often will not correspond exactly to the internal structure of the corresponding adult categories.

2. Maternal accommodation to her child's categorization scheme is a function of maternal perception of her child's competence. Mothers of young normal children tend to follow their children's initiatives when interacting with their children. Therefore, these mothers should often label objects according to their child-basic category assignments when speaking to their children (once the mothers realize the differences between their categorization schemes and their children's categorization schemes). Once the children begin to talk, the mothers should accept their children's uses of child-basic labels for objects. However, the mothers should reject the use of a label to refer to an object not included in the child-basic category labeled by that word.

3. Mothers of young handicapped children tend to demand that their children follow the mothers' initiatives. Therefore, these mothers should use adult-basic labels for objects when talking to their preverbal children. However, once the children begin to talk (or sign), the mothers should perceive their children to have suddenly increased in competence, and the mothers should therefore become less intrusive and less demanding. Consequently, they should begin to use child-basic names for objects when talking to their children, and should accept these labels from their children.

4. Child-basic categories that initially do not correspond exactly to adult-basic categories must eventually evolve to correspond to the adult categories. The first step in this evolution occurs when a child comprehends the adult-basic name for an object previously included in only an initial child-basic category. The mother plays an important role in initiating this evolution; the manner in which she introduces adult-basic names is the major determinant of whether the child will comprehend the name. Introduction of these names accompanied by a concrete demonstration of crucial form and/or function attributes that serve to differentiate the object from other members of the child-basic category is most likely to lead to successful comprehension of the name by the child. Very young children are extremely unlikely to comprehend the new name based on presentation of the name alone.

5. All the categories that will ultimately be derived from an initial child-basic category will not emerge simultaneously. The first categories to be acquired should be those whose exemplars are least similar to the best example of the old category. These same categories should be the first ones to separate completely from the initial child-basic category.

6. Once the breakdown of an initial child-basic category begins, the separation of the new category(ies) from the initial category is gradual. Thus, some categories that are mutually exclusive from an adult perspective will be overlapping from the young child's perspective.

A great amount of work remains. First, several of the hypotheses that received preliminary support based on an analysis of the transcripts of the play periods would perhaps be more convincingly supported by the results of formal experiments. For example, the hypothesis concerning the relative effectiveness of various methods of introduction of adult-basic labels could be tested by systematically varying the three alternative maternal methods. Children of different ages and vocabulary levels could be included. Experiments are necessary, and are currently being planned. However, the importance of description must not be forgotten during the quest for proof of causal relationships. Observational studies such as the one presented in this chapter provide a description of what mothers and children actually do, and how they actually interact, during the process of lexical development. Thus they are mandatory scientific prerequisites, for they point to the essential variables for which causal relationships may be sought subsequently. Evidence for causal relationships that do not naturally occur is pointless if what one is interested in is the naturally occurring process of development.

Second, certain parts of the theory are not well specified. For example, the correction strategies that mothers use when children label an object with a word the mother wishes to correct, and the role of these corrections in the eventual evolution of the child's conceptual system to correspond to the adult system, have hardly been considered. Initial hypotheses concerning correction strategies can be generated based on the data contained in the transcripts from the present study. Similarly, the relationship between comprehension and production has not been specified, although once again the transcripts from the present study should provide a basis for hypothesis generation. The incidence of overly narrow initial child-basic categories was not adequately tested, because objects that might be excluded from a child-basic category even though they were included in the corresponding adult-basic category were not introduced into the study until the fifth session, by which time many of the children had already begun to comprehend the three target words. Further observational and/or diary studies, accompanied by systematic comprehension and production testing, would be useful. Finally, study of older children is necessary in order to expand the scope of the theory.

The theory so far has only been concerned with categories of concrete objects. I would like to suggest, via example, that parts of the theory are likely to be applicable to abstract noun categories and to verb categories. The entities referred to by many abstract nouns are likely to differ for young children and adults for the same reason (lack of knowledge of culturally appropriate functions and their correlated form attributes, and consequent attention to different attributes than adults for the same entity) as these differences occur for concrete object categories. Adults who are aware of these differences are likely to respond by adopting the child's perspective. For example, when talking to my 5-month-old son, several people have used the word "friend" to label inanimate objects (e.g., a lit chandelier or his favorite rattle) in which Ariel seems to take particular joy. Similar differences occur for certain verb categories, and adults respond in the same way. For example, a number of people have told Ariel that he was talking, in response to babbles. Among the other sentences including "talk" that have been addressed to Ariel are "Bear is talking to you." after his father turned on Ariel's rock-a-bye bear (which contains a recording of intrauterine sounds) and "Rattle can talk very loud." as his mother vigorously shook Ariel's rattle. (See Bowerman, 1976, for additional examples of child-adapted verb usage.) The study of children's early acquisition of verbs is just beginning (see Huttenlocher, Smiley, & Ratner, 1983). The theory offered in this chapter may provide some guidelines for further research.

This work has implications for broader issues in the study of child development. We now know something about the contributions of mother and child with regard to early lexical development. First, the initial extension and internal structure of young children's categories is determined by the child, on the basis of his or her cognitive structures. These initial categories are not influenced by the manner in which mothers label objects for their children. Second, mothers, along with their children, play a major role in initiating the evolution of the child's category scheme to conform to the adult scheme. Without the help of the mother (or other adults), the child is likely to acquire the adult scheme slowly, if at all. When the mother introduces an adult-basic name for an object, the manner in which this introduction is made is the major determinant of whether the child will accept the new label, and thus allow conceptual evolution to begin. The child gradually constructs the adult categorization scheme for him- or herself, on the basis of his or her own cognitive structures and the influence he or she allows his or her mother (or other adults) to have on these structures.

The results of this research also demonstrate that it is an oversimplification to say (as has often been said; see Miller, 1982; Slobin, 1972) that mothers do not correct syntactic errors but do correct semantic ones. What mothers actually seem to do is to gain an insight into their children's cognitive structures, and then correct semantic errors that are outside the reasonable bounds of these structures.

Finally, it is clear that theorists can push the idea of the competent child too far. After all, young children are in many ways quite different from adults. In the present study, young children thought that all felines were *kitties* and that a round bell, candle, bank, and bead were *balls*. Children are competent in the sense that the principles of categorization are the same for them as for adults. The material that these principles work upon is initially quite different for children, however; and the development to adult categorization requires constant interaction between the child, the physical world, and the social world.

ACKNOWLEDGMENTS

I would like to thank the mother–child dyads who participated in the longitudinal study for their devotion to the research. Kimberlee Chamberlain, Patricia Christiansen, and

Julie Nakamura assisted me with the study. Cindy Mervis and Cláudia Cardoso-Martins have contributed to the research from its inception. Rachel Clifton, Nancy Myers, and especially John Pani provided helpful comments on previous drafts of this chapter. Finally, I thank Ariel Pani, who has given me the opportunity to consider the applications of my theory to the domains of abstract noun concepts and verb concepts. The support of the National Science Foundation, grants No. BNS 79–15120 and BNS 81–21169, and of the Department of Education, grant No. DEG 008002485, is gratefully acknowledged.

REFERENCES

Barrett, M. D. Lexical development and overextension in child language. *Journal of Child Language*, 1978, *5*, 205–219.

Barrett, M. D. Distinguishing between prototypes: The early acquisition of the meaning of object names. In S. A. Kuczaj, II (Ed.), *Language development* (Vol. 1: Syntax and semantics). Hillsdale, N.J.: Lawrence Erlbaum Associates, 1982.

Bell, R. Q. The effect on the family of a limitation in coping ability in the child: A research approach and a finding. *Merrill-Palmer Quarterly*, 1964, *10*, 129–142.

Bell, R. Q., & Harper, L. V. *Child effects on adults*. Hillsdale, N.J.: Lawrence Erlbaum Associates, 1977.

Bowerman, M. Semantic factors in the acquisition of rules for word use and sentence construction. In D. Morehead & A. Morehead (Eds.), *Directions in normal and deficient child language*. Baltimore: University Park Press, 1976.

Brown, R. How shall a thing be called? *Psychological Review*, 1958, *65*, 14–21.

Brown, R. A new paradigm of reference. In G. A. Miller & E. Lenneberg (Eds.), *Psychology and biology of language and thought: Essays in honor of Eric Lenneberg*. New York: Academic Press, 1978.

Clark, E. V. What's in a word? On the child's acquisition of semantics in his first language. In T. E. Moore (Ed.), *Cognitive development and the acquisition of language*. New York: Academic Press, 1973.

Clark, E. V. Meanings and concepts. In P. H. Mussen (Ed.), *Charmichael's manual of child psychology* (Vol. 3: Cognitive development). New York: Wiley, 1983.

Cardoso-Martins, C., & Mervis, C. B. *Maternal speech to prelinguistic Down syndrome children*. Paper presented at the Gatlinburg Conference for Research in Mental Retardation/Developmental Disabilities, Gatlinburg, Tennessee, March 1981.

Daehler, M. W., Lonardo, R., & Bukatko, D. Matching and equivalence judgments in very young children. *Child Development*, 1979, *50*, 170–179.

Dougherty, J. W. D. Salience and relativity in classification. *American Ethnologist*, 1978, *5*, 66–80.

Gillham, B. *The first words language programme*. London: Allen & Unwin, 1979.

Huttenlocher, J., Smiley, P., & Ratner, H. H. What do word meanings reveal about conceptual development? In T. Nammenmacher & W. Seiler (Eds.), *The development of word meanings and concepts*. New York: Springer-Verlag, 1983.

Jones, O. H. M. Mother-child communication with pre-linguistic Down's syndrome and normal infants. In H. R. Schaffer (Ed.), *Studies in mother–infant interaction*. New York: Academic Press, 1977.

Jones, O. H. M. A comparison study of mother–child communication with Down's syndrome and normal infants. In H. R. Schaffer & J. Dunn (Eds.), *The first year of life: Psychological and medical implications of early experience*. New York: Wiley, 1979.

Jones, O. H. M. Prelinguistic communication skills in Down's syndrome and normal infants. In T. M. Fields, S. Goldberg, D. Stern, & A. M. Sostek (Eds.), *High risk infants and children: Adult and peer interactions*. New York: Academic Press, 1980.

Kogan, N. Educational implications of cognitive style. In G. Lesser (Ed.), *Psychology and educational practice*. Glenview, Ill.: Scott Foresman, 1971.

Lewis, M. M. *Infant speech: A study of the beginnings of language*. London: Kegan Paul, Trench, Trubner, & Co., 1936.

Mervis, C. B. *Tigers and leopards are kitty-cats: Mother–child interaction and children's early categories*. Paper presented at the Interdisciplinary Conference, Park City, Utah, January 1981.

Mervis, C. B. *Mother–child interaction and early lexical development*. Paper presented at the Annual Meeting of the Midwestern Psychological Association, Minneapolis, Minnesota, May 1982.

Mervis, C. B., & Canada, K. On the existence of competence errors in early comprehension: A reply to Fremgen & Fay and Chapman & Thomson. *Journal of Child Language*, 1983, *10*, 431–440.

Mervis, C. B., & Crisafi, M. A. Order of acquisition of subordinate, basic, and superordinate level categories. *Child Development*, 1982, *53*, 258–266.

Mervis, C. B., & Mervis, C. A. Leopards are kitty-cats: Object labeling by mothers for their 13-month-olds. *Child Development*, 1982, *53*, 267–273.

Mervis, C. B., & Rosch, E. Categorization of natural objects. *Annual Review of Psychology*, 1981, *32*, 89–115.

Miller, J. F. Early language intervention: When and how. In M. Lewis & L. T. Taft (Eds.), *Developmental disabilities: Theory, assessment, and intervention*. New York: SP Medical and Scientific Books, 1982.

Nelson, K. Structure and strategy in learning to talk. *Monographs of the Society for Research in Child Development*, 1973, *38*, (Serial No. 149) 1–2.

Nelson, K. Concept, word, and sentence: Interrelations in acquisition and development. *Psychological Review*, 1974, *81*, 267–285.

Piaget, J. *The construction of reality in the child*. New York: Basic, 1954.

Rosch, E., & Mervis, C. B. Family resemblances: Studies in the internal structure of categories. *Cognitive Psychology*, 1975, *7*, 573–605.

Rosch, E., Mervis, C. B., Gray, W. D., Johnson, D. M., & Boyes-Braem, P. Basic objects in natural categories. *Cognitive Psychology*, 1976, *8*, 382–439.

Slobin, D. I. Children and language: They learn the same way all around the globe. *Psychology Today*, 1972, *6*, 71–74, 82.

Tversky, B., & Hemenway, K. Objects, parts, and categories. *Journal of Experimental Psychology: General*, in press.

Uzgiris, I. C., & Hunt, J. McV. *Assessment in infancy: Ordinal scales of psychological development*. Urbana: University of Illinois Press, 1975.

13

The Acquisition and Hierarchical Organization of Categories by Children

Ellen M. Markman
Stanford University

Children are faced with two major problems in trying to learn the conventional object categories of their culture. The first problem has to do with the acquisition of single categories. First the child must figure out what the criteria are for grouping objects into categories. Because there are an unlimited number of possible ways of forming categories, how is it that the child comes up with the conventional categories encoded by his or her culture? The second problem has to do with the relations between categories that the child has formed. Human categories tend to be organized into systems, in particular into hierarchically organized class-inclusion relations. This kind of hierarchical organization poses special problems for children that they must somehow overcome.

In this chapter, I consider both of these problems—the acquisition of single categories and the organization of categories into hierarchical class-inclusion relations. In each case, I describe some of what children must accomplish and what problems children must solve. Also, in each case I suggest ways in which the child's knowledge of natural language may provide a partial solution to these problems.

ACQUISITION OF SINGLE CATEGORIES

A common way in which children learn their first category terms is through ostensive definition. That is, a parent or other teacher points to an object and labels it. Especially in the early phases of language acquisition, when children do not know enough language that one could describe a category to them, children's learning of new category terms must depend heavily on ostensive definition.

Given that an adult points to an object and labels it, how is it that the child settles on an interpretation? At first sight this would seem to be a quite simple problem and, in fact, children make hundreds of such inferences correctly when acquiring new vocabulary. This apparent simplicity belies an incredibly complex inferential problem that was formulated by Quine (1960) in his well-known argument about translation. Imagine that someone points to a dog and says *chien,* and our job is to figure out what *chien* means. Obviously, our first hypothesis is that it means *dog.* But this is not necessary. It could mean *furry object,* or *brown object,* or *medium-sized object,* and so on. To decide if the new term refers to dog, we might set up certain test situations in which we could point to various objects and ask whether or not *chien* applies. Quine's point is that no matter how many test situations we construct, there will always be more than one hypothesis for the meaning of a new term that is consistent with the existing evidence.

Young children beginning to acquire their native language continually face this problem of narrowing down the meaning of a term from an indefinite number of possibilities. Someone points in some direction and and then utters a word. On what grounds is the child to conclude that a new unfamiliar word—for example, *dog*—refers to dogs? What is to prevent a child from concluding that *dog* means furry object or brown object or any number of other characteristics that dogs share? And finally, what prevents the children from concluding that *dog* means something like ''the dog and his bone'' or ''the dog next to the tree'' or ''mother petting the dog.'' These last examples of thematic relations pose a particular problem because children are very interested in such relations and may find them more salient than categorical relations. Before continuing to discuss how children narrow down the possible meanings of terms, I would like to briefly review the work on classification showing children's fascination with thematic relations.

Classification Studies

One widely used procedure for studying how children form categories of objects is to ask them to classify objects by sorting them into groups. Typically, children are presented with objects from several different categories—for example, vehicles, animals, clothing, and people—and they are instructed to put together the objects that are alike or that go together. There are other variants of the procedure that are also frequently used, one being an oddity task. In this case, children would be presented with three objects, two from the same object category and one from a separate object category, and they would be asked to find the two that go together. The rationale for using these procedures is straightforward. We want to find out on what basis children form categories, or what principles of organization they use. One way to do this is to present children with various objects and give them relative freedom to sort the objects as they like. In this way, the child's own organizational preferences might be found.

Here is a somewhat oversimplified summary of what is often found in these studies. Children older than 6 or 7 sort objects on the basis of the object's taxonomic category. For example, they place all and only the vehicles together, all and only the clothing together, and so on. Younger children sort on some other basis. Sometimes, especially when geometric figures are used, young children create spatial configurations with the objects, arranging them into designs or patterns. When more meaningful objects are used, children represent causal and temporal relations among the objects as well as spatial relations. These thematic relations emphasize events rather than taxonomic similarity. For example, children might sort a man and a car together because the man is driving the car. Or they might place a boy, a coat, and a dog together because the boy will wear his coat when he takes the dog for a walk. This attention to relations between objects rather than to how objects are alike is a common finding replicated in many studies. In fact, this thematic bias shows up in various studies of memory and word association (see Markman, 1981) in addition to studies using classification and oddity procedures. From these studies of classification, we can conclude that children are more interested in the thematic relations among objects, or that thematic relations are simpler or more readily constructed than categorical relations.

It is not surprising that children notice these thematic relations. They are obviously very important for making sense of the world for adults and children alike. As we move about in our daily lives, we observe people interacting or using tools, machines, or other artifacts to accomplish some goal. We view natural occurrences such as storms, and we admire scenery. Much of our perception is interpretive, making sense of what we encounter, trying to figure out what is happening and how. Thus, these eventlike meaningful structures are a fundamentally important and natural way of organizing information. Even infants tend to place causal interpretations on events they perceive (cf. Gibson & Spelke, 1983). Moreover, there seem to be fewer developmental and cross-cultural differences in understanding this type of organization (Mandler, Scribner, Cole, & DeForest, 1980). This is in marked contrast to the cross-cultural and developmental differences found in studies of classification. In sum, interest in thematic relations is not limited to young children. Nor should attention to thematic relations be viewed as a useless or nonproductive bias. Noticing the way in which objects interact, attending to causal, spatial, and temporal relations between objects, is essential for understanding the world. It is the failure to notice categorical relations and not the child's attention to thematic relations that changes with development.

Although children are biased toward organizing objects thematically, single words, in particular count nouns, rarely encode thematic relations. English does not have a single noun for thematically related objects such as *a boy and his bike, a spider and its web,* or *a baby and its bottle.*

Thus, to return to Quine's problem of induction, we are faced with a kind of paradox here. Children seem to readily learn terms that refer to object categories. Their vocabularies are filled with words such as *ball* or *dog,* simple concrete nouns referring to object categories. Yet, children tend to notice and remember thematic relations between objects more readily than the objects' categories. How is it that children readily learn labels for categories of objects if they are attending to these relations between objects instead? To take a concrete example, imagine a mother pointing to a baby and saying "baby." Based on the classification studies, we should assume that the child will be attending to the baby's shaking a rattle, or to the baby's being diapered. Why, then, does the child not infer that *baby* means something like *baby and its rattle* or *baby and its diaper?*

Hutchinson and I (Markman & Hutchinson, 1984) have proposed that the solution to this problem is that children, even extremely young children, constrain the possible meanings of words. Regarding Quine's problem of induction, children rule out many possible meanings of a new term, in particular many thematic meanings. That is, they do not consider thematic relations as possible meanings and focus instead on categorical relations.

We know that under simplified conditions, children are able to understand categorical organization (see Carey, 1982; Gelman & Baillargeon, 1983; Horton, 1982; Markman & Callanan, in press for reviews) even though they prefer thematic relations. To take one example, Smiley and Brown (1979) tested whether 4- and 6-year-old children could understand taxonomic relations even though they prefer thematic ones. They presented children with a target picture and two choice pictures. One of the choices was thematically related to the target, and one of the choices was taxonomically related to the target. For example, children were shown a spider (target), a spider web (thematic choice), and a grasshopper (taxonomic choice). The experimenter pointed to the spider and asked for "the one that goes best with this one." As usual, these young children tended to pick the spider web, rather than the grasshopper, thereby indicating a thematic relation. Nevertheless, when they were asked about the grasshopper, all of the children except the very youngest could explain the taxonomic relation. Thus, children have a rudimentary ability to organize objects taxonomically, but it is often obscured by their attention to thematic relations.

Hutchinson and I (Markman & Hutchinson, 1984) proposed that children have implicit hypotheses about the possible meaning of words that help them acquire words for categories. Children may well prefer to structure the environment in a way that conflicts with the way that language is organized. But even very young children may be aware of the constraints on word meaning so that when they believe that they are learning a new *word,* they shift their attention from thematic to categorical organization.

The first study we conducted investigated whether hearing a novel word will cause 2- to 3-year-old children to shift their attention from thematic to categorical relations. Basic-level categories (Rosch, Mervis, Gray, Johnson, & Boyes-

Braem, 1976), such as *dog* or *chair,* were used with these young children rather than general superordinate-level categories, such as *animal* or *furniture.*[1]

Three-year-old children participated in the study. Children were assigned to one of two conditions. In one of the conditions children were asked to find a picture that was the same as the target. The other condition was the same except that a nonsense syllable was used to label the target picture.

In both of the conditions, children were first shown the target picture. They were then shown two other pictures and had to select one of them as being the same as the target.

No-Word Condition. To begin, children were introduced to a hand puppet and they were told to put the picture they chose in the puppet's mouth. On each trial, the experimenter pointed to the target card and told the child, "Look carefully now. See this?" as she pointed to the picture. Then the experimenter placed the two choice pictures on the table and told the child to "find another one that is the same as this," as she continued to point to the target picture.

One of the choice pictures was a member of the same basic-level category as the target—for example, the target might be a poodle and the choice a German shepherd (both dogs). We attempted to make the two category exemplars fairly dissimilar yet still readily identifiable to these young children. The other choice card was a strong thematic associate to the target, in this case, dog food. There were 10 such triads in all. They are listed in Table 13.1.

Novel-Word Condition. Everything about the novel-word condition was identical to that of the no-word condition, with one exception. Children in this condition were told that the puppet could talk in puppet talk. They were instructed to listen carefully to find the right picture. The puppet gave the target picture an unfamiliar name and used the same name in the instructions for picking a choice picture. For example, the puppet might say, "See this? It is a sud. Find another sud that is the same as this sud."

---

[1]Rosch et al. (1976) showed that 3-year-old children are capable of using category membership to sort objects at the basic level of categorization, even though they fail to sort objects taxonomically at the superordinate level. In Rosch et al.'s (1976) study, children were presented with two objects related at the basic level, along with an unrelated distractor, and they were asked to find the two that were alike. Three year-olds almost always selected the two category members over the unrelated distractor. Because this study failed to include any competing thematic relations, however, it did not establish the relative salience of thematic and categorical relations. In a preliminary study, we demonstrated that when a competing thematic relation is present (e.g., a baby and a bottle), 2 and 3 year-olds often select it over the basic-level category (e.g., two babies). When an unrelated distractor was used, children selected the categorical associate 94% of the time, as in Rosch et al.'s (1976) study. When a thematically related distractor was used, however, children selected the categorical associate only 56% of the time. This finding allowed us to address the main question about the role of a word in inducing categorical organization.

TABLE 13.1
Stimulus Materials for Experiment 1

Standard Object	Taxonomic Choice	Thematic Choice
Police car	Car	Police officer
Tennis shoe	High-heeled shoe	Foot
Dog	Dog	Dog food
Straight-backed chair	Easy chair	Man in sitting position
Crib	Crib	Baby
Birthday cake	Chocolate cake	Birthday present
Blue jay	Duck	Nest
Outside door	Swinging door	Key
Male football player	Man	Football
Male child in swimsuit	Female child in overalls	Swimming pool

When children in the no-word condition had to select between another category member and a thematically related object, they selected other category members 59% of the time. When the target picture was labeled with an unfamiliar word children were significantly more likely to select categorically. They now chose the other category member a mean of 83% of the time. This effect held up over every item. As predicted, when children think they are learning a new word they look for categorical relationships between objects and suppress the tendency to look for thematic relations. These results supported the hypothesis at least for very young children and basic-level categories.

Two further studies were conducted to test the hypothesis that hearing a new word will induce older preschoolers to look for taxonomic relations rather than thematic relations at the superordinate level of categorization. I report the results of only one of the studies here (Study 3 of Markman and Hutchinson, 1984), but both studies showed the same pattern of results.

Four-year-old children participated in the study. They were assigned to one of three conditions.

No-Word Condition.   The procedure used in this condition was very similar to that used in the no-word condition of the first study, except that now superordinate-level categories were used. Associated with each of the target pictures were two choice pictures. One of the choice pictures was related in a thematic way to the target—for example, as milk is to cow. The other choice picture was a member of the same superordinate category as the target—for example, as pig is to cow. An attempt was made to use a variety of thematic relations rather than just one, so as not to limit the generality of the results. Examples of the materials used are shown in Table 13.2.

On each trial in the no-word condition, the experimenter, using a hand puppet, said, "I'm going to show you something. Then I want you to think carefully

TABLE 13.2
Stimulus Materials for Experiment 2

Standard Object	Taxonomic Choice	Thematic Choice
Cow	Pig	Milk
Ring	Necklace	Hand
Door	Window	Key
Crib	Adult bed	Baby
Bee	Ant	Flower
Hanger	Hook	Dress
Cup	Glass	Kettle
Car	Bicycle	Car tire
Sprinkler	Watering can	Grass
Paintbrush	Crayons	Easel

and find another one.'' The experimenter then placed the target picture face up on the table directly in front of the child, and said, ''See this?'' She placed the two choice pictures to the left and right of the target, then said, ''Can you find another one?'' After children made choices, they were asked to justify their responses: ''How did you know it was this one?''

Novel-Word Condition. Everything about the procedure for this condition was identical to that of the no-word condition, except that the target picture was now labeled with a novel word. Children were told that the puppet could talk in puppet talk, and that they were to listen carefully to what the puppet said. The instructions now included an unfamiliar label for the target: ''I'm going to show you a dax. Then I want you to think carefully and find another dax. See this dax. Can you find another dax?'' Children were asked to justify their choices.

We predicted that children in the novel-word condition, because they were given a label, should choose the taxonomically related choice picture more often than children in the no-word condition.

An additional condition was included to evaluate an alternative explanation for increased taxonomic responding in the novel-word condition. We are arguing that when children hear a word, they focus on categorical relationships because of general knowledge of what count nouns encode, and not because of specific knowledge about a particular word's meaning. But children already knew real-word names for the target pictures and they conceivably could have translated the unfamiliar labels. We could not control for the possibility that children were translating. However, when children were explicitly asked to translate the terms, they sometimes translated them into basic-level terms, but they virtually never translated them into superordinate-level terms.

Basic-Word Condition. If children are going to translate at all, it will be into a basic-level category term. The basic-word condition tested whether translation into a basic-level word would facilitate taxonomic responding.

The materials and procedure for this condition were identical to those in the novel-word condition. The instructions simply substituted the basic-level word for the target, in place of the unfamiliar label. For the example with the cow target, the experimenter said: "I'm going to show you a cow. Then you'll have to think carefully and find another cow. See this? It's a cow: Can you find another cow?" Children were asked to justify their choices.

As is typical for children this age, when no word was present they did not often make categorical choices. When children in the no-word condition had to select between another member of the same superordinate category and a thematically related object, they chose the categorical relation only 25% of the time. As predicted, the presence of a new word caused children to seek taxonomic relations. When the target picture was labeled with an unfamiliar word, children hearing that word were much more likely than children hearing no label to select categorically. They now chose the other category member 65% of the time. This effect held up over every item.

More support for the hypothesis came from the justifications that children gave for their choices. Even when children chose thematically in the novel-word condition, they seemed reluctant to justify the thematic choice with a thematic explanation. When they heard a new word, they justified thematic choices with a thematic explanation only 44% of the time. The children seemed to be in conflict between having chosen thematically but believing that the word implied a taxonomic relation. These children were now unable to justify their selections in the most natural way. When children in the no-word condition selected thematically they did not have the same conflict and were quite willing to give thematic justifications. These children, who did not hear a word, justified their thematic choices thematically the majority (79%) of the time. Thus children in the novel- and no-word conditions differed in their willingness to give thematic justifications even for their thematic choices.

In sum, when young children are asked to classify things, they often classify them thematically. But hearing a new word induces children to look for categorical relationships instead of thematic relationships. These results, although supporting the hypothesis, need to be interpreted in light of the results from the basic-word condition. Children in the basic-word condition gave just as many taxonomic responses as children in the novel-word condition. The mean percentage of taxonomic responses in the basic-word condition was 62%, as compared to 65% for the novel-word condition. The question is, were children in the novel-word condition really translating into basic-level words?

A closer examination of the data suggests that translation into basic-level words is not accounting for the advantage of the novel-word over the no-word condition. That is, the novel-word condition and basic-word condition differ in several ways (see Markman & Hutchinson, 1984, for more details).

For example, children who heard basic-level words did not seem as reluctant to justify thematic responses thematically as children who heard unfamiliar words. The proportion of thematic responses justified thematically was 70% in the basic-word condition as opposed to 44% in the novel-word condition. Thus, the justification data show that the basic-level word did not focus children's attention on taxonomic relations as much as the unfamiliar word did. One possible explanation for this is that children in the novel-word condition were trying to figure out the meaning of a new word and were, therefore, more aware that a word was involved. Consequently, they were more aware than children in the basic-word condition that they should be searching for categorical relations.

In sum, hearing new words overrides children's tendencies to look for thematic relationships, and causes them to look for categorical relationships instead. If children were translating the terms into basic-level words for the objects, that would have helped them to choose categorically related objects. However, the justifications from children hearing novel words differed from those of children hearing basic-level words, suggesting that translation into known terms was not accounting for the results. Thus, there is at least some evidence that children focus on categorical relationships because of the sheer presence of the words, and not because of any particular knowledge about the meanings of the words.

This next study was designed to provide additional evidence that children use abstract knowledge about words rather than specific known meanings to facilitate taxonomic responding. In this study, pictures of artificial objects were used instead of real objects. Children are not likely to translate unfamiliar names for these pictures into known words, because they do not know real word names for them. If the presence of an unfamiliar word still causes children to shift from thematic to taxonomic responding when the materials are also unfamiliar, then this would rule out translation as an explanation for the effect.

Four- and 5-year-old children participated in the study. The design and procedure for this study were essentially the same as that of the previous study. The main difference was that the experimenter first taught children the taxonomic and thematic relations for the artificial objects before asking them to select the picture that was like the target.

No-Word Condition.   Children were shown eight sets of pictures. Each set included a target picture and two choice pictures, one thematically related and one taxonomically related to the target. Before children saw the target picture and the two choices, they were shown two training pictures that illustrated how the target picture related to each of the choice pictures. One picture showed the target object and the taxonomic choice, side by side. For these pairs, children were told a common function that the two objects shared. An example taxonomic-training picture is shown in Fig. 13.1.

For this example, the experimenter said, "This swims in the water" (pointing to the left-hand object). "This swims in the water" (pointing to the right-hand object).

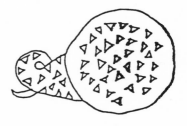

FIG. 13.1.   Sample taxonomic training picture.

A second training picture showed the target and the thematic choice in an interactive relationship. The experimenter told the children how the two objects interacted. The thematic training picture for the set just given is shown in Fig. 13.2. For this example, the experimenter said, "This catches this" (pointing to the objects she was referring to as she said the sentence).

A second example taxonomic training picture is shown in Fig. 13.3. For this example, the experimenter said, "This pokes holes in things" (pointing to the left-hand object). "This pokes holes in things" (pointing to the right-hand object). The thematic training picture for the same set is shown in Fig. 13.4. For this picture, the spoken information was, "You keep this in here."

After children saw the two training pictures in a set, the pictures were removed from the table. The procedure for the rest of the trial was identical to the

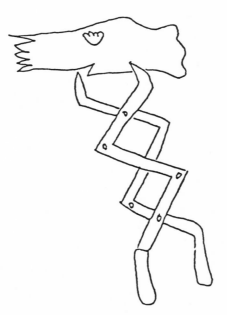

FIG. 13.2.   Sample thematic training picture.

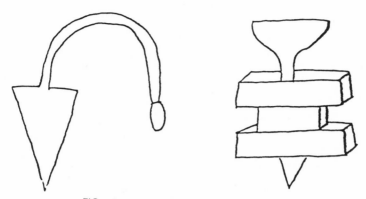

FIG. 13.3.   Sample taxonomic training picture.

procedure in the no-word condition of the previous experiment. The experimenter said, "I'm going to show you something. Then I want you to think carefully, and find another one." The experimenter then placed the target picture face up on the table, directly in front of the child, and said, "See this?" She placed the two choice pictures to the left and right of the target, and then said, "Can you find another one?" Note that the choices were pictures of the individual objects as in the previous studies, rather than pictures of two objects together.

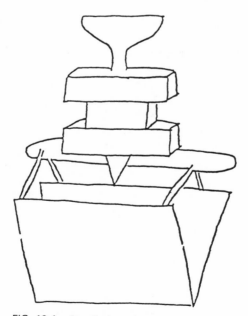

FIG. 13.4.   Sample thematic training picture.

Novel-Word Condition.   The materials and procedure for this condition were identical to those of the no-word condition, except that a novel word was used to label the target picture. After children saw the training pictures, the experimenter said, "I'm going to show you a dax. Then I want you to think carefully, and find another dax. See this dax? Can you say dax? Can you find another dax?" A different unfamiliar word was used for each set.

The results for the choices were parallel to those of the previous studies. As usual, when children in the no-word condition had to select between another member of the same superordinate category and a thematically related object, they often chose the thematic relation. They selected the other category member a mean of only 37% of the time. When the target picture was labeled with an unfamiliar word, children were more likely to select categorically. They now chose the other category member a mean of 63% of the time. Children hearing a novel word were significantly more likely to select an object from the same category than children not hearing a label. Moreover, the difference held up over every item.

The hypothesis tested by these studies is that children place an abstract constraint on what single nouns might mean. Children limit count nouns to refer mainly to objects that share some property or function rather than allow them to refer to objects that are united by thematic relations. This would help explain how children acquire words that refer to categories even though, in many other situations, they seem to find the thematic associations between objects to be more salient. That is, the simple presence of a noun, even an unfamiliar one such as *dax*, should cause children to search for objects that share some perceptual or functional properties. Thus, labeling a picture as *dax* and asking children to find "another dax" should help override their preference for choosing thematically.

The results from several studies supported the hypothesis. Even children as young as 2 and 3 years of age place constraints on what an unfamiliar word might mean. When presented with two basic-level objects, such as two different kinds of dogs, and a third object that was thematically related, such as dog food, very young children would often select a dog and dog food as being the same kind of thing. If, however, one of the dogs was called by an unfamiliar label such as *dax* and children were told to find another dax, they were now much more likely to select the other dog.

By the time children are 4 or 5 years old a word induces them to search for categorical relations even among objects that can only be related at the superordinate level of categorization. For example, with no word present, children often selected a dog and dog bone as being the same kind of thing because of the strong thematic association between dog and bone. When one of the dogs was called a *dax*, however, and children were asked to find another dax, they more often selected a dog and a cat as being the same, because they are both in the same superordinate category, animals.

These older children's justifications corroborated their choices. Children who heard novel words tended to give more justifications that referred to the categorical relations between the objects, whereas children who did not hear labels for the objects referred more to thematic relations. Even when children chose thematically in the novel-word condition, they seemed reluctant to justify the thematic choice with a thematic explanation. For example, when children select a dog and a dog bone as being the same, they ordinarily justify this by saying that the dog eats the bone. However, those children who had heard the dog labeled with an unfamiliar term, yet nevertheless selected the dog bone, would now justify their choices by saying that the dog and the bone were both white, for example, or they would refuse to explain their selections. There was no such reluctance to justify thematic choices thematically when no label was given.

The hypothesis is that the presence of an unfamiliar word shifts children's attention to taxonomic relations because of an abstract constraint children place on possible word meanings, and not because they know the meaning of the word. Thus, we would like to rule out translation into a known word as accounting for the effect.

Had children been translating into basic-level terms, it would have helped them select taxonomically. Yet, there are a number of sources of evidence that the increase in taxonomic responding when children heard novel words cannot be fully accounted for by translation of the unfamiliar word into a basic-level term.

The most compelling evidence that translation into known terms cannot account for the results comes from the last study, in which unfamiliar objects, as well as unfamiliar words, were used. Here, children were shown three novel objects. They were taught a taxonomic relation for two of the objects and a thematic relation for two. When no label was used children often selected the two objects that were related thematically as being the same. When an unfamiliar word was used to label the target picture children now selected the two objects that were related taxonomically. Children could not have been translating in this study, because they did not know what these unfamiliar objects were and had no familiar labels for them. Nevertheless, the results from this study replicated the results from the studies that used familiar objects. Again, the presence of an unfamiliar meaningless word caused children to shift from selecting objects that are thematically related to selecting objects that are taxonomically related. This suggests that children have placed an abstract constraint on what words can mean that is not mediated by the meaning of known terms.

These findings raise the question of how children come to constrain their hypotheses about what words can mean. What leads children to assume that words are likely to refer to objects that are similar in some way rather than to objects that participate in the same event or context? There are at least two possibilities. One is that sensitivity to the constraint is innate—from the start, children assume words will refer to categories of similar objects. Having such implicit knowledge would provide children with an entry into the formidable problem of learning language. Children would at least be able to readily acquire count nouns, and once they had a reasonable vocabulary of category terms, they could then begin to comprehend other linguistic forms. In fact, the huge majority of children's first words are count nouns (Clark, 1983; Huttenlocher, 1974; Nelson, 1973).

Another possibility is that the constraint is induced from early language experience. Having learned many count nouns, almost all of which refer to objects that are taxonomically related, children may come to expect this to be true of subsequent terms they learn. If so, then this induction must take place fairly rapidly at an early point in language acquisition, because Hutchinson and I found that even 2-year-olds believe that count nouns are more likely to refer to objects that belong to the same category than to objects that are thematically related.

It is not clear whether or not very young language learners limit the constraint to count nouns. Particularly if children have some innate knowledge of the constraint, they may at first overextend it, indiscriminately believing that any word they hear must refer to a taxonomic category. Only somewhat later might they become sensitive to form class and expect count nouns to be more likely than other classes of words to refer to categorical relations.

Children's sensitivity to this constraint raises the possibility that language may help children acquire new categories. In contrast, it is often argued that words must map onto concepts that have already been worked out nonlinguistically (Clark, 1973; Huttenlocher, 1974; Macnamara, 1972; Nelson, 1974; Wittgenstein, 1953, 1958). On this view, language plays little role in concepts learning. But this view may underestimate the importance of language. Young children may create concepts to fit new words, guided by abstract constraints on word meaning. This alternative view is a mild form of linguistic determinism (Whorf, 1956), in that language is believed to shape thought. It is quite different, however, from Whorf's conception that each language imposes a particular world view on its speakers, and that cognition is determined and limited by the specific language one speaks. First, all languages are likely to share similar constraints on possible meanings for count nouns. Thus, the hypothesis is that, regardless of native language, children look for categories of similar objects when they hear new nouns. Second, although nouns help focus children's attention on categorical relations, Hutchinson and I are not arguing that children would be incapable of forming categories without exposure to language.

The small amount of research that bears on this milder form of linguistic determinism suggests that children can use abstract knowledge of the semantic correlates of form class to help them discover the concept to which a word refers. Brown (1957) found that 3- to 5-year-old children interpreted an unfamiliar count noun (a *dax*) as referring to a new concrete object, whereas they interpreted an unfamiliar mass noun (some *dax*) as referring to a novel undifferentiated mass. In a study by Katz, Baker, and Macnamara (1974), children as young as 18-months-old interpreted an unfamiliar proper noun (*Dax*) as referring to an individual. At the same time, these young children understood an unfamiliar count noun (a *dax*) as referring to a category of similar objects.

To return to our findings, hearing a noun caused children to shift their attention from thematic to taxonomic organization. These results led Hutchinson and me to speculate that linguistic input may serve more generally to shape the conceptual structure of the child in the direction of greater taxonomic organization. A word may draw members of a category together for a child, highlighting their common category membership. Language may thus play a direct role in making categorical relations a salient and highly structured mode of organization.

The question arises as to why language is organized this way. Why don't words refer typically to objects that are thematically related? As pointed out earlier, thematic relations between objects are certainly important for adults as well as for children. In naturally occurring situations, objects are not found organized by category, but rather are embedded in spatial, temporal, and causal contexts. Such relational structures as events and themes are a common way of organizing information to make sense of what we encounter (cf. Mandler, 1979; Markman, 1981).

Given that these thematic eventlike organizations are a natural way of construing the world, why should languages force a taxonomic or categorical structure rather than capture this thematic bias? Why do we not have single words to refer to a boy or his bike, a baby or its bottle, a spider or its web? One reason may be that if nouns referred exclusively to relations such as a baby and its bottle, or a boy and his bike, there would be no easy way to express hierarchical taxonomic relations. Because a taxonomy groups objects into categories nested within broader categories, it allows deductive inferences to be made that go beyond the first-hand knowledge one has about a specific object. If one knows, for example, that a particular object is an animal, one can be fairly sure that it takes in food, moves about, reproduces, and has internal organs. In contrast, knowing that something is a *dax*, when *dax* could be a boy or his bike, tells one very little else about it. One reason why nouns tend not to refer to thematically related objects, then, may be because of the advantages of hierarchical organization.

Another more important reason may be that if a language had single nouns refer exclusively to pairs of thematically related objects, it would be at great cost. The enormous expressive power of language would be lost. The expressive power of language derives from its ability to convey new relations through combinations of words. There are a potentially infinite number of thematic relations that one might want to express. The many thematic relations can easily be described through combinations of words—for example, sentences and phrases. If single words referred only to thematic relations, however, there would be an extraordinary proliferation of words, probably more than humans could learn. One would need separate words for a baby and its bottle, a baby and its crib, a baby and its mother, a baby and its diaper, and so on. Thus, the combinatorial power of language would be wasted. This, then, may be the major reason why nouns refer primarily to taxonomic categories rather than to thematically related objects.

In conclusion, young children possess the knowledge that single nouns are more likely to refer to objects that share perceptual or functional properties than to objects associated by their participation in a common event or theme. This knowledge helps explain how children acquire new words. By constraining the meaning of a term to categorical relations, children are able to rule out a huge number of other potential meanings for any given term. For example, suppose an adult points to a cup and says *cup*. With no constraints on possible meanings, a child would have to consider that *cup* might mean *the cup is on the table,* because the cup was on the table, or *coffee in the cup,* because the cup was filled with coffee, or *mother lifting the cup,* because mother was lifting the cup. All of these relational meanings would be eliminated from consideration by the constraint that nouns refer to object categories. By limiting the number and kind of hypotheses that children need to consider, this constraint tremendously simplifies the problem of language learning.

HIERARCHICAL ORGANIZATION OF CATEGORIES

In this past section, I argued that children's knowledge of natural language helps them acquire category terms. I now turn to the problem of how children organize categories with respect to each other, in particular, into hierarchically organized class-inclusion relations. Here too, I argue that children's knowledge of natural language can help them to structure categories into hierarchical systems, but in a quite different way.

On striking characteristic of human categories is that they tend to be organized into systems in which the categories are related to each other in various ways rather than each concept's being represented in isolation. Many categories form hierarchies that consist of more and more general levels of categorization (e.g., delicious apple, apple, fruit, food; poodle, dog, mammal, animal). It is the systematic organization of categories that Callanan and I argued (Markman & Callanan, in press) to be the major intellectual achievement of human conceptualization.

Assuming hierarchical organization is a major intellectual achievement, one needs to consider what would count as evidence that someone had represented categories hierarchically. The minimal criterion would be that the child can recognize that an object that can be seen to be at one level of categorization—for example, a chair—is also a member of a more general category—for example, furniture. The problem with this criterion is that it is trivially fulfilled by any concept whatsoever. The minimal criterion for simply having a concept is that discriminably different objects be treated as similar. For example, a pigeon who can tell the difference between large and small circles yet learns to peck at all circles to receive a reward would have the concept *circle*. This pigeon could be said to know that a given object is a large circle and that it is a circle and would therefore be credited with understanding inclusion on this criterion.

In the example with circles, both levels of the hierarchy are given perceptually. That is, the fact that the object is a large circle and that it is a circle can both be seen by inspecting the object. Perhaps one should require that one level of categorization be nonperceptually based. However, the nonperceptual criterion also fails to differentiate between a true understanding of inclusion and a trivial one. First, even animals have nonperceptually based concepts. For example, omnivorous animals have a concept of edible object that includes berries and small animals. These animals would therefore automatically be credited with understanding class inclusion. Second, a child could rote memorize instances of a category, such as *furniture* or *animal*, without understanding the hierarchical organization.

What is required is evidence that the child understands the inclusion relation and not just that the child can apply two labels to the same object. Someone who understands class inclusion should show some appreciation of what the relation entails. Inclusion is an asymmetric transitive relation. The asymmetry of the relation means that if a class A is included in a class B, then all of the members of A are members of the more general class B, but not vice versa. To take a concrete example, if a child understands the relation between dogs and animals, he or she should know that all dogs are animals and that not all animals are dogs. The transitivity of the relations means that if class A is included in class B and if class B is included in class C, then class A is included in class C. If someone understood the transitivity of the relation, then from all dachshunds are dogs, they should be able to conclude that all dachshunds are animals. Further, if one knows a property is true of the more general category—for example, that all dogs bark—then one should be able to conclude that the class included also has the property—for example, that all dachsunds bark. The converse, however, is not true. From all dogs have claws, one cannot conclude that all animals have claws.

To summarize, simply being able to categorize the same object in two different levels of a hierarchy is only a very primitive form of hierarchical organization. That criterion is trivially satisfied by any concept at all. What seems to be required before we can conclude that someone has a hierarchical organization is evidence for understanding that the relation between the categories is an asymmetric and a transitive one.

With these criteria in mind, Callanan and I (Markman & Callanan, in press) reviewed the literature. We found that only a very few studies have directly examined children's understanding of the asymmetry and transitivity of inclusion. However, an enormous amount of research has been conducted to study the conceptual organization of young children. According to some studies it is not until children are 7 or 8 years old that they show evidence of hierarchical organization. Yet according to other studies, even infants show abilities to classify objects into taxonomic categories. Obviously, depending on the difficulty of the task one selects to measure classification abilities, performance will vary. But what we were especially concerned with was whether or not the studies provide evidence for an appreciation of inclusion. Several different types of procedures used to study classification have been used. Some of the tasks, for example the Piagetian class-inclusion problem and object-sorting tasks, are overly demanding. That is, a child could fully understand the asymmetric transitive nature of class inclusion and still fail these problems. Other tasks used to measure classification, such as habituation studies of infants or or memory procedures used with preschoolers, are overly lenient. That is, a child could solve these problems without genuinely understanding inclusion.

From these studies, Callanan and I concluded that there was little evidence for infants' or very young children's understanding of inclusion. Children may have only a fragmentary grasp of the asymmetry and transitivity of inclusion by 4 or 5 years of age. On the other hand, there is evidence from work contrasting collections and classes that when the asymmetry of the relations is made more salient, as in the part–whole structure of collections, children become better able to deal with hierarchical organization.

COLLECTIONS VERSUS CLASSES AS HIERARCHICAL ORGANIZATION

I turn now to describe work that has contrasted the hierarchical structure of classes with a different type of hierarchical structure: the part–whole structure of collections. Collections are the referents of collective nouns—for example, forest, pile, family, army—and they are structured into part–whole hierarchies—for example, a tree is part of a forest, a block is part of a pile, a child is part of a family, and so on. I argue that collections form a simpler hierarchy for children to deal with because the asymmetry of part–whole relations is easier to maintain than that of class inclusion.

One of the reasons that the asymmetry of collections may be easier to maintain than that of classes is that the two levels of a collection hierarchy are clearly distinct, whereas the levels of a class-inclusion hierarchy are more similar, and thus more confusable. For class inclusion, both levels of the hierarchy involve the same *is a* relation. A poodle *is a* dog and *is an* animal. This may contribute to the child's confusion of levels and difficulty in keeping track of the asymmetry. For part–whole structures, the relations differ at the two hierarchical levels. A boy *is a* child but is *part of* a family. An oak *is a* tree but is *part of* a forest. If there were less confusion between part and whole than between subclass and superclass, then the asymmetrical relations of collections would have greater psychological stability and would not so readily degenerate into symmetrical relations.

Because collections are predicted to help children maintain the asymmetry of the hierarchy, one might think that collections should also help children appreciate transitivity. This does not follow, however, because the part–whole relations of collections are not transitive. A property true of the whole will not necessarily be true of the part. For example, if we know that the family is large, it does not follow that the child in the family is large. If we know that a pile of bricks is U-shaped, it does not follow that the bricks in the pile are U-shaped. Because the two levels of the collection hierarchy are defined by different relations, transitivity is violated but the asymmetry should be simpler for children to establish and maintain.

Here are some further ways in which these two types of hierarchies differ:

1. *How Membership is Determined:* Membership in a class can be determined by evaluating an object against the defining criteria of the class. To know whether an object is a toy block, for example, one must examine it for its size, shape, material, or function, and so on. To know whether an object is a member of a collection, however, one needs to know something about its relationship to other members of the collection. To determine whether a block is part of a pile of blocks, for example, one must examine its relation to other blocks in the pile. Although spatial proximity is not necessary for membership in a family, a team, or a club, some type of relationship is still required.

2. *The Nature of their Part–Whole Relation:* Collections have more literal part–whole relations than do classes. A dog, for example, is a kind of (or type of or example of) an animal, not part of an animal. In contrast, children are parts of families, not kinds of (or types of or examples of) families.

3. *Internal Structure and the Nature of the Whole Formed:* The internal structure of collections results in their greater psychological coherence compared to classes. Collections have an internal organization that results in a coherent structure. A random set of people does not make a family. To be a family, the people must be related to each other. Intuitively it seems fairly natural to consider a family, a pile, or a crowd as a single thing. English captures this intuition in that collective nouns are singular in form.

To summarize, collections and classes are both hierarchically organized concepts but they differ in their structural principles. The part–whole structure of collections is a type of relational structure that confers psychological coherence on the higher-order aggregate formed and may thereby enhance the asymmetry of the relation. If this analysis is correct, then organizing items into collections should help children solve problems that require dealing with two levels of the hierarchy at the same time. I summarize some of this work later in this chapter, but for a more complete discussion see Markman (1981).

The Piagetian Class-Inclusion Problem

Some evidence for the greater coherence of collections over classes comes from work on the Piagetian class-inclusion problem, in which children are asked to make a quantitative comparison between a superordinate set and the larger of its subordinate sets (Inhelder & Piaget, 1964). For example, a child might be shown pictures of five boys and three girls and be asked: "Are there more boys or more children?" Although children are asked to make a part–whole comparison (boys versus children) they make part–part (boys versus girls) comparisons instead. In devising this task, Inhelder and Piaget were concerned, in part, with children's abilities to recognize the asymmetry of class inclusion—for example, that all boys are children but that not all children are boys. To answer the class-inclusion question correctly, children must maintain the whole class in mind while simultaneously attending to its subclasses. This division of the superordinate class into subordinate classes strains children's ability to keep the whole class in mind. If part–whole relations of collections are easier for children to represent, then children should be better able to keep the whole class in mind even while focusing on the parts.

In several studies, children have consistently revealed a superior ability to make part–whole comparisons with collections than with classes (Markman, 1973; Markman & Seibert, 1976). In each of the studies, the objects children viewed and the questions they were asked in the two conditions were identical. The only difference in the two conditions was in the description given the higher level of the hierarchy. As one example, for the "boys–children" comparison in the class condition, children were told, "Here are some kindergarten children. These are the boys and these are girls and these are the children." They were then asked, "Who would have a bigger birthday party, someone who invited the boys or someone who invited the children?" As usual, young children often answered incorrectly, claiming that there were more boys. The collection version of this question was identical except that "kindergarten children" was changed to "kindergarten class" (note that *class* is a collection term). So the question became, "Who would have a bigger birthday party, someone who invited the boys or someone who invited the class?" With this change of how the higher-level category was labeled, children became better able to solve the part–whole comparison that they usually find so difficult. For further discussion of this work and some possible objections, see Markman and Callanan (in press).

Cardinal Number

The studies summarized here demonstrate that children are better able to deal with cardinal number when objects are conceptualized as belonging to collections rather than classes. The argument here is that dealing with cardinal number implicitly requires a part–whole analysis and that children should be better able to solve number problems when they conceptualize the objects as organized into the part–whole structure of collections.

The cardinal number of a given set of items is not a property of the individual items themselves. Number is a property of the set taken as a whole and not a property of the elements that compose the set. To see why, consider the following syllogism: "Men are numerous. John is a man. Therefore, John is numerous." The syllogism is absurd because numerosity does not distribute over each element of a set, but is a characteristic of sets themselves. To take another example, "There are five books" does not imply that any one of the books is five. "Five" applies only to the group, not to the individuals in it. Of course, one cannot ignore individual members when calculating the numerical value of a set. Individuals must be counted or otherwise enumerated—that is, the "parts" must be noticed. But it is not enough to focus on just the individuals; one must also consider the set taken as a whole. Because collections should promote conceptualization of individual objects as aggregates and because cardinal number applies to aggregates, not individuals, collections should facilitate numerical reasoning about discrete objects. There are many well-known problems that young children have in dealing with cardinal number (e.g., number conservation). Young children should be better able to solve these problems when the objects are thought of as collections rather than classes. This hypothesis was investigated in several studies (Markman, 1979) that focused on different aspects of a full appreciation of cardinal number. I summarize some of the findings here, but see Markman (1979) for a complete discussion.

Number Conservation: Understanding the Irrelevance of a Length Transformation. In the standard conservation task (Piaget, 1965) two equal rows of pennies, or other items, are lined up in one-to-one correspondence. A 4- to 5-year-old child will judge the rows to be equal. One of the rows is spread out in front of the child, who then typically judges that the lengthened row now has more pennies, though no pennies have been added or subtracted from either row. A child must correctly interpret the original judgment in terms of number and must attend to number per se throughout the physical transformation in order to realize that the quantities remain the same. Collection labels, by making it easier for children to think about the aggregate and thus about number, might help them to conserve.

This hypothesis was tested by having 4-year-old children solve conservation problems in which the objects were given either class or collection labels. Half of the children received class questions and half received collection questions. Each child was given four conservation problems. The only difference between conditions was that a collection label (e.g., *army*) was substituted for a class label (e.g., *soldiers*) for the rows. For example, a child in the class condition saw two rows of soldiers lined up in one-to-one correspondence and heard: "These are your soldiers and these are my soldiers. What are more: my soldiers, your soldiers, or are they both the same?'' A child in the collection condition saw the identical two rows and heard: "This is your army and this is my army. What's more: my army, your army, or are they both the same?'' Then in both conditions, the experimenter spread out one of the rows and repeated the question.

The children in the two conditions were presented with identical perceptual information and were asked virtually identical questions. Yet, simply relabeling the objects as collections helped children to conserve. Children hearing the objects described as classes answered correctly an average of only 1.46 out of four problems. Children hearing objects described as collections correctly answered an average of 3.18 problems.

Understanding the Relevance of Addition and Subtraction.   The study reported next addressed whether children who have heard objects described as collections would be more likely to realize that the addition or subtraction of an object does in fact change the number.

After a child has seen someone add or subtract an object from one row, he or she will strongly tend to judge that two initially equal rows differ. Even in the standard conservation task, children judge that the rows are different when the rows are, in fact, the same. When an object is actually added or subtracted from a row children will certainly judge the rows to differ. Now, however, "different" is the correct answer, so children could respond correctly without attending to number per se. One way to determine whether or not children base a judgment on number is to examine their justifications for their responses.

Four-year-old children were asked to solve addition and subtraction problems in which the objects were given either class or collection labels. Half of the children were in the class condition and half were in the collection condition. The procedure in this study was identical to the conservation procedure in the previous study except that instead of lengthening a row, the experimenter added or subtracted an object from a row.

As expected, after witnessing an addition or subtraction, children in both conditions almost always judged that the two rows were no longer equivalent. However, differences emerged once children's justifications were taken into account. The main difference was that children in the collection condition based their answers on numerically relevant information relatively more often, whereas children in the class condition gave relatively more irrelevant explanations.

The Cardinality Principle.   Three- and 4-year-old children are generally able to count an array of five toys. However, when they are then asked, "How many toys are there?" they often count again rather than answering "five." This is a reflection of the child's difficulty with the cardinality principle, the failure to appreciate that the last number counted becomes the cardinal number of the set (Gelman & Gallistel, 1978; Schaeffer, Eggleston, & Scott, 1974). If part of the child's problem with the cardinality principle is a difficulty in thinking of the individual items as a set to which cardinal number applies, then helping the child think of the arrays as collections might promote correct use of this principle.

Three- and 4-year-olds participated in a study designed to test this hypothesis. Half of the children were assigned to the class condition and half to the collection condition. In both conditions children viewed some objects, were instructed to count the objects, and then were asked how many objects there were.

When children heard a class description—for example, "Here are some pigs, count the pigs"—they counted "one, two, three, four, five." When they were then asked, "How many pigs are there?" they tended to count again, "One, two, three, four, five." In marked contrast, when children in the collection condition heard, for example, "Here is a pig family, count the pigs in the family," they counted. But when asked, "How many pigs are in the family?" they very often correctly responded "five."

In summary, I have argued that number is a property of a set of objects and not of objects themselves. If thinking about individuals as collections helps children focus on the aggregate as well as on the individual, it should thus facilitate numerical reasoning. As predicted, thinking of objects as collections helped children solve numerical problems they otherwise would have failed. It helped them conserve number in the face of an irrelevant change. It helped them access and verbalize a numerically relevant basis for their judgments of equality and of difference and it promoted their use of the cardinality principle.

Learning Hierarchical Relations

In the previous studies on the Piagetian class-inclusion problem and on cardinal number, the experimenter determined what type of organization the child should impose on the objects by labeling the array for the child. These studies found that the part–whole structure of collections is easier for children to represent and deal with than the class-inclusion relations. In the studies reported now, we did not manipulate the organization ourselves, but rather examined what kind of organization children would impose on their own. If children find the structure of collections simpler than that of class inclusion, then they might organize objects into collections rather than classes when they need to construct a hierarchy. If so, this would run counter to what one would expect based on the familiarity or frequency of words in English. Class terms are far more frequent in the language and children must have encountered many more of them. Although collective nouns are scarce relative to class terms, it still could be that the collection hierarchy is easier for children to construct. When children are relatively free to impose their own structures on novel hierarchies, they might prefer collections to class organizations.

This hypothesis was tested by contriving a situation in which children were presented with only minimal information about a hierarchical relation (Markman, Horton, & McLanahan, 1980). This study was designed to see how children would spontaneously interpret the relations when given relative freedom. In actuality, the relations were novel class-inclusion hierarchies, analogous to the relations between oaks, pines, and trees. Ostensive definition (pointing and labeling) was used to achieve a minimal specification of the relationship. To illustrate, imagine that oaks and pines are lined up in a row in front of the child. As the experimenter points to the oaks, he says, ''These are oaks,''; as he points to the pines, he says, ''These are pines.''; and as he points to the trees, he says, ''These are trees.'' When he described trees in the plural—''these are trees''—it means that each individual tree is a tree. Thus the use of the plural establishes the class-inclusion relation. The singular would have to be used to establish a collection—for example, ''This is a forest.'' Though the ostensive definition provides only minimal information, it does establish that the objects presented form a class-inclusion hierarchy.

Suppose children misinterpret the class-inclusion relation as a collection hierarchy. What errors should they make? They should erroneously believe that several of the items together form an instance of the concept at the higher level of the hierarchy (trees in the example) and should not believe that any single item is an instance. To see why, consider what the correct response would be had children actually learned a collection—for example, *forest*. If asked to point to the forest, the child should point to many trees but should deny that a pine or any other single tree is itself a forest.

Children from 6 to 17 years old participated in the study. Each child learned four novel categories, one at a time, each composed of two subcategories. All of the category exemplars were small construction-paper figures of novel shapes or novel animate figures. Nonsense syllables were used as names for the novel figures.

The results of this study revealed that children, until a surprisingly late age, tend to misinterpret class-inclusion relations as collections when only minimal information is provided. When novel class-inclusion relations were taught by ostensive definition, children as old as 14 often mistakenly interpreted the relations as collections. When asked what would be analogous to ''Show me a pine,'' children correctly picked up a single pine. When the experimenter, while pointing to a pine, asked, ''Is this a pine?'' children responded correctly. The errors occurred almost exclusively on the upper level of the hierarchy. When asked, ''Show me a tree,'' children scooped up a handful rather than just one. When the experimenter, while pointing to a tree asked, ''Is this a tree?'' children often said ''No.'' This is exactly as one would expect if children were answering questions about a collection.

Because collections form more stable hierarchies, it may be easier for children to keep the two levels of the hierarchy distinct. At least in the somewhat artificial conditions of the present study, children found it simpler to impose a collection structure on a novel hierarchy than to correctly interpret it as inclusion. This is true even though children must certainly have more experience learning inclusion relations, because collective nouns are relatively rare. Because this was an unusual way to learn novel concepts, collection errors may be unlikely in natural situations. However, there is some anecdotal (Valentine, 1942) and experimental (Macnamara, 1982) evidence suggesting that such errors may be found in a naturalistic context. Callanan and I have conducted more controlled studies to investigate this possibility (Callanan & Markman, 1982). We questioned 2- and 3-year-old children about five categories: toys (balls and dolls), animals (horses and cows), drinks (milk and juice), children (boys and girls), and cars (racing cars and Volkswagens). In general there was a very low error rate, in part because these category terms were pretested to ensure that children knew them (in the plural). However, there was a significant tendency for children to interpret the terms as collections. Children agree, for example, that a set of toys is toys, but deny that a single toy (a doll, for example) is itself a toy and they pick up several toys when asked for one. These findings suggest that in first acquiring superordinate terms, young children distort some class-inclusion relations into collections. Thus, even in naturally occurring contexts, very young children may find it simpler to impose a collection structure on what are actually inclusion hierarchies they are trying to learn.

The Role of Language in Helping Children Construct Hierarchies

These findings suggest that if superordinate category terms were represented by collective nouns, then children would find them easier to learn. But collective nouns cannot themselves serve as superordinate terms for the very reason that they express a different relation. And this difference is extremely important when one considers the function of taxonomies. One of the main purposes of taxonomies is to support inductive and deductive inferences. For example, if I know something that is true of all mammals (e.g., that they breathe, eat, are warm blooded, and so on), once I learn that a previously unfamiliar animal is a mammal I can transfer all of this knowledge to the newly learned animal. Collections do not support inferences in the same way. Properties true of the forest may not be true of individual trees. Nor will similarities that exist between the trees allow an inductive inference that the properties will also be true of the forest. Thus, although the part–whole organization of collections is simpler for children to learn, it is not a useful substitute for the inclusion relation that defines taxonomies. Mass nouns, however, may provide an appropriate substitute for collective nouns.

Many superordinate category terms in English are mass nouns (e.g., *furniture, jewelry, money*) though conceptually they refer to diverse, discrete, countable objects. This violates the common intuition that mass terms refer to masslike, homogeneous substances, such as milk or clay, or to substances made of small, virtually identical particles, such as sand or grass. That is, the homogeneity of the substance and the difficulty of individuating elements of the substance characterize the semantic basis of many typical mass terms. Yet, *furniture,* for example, refers to heterogeneous, readily individuated objects. I argue for a functional explanation for this violation of the semantic basis of mass terms. There are, however, many other exceptions to this oversimplified semantic rule (cf. Gordon, 1981) that may reflect only unprincipled vagaries of English. For example, some (but not all) abstract concepts are referred to by mass nouns (e.g., justice); some seemingly countable objects are referred to by mass nouns (e.g., toast, paper); and some substances are referred to by mass nouns (e.g., gravel), whereas some very similar substances are referred to by count nouns (e.g., pebbles). There may not be any cogent explanation for all of these idiosyncrasies. But I argue that the exception for superordinate categories is a principled one.

By referring to superordinate categories as mass nouns, languages may help speakers learn hierarchical relations between the superordinate and lower-level categories. Mass nouns may, like collective nouns, help keep the top level of a hierarchy more stable and distinct but, unlike collective nouns, they may be able to accomplish this while still maintaining a taxonomic organization. In a sense, mass nouns can be viewed as a compromise between collections and classes, or, to be more precise, as a compromise between *part–whole* and *is a* relations. Consider a typical mass such as clay. A piece of clay is part of the whole mass of clay. This is similar to the part–whole organization of collections, in which each tree, for example, is part of the forest. On the other hand, each piece of clay is itself clay. This is more like the *is a* relation of class inclusion, in which each oak is a tree.

By referring to discrete objects with mass terms, a language might be able to provide some of the stability that the part–whole organization of collections would have achieved, yet remind the speaker that an inclusion relation is still involved.

This analysis predicts that this peculiarity should not be limited to English. Other languages with a count–mass distinction should also have this type of aberration. Further, if these aberrations serve the purpose of helping to give stability to hierarchically organized categories, then such "inappropriate" mass terms should occur mainly on superordinate or relatively high levels of the hierarchy, not on relatively low levels. That is, languages should contain terms that require one to say "a piece of furniture" or "a piece of vehicle" when one wants to refer to a single piece of furniture or a single vehicle. But they should not require speakers to say "a piece of chair" or "a piece of car" when one wants to refer to a single chair or a single car. This hypothesis was tested in Markman (1983) by asking native speakers of various languages to judge whether terms were count nouns or mass nouns in their languages.

All of the participants in this study were speakers of English as a second language. Informants were asked to translate English category terms into their

TABLE 13.3
Number of Languages
($N = 19$) Treating
Each Superordinate Term as a
Mass Noun

Term	Number of Languages
Money	17
Food	16
Clothing	13
Furniture	11
Reading material	11
Sports equipment	11
Jewelry	10
Silverware	9
Fruit	9
Vegetable	9
Footwear	6
Headgear	6
Linen	5
Weapon	6
Human dwelling	6
Tools	5
People	5[a]
Toy	2[a]
Building	1
Musical instrument	2
Flowers	1
Vehicle	1[a]
Tree	0
Animal	0
Bird	0

[a]One additional language had an optional mass usage.

native languages and to judge whether or not the terms could be used in a phrase in which the objects were counted directly, such as "two pencils," or whether they required a quantificational phrase, as in "two cups of sugar." Informants were asked to translate terms for 25 higher-level categories that are relatively common in English. All of the object categories that appeared in Rosch et al. (1976) and Rosch (1975) that fulfilled Rosch's criteria of superordinate categories were used in this study. Several other high-level categories were added. The left-hand column of Table 13.3 presents these categories. For each of these 25 categories, two lower-level terms were also selected to be translated. One lower-level category was selected to be a very common, high frequency, exemplar, whereas the other was somewhat less frequent. So, for example, for the category

TABLE 13.4
Number of Languages (*N* = 19) Treating Each Lower-Level Term as
a Mass Noun

Term	Number of Languages	Term	Number of Languages
Dollar	0	Towel	0
Penny	0	Gun	0
Egg	0	Sword	0
Shirt	0	House	0
Belt	0	Apartment	0
Chair	0	Hammer	0
Mirror	0	Saw	0
Book	0	Man	0
Magazine	0	Woman	0
Ball	0	Doll	0
Racquet	0	Church	0
Ring	0	School	0
Bracelet	0	Piano	0
Fork	0	Guitar	0
Spoon	0	Rose	0
Apple	1	Daisy	0
Melon	1	Car	0
Carrot	2	Airplane	0
Onion	2	Oak	1
Shoe	0	Palm	0
Skate	0	Dog	0
Hat	0	Pig	0
Scarf	0	Robin	0
Sheet	0	Eagle	0

vegetable informants would judge whether *carrot* and *onion* were mass or count nouns in their native languages. Due to an error, two terms were omitted, leaving 48 rather than 50 lower-level judgments. Thus, there were almost twice as many opportunities for lower-level terms to be judged as mass nouns as for superordinate terms. Table 13.4 presents the 48 lower-level categories used, arranged to correspond to the higher-level categories of Table 13.3.

Table 13.5 presents the languages that were included in this study, classified according to their language family and subgroup. Nineteen languages, at least 11 different subgroups, and seven different language families were represented (Katzner, 1975; Voegelin & Voegelin, 1977). American Sign Language (ASL) was included in the sample. It should be noted that the superordinate terms in ASL are not finger-spelled English terms. Quite often they are compound signs such as *knife–fork* for *silverware* (Newport & Bellugi, 1978).

The results of this study strongly support a functional explanation for why superordinate terms are often mass nouns. As can be seen in Table 13.5, in every

TABLE 13.5
Percentage of Superordinate and Basic-Level Terms That Are Mass
Nouns in Each Language

Family	Subgroup	Branch	Language	Higher-Level Category	Lower-Level Category
Indo European	Germanic	Western	Afrikaans	44	0
Indo European	Germanic	Western	Dutch	48	0
Indo European	Germanic	Western	English	48	0
Indo European	Germanic	Western	German	40	0
Indo European	Romance		French	36	0
Indo European	Hellenic		Greek	16	0
Indo European	Slavic	Eastern	Ukranian	16	0
Indo European	Indo-Iranian		Urdue	44	0
Uralic	Finno-Ugric	Finnic	Finnish	16	0
	Finno-Ugric	Ugric	Hungarian	24	0
Altaic	Turkic	Southwestern	Turkish	44	0
Independent			Japanese	28	0
			Korean	24	0
Afro-Asiatic	Semitic	North Arabic	Arabic	44	2
		Camanitic	Hebrew	20	0
African			Guro	32	8
			Nzema	20	0
—	—	—	American Sign Language	68	4
Mean Percent				34	0.7

language family, in every language subgroup, and, in fact, in every language, some superordinate categories were represented by mass nouns. In marked contrast, lower-level category terms are almost always represented by count nouns. Overall, languages represented an average of 34% of the superordinate categories as mass nouns. In marked contrast, languages represented an average of less than 1% of the lower-level terms as mass nouns. Every one of the 19 languages studied had more superordinate terms as mass nouns than lower-level terms as mass nouns.

Table 13.3 presents the number of languages out of 19 that represented each of the 25 superordinate categories as a mass noun. With the exception of *tree, animal,* and *bird,* every superordinate category was represented by a mass noun in at least one language. In contrast, as can be seen in Table 13.4, of the 48 lower-level category terms, only 5 were treated as mass nouns in any language.

In summary, these findings reveal a striking tendency for languages to refer to higher-level but not lower-level categories with mass nouns. Moreover, the procedure used probably underestimated the magnitude of the effect. Although the 25 category terms selected were familiar to English-speaking cultures, they were not always important in other cultures. For example, there were 13 categories with no translation into Nzema; 10 with no translation into Ukranian; 7 with no translation into Turkish. Thus, the proportion of superordinate categories that were mass nouns is greater when considered as a proportion of the easily translatable categories than as a proportion of the total number of categories. If superordinate categories had been selected that were more frequent in these various cultures, even more of them may have been referred to by mass nouns.

This study established that it is not just English that refers to superordinate categories with mass nouns. There is a systematic tendency across languages to use mass nouns to refer to these categories. This finding provides indirect support for the hypothesis that having superordinate categories referred to by mass nouns should help speakers learn the categories. A second study in Markman (1983) tested the hypothesis more directly by comparing how well children learn a new category when it is labeled by a mass versus a count noun. Preschool children were taught a new superordinate category for familiar objects. For example, they were taught the new category *vehicle* for a bicycle, a boat, a plane, and a firetruck. There were two training conditions. In one, the category was referred to with a mass noun, in the other with a count noun. Otherwise the training procedures and categories taught were identical. The prediction is that children who hear, for example, *A car is a piece of vehicle, This (a boat, a plane, a bicycle, and a firetruck) is some vehicle,* and *How much vehicle is here?* should be better able to learn the category than children who hear, *A car is a vehicle, These (a boat, a plane, a bicycle, and a firetruck) are vehicles,* and *How many vehicles are here?*

Four-year-old children participated in this study. These children are quite young to be taught superordinate-level categories. They may be the youngest children who both understand the basic object categories well enough to begin to learn superordinate-level categories and who could master the mass–count distinction. Three and 4 year olds were selected because the procedure was feasible with them and there is evidence that children this young can learn the mass–count distinction even when it is taught as a syntactic distinction—that is, without semantic support (Gordon, 1981).

Children were taught one of three categories: *sports equipment, vehicles,* or *bathroom supplies.* Four exemplars were used to first teach the category. For example, for the category *sports equipment* children were shown a racquet, a helmet, a hockey stick, and a baseball mitt. In the subsequent tests children were shown new exemplars and distractors for each category. Some of the exemplars were very similar to the training exemplars—for example, a different helmet. Some of the exemplars were novel—for example a soccer ball. Some of the distractors were designed to be simple to reject—that is, they were quite distinct from the category exemplars—whereas others were designed to be more difficult to distinguish from the exemplars.

Children were introduced to a puppet and they were told that the puppet was going to play a game with them in which she would teach them a special puppet word for some of the pictures they would see. Children were given training to learn the new category, were tested on their ability to distinguish category exemplars from distractors, were retrained, and then were retested. The only difference between the two conditions was that children in the mass noun condition always heard the new term (a nonsense syllable) used as a mass noun whereas children in the count noun condition always heard the new word used as a count noun. To illustrate, if the new word was *veb* and the category was bathroom supplies, some of the training items for the two conditions were: (1) the puppet would point to the four exemplars (soap, shampoo, comb, and toothpaste) and say *This is veb* for children in the mass noun condition and *These are vebs* for children in the count noun condition; (2) the puppet would point to several of the items, saying *Here are some pieces of veb* for the mass noun condition and *Here are some vebs* for the count noun condition; (3) the puppet would ask *How much veb is here?* for children in the mass noun condition and *How many vebs are here?* for children in the count noun condition.

In general, these 4-year-old children found these superordinate categories difficult to learn. This is to be expected given the well-known difficulty that young children have with superordinate categories and that this procedure provided only minimal training. Nevertheless, having the categories encoded by mass nouns rather than count nouns helped children learn them. Although the effects were small, children who heard mass nouns were significantly better able to discriminate category exemplars from distractors, especially after the second training session. These findings were replicated in a similar study reported in Markman (1983).

To summarize, I observed that in English many superordinate categories are referred to by mass nouns although conceptually they encompass discrete countable objects. Why should we have to say *two pieces of jewelry* instead of *two jewelries* or *two pieces of furniture* instead of *two furnitures?* The argument is that this construction is not just an accident of English but instead may have evolved to help speakers learn and represent hierarchically organized category terms. This hypothesis derives from the findings with collective nouns that demonstrated that children find part–whole hierarchies of collections simpler than class-inclusion hierarchies. Collective nouns could not, however, serve as superordinate terms in a language because they form a different type of hierarchical structure. Mass nouns can be viewed as a type of compromise between collective and count nouns. A piece of clay is part of the mass of clay (as a tree is part of a forest) but a piece of clay is itself clay (as an oak is a tree). Thus mass nouns can encode superordinate categories in a way that simplifies the hierarchical representation yet remains faithful to the inclusion relation.

The hypothesis here is that children rely on the mass nouns as a way of bootstrapping a class-inclusion hierarchy from a part–whole hierarchy. Children can first work out the asymmetry of the hierarchical structure based on the simpler part-whole organization and then use the similarity of the objects at both levels to draw the relevant transitive inferences.

If there is a psychological explanation for why superordinate category terms become distorted into mass nouns, then it should not be limited to English. Languages that have a count–mass distinction should tend to represent superordinate category terms as mass nouns even though this violates the semantic basis of mass nouns. An examination of 19 languages, spanning several distinct language families and subgroups, confirmed this prediction. The tendency to use mass nouns as category terms was limited to the higher-level categories, as it should be if it were to help speakers learn the hierarchy.

Two training studies provided a more direct test of the hypothesis. Four-year-old children were taught superordinate categories in one of two ways: the category was labeled with either a mass noun or a count noun. In every other respect the training procedure used and the categories taught were identical in the two conditions. As expected for children this young, they found it difficult to learn these superordinate-level categories. Yet, in two studies, children were better able to learn a category when it was labeled with a mass noun than when it was labeled with a count noun. Thus, for example, children were better able to learn the category *vehicle* when they heard statements such as: *A bus is a piece of vehicle.* and *How much vehicle is here?* than when they heard *A bus is a vehicle.* and *How many vehicles are here?*

Taken together, the results from these three studies indicate that languages tend to use mass nouns to refer to superordinate categories because it helps children to learn them. In other words, children can capitalize on their knowledge of the count–mass distinction to help them organize categories into hierarchies.

GENERAL DISCUSSION

In this chapter, I have considered two ways in which children's knowledge of natural language can help them acquire and organize categorical knowledge. The first way is that children place constraints on possible word meanings. In a neutral context, children find thematic relations of interest, often of greater interest than categorical similarity, focusing, for example, on relations such as a spider and its web, or a boy and his bike. Yet, they acquire many words referring to categories. Children are able to acquire category terms despite their interest in thematic relations, in part because they limit the possible meanings of nouns to refer to categorically related items (Markman & Hutchinson, 1984). So when hearing a new word, a child supresses the tendency to look for thematic relations and looks for categorical relations instead.

The second way in which children's knowledge of natural language helps in acquiring category knowledge is in the construction of hierarchically structured class-inclusion relations. Children rely on their knowledge of mass nouns to bootstrap their way into hierarchical relations. I argued that this is why so many superordinate-category terms are mass nouns—for example, *furniture, clothing, food,* and *fruit.* There is a substantial amount of evidence that children find the part–whole hierarchies of collections (e.g., a tree is part of a forest) simpler to represent and understand than the inclusion relation of classes (e.g., an oak is a tree). Very young children may even misrepresent high-level category terms as collections. If superordinate categories could be encoded by collective nouns, children would find them easier to learn. Collective nouns could not serve as superordinate terms, however, because they do not allow for the transitive inferences important in a taxonomy. That is, something true of the whole will not necessarily be true of the parts. Yet one of the major functions of taxonomies is to support such transitive inferences so that something true of the more general class (e.g., mammals) will be true of more specific classes within it (e.g., dogs). Mass nouns would be effective superordinate terms because they are a hybrid of collective and count nouns. That is, mass nouns refer to a part–whole structure as do collective nouns (e.g., a piece of clay is part of the whole mass of clay), but they also encode an *is a* relation as do count nouns (e.g., a piece of clay is itself clay). In the special case of mass nouns, therefore, properties of the whole can be transmitted to the parts. Thus, children's knowledge of the count–mass distinction helps them organize categories into hierarchies.

These two ways in which natural language helps children acquire categories need to be reconciled and integrated with each other. The argument about mass nouns is based on children's preferences for a collectionlike organization. Collections defined by their part–whole structures are a kind of relational concept. To be sure, they are a relation defined on similar objects—for example, trees in a forest, soldiers in an army—and not objects as diverse as a baby and its bottle, or a dog and its bone. But they are relational nonetheless. By the argument that Hutchinson and I made earlier, one would expect children to avoid interpreting category labels in this way. Yet, when children work out hierarchical categories they may first consider this kind of relational concept, although it is important to keep in mind that it is a relation uniting similar objects.

We can make sense of this problem by considering a developmental progression in the kinds of problems children are trying to solve. In the first case, children are trying to acquire a single new category. In the second case, children are attempting to work out a hierarchical relation between categories, one of which they have already interpreted as having a categorical organization.

To clarify the problem, I would like to make explicit two assumptions that I believe children make when first acquiring category terms:

1. *The Assumption of Categorical Relations.* Children assume that category terms refer to objects that are similar or like each other in some way, rather than to objects organized thematically. This is the assumption tested by Markman and Hutchinson (1984).

2. *The Assumption of Mutual Exclusivity.* Children assume that category terms will tend to be mutually exclusive. It would be reasonable for children to make this assumption. First, in order for categories to be useful they will tend to

exclude each other to a fair degree. If an object could be a member of just about any category, then the categories would tell us little about the objects. In contrast, to the extent that categories are informative about objects, to the extent that they contain much correlated information, they tend to be mutually exclusive. For example, an object cannot be a cat *and* a dog or a bird or a horse, and so on. Thus, categories tend to be mutually exclusive, especially at the basic level of categorization. Moreover, it is the basic-level category terms such as *dog,* and *apple,* and *car* that children tend to learn first. Only after acquiring basic-level terms do they then learn subordinate and superordinate categories. Inspection of early vocabulary norms (e.g., Goldin-Meadow, Seligman, & Gelman, 1976) reveals that they consist of object category labels that are largely mutually exclusive.

There is, however, tension between these two principles and the hierarchical organization of categories. In a class-inclusion hierarchy, of course, one category is included in another and both category names can refer to the same object. That is, the subordinate and superordinate categories are not mutually exclusive in such a hierarchy.

From the child's point of view, then, class-inclusion hierarchies pose special problems. The child knows that a particular object, a doll, say, *is a* doll. Now the child hears that the object *is a* toy. The child will be puzzled, on the assumption of mutual exclusivity, as to how a given object can both be a doll and be a toy. Of course, the child will eventually weaken or relinquish this assumption and work out the class-inclusion relations. But as I have already argued, class inclusion is a difficult relation, in part because it violates mutual exclusivity, but also because the asymmetry of inclusion is difficult to understand and represent for children. To resolve this problem, children may begin by weakening the categorical assumption instead and allow a collection interpretation. If children form a collection hierarchy, they do not need to violate the assumption of mutual exclusivity. In a collection structure, a particular object is not given two labels. Something *is an* oak, for example, but is *part of* a forest. (Although children's early vocabulary does not contain overlapping category terms, it does contain many terms that can be organized into part–whole relations, such as mouth and lips.) In sum, the part–whole organization finesses the problem of two labels for the same object and maintains the exclusivity assumption. It accomplishes this, however, at the expense of the first assumption of not allowing relational organization.

Thus, one or the other of these assumptions must be weakened to acquire hierarchically related terms. Which assumption is relinquished probably depends on the relative difficulty of fulfilling each. When the similarity among the objects is great and easy to perceive, then children will likely preserve the assumption of categorical relations and violate the assumption of mutual exclusivity. This would suggest that children should not be very likely to misinterpret a hierarchy of subordinate–basic-level categories as having a collection structure. It also suggests that mass nouns should not be helpful for representing the higher-level category of a subordinate–basic hierarchy. Thus, in relations such as poodle–dog or rocking chair–chair, it would not benefit children to have *dog* or *chair* be mass nouns. When the category similarity is difficult to discern, as in superordinate-level categories, then imposing a part–whole structure would simplify the hierarchy and preserve the assumption of mutual exclusivity. It does this, however, by allowing relational meanings of the category term. Nevertheless, it still might work to the child's advantage to be able to construct a part–whole scaffolding on which to build an asymmetric hierarchical relation, which can later be transformed to support transitive inferences.

ACKNOWLEDGMENTS

This chapter was completed while I was at the Center for Advanced Study in the Behavioral Sciences. I am grateful for support from NSF Grant No. BNS8206304 and the Spencer Foundation.

REFERENCES

Brown, R. Linguistic determinism and the part of speech. *Journal of Abnormal and Social Psychology*, 1957, *55*, 1–5.

Callanan, M. A., & Markman, E. M. Principles of organization in young children's natural language hierarchies. *Child Development*, 1982, *53*, 1093–1101.

Carey, S. Semantic development, state of the art. In L. Gleitman & E. Wanner (Eds.), *Language acquisition, state of the art*. London: Cambridge University Press, 1982.

Clark, E. V. What's in a word? On the child's acquisition of semantics in his first language. In T. E. Moore (Ed.), *Cognitive development and the acquisition of language*. New York: Academic Press, 1973.

Clark, E. V. Meanings and concepts. In J. H. Flavell & E. M. Markman (Eds.), *Cognitive development* (Vol. 3, Gen. Ed. P. H. Mussen, *Handbook of child psychology*). New York: Wiley, 1983.

Gelman, R., & Baillargeon, R. A review of some Piagetian concepts. In J. H. Flavell & E. M. Markman (Eds.), *Cognitive development*, Vol. 3, P. H. Mussen (Gen. Ed.) *Handbook of child psychology*. New York: Wiley, 1983.

Gelman, R., & Gallistel, C. R. *The child's understanding of number*. Cambridge, Mass: Harvard University Press, 1978.

Gibson, E. J., & Spelke, E. S. The development of perception. In J. H. Flavell & E. M. Markman (Eds.), *Cognitive development* (Vol. 3, Gen. Ed. P. H. Mussen, *Handbook of child psychology*). New York: Wiley, 1983.

Goldin-Meadow, S., Seligman, M. E. P, & Gelman, R. Language in the two-year-old. *Cognition*, 1976, *4*, 189–202.

Gordon, P. *Syntactic acquisition of the count/mass distinction*. Paper presented at the Stanford Child Language Research Forum, 1981.

Horton, M. S. *Category familiarity and taxonomic organization in young children*. Unpublished doctoral dissertation, Stanford University, 1982.

Huttenlocher, J. The origins of language comprehension. In R. L. Solso (Ed.), *Theories in cognitive psychology: The Loyola symposium*. Hillsdale, N.J.: Lawrence Erlbaum Associates, 1974.

Inhelder, B., & Piaget, J. *The early growth of logic in the child*. New York: W. W. Norton, 1964.

Katz, N., Baker, E., & Macnamara, J. What's a name? On the child's acquisition of proper and common nouns. *Child Development*, 1974, *45*, 469–473.

Katzner, K. *Languages of the world*. New York: Funk & Wagnals, 1975.

Macnamara, J. Cognitive basis of language learning in infants. *Psychological Review*, 1972, *79*, 1–13.

Macnamara, J. *Names for things: A study of human learning*. Cambridge, Mass.: MIT Press, 1982.

Mandler, J. M. Categorical and schematic organization in memory. In C. R. Puff (Ed.), *Memory organization and structure*. New York: Academic Press, 1979.

Mandler, J. M., Scribner, S., Cole, M., & DeForest, M. Cross-cultural invariance in story recall. *Child Development*, 1980, *51*, 19–26.

Markman, E. M. Facilitation of part–whole comparisons by use of the collective noun "family." *Child Development*, 1973, *44*, 837–840.

Markman, E. M. Classes and collections: Conceptual organization and numerical abilities. *Cognitive Psychology*, 1979, *11*, 395–411.

Markman, E. M. Two different principles of conceptual organization. In M. E. Lamb & A. L. Brown (Eds.), *Advances in developmental psychology* (Vol. 1). Hillsdale, N.J.: Lawrence Erlbaum Associates, 1981.

Markman, E. M. *Why superordinate category terms can be mass nouns*. Unpublished manuscript, Stanford University, 1983.

Markman, E. M., & Callanan, M. A. An analysis of hierarchical classification. In R. Sternberg (Ed.), *Advances in the psychology of human intelligence* (Vol. 2). Hillsdale, N. J.: Lawrence Erlbaum Associates, in press.

Markman, E. M., Horton, M. S., & McLanahan, A. G. Classes and collections: Principles of organization in the learning of hierarchical relations. *Cognition*, 1980, *8*, 227–241.

Markman, E. M., & Hutchinson, J. E. Children's sensitivity to constraints on word meaning: Taxonomic vs thematic relations. *Cognitive Psychology*, 1984, *16*, 1–27.

Markman, E., & Seibert, J. Classes and collections: Internal organization and resulting holistic properties. *Cognitive Psychology*, 1976, *8*, 561–577.

Nelson, K. Structure and strategy in learning to talk. *Monographs of the Society for Research in Child Development*, 1973, *38* (Serial No. 149).

Nelson, K. Concept, word and sentence: Interrelations in acquisition and development. *Psychological Review*, 1974, *81*, 267–285.

Newport, E. L., & Bellugi, U. Linguistic expression of category levels in a visual–gestural language: A flower is a flower is a flower. In E. Rosch & B. B. Lloyd (Eds.), *Cognition and categorization*. Hillsdale, N.J.: Lawrence Erlbaum Associates, 1978.

Piaget, J. *The child's conception of number*. New York: Norton, 1965.

Quine, W. V. O. *Word and object*. Cambridge, Mass.: MIT Press, 1960.

Rosch, E. Cognitive representations of semantic categories. *Journal of Experimental Psychology: General*, 1975, *104*, 192–233.

Rosch, E. H., Mervis, C. B., Gray, W., Johnson, D., & Boyes-Braem, P. Basic objects in natural categories. *Cognitive Psychology*, 1976, *3*, 382–439.

Schaeffer, B., Eggleston, V. H., & Scott, J. L. Number development in young children. *Cognitive Psychology*, 1974, *6*, 357–379.

Smiley, S. S., & Brown, A. L. Conceptual preference for thematic or taxonomic relations: A nonmonotonic age trend from preschool to old age. *Journal of Experimental Child Psychology*, 1979, *28*, 249–257.

Valentine, C. W. *The psychology of early childhood*. London: Methuen, 1942.

Voegelin, C. F., & Voegelin, F. M. *Classification and index of the world's languages*. New York: Elsevier, 1977.

Whorf, B. L. *Language, thought and reality*. Cambridge, Mass.: MIT Press, 1956.

Wittgenstein, L. *Philosophical investigations*. New York: Macmillan, 1953.

Wittgenstein, L. *The blue and brown books*. New York: Harper and Brothers, 1958.

14 Commentary: Where Do Categories Come From?

Brian MacWhinney
Carnegie-Mellon University

One cannot avoid being impressed by the importance of the study of the development of categorization to large areas of developmental psychology, perceptual psychology, psycholinguistics, linguistics, and philosophy. This topic means a great deal to many disciplines, and the requirements that have been placed on the nature of what constitutes a good explanation of development are more intense than in any other area that I have ever studied. Because of this centrality, students of child categorization must deal with fundamental problems in the theories of reference, semantics, information processing, memory, and even psychobiology. They must conduct their work within the edifice of a theory of semantics that not only has holes in its roof, but often seems to be missing some major walls and supporting pillars. Despite a great deal of current interest in the description of semantic structures, we still have only a few bits and pieces of formal analyses of a few semantic spaces. As a result, it is often difficult to know how to control and properly select experimental stimuli. While they are dealing with these theoretical problems, researchers must also deal with practical problems involved in working with subjects whose verbal abilities are either nonexistent or incomplete in the particular areas under investigation. They must often utilize tasks that provide only weak evidence that stimuli are being categorized in more than just a peripheral way. Whether gathering experimental or observational data, investigators must concern themselves deeply with the social milieu within which children learn and within which they demonstrate the state of their knowledge.

Given the problems confronting progress in this area, we must admire all the more deeply the accomplishments of our three contributors—Bornstein, Mervis, and Markman. Each of their chapters constitutes a significant contribution toward furthering our understanding of the development of categorization. To-

407

gether, they show us that, despite the difficulties inherent in this area, we can expect to encounter progressively more intelligent answers to the basic question about the development of categorization: ''Where do categories come from?'' Even more importantly, they show us that the really interesting issues in this area arise exactly at those points at which their ideas intersect.

The reader may have noted that Bornstein's focus has been on the period of infancy, that Mervis' has been on the period of the first words, and that Markman's has been on the preschool period. Each of these three researchers has been working within a somewhat different set of theoretical assumptions. It is my impression that these differences in approach are not at all accidental, but that they are direct reflections of changes in the fundamental nature of categories as children mature. I am not imagining that the core mechanisms of the categorization process change with age; rather it seems to me that change focuses on the modification of the shape of the semantic spaces upon which the categorization process operates. Also, as Markman suggests, children seem to acquire a number of additional procedures that supplement the basic categorization process. If we look at a 10-year-old schoolchild, we find a vast array of categories and subcategories, organized according to a variety of principles. In a sense, this child represents the end state of the process of categorization development that we are studying. Somewhat unrealistically, let us imagine that we can get a reasonably accurate mapping of the category system of this 10-year-old. We may then ask ourselves the basic question in this area: Where did these categories come from? How did this particular 10-year-old develop exactly this set of categories and not those of some other 10-year-old in some other culture? There are a number of answers to these questions. Each of these answers focuses on a particular period of human development. There are four sources of categories that I would like to consider: biological substrates, attribute clustering, social interaction, and language. These are the four major forces that are generally discussed in the literature and they are also the four that are examined by our three participants. Let us begin with the question:

IN WHAT WAYS DO CATEGORIES ARISE FROM BIOLOGICAL SUBSTRATES?

All of us realize that there must be a certain neurological substrate upon which categorization depends. However, opinion is sharply divided regarding the exact ways in which innate biological substrates determine higher levels of categorization. Addressing this issue, Bornstein advances an ontogenetic typology of categorization processes that posits a loose linkage between children's age or developmental levels and their use of the four possible categorization processes. It seems to me that Bornstein's most important contribution here is the articulation of a typology of categorization processes. This typology, which is much like that we find in Kant, is now articulated with new data from infancy research. However, I believe that there is still some room for further differentiation of this typology. The importance of identity equivalence as separate from referent equivalence is unclear, as Bornstein himself notes. Referent equivalence needs to be differentiated into equivalence processes across various types of transformations. The overlap between acquired perceptual equivalence and conceptual equivalence needs to be clarified. With further modifications and elaborations of this type, a typology of categorization processes would become increasingly useful.

The degree to which this typology of categorization processes can also serve as a guide to sequence in ontogenesis is unclear. As Bornstein himself notes, the evidence currently available indicates that the three most primitive categorization processes—categorization by identity, categorization by referent equivalence, and categorization by perceptual similarity—can all be demonstrated either at birth or within the first 2 months. On the other hand, children cannot demonstrate evidence of categorization by conceptual/linguistic equivalence until the end of the first year. Thus, rather than motivating a four-stage progression, the data on levels of categorization only seem to motivate a distinction between categorization that can be achieved at the onset of infancy and categorization that occurs during the period preceding the onset of language. One could argue that children's abilities to use the first three categorization processes in the first months of life simply reflect the ease with which categorization processes of this type are learned. Alternatively, one could argue that children's command over categorization in these first few months is given to them as a part of their biological inheritances. It seems to me most unlikely that abilities that emerge so uniformly across children in the first 2 months could have anything less than a major biological component. If we are to believe that learning plays any major role in the acquisition of the most fundamental categorization processes, we will need to see something in the way of a plausible account of how the various types of referent equivalence might be learned. This would be an extremely interesting line of research for infancy researchers.

The second source of categories that we should consider is children's cognitive processing of direct perceptual interactions with the world. Thus, the next question we try to address is:

IN WHAT WAYS DO CATEGORIES ARISE FROM CHILDREN'S DETECTIONS OF PERCEPTUAL REGULARITIES?

Mervis advances a series of interesting and clear-headed claims regarding the origins of the categories underlying children's first words. The most crucial assumption is stated in this way:

As with adult-basic-level categories, child-basic categories are characterized by gradients of goodness-of-example. . . . Thus, the most representative exemplars are those that share large numbers of attributes with many other exemplars of the category, while at the same time sharing few attributes with exemplars of related categories.

Mervis' formulation of category membership is essentially correct. Following this formulation, we can think of categories as areas of local density in a multidimensional semantic space. For example, things that are round can also be rolled, bounced, and thrown. This correlation of the attributes of roundness, rollability, bounceability, and throwability defines a nexus of properties in semantic space. As Mervis clearly notes, the child's idea of what this space looks like may differ in very reasonable ways from the adult's. For the child, a round bank may be categorized as a ball simply because of the strength of *roundness* as a feature in the computation of *ballness*.

If we could view all child-basic categories as local maxima in the density of correlation of attributes, we could construct a rather straightforward account of the development of categorization prior to acquisition of words. Following Bornstein, we could imagine that the child categorizes experiences into objects by using categorization by identity, reference equivalence, and perceptual equivalence. Each object that is categorized in this way is then stored in the child's memory along with its attributes. When a large number of objects begin to occupy points in semantic space that are extremely close to each other, a local maximum arises that then constitutes a child-basic category.

There are three qualifications that must be made on this analysis. The first, and most important, is that it is not at all clear that we can think of semantic space as a tabula rasa upon which experience writes at will. As both Eleanor Rosch and Mervis herself have pointed out, there may be certain universal natural prototypes in domains such as color and shape. Thus, although the Dani distinguish only two basic colors (mili and mola), when exposed to a series of red color chips they tend to remember best those colors that are closest to what Americans judge to be "good" reds. Although we would not imagine that there is a biological basis for the prototypical chair, we might well imagine that among the class of *balls* the nonprototypicality of the rugby ball might be at least in part a consequence of the importance of a universal natural type for "complete sphericality." In general, it is clear that once experience begins to write on semantic space it becomes highly nonuniform. However, it also seems to be the case that semantic space may not be uniform even at birth.

The second qualification we must make is that the notion of local maxima may become difficult to apply when there is extreme category overlap or embedding. Stated somewhat more abstractly, we can say that the prelinguistic child's semantic space may well contain dense, narrow maxima embedded within larger, broader maxima. For example, within the broad local maximum for *ball,* there may also be narrower local maxima for *balloon* and *marble*. When the parent gives the name *balloon* to an object, it may be that the child judges it to be actually a *balloon*. This should occur if the current exemplar of a balloon is a good example for the local maximum for the concept *balloon*. However, if the current exemplar is not a good balloon, will it be judged to be a ball, thereby leading the child to believe that the name for balls is *balloon?* In other words, if a referent fits within two child-basic category levels, one of which is embedded within the other, how does the child decide which level relates to the verbal label? Mervis and Roth (1981) have considered issues like this in the context of adult color categorization, but they have not yet considered the impact of these considerations on child categorization.

The third qualification on the role of correlated attributes in the emergence of the categories underlying words is that many words do not demonstrate the intense correlation of attributes that we see in common nouns. In particular, as Huttenlocher and others have argued, the actions underlying verbs involve great variance in the identity of the positions in which they occur, the instruments they utilize, the agents that conduct them, and the objects upon which they are performed. However, it is not at all clear that we cannot categorize actions. Rather, it appears that the basis of that categorization is fundamentally different from the basis for categorization of objects.

These problems with the use of correlated attributes to explain the ontogenesis of categories are not fatal flaws. Rather, they are qualifications that need to be made in our application of the notion of correlated attributes.

We can turn now to a consideration of the third major source of category structure in young children: social interaction with their parents and peers. Here the question we wish to address is:

IN WHAT WAYS DO CATEGORIES ARISE FROM SOCIAL INTERACTION?

Although the role of the adult in focusing the child's attention on attributes of objects may be relatively slight in the first year, it grows in importance with time. Mervis has been instrumental in drawing our attention to the importance of social interaction as a source of category development. Her work has also underlined the complexity of the relation between parent–child interaction and the child's underlying category structure.

In the current chapter, Mervis has focused her attention on a very particular type of social interaction: one in which the mother and child are expected to repeatedly name a small set of objects under the watchful eye of the experimenter. It is my impression that the unique demand characteristics of this situation have led to results that may not be representative of other interactions between the mother and the child. Because the emphasis here is on producing play and entertainment, it may be that mothers tend to relax the precision of their naming behavior in this situation. The fact that mothers of Down Syndrome children do not show such relaxation may be a consequence of particular social pressures placed upon these parents by medical counselors who encourage them not to use "baby talk." I should note that I have no hard evidence to back up these claims. They derive simply from my own impressions obtained while playing with children and watching others play with children.

Another rather subtle aspect of this experimental situation may be the lessening of the importance of episodic encoding of particular exemplars as a source of category information. In Mervis' experimental situation, all objects appear as toys, rather than as objects serving their normal functions. For example, if a round wax candle is perceived in the middle of a formal table setting, I would imagine that even a toddler would be less likely to think of it as a *ball*. In normal word learning, a child is presented with highly distinct exemplars embedded in a rich and distinctive context. Researchers such as Anglin (1977), Macnamara (1982), and myself have argued that much of early lexical acquisition involves the acquisition of highly undergeneralized terms. Macnamara relates this process to the acquisition of proper nouns—that is, words that refer to particular episodic encodings for objects. Nelson, Rescorla, Gruendel, and Benedict (1978) report that some 30% of children's early words are overgeneralized. However, both Macnamara and I have found levels of overgeneralization closer to 5%. Of course, both of us admit to being a bit pedantic in terms of the way we named objects for the children. But the point is that calling a tiger a *kitty* is neither a universal of parental speech nor a particularly efficacious teaching strategy. The use of this strategy in the context of Mervis' experiment may arise more from boredom and the limitation of options than from the mother's normal teaching practice. As Mervis and Pani (1980) have argued, presentation of good exemplars is the best form of instruction and the one that the mother would no doubt prefer.

I believe that Mervis is correct in holding that children come to the word-learning task with certain preconceptions regarding the shapes of categories for which they would like to learn names (MacWhinney, 1978). However, unlike Mervis, I believe that at least some children are extremely sensitive to the shapes of the categories presented to them by adults. If adults present such children with consistent category labels, they will be willing to abandon their own hypotheses and acquire the labels sanctioned by the adult language. That at least some children show very low levels of overgeneralization sets important limits on Mervis' claims regarding the pervasiveness of child-basic categories and indicates that the process of social interaction with adults may be an equally powerful source of the acquisition of categories.

I return to the issue of the acquisition of undergeneralized terms in a moment. Here, I should simply note that there are, of course, many other issues to be considered in the area of social interaction and its influence on categorization.

Topics such as adults' reactions to overgeneralization and undergeneralization and the role of monitoring in the children and the adults should be considered. But our time is short and we must move on to examining the last major source for categories: language.

IN WHAT WAYS DO CATEGORIES ARISE FROM LANGUAGE?

Markman maps out two major areas in which language seems to influence the acquisition and organization of categories. She rightly considers the first area as relevant to a resolution of Quine's classic induction problem. She argues that children assume that the referents of new words are simple objects rather than complex thematic relations. Markman looks at this strategy in terms of a universal constraint on what children do not consider. I believe that it is more profitable to look at language-specific influences on the shape of what children do consider as possible referents for words. Evidence for a general class of semantic-induction strategies has been offered by Braine, Carey, Macnamara, MacWhinney, Maratsos, Pinker, and many others. An example of a strategy of this type is encoding of the verbal material that occurs between the auxiliary verb *is* and the progressive suffix *-ing* as referring to a process, as in *Bill is nibbing* where *nib* is judged to refer to a process. If the nonce word is followed by a noun, the child infers that the word is an action, as in *Bill is nibbing the table.* There are, of course, as many strategies of this type as there are syntactic frames in the language the child is learning. In the novel-word condition in Markman's experiment, the context is the indefinite article *a*. This context forces induction of the attribute or semantic feature ($+$object) into the lexical entry for the nonce word as Katz, Baker, and Macnamara (1974) have demonstrated. In the so-called no-word condition, the referent is identified by the indefinite pronouns "something" and "another one." One possible rule-governed binding of these pronouns is to the whole photographs including the action, rather than the individual elements within the photographs. Thus, it is not at all clear, in the no-word condition, that there is real evidence for a predisposition to categorize in terms of thematic relations.

Having introduced the general notion of the induction of attributes from syntactic frames, we are now in a position to consider how the four factors I presented at the beginning interact in early lexical acquisition. Let us take as an example a situation in which a child sees a wet dish towel lying on a redwood table, and hears his or her father say, "Could you bring me the towel?" The child has not yet learned the word *towel,* but he or she has seen towels frequently and has developed a weak cluster from the correlated attributes of towels, as opposed to other household objects and things made of cloth. Biological substrates have already operated in a variety of ways in shaping this cluster. They provide the child with dimensions of texture to judge the quality of towels. They allow the child to perceive the identity of the towel through transformations of folding and getting wet. Now the child hears the not-yet-learned form *towel* and, as argued in MacWhinney (1978, 1982), seeks to associate this form with some function. In doing this the child can be aided by language and social interaction, as well as by the presence of already-present attribute clusters. From language, the child learns that, because the word *towel* follows the word *the* it must refer to a countable nonproper object. Although the child has made a complete episodic encoding of the towel along with the redwood table, he or she now realizes that, because they are clearly separate objects, the word *towel* must refer to only one. Furthermore, because there is only one of the objects that could reasonably be the object of the verb *bring,* the label *towel* must relate most closely to the cloth object on the table. The syntactic frame also encourages the child to assume that the word *towel* is a common and not a proper noun. Thus, although the child first encodes *towel* as referring to this nonprototypical dish towel, this encoding is accompanied with the information that *towel* must eventually be generalized to a broader range of referents. If the dish towel is close enough to the core of the *towel* attribute cluster, and if that cluster is sufficiently strong, the child will be more likely to simply identify the new object as an instance of the cluster and learn the name as the name of the cluster. However, if the nearby cluster already has a name, the child will attempt to maintain his or her encoding of the new object and new label. The closer the object is in semantic space to some attribute cluster, the more difficult it will be to maintain this encoding. The child will attempt over time to discover attributes of the new item that will allow him or her to eliminate the potential synonymy. To the degree that adults help the child in identifying such distinguishing attributes, his or her task will proceed quickly and with minimal error.

This analysis also has consequences for Markman's work on class inclusion. If we call something a *dax* we are treating it as a count noun; if we speak of a *piece of dax* we are treating *dax* as a mass noun or a collection noun. The finding that we need to explain is why the class-inclusion problem becomes easier when the superordinate is a collection noun. It seems to me that collection nouns differ from other superordinates in that they contain specific instructions that encourage the listener to think of the member types of the set. Unlike nouns such as *toys,* which do not evoke any small set of members, nouns like furniture and silverware evoke a small set of potential members. I would guess that it is this evocation supported by words like *piece of* that support the child's superior performance on the class-inclusion task with collection nouns.

In summary, we have seen that a full picture of the development of categorization must not only show us how categorization arises from biology, from cognition, from social interaction, and from language, but a full picture must also show us how these very different impacts on categorization compete and coexist. It is precisely when we consider these interworkings that we realize that we are in the deepest ignorance and it is here that the issues seem the most fascinating.

REFERENCES

Anglin, J. M. (Ed.). *Word, object, and conceptual development.* New York: W. W. Norton, 1977.

Katz, N., Baker, E., & Macnamara, J. What's in a name? A study of how children learn common and proper names. *Child Development,* 1974, *45,* 469–473.

Macnamara, J. *Names for things.* Cambridge, Mass.: MIT press, 1982.

MacWhinney, B. The acquisition of morphophonology. *Monographs of the Society for Research in Child Development,* 1978, *43* (Whole No. 1).

MacWhinney, B. Basic syntactic processes. In S. Kuczaj (Ed.), *Language acquisition* (Vol. 1: *Syntax and semantics*). Hillsdale, N.J.: Lawrence Erlbaum Associates, 1982.

Mervis, C., & Pani, J. Acquisition of basic object categories. *Cognitive Psychology,* 1980, *12,* 496–522.

Mervis, C., & Roth, E. Basic and non-basic color categories. *Language,* 1981, *57,* 384–405.

Nelson, K., Rescorla, L., Gruendel, J., & Benedict, H. Early lexicons: What do they mean? *Child Development,* 1978, *49,* 960–968.

IV GENERAL COMMENTARY

15

Construction, Deconstruction, and Reconstruction of the Child's Mind

William Kessen
Yale University

Imagine my receiving a letter from Catherine Sophian some time ago:

> Dear Professor Kessen,
>   We are pleased that you will attend the 18th Annual Carnegie Symposium on Cognition. Of course, we must ask that you speak for no longer than 30 minutes; I trust that time will be sufficient for your commentary on the Old Testament.
>   Sincerely yours,

Fortunately, a good part of my task has already been done; the first cluster of chapters on Exodus, the second on Numbers, and the third's distinction between Chronicles and Kings simplify my assignment. And, because Bornstein has claimed Genesis, I am left to write at some length in the manner of Psalms and only a little in the manner of Jeremiah.

My first newborn research subject is, by now, older than most of the people who attended the Symposium; I claim thereby the greybeard's privilege of singing Psalms of praise. The chapters appearing here constitute a celebration of keen analysis, close attention to method, and elegant presentation. Congratulations to all the symposiasts and, from me as student, thanks.

The chapters we have read, perhaps because of their necessary diversity, reveal and illuminate several significant issues facing the student of cognitive development. But I want to claim even more for the importance of this volume. Over the last several years, the study of cognitive development has undergone a series of changes that came on us so gradually that we may not have recognized their full consequence; in truth, we stand at a watershed where the paths we took up the hill are misty and the paths that lay down the hill are not yet cleared. I cannot hope to do much about the future, either to predict or to control it, but it may be useful for me to try to blow away some of the mist over the recent past and to use the evidence of the chapters here to suggest the shape of cognitive-developmental research at the present moment. I organize my comments around five issues that seem critical to our understanding of our shared work in 1983: the issues of the *overstuffed infant, developmental goals and finished forms,* the *virtues of unfinished forms, mechanisms of transition,* and, more briefly, the relation between *plurality and modularity.* You should also know, at the outset, that my prejudices have for long been those of the constructionist in child psychology. However, my commitment was sorely tested by the Symposium and, as you see here, there is some danger that I went to Pittsburgh a constructionist and left a deconstructionist, sighing for a new builder.

THE OVERSTUFFED INFANT

Initial Structures

What is in the newborn and young infant? The language of reference has changed over the years, but most of us agree that the baby possesses initial or *early-formed structures,* what Klahr has called the "innate kernel," the initial values of the cognitive system. The search for initial values has occupied the attention of generations of researchers and, throughout the last century, there has been a continuing debate between the minimalists and the maximalists. By and large, this volume adds new evidence to the claims of the maximalists, the position that Sophian calls the "early-competence model." Lockman and Pick speak of "optimizing principles" at work in the young child to make the 18-month-old spatially efficient; DeLoache tells us of feats of infantile memory, and Bornstein documents perceptual categorization in the first halfyear of life. Nowhere is the recent dominance of the maximalists more evident than in the study of number cognition. From confident statements that the child in the first 5 years of life had only a primitive sense of number we have got to the present-day expectation that we will soon hear from the infant looking up at the tending parent to sing:

> One, two, who are you?
> Three, four, count some more.

It is almost comforting for Miller to remind us of the possibility that "number may be a special, limited area of early competence, with little meaning for cognitive development in general."

But, whatever the exaggerations of the folks who believe less is more and the folks who believe more is beautiful, the last decades have seen astonishing advance, especially in early perceptual development, in precision of method and coherence of findings. What will surely last from this volume to the next Carnegie-Mellon Symposium on development is the assembly of confirmed and replicated observations. Those observations surely persuade us that the young human infant is more active and more of a hypothesis generator than we dreamed before 1960. Let me propose only one cautionary note about the way we have stuffed our babies with smarter and smarter initial structures: the problem of the baby in a Cartesian world.

Much, although not all, research on infantile cognitive structures has implicitly assumed that the baby is confronted with a Cartesian universe of fragments (stimuli, features, . . .) which the infant reassembles to the synthesized world of objects and people. The present volume contains interesting evidence that the older emphasis on the reassembling child is in a decline and that researchers are again recognizing (or postulating) that, from the beginning, the child lives in a world of *privileged events* that, whatever they are, are not Cartesian fragments. A short list of privileged events would probably include human face, human voice, sweet things, an early-emerging sense of self, and medium-sized objects that move against a stable background. Mervis' somewhat mysterious "child-basic" categories, for example, seem also to be a kind of privileged event. In any case let me state in a general form a proposition that was foreshadowed and given outline by the notion of affordance: We will not understand the origins of the baby's world until we confront the problem of privileged events and the entailed problem of the relation between figure and ground in the early months and years of the child's life. However, even as an unconfident constructionist, I hope that we will not solve the problem by a naive–realistic epistemology that assumes that the child has only to discover what is *really* out there.

Functional Mechanisms

When compared to our excitement and sense of achievement about initial and early structures, we may feel uneasily disappointed about our recent (and not so recent) treatment of the mechanisms or procedures of processing and of change that we assign to the infant and young child. Later in this chapter, I comment a bit more about mechanisms, particularly those mechanisms that are supposed to explain developmental change in a childish mind, but, for now, as we contemplate the overstuffed infant, I want only to call attention to a peculiarity of much work on cognitive development—the assumption of uniform mechanisms.

Again, there are sweet exceptions, but many of us have assumed that whatever mechanism of change we assign the baby—maturation, learning, adaptation, problem solving, and so on—is much the same kind of fundamental process that we can see throughout life, even, for thinkers as significant and fecund as Piaget and Skinner, throughout living tissue. You will anticipate my conclusion that Symposium 18 and this volume stand as clear markers of a retreat from such simplifying premises. Let me state the case in brief form. Functional mechanisms working in children are not necessarily uniform across age or across cognitive domain, nor are they likely to be. Much of the current discussions of metathings is a move toward characterizing a cognitive system that operates under different procedures at different times and for different systems. The infant is a frustrating and important case in point because the infantile cognitive system changes so fast and under so various a collection of proposed mechanisms. Miller again catches the issue at the center when he writes, "Young children . . . [measure] . . . an invariance, although the invariance [is] not the same as that adults would measure in similar circumstances." A last point: If mechanisms and procedures of the cognitive system vary across age and across domain of thought, as this volume amply suggests, the age-indifferent and domain-indifferent theoretical systems of cognitive development (almost all of them *are*) require reconstruction.

Thus, we may have overstuffed our infant friend with initial structures and we have surely left the baby inadequate ways of relating, organizing, selecting, and executing the structures. But we cannot clearly see the baby, overstuffed or not, without first considering that other being we tend to overestimate, the human adult.

DEVELOPMENTAL GOALS AND FINISHED FORMS

The study of child psychology in general and of children's cognition in particular has been dominated by two assumptions about development. The first assumption has been that all development has a goal; it is going somewhere. The second assumption has been that the goal toward which child development is heading is represented by finished adult forms, the thought of the rational adult.

Let me say just a word in passing about the first assumption, the one that presupposes directional, inevitable, and progressive change. The notion has at least four possible warrants and I suppose that most believers in development would call on all of them. First, it serves a descriptive function. We gather all our observations on the way children deal with countable arrays and call the whole package "number development." Second, the idea of developmental goal is warranted by its analogy with evolutionary theory or, more accurately, with a somewhat discredited misreading of evolutionary development that sees phylogenetic change as adaptational and progressive. Third, development toward a goal can stand proxy to a commitment to biological inevitability (as Gesell and other maturationalists would have the case). Finally, and more recently revived, inevitable development may represent any particular culture's requirement that children in its purview run through a prescribed set of cognitive exercises. Because all of these warrants, and the first two a fortiori, are intellectually suspect, we may soon find ourselves facing the prospect of trying to construct a child psychology that dispenses with the notion of development. I will be fascinated to observe the status of the notion of development at, say, the 25th Symposium.

But the second major assumption of developmental goals is more closely related to the work of this volume. Throughout the preceding chapters, implicitly or explicitly, the goals, the end points, toward which the baby and child are pointing are the ratiocinations of the Western analytic scientist. The child is *assumed* to represent a series of way stations en route to being like adults. Why do we find this camel of an assumption so easy to swallow? And, to call on Jeremiah for a moment, what are the limitations of believing in the inevitable approach of child cognition toward adult finished forms of thought?

Historical Justification

For hundreds of years, Western cultures have been committed to the notion of progressive improvement—whether God or Nature or Evolution or Science or Development was implicated as agent, there has been an unwavering belief that change was progressive. It is hardly surprising that human development did not escape the analogy; if adults were the end of the line, then all prior conditions were part of an approach to the adult forms. Piaget, in his Bergsonian optimism and his addiction to theoretical simplicity, insisted that we see the cognitively messy child from the standpoint of the cognitively well-scrubbed adult.

However persuaded we may be of the child as incomplete adult, we ought to be careful about grounding our belief in what is, at best, an analogy.

Justification by Method

If the research task is taken to be the search for childish forms that precede adult forms, then the ponderous problem of limiting the scope of research is readily solved. In the simplest form of the argument by method, the measure of the child's performance is taken to be *discrepancy from adult forms.* Now, it is true that all research domains must be limited in some way in order to prepare feasible studies, but it may be well for us to look at some implications of the discrepancy rule for defining domain boundaries. If you, in a sense, look backward from the adult behavior to find its precursors in children, even in infants, an enormous array of data is thereby omitted from consideration. It is a bit like going from Boston to San Antonio by way of a group of cities that more and more resemble San Antonio. In short, the specification of research domain as discrepancy from adult forms makes inaccessible a large number of potentially relevant observations. And, of course, some of the most important of the potentially relevant observations are those that would serve to disconfirm the hypotheses governing the research. One must limit the research domain, to be sure, but some care must be taken not thereby to reduce significantly the chances of seeing disconfirming evidence.

Empirical Justifications

But, someone will surely assert, all the cautions of the last paragraphs are irrelevant if we have *demonstrated* that certain childish forms systematically approach the finished adult forms. Correct; there is no better response to a question about method than an answer with secure data. But, the testimony of this volume and of the new *Handbook of Child Psychology* can be read as casting substantial doubt on the claims of continuous (or saltatory) movement toward adult cognition; assertions of continuity seem as often formulaic as they are confirmed. I fully recognize that someone else may read the evidence in a different way; my intention is to make more likely a highly critical view of the available evidence for progressive development.

There is one peculiarity in the story of cognitive development that I would like to mention in passing. In grim parallel to the evidence that infants and young children are smarter than we had thought is the evidence that adults are a good deal stupider than Piaget's claims, for example, would have them be. We need only take notice of Klahr's example of counting to December without your fingers to do the work or Markman's high-school students who do not know their forests from their oaks or Gamble's (personal communication) finding that common kinship patterns (aunts, grandparents, cousins, . . .) are extraordinarily difficult to learn if the patterns are cast into an abstract characterization. Caught between brilliant infants and stupid adults, cognitive development may be squeezed dry.

THE VIRTUES OF UNFINISHED FORMS

The changing landscape of research on the childish mind is marvelously demonstrated in this volume's shared attention to the positive virtues of studying unfinished forms of human cognition. Almost every chapter presented here could be drawn on to demonstrate the thesis, so that I must be sparsely selective in my citations. Permit me to approach such wealth by laying out several themes in the argument for unfinished forms and then commenting briefly on each.

The Integrity of Relatively Short Periods of Cognitive Change

Partly because our specialized knowledge of cognitive change is growing so fast and partly because we are worried about sweeping claims of change over long periods, researchers have pared their preparations down to comprehensible size. Many of my cautions about the cost of viewing development from the adult end are reduced or disappear when short-term studies of change are under scrutiny. Almost all of the authors have bitten off discretely chewable problems, a welcome change from a more ambitious past.

The Growth of a Psychology of Natural Kinds

Without the command to see human development as the emergence of grand and inclusive principles of logic and mathematics or as a succession of content-free processes, researchers are freer to explore the kinds of activities engaged by children in the orginary course of their lives. It is good to be reminded that, as psychologists, we start with and must return to *what human beings in fact do*.

There is another aspect of the new psychology of natural kinds—a recognition of the importance of the contexts of cognitive development and of the critical status of decontextualization in cognition.

Matter of fact, Catherine Sophian could as well have named the Symposium *Exercises in Cognitive Context and Decontextualization*. Cooper on the child's task-relevant appreciation of number, Markman's attention to the natural-language guides to categorization, DeLoache's caution that precocious memory skills appear "when the object is hidden in the natural large-scale environment," Lockman and Pick's comments about the importance of comprehensible scale, Huttenlocher's evidence that the child's encoding resists logical equivalence, concepts such as "framework" or "landmark"—all pile up persuasive arguments for the importance of "practical intelligence" and the slow, perhaps never-ending, process of decontextualization that has been heralded as the only valid marker of adult intelligence. Strauss and Curtis show the way toward liberation from precocious rationality: " . . . it could be argued that . . . practical or sensory-based knowledge is a vital aspect of all cognition." Perhaps we should accept, at least as a working hypothesis, that we solve problems in two modes: one practical, everyday, unfinished; the other school carried, formal, and rare.

And the decontextualization is double at that: the decontextualizing activity of the researcher in the selection of the defining research preparation or problem *and* the decontextualizing activity of the child who must find what uniquely and efficiently defines object, category, dimension of space, and, above all, number. At several points in the discussions of these chapters there appeared the fascinating question of the relation between the two decontextualizations; how and to what degree are the cognitive processes in use by the investigator giving the research problem a specific form, on one hand, and the cognitive processes of the child attempting to solve the problem, on the other, related to one another?

The Methodological Therapy of Bounded Propositions

There is a curious human tendency, amplified by those of us still infected by positivism, to turn what we think we know into universal propositions. Our present attention to bounded domains and limited problem sets supports the recognition of plurality in explanatory propositions as well as plurality in behavior. The foregoing chapters contain a wealth of ingenious preparations and interesting observations without twitching distress by anyone about the need to sew everything together in a universalistic summary. I, for one, doubt that we are ready for universalistic propositions about children's cognition and that it is both necessary and healthy that we concentrate on local solutions to well-defined research problems.

Domains of Research are not Cleanly Separable

The letch for intellectual order leads us to organize symposia and conventions and programs in child psychology into (of course) categories—number development, spatial development, category development, and the like. But the same forces that make nonuniversalistic propositions essential also work against the establishment of domain boundaries that are fixed and firm. There are problems with drawing such messy maps and I address some of them in my closing commentary, but I believe that we are as unready for a taxonomy of developmental research as we are for a general theory of development.

Particular Bounded Studies May Show Importance of Social Factors

Until Mervis' chapter, I was sensitive to a troublesome omission in this volume, to an insufficient attention to the child as social construction as well as biological. Yet social interaction may be the fuel for the cognitive machine, and the place of the social partners in cognitive development is richly complicated and woefully understudied. I would like to flag several issues for future attention because they bear so closely on the research presented in this volume.

1. The cognitive implications of social change. When adult and child address each other in dialogue, gestural or spoken and particularly in the first months and years of life, there are *represented* in the conversation many of the processes that we have habitually called "cognitive." It seems almost obligatory to examine the *social* or dialogual forms of reciprocity, stability or relations, procedures for decontextualization, and the importance of matching; we know too little about how these rough-and-ready exchanges are related to the processes of the same names that we assign to the child's cognitive apparatus. Miller's contention that numerical equality is related to, or even derivative from, the American doctrine of fairness is an especially poignant example.

2. The adult as selector. The world is full of a number of things, to be sure, and it is unlikely that the touted intelligence of human beings is adequate to know everything about everything. The adult caretaker plays an important role in *selecting* for the child those aspects of the environment that matter, however "mattering" be defined. As I read the fine contributions of the symposiasts, I wondered about how a caretaking adult teaches a child *how* to distribute attention and *toward what* the child's attention is directed.

3. The adult as culture guide. An offshoot of the foregoing point, this proposition can be separated out to emphasize that one of the most mysterious aspects of the caretaker's control of the child's attention distribution is the representation in action of some culture-defined cognitive values and tasks. Unless we accept a biologically driven cognitive development, we will have to look closely at how parents and other mentors define the cognitive space of children. In Markman's formulation of the issue, "Because there are an unlimited number of possible ways of forming categories, how is it that the child comes up with the conventional categories encoded by his or her culture?"

How can the case sketched here be presented starkly? I maintain that a good part of what we call cognitive development is dependent on the selection by caretakers among possible lines of development in children. In content we can, as holders of the culture, select physics or music, and in strategy we can emphasize social-interactional solutions to problems or we can emphasize analytic-"scientific" solutions. Most of the researchers who have studied cognitive development, Piaget beyond all others, have chosen to emphasize physics as a typical problem and science as a typical method. I want only to point out that there is no epistemological or moral warrant for those choices. They are valuative judgments and are as subject to critique and study as other, more visible parts of our presuppositions.

MECHANISMS OF TRANSITION

Whatever we assign to the baby by way of cognitive structures on one side and the developmental goal on the other, we are compelled to propose mechanisms by which children get from here to there, from birth to maturity. Not much time was spent in this volume on the issue of the mechanisms of transition. Unless I missed the words, many of the captivating phenomena described by members of Symposium 18 are apparently unmotivated—they just happen. The most laudably ambitious attempts to write about change—Sophian's, Cooper's, Miller's—turn out to be more like organized and wise description than like transitional mechanisms.

There were, I believe, hints of the Classical Four Mechanisms—maturation, contingent reinforcement, modeling, and adaptation or discrepancy reduction—but no one took on the task of considering new mechanisms or revisions in the Four. I find the omission interesting because the traditions of American psychology have been so strongly linked to accounts of transitional mechanisms and because the scholars of this book are so splendidly ingenious.

There are two brief points I would like to append to any consideration of mechanisms of transition. First, the bad news. Theories of contingent reinforcement provide no warrant or expectation for inevitable, progressive, or uniform cognitive change over age, a fact that has made such theories peculiarly unfit for the explanatory language many of us use. But adaptational theories—either in phylogenetic or ontogenetic shape—also do not provide warrant or expectation for inevitable, progressive, or uniform cognitive change. Piaget believed that adaptation was progressive and we have tended to follow him somewhat uncritically, but evolutionary theory, construed as Darwin did, can go in any direction or, more accurately, goes in no direction at all. Further, a similar and parallel argument using social mechanisms of change can be made. Are we left, then, with maturation alone as a guaranteed mechanism for getting the child through his or her cognitive developmental paces? It may be the confrontation with that possibility that has been sending some researchers, willy nilly, toward a commitment to the Fodorian child. The only intellectually sound argument to be made to counter the *philosophically* overstuffed child is to present powerful and explicit new proposals for the mechanisms of cognitive change.

Now, the good news. Whether one is guided by reinforcement or adaptational models, the researcher is required to state the initial position of the cognitive system, the mental structure that is to be modified. In the past, the required specifications have often been absent, incomplete, or vague. It may be that the most solid achievement of the construal of cognitive development as information processing lies in the inescapable requirement of that construal for a fully explicit statement of initial, intermediary, and final structures. Siegler and Shrager's meticulous account of the successive structures of number understanding and Bornstein's rigorous typology of categorization are models for all of us in making sure that we know what we are postulating as structures. These achievements are very good news indeed and may provide us with the patience to await the breakthrough on transitional mechanisms.

PLURALITY AND MODULARITY

There is a refreshing novelty in avoiding universalisms and studying unfinished forms, local solutions, and natural kinds; the heavy hand of large-theory positivism is off us. Several research groups—settlements in the vast developmental domain—exist; each busily working with its favored research preparation and its favorite content domain, natural or decontextualized; each proposing its own initial structures and processes for change; each with its own sense of the developmental endpoint. By the way, the recent popularity of claims for cognitive modularity may be little more than turning a social fact—the existence of groups of scholars independent from one another—into a scientific principle about mind!

But with the new openness there comes a cost: the reduction of a common ground for communication, critical evaluation and comparison, and the positive search for connections and combinations of ideas from different laboratories. In fact, it is probably true that the present openness of research in cognitive development is an unstable condition; the fragmentation will be institutionally and intellectually insupportable. But this volume presents bits of hope. Against the dangers of Babelism, Siegler and Shrager write of domain-general "common processes"; Markman finds order in the variation of languages; Lockman and Pick find connections among spatial cognition, quantitative skills, and representation; Bornstein claims universality for the categorical impulse.

Even with such smart, sensitive help, I do not dare to predict the short future of cognitive-developmental research and thinking. What I do dare to recommend is the continuation of meetings like the Symposium that formed the basis of this volume. Whatever we may guess about the next years, we can be sure that successful systematic science is a social enterprise, depending on competence, mutual respect, and communication. Particularly in a time when our preparations vary, when we become increasingly specialized, when the onrushing tidal wave of publications threatens to drown us all, we need conversations at the boundaries, talk over the fences of our special interests. We may, thereby, have to display our ignorance or even to change our minds, but respectful conversation among colleagues is a necessary condition for serious science.

A LAST WORD

The deconstructionists in contemporary literary criticism tell us that the history of literature is a history of misreadings by authors of their forerunners and ancestors. Psychologists seem to believe that progress requires assassination of their forebears. The number of references to Piaget among the chapters in this volume is tellingly low; still, for all our disavowals, Piaget is with us still, listening, occasionally wincing, but I have a strong hunch that, as we conclude our conversation, he would applaud.

REFERENCE

Gamble, T. J. *The development of representation for social inference.* Personal communication, 1982.

Author Index

Subject Index